THE POLITICS OF ONTARIO

Contents

List of Figures and Tables   vii

Preface   ix

Contributors   xi

1 What Is Ontario?   1
 JONATHAN MALLOY

2 The Political Economy of Ontario: How Did Ontario Get So Rich? And Why Are There So Many Poor Ontarians?   15
 PETER GRAEFE

3 "Business as Usual": The Relationship Vacuum between Ontario and Indigenous Peoples   37
 REBECCA MAJOR

4 A Brief History of the Procedure at the Ontario Legislature   53
 TOM McDOWELL

5 The Ontario Executive   72
 ANDREA MIGONE

6 Local Government and Politics in Ontario   91
 ZACHARY SPICER

7 Ontario Federal-Provincial Relations: Still a Responsible Partner in Confederation? 110
JULIE M. SIMMONS

8 Government-Media Relations in Ontario: Political Communication in the Time of the COVID-19 Pandemic 134
TAMARA A. SMALL

9 Ontario's Political Parties and the Party System 157
ANNA LENNOX ESSELMENT

10 Progress Stalled ... Again: Women, Gender, and Party Politics in Ontario 175
CHERYL N. COLLIER

11 Northern Ontario 195
GINA S. COMEAU

12 Race and Ontario Politics 216
ASIF HAMEED

13 "Just Want a Regular Life": Race and the Educational Credentials of Black Youth 238
CARL E. JAMES

14 The Environment, Climate Change, and Market Populist Politics 262
MARK WINFIELD

15 The Shifting Landscape of Party-Union Relationships in Ontario 287
LARRY SAVAGE

16 Toronto and the GTA: Governing Ontario's Global City 310
MARTIN HORAK

17 Ontario Health Policy and Politics 329
RAISA B. DEBER AND GREGORY P. MARCHILDON

Index 349

Figures and Tables

Figures

5.1 Ontario Emergency Orders 82
6.1 Revenue Sources – Ontario Municipalities, 2020 99
6.2 Expenditures – Ontario Municipalities, 2020 100
10.1 Percentage of Women in Party Caucuses, 1945–2022 179
13.1 Highest Level of Education of Black Youth, Ages 25–9, 2021 247
13.2 Generational Status by Race and Gender, Ages 25–9, in Canada 247
13.3 Generational Status by Race and Gender, Ages 25–9, in Ontario 248
14.1 Average Global Adjustment vs. Average Market Electricity Price, 2009–19 267
15.1 Union Campaign Donations by Party in Dollars 292

Tables

2.1 Share of Gross Domestic Product by Industry, 1997–2021 21
2.2 Share of Employment by Industry, 1997–2021 22
2.3 Ontario Share of Canadian GDP by Industry 23
2.4 Average Income in 2015 Dollars by Racialized Status, Toronto and Region, 1980–2015 27
4.1 Time Allocation at the Ontario Legislature, 1981–2023 66
4.2 Time Allocation under the Ford Government, 2018–2023 68

5.1 The Composition of the Ontario Public Sector, Select Years 75
5.2 Orders in Council – Ontario 81
8.1 Queen's Park Press Gallery Membership 138
8.2 News Organizations with Active Members in Queen's Park Press Gallery, April 2022 139
10.1 Women Elected by Each Party, 1945–2022 178
10.2 Percentage and Number, in Brackets, of Women Candidates by Party 180
10.3 Women Cabinet Ministers in Ontario, 1970–2022 184
13.1 Highest Level of Education by Race, Ages 25–9, 2021 246
13.2 Highest Level of Education of Black Youth, Ages 25–9, by Generational Status and Gender, 2021 249
14.1 Discursive Orientation and Public Salience of Environmental Issues 275
16.1 Population Growth of Toronto Area in Millions, Percentage of Ontario Population, 1986–2021 312
16.2 Distribution of Seats in Legislature by Major Party, 1990–2022 312

Preface

Cheryl N. Collier and Jonathan Malloy

Ontario keeps evolving. This new edition of *The Politics of Ontario* builds on both the earlier 2017 edition as well as the five volumes of *The Government and Politics of Ontario*, edited by Donald C. Macdonald and later Graham White, first published in 1975. A look back at those books over five decades shows the evolution of Ontario as a political society. While there are clear patterns of continuity, there are also important changes.

The first edition of *The Politics of Ontario* in 2017 emphasized the changing economic patterns of Ontario that had undermined its traditional manufacturing identity and assumption of pre-eminence in Confederation. This edition brings new focus to the continually growing diversity of Ontario. New chapters on race and Ontario politics by Asif Hameed and on the specific experiences of Black Ontarians by Carl E. James highlight important dimensions of a province in which a third of residents are racialized. We have also added a long-overdue focus on the relationship between the Indigenous Peoples and Ontario by Rebecca Major. These are joined by a mix of returning and new authors who have each drawn from their expertise to analyze Ontario's complex and fascinating politics. Particular attention has been given to the COVID-19 pandemic and how it both disrupted and, in other ways, maintained the patterns of Ontario politics.

We thank each author for their contributions and the many other people that made this edition possible. Progress on the book has been supported by the resources of the Bell Chair in Canadian Parliamentary Democracy at Carleton University, including sponsoring a workshop at Toronto Metropolitan University in the summer of 2022, where authors presented and discussed initial drafts. We also thank two Carleton University students: Erin Kinzie and Jayden Dill, for their assistance at various stages of the manuscript. We thank the University of Toronto Press for its continuing support of the series, especially acquisitions editor Rebecca Duce and associate managing editor Mary Lui, as well as Alicia Hibbert and Melissa MacAulay for their skilful copy-editing and proofreading. Finally, we thank readers and welcome them to this new edition of *The Politics of Ontario*.

Contributors

Cheryl N. Collier is a professor of political science and dean of the Faculty of Arts, Humanities, and Social Sciences at the University of Windsor. Her work focuses on gender and politics, social movements, federalism, and provincial politics. She is co-editor of the *Handbook on Gender, Diversity and Federalism* and also studies sexism and sexual harassment in Canadian politics and legislatures.

Jonathan Malloy is a professor of political science and the Honourable Dick and Ruth Bell Chair in Canadian Parliamentary Democracy at Carleton University. He is a former Ontario legislative intern, and his teaching and research focus on Canadian political institutions and Ontario politics. His other books include *The Paradox of Parliament* (UTP).

Gina S. Comeau is a political scientist whose work focuses on Canadian politics and public policy. She has published extensively on sport policy and francophone minorities in Canada. She was a professor of political science at Laurentian University.

Raisa B. Deber is a professor in the Institute of Health Policy, Management and Evaluation at the University of Toronto. She is the author of many articles and several books, including *Case Studies in Canadian Health Policy and Management* and *Treating Health Care*. She is a recipient of the Emmett Hall

Memorial Lectureship, and she is a fellow of the Canadian Academy of Health Sciences and the Royal Society of Canada.

Anna Lennox Esselment is an associate professor in the Department of Political Science at the University of Waterloo. Her areas of research focus on Canadian politics, particularly political parties, campaigns and elections, and political marketing.

Peter Graefe is an associate professor in the Department of Political Science at McMaster University. His research deals with the political economy of public policy in Ontario and Quebec, as well as intergovernmental relations in social policy. He is co-editor (with Julie Simmons and Linda White) of *Overpromising and Underperforming: Understanding and Evaluating New Intergovernmental Accountability Regimes*.

Asif Hameed is a PhD candidate and instructor at Carleton University's Department of Political Science specializing in Canadian and Comparative Politics. A member of the Digital Democracy Project – a collaborative research project featuring the work of select political sociologists from across the country – his research looks at the intersection of digital and democratic engagement. He also works on the politics of race, federalism, and comparative provincial politics in Canada, and the politics of the alt-right.

Martin Horak is an associate professor of political science and associate director of the Centre for Urban Policy and Local Governance at Western University. His teaching and research focus on the Canadian and comparative urban politics and governance. His publications include *Governing the Post-Communist City* and *Sites of Governance: Multilevel Governance and Policy Making in Canada's Big Cities*.

Carl E. James is the Jean Augustine Chair in Education, Community & Diaspora at York University. The 2022 Killam Prize Laureate in Social Sciences, his work explores the ways in which institutional structures through policies, programs, and practices mediate the educational trajectories, economic opportunities, and civic engagement of racialized youth. His recent publications include *Colour Matters: Essays on the Experiences, Education, and Pursuits of Black Youth* (UTP).

Rebecca Major is an associate professor and NVD research chair in the Indigenous Governance Program at Yukon University. Her teaching and research focus on Canadian public policy and Indigenous governance, identity, and land claims. She has also served as a community leader and policy advisor for Métis organizations.

Gregory P. Marchildon is a professor emeritus at the Dalla Lana School of Public Health and the Munk School of Global Affairs and Public Policy at the University of Toronto. A former senior public servant, he was the executive director of the Commission on the Future of Health Care (the Romanow Commission). He became a member of the Order of Canada in 2021.

Tom McDowell is an instructor in the Department of Politics and Public Administration at Toronto Metropolitan University. A former Ontario legislative intern, Tom is the author of *Neoliberal Parliamentarism* (UTP) as well as several articles about the evolution of parliamentary government. His work takes a critical approach to the study of institutional and policy structures, emphasizing the impacts of neo-liberalism on socio-political phenomena.

Andrea Migone is an assistant professor in the Department of Politics and Public Administration at Toronto Metropolitan University. His research and publications focus on the intersection of public administration, public policy, and the role of institutions. He is a past research director at the Institute of Public Administration of Canada.

Larry Savage is a professor of labour studies at Brock University. His teaching and research focus on the politics of labour in Canada. He is also the author of *Socialist Cowboy: The Politics of Peter Kormos* and co-author with Charles W. Smith of *Unions in Court: Organized Labour and the Charter of Rights and Freedoms*.

Julie M. Simmons is an associate professor in the Department of Political Science at the University of Guelph. She teaches and researches in the fields of Canadian politics, federalism, public policy, and administration. She particularly focuses on issues of democracy and accountability in federal-provincial relations. She is co-editor of *Open Federalism Revisited: Regional and Federal Dynamics in the Harper Era* (UTP).

Tamara A. Small is a professor in the Department of Political Science at the University of Guelph. She is a leading expert on Canadian politics with a particular research focus on digital politics. She is the co-editor of *Digital Politics in Canada: Promises and Realities* (UTP). She held a Fulbright Visiting Research Chair at Vanderbilt University.

Zachary Spicer is an associate professor in the School of Public Policy and Administration at York University, where he also serves as the head of New College. He previously served as a senior policy advisor for the province of Ontario's Ministry of Municipal Affairs and Housing and conducts research in the areas of local government, public sector management, and innovation policy.

Mark Winfield is a professor of environmental and urban change at York University. He is also co-chair of the faculty's Sustainable Energy Initiative and coordinator of the Joint Master of Environmental Studies/Juris Doctor program offered in conjunction with Osgoode Hall Law School. He is the author of *Blue-Green Province: The Environment and the Political Economy of Ontario* and a co-edited volume on *Sustainable Energy Transitions for Canada*.

1

What Is Ontario?

Jonathan Malloy

What is Ontario? This is both a simple and difficult question to answer. Ontario exists as a jurisdiction, a province, and a constitutional and legal reality. But is it more than that? What actually makes Ontario ... Ontario? Is it a distinctive polity and society? This is a perennial question when attempting to describe and analyze the politics of Ontario.

Ontario is big and diverse. The east-west distance across the province, from its most easterly point near Montreal to the Manitoba border, is approximately 2,000 km and would take twenty-four continuous hours to drive. Toronto and the surrounding Greater Toronto Area (GTA) is by far the largest metropolitan centre in Ontario, and Canada, but the province has four other urban areas with at least a half-million people (Ottawa, Hamilton, Kitchener-Waterloo-Cambridge, and London). And while Ontario cities struggle with sprawl and affordable housing, more rural and remote areas grapple with aging and diminishing populations.

The Ontario population is increasingly racially diverse. Yet, it is an uneven distribution, especially between urban and rural areas. The Ontario economy is broad and multi-faceted, with strong primary, secondary, and tertiary industries, but prosperity is unequal both between and within regions and cities. And while more Indigenous people live in Ontario than any other province, they comprise only a small proportion of the total population, and the Indigenous reality of Ontario is often overlooked.

The lines between Ontario and Canada as a whole have long been blurry. Ontario is centred in the middle of the country. It contains over 40 per cent of the Canadian population, the national capital, and the country's largest city. The rest of the country feels, often with justification, that Ontarians mistakenly equate whatever is good for their province with what is good for Canada as a whole. And indeed, Ontarians are proud Canadians who exhibit a low level of identity with their province. Being Ontarian often seems little more than a jurisdictional label on one's health card or driver's licence, not a point of intense pride. Few think of themselves as Ontarians first. Hardly anyone flies the provincial flag outside of official locations. Ontario provincial licence plates for decades have been unsurpassed in their generic slogans – "Keep it Beautiful"; "Yours to Discover"; and "A Place to Grow" – that could apply to absolutely anywhere.

Ontario lacks unifying symbols and icons distinct to the province. Often, they tend to be ascribed to Canada as a whole. The most recent three Canadian prime ministers, Justin Trudeau, Stephen Harper, and Paul Martin, were all born and raised in Ontario, but then moved to other provinces where they built their careers and political identities. The first Tim Hortons restaurant was in Hamilton, co-founded by and named after Toronto Maple Leafs player Tim Horton, who was born in the Northern Ontario town of Cochrane. But no one thinks of the eponymous chain as a specifically Ontario – rather than Canadian – icon. Even the souvenir and memento business struggles for an iconic symbol or image of Ontario. The downtown Toronto skyline with the CN Tower usually wins out, but this is arguably a symbol of the city more than the province.

In 1968, historian Arthur Lower wrote an essay titled "Ontario: Does It Exist?"[1] Lower's point was to illustrate the lack of a clear Ontario identity. Many years later, the question takes on even greater impact, especially when trying to understand the politics of the province.

For much of the nineteenth and twentieth centuries, there arguably was a dominant Ontario identity, tied closely to its colonial history as a British and primarily Protestant Christian settler society. Ontario was shaped as a colonial jurisdiction by the American Revolution (1775–83) and the War of 1812, in which the colony repeatedly resisted American incursions. While most of Ontario's Indigenous heritage has been ignored in provincial history, exceptions were made for individuals like Thayendanegea (Joseph Brant) and Tecumseh, who fought on the British side against the Americans, thus fitting into the dominant colonial narrative. This colonial history underpins the provincial motto of *Ut incepit fidelis sic permanent*, translated as "Loyal She Began, Loyal She Remains."

This colonial embrace continued. The Ontario flag still includes the British Union Jack banner, which was discarded from the Canadian flag in 1965. In the 1920s, in a burst of royal enthusiasm, the Ontario Conservative government of the day renamed the fledgling provincial highway network as *The King's Highways*, and a distinctive crown is still observable at the top of every highway sign in the province.

Before Confederation, Ontario served as one half of the Province of Canada with Quebec as the other contrasting half; one predominantly French and Catholic, and one English and Protestant. This duality and pairing continued after Confederation, even as new provinces were added. Teaching in French in Ontario public schools was notoriously outlawed entirely in 1913, and it was only amid the pressures of Quebec nationalism and national unity crises that Ontario began to gingerly embrace bilingualism in the late twentieth century.

One of the most unique aspects of Ontario today is its maintenance of a dual publicly funded school system – both "public" and "separate" Roman Catholic schools. This is not merely an ancient nineteenth-century anachronism. The system gradually developed throughout the twentieth century, with the final phase not introduced until 1985. Most provinces never developed such a full, parallel denominational system, and ones that did, like Quebec and Newfoundland and Labrador, abandoned them by the 1990s. But there has never been a serious attempt in Ontario to unify the system; the closest was in the 2007 election when the Opposition Progressive Conservatives proposed similar funding for other faith-based schools but were defeated by the Liberals who championed the current arrangement. Religion and morality coloured the province in other ways. One of the hottest public issues in Ontario in the 1980s and early 1990s was the once heretical idea of Sunday shopping, and in sharp contrast to Quebec in particular, the province has always kept a tight rein on alcohol sales, only allowing the sale of beer and wine in grocery stores in 2016.

So perhaps there was once an Ontario identity, at least for the dominant population: a prosperous, somewhat prudish, deeply colonial, and Christian place. But what relevance does this have to twenty-first century Ontario – a place where many people have little or no religious identity; where almost a third are of a racialized background, and a minority are of British heritage; and where there is increasing though uneven recognition of the Indigenous population in Ontario? This returns us to the opening question: what is Ontario?

GEOGRAPHIC, SOCIAL, AND ECONOMIC DIVERSITY

Ontario is a geographically diverse province. Within Canada, only Quebec and British Columbia come close to approximating the variety of physical landscapes and economic and social patterns found in Ontario. Yet with most of the population huddled in the South, primarily around Lake Ontario, the province arguably has the worst of both worlds – neither a firm geographic identity nor a truly clear sense of distinctive parts.

The province has regions, sometimes delineated by neat administrative boundaries. But it can be more difficult to identify socially agreed-upon boundaries that people identify with, as opposed to purely jurisdictional ones. "Eastern Ontario" arguably starts around Peterborough or Belleville, but maybe not until Kingston; "Southwestern Ontario" probably begins at London or maybe Woodstock; "central Ontario" usually consists of whatever is left over. And despite the overall provincial heterogeneity, there is a certain sameness to much of Southern Ontario. The mighty 401 highway that connects the province is perhaps the dullest drive in Canada, a mix of undistinguished countryside and low-rise industrial areas, lacking the spectacular Big Sky of the flat western Prairies.

The one consistent agreement is that there is something called *Northern Ontario*. More than any other Canadian province, the northern portion of Ontario feels and looks on a map to be distinctly cut off from the southern part, divided by a narrow isthmus between Georgian Bay and the Quebec border. The North can then be divided into Northeastern and Northwestern Ontario and even further divisions, but together it does have a consistent identity, one of alienation from the southern part of the province that contains only a sliver of provincial land but more than 90 per cent of the provincial population.

The constant expansion outward from Toronto in all directions has further reduced a sense of regional distinctions. Cities like Oshawa or Burlington once stood alone as their own separate communities, but have been surrounded and swamped by the general urban expansion, along with formerly small towns like Milton or Newmarket. Rising real estate prices have driven families further and further from the core in search of affordable homes, so that even large cities like Hamilton and Kitchener-Waterloo are increasingly being sucked into the Toronto orbit. The same types of housing developments, chain restaurants, and big-box stores dot the landscape everywhere, creating a generic suburbia of consumer culture and increasingly a limited sense of community differences.

There is more distinctiveness in racial settlement patterns. About 56% of the city of Toronto residents are non-white racialized individuals,[2] compared to 34% of the province as a whole. This is much higher than any other major Ontario city such as Ottawa (32%), London (29%), or Hamilton (25%). Yet racial diversity is even higher in some cities surrounding Toronto. In Markham, 82% of people are non-white, as is 81% of Brampton and 66% of Richmond Hill. In contrast, some GTA cities are still majority white, such as Oakville (42% racialized), Vaughan (41%), or Whitby (35%). There are also distinctive patterns; for example, 48% of Markham residents are of Chinese ethnicity, while 52% of Brampton residents have a South Asian background. But as one moves outward from the GTA, the racialized portion of the population grows smaller and smaller. Thus, race is increasingly the most obvious way in which Ontario communities can be distinguished from each other, a fact with many implications. (Race also has strong implications within cities, especially the stark racial distribution patterns in Toronto that correlate with income and wealth).

If there is an Ontario "heartland" in the twenty-first century, it may as well be Mississauga, the city west of Toronto. Almost 800,000 people live in Mississauga, making it more populous than three Canadian provinces and itself the sixth-largest municipality in Canada, ahead of Winnipeg and the city of Vancouver. Mississauga is also deeply diverse, with 57 per cent of its population racialized. Yet Mississauga, like Ontario itself, lacks a clear identity or distinctiveness separate from the other cities bumping up against its borders – despite valiant attempts to give meaning to the words "downtown Mississauga" – and was itself cobbled together from different historic towns like Streetsville and Port Credit. Mississauga exists, but like the province, it is sometimes more a jurisdiction than a cohesive and distinct society of its own.

More Indigenous people live in Ontario than any other province. But their proportion of the overall population is among the smallest in Canada – only 2.8 per cent.[3] The Indigenous reality of Ontario is often muted and overlooked despite the presence of one of the largest reserves in Canada, Six Nations, ninety minutes from downtown Toronto. Indigeneity is more visible in Northern Ontario, in the northern cities as well as in isolated and often fly-in communities. But this can make Indigenous issues seem like an exclusively northern affair, unconnected on a day-to-day basis to the Ontario southern metropolis. Only in times of confrontation and conflict, such as the Tyendinaga rail blockade of 2020 or the long-running Caledonia housing development dispute, do most non-Indigenous Ontarians consider Indigenous issues to be a local matter.

Franco-Ontarians are another often overlooked aspect of Ontario society, with 3.6 per cent of Ontarians speaking French as their first language. This is often forgotten, especially in the Greater Toronto Area, where many people speak a mother tongue other than English or French. Yet French is the majority language in many towns and communities in Eastern Ontario, from Alexandria in the east to Hearst in the north. Cities like Sudbury, Cornwall, and Ottawa all have strong French-speaking populations; Windsor also has a small but important French legacy, though it is rapidly diminishing. Thus, for part of Ontario, the "French fact" is an everyday reality, but much of the province is oblivious to it.

Economically, the Ontario identity was once closely tied to its predominance in manufacturing. The twentieth-century economic icons of Ontario included the General Motors complex in Oshawa, which employed 22,000 workers at its peak, and the competing steel concerns of Stelco and Dofasco that dominated Hamilton Harbour. But the Oshawa GM plant now employs only a fraction of its once huge workforce, and halted production entirely for a period from 2018 to 2020. Stelco and Dofasco are still operating, but with far fewer workers, and they were long ago acquired and renamed by foreign multinationals (though Stelco returned to Canadian ownership and its original name in 2016).

Ontario remains a strong centre of manufacturing. The automotive sector continues to be the largest employer in cities like Windsor, where the Ambassador Bridge spanning the border carries a quarter of all Canada-US trade, most of it manufactured goods. But manufacturing itself has changed, with an ever-increasing focus on technology over labour, especially unskilled labour. For a brief period in the early 2000s, Waterloo was the centre of the global technological universe with the invention and manufacturing of the BlackBerry, the first widespread smartphone, by local entrepreneurs Mike Laziridis and Jim Balsillie. Although the BlackBerry was eclipsed by the iPhone and other devices, Kitchener-Waterloo remains a strong centre of technological innovation. Ontario still builds things, but with a much smaller and more specialized workforce.

Ontario also retains a strong primary economy – the farms that dot Western Ontario, forestry in the east and north, and mining. But again, technology is replacing labour. Agriculture, in particular, is increasingly big business, a far cry from the small family farms of the past. And like all modern societies, Ontario has developed a tertiary service economy that can be lucrative and prosperous, but often uneven, providing well-paid jobs for some but an uncertain "gig economy" for others. Overall, the Ontario economy is huge and broadly based, so that unlike some provinces, Ontario is not prone to booms and busts in commodities like oil or fish. The challenge instead is to keep the broad base growing in all directions, maintaining the diverse and varied Ontario economy.

In short, there is no single "Ontario." The province is diverse geographically, socially, and economically. Yet the differences are often fuzzy and blend together. The sharpest distinction is between the GTA, especially its racial diversity, and the rest of the province. But in practice, even this divide is gradual. And the continuing growth of sprawl means everything is converging more than diverging, without a clear sense of what makes Ontario.

ONTARIO IN CONFEDERATION

Ontario's identity within Canada is also unclear. Ironically, the rest of Canada may have a stronger distinct impression of Ontario than Ontarians do of themselves – though often a negative one. For much of Canada, Ontario is the 800-pound gorilla of Confederation; the fat-cat province. Non-Ontarians see it as the province that sucks up the majority of resources and attention, overshadowing the different needs of other regions, often out of sheer ignorance.

When the rest of Canada thinks about Ontario, they likely think primarily of downtown Toronto – the centre of the Canadian financial industry and English-language media and communications. More broadly, some speak of the "Laurentian Elite" centred in Toronto and Ottawa (and also Montreal) that has had a predominant voice in Canadian public and economic affairs. Yet Ontario is much more than downtown Toronto and urban elites. Non-Ontarians might be surprised at the number of Ontario communities where pickup trucks are the vehicle of choice and workplaces shut down for hunting season. In fact, much of the province has its own resentments about Torontonian arrogance and GTA-centrism. But what is true is that Ontarians, virtually alone among Canadian provinces, have no sense of general alienation from the federal government, nor do they feel peripheral and neglected by other parts of Canada.

This is not to say that Ontario does not have grievances and disputes in the federation. It has many, going back to the nineteenth century when Ontario premier Oliver Mowat was the leading champion of provincial rights and regularly took the federal government to court over jurisdictional disputes. These disputes carried into the twenty-first century, when the Dalton McGuinty government took out advertising demanding a "Fair Share" of federal dollars for Ontario. Ontario also has long-running disputes with other provinces, particularly Quebec, over cross-border trade issues.

But Ontario's disputes are overwhelmingly technical in nature: a matter of funding formulas and finely tuned constitutional arguments. They are driven by governments more than popular feeling, and in most cases these disputes are solely about money, not larger principles and ideals. Individual Ontarians may dislike a particular prime minister or governing party, but there is no general reservoir of overall estrangement and skepticism towards the federal government among Ontarians, as there is to at least some degree in every other Canadian province. (The exception is Northern Ontario, where such a reservoir of resentment, complaints, irritations, and general feelings of neglect does exist, but is directed primarily *within* the province, at Southern Ontario.)

Historically, Ontario saw itself as the honest broker of Confederation – the province that brought few demands of its own to the bargaining table and thus could facilitate agreement among everyone else. This was particularly the case in the great constitutional negotiations of the 1960s to 1990s. For example, in 1980, when then-prime minister Pierre Trudeau attempted to unilaterally patriate the Constitution, eight provinces opposed him, and many took the federal government to court. But Ontario, under Bill Davis (along with New Brunswick), supported the federal side. Two years later, Davis agreed to a re-adjustment of the federal Equalization formula to exclude Ontario, even though the province qualified for its own payments under the current formula. While more recent premiers have been less deferential, Ontario still prefers to see itself in this disinterested facilitator role, making sure everyone else gets along.

The rest of Canada has a less benign view of Ontario, and in any event, the honest broker role is again an elitist, government-driven identity. But this returns us to the question of what is Ontario? Having grievances at least builds shared identity and solidarity among a population. But because Ontario lacks a strong sense of its place within Confederation, other than entitlement and self-satisfaction, it is again unclear exactly what makes Ontario Ontario, especially as a political society.

THE ONTARIO POLITICAL CULTURE

Ontario has never been seen as a laboratory of political change. "Ontarians have a reputation for political immobility. At most, they have been content to nibble at innovation," wrote Desmond Morton in 1975,[4] and Peter Woolstencroft wrote in 2016 that "Ontarians are conservative and politically indifferent people. Political interest is episodic and sporadic, and political conversations seem to be rare."[5] The most important public policy innovation in Ontario is over a century old, when it became the first jurisdiction in North America to create a publicly owned electricity utility, long known as Ontario Hydro. (The province also relies on nuclear power far more today than any other province, a controversial distinction it does not trumpet.) But it is difficult to identify more recent innovations of the same scale.

Most Ontario political leaders are also unremarkable. There are exceptions, notably the current premier Doug Ford, who is the most colourful Ontario premier since Mitch Hepburn, premier from 1934 to 1942. Hepburn was a brash Depression-era populist who auctioned off the previous government's ministerial limousines at Varsity Stadium in downtown Toronto and later sold off the contents of the lieutenant governor's residence. But most Ontario leaders have tended towards "bland," the famous label of Bill Davis, premier from 1971 to 1985.

Is this blandness itself a distinctive aspect of Ontario? For many years, there has been an interest in whether Ontario has a distinct "political culture" compared to the rest of Canada. The entire concept of political culture – a sense of enduring values that guide political expectations and norms, distinct from short-term election patterns – is somewhat problematic and prone to overgeneralizations and stereotypes. Nevertheless, Ontario did seem to display a distinctive political culture for much of the twentieth century, especially when a single party, the Conservatives (renamed the Progressive Conservatives in 1942 as part of a general renaming across Canada), held power almost continuously from 1905 to 1985, including a forty-two-year unbroken streak from 1943 to 1985.

The ability of the "PC dynasty" to continuously reinvent themselves and stay in power for this extended period, despite massive changes in the Ontario economy and society, suggested they had managed to find and maintain an enduring sweet spot in the provincial political culture. In 1980, John Wilson argued that Ontario was the "Red Tory province" that truly embodied the oxymoronic Canadian values of "progressive conservatism," and "in Ontario we don't believe in change for the sake of change; we prefer order, stability, and continuity. And as long as the Conservatives can prove that – with just a touch of reform when the times demand it – they can go on at Queen's Park for ever."[6]

Wilson listed the prevailing Ontario political culture values as "ascriptive," "elitist," "hierarchical," "stable," "cautious," and "restrained."[7] These arguably also described the Ontario PC party, especially under the aforementioned Bill Davis, who really did proclaim that his cautious style of politics was effective and that his slogan could be "bland works." This pragmatism was key for political leadership; Noel argues that, "more than the people of any other province, and perhaps more than any people anywhere, Ontarians tend to define political leadership in terms of managerial capability rather than other qualities such as personal charisma."[8]

But the PC dynasty ended long ago, in 1985. Does that mean the Ontario political culture shifted or shattered as well? There are two competing interpretations, again triggering broader questions about what constitutes Ontario, especially its politics.

One interpretation has a simple answer: yes, everything has changed. Indeed, Ontario politics has lurched in many directions since 1985, suggesting an unstable and evolving political culture and polity. The period 1985–95 was a rollercoaster decade in Ontario politics, seeing three successive parties in power: the Liberals under David Peterson, the NDP under Bob Rae, and a reinvented PC party under Mike Harris, which took power in 1995 with an aggressive and populist "Common Sense Revolution" platform and style very different from its dynastic predecessors. The 1990s thus saw substantive turmoil and polarization in Ontario politics. The PCs were then succeeded in 2003 by the Liberals under Dalton McGuinty, who won three elections but resigned amid declining popularity and scandal. He was succeeded by Kathleen Wynne, who won re-election in 2014 but was then badly defeated in 2018, her party nearly wiped out. Wynne was replaced by the bombastic Doug Ford, an unexpected newcomer to provincial politics with a personal style that seems the complete opposite of "bland."

In sum, under this interpretation, Ontario politics in recent decades has become lurching and unpredictable, suggesting that the underlying political culture of the past, if it did exist, is long gone. Contrarian analyses of Ontario's political culture have arisen. In 2013, McGrane and Berdahl reported survey findings that Ontarians were in fact more restless and unstable compared to other Canadians: "residents of Ontario feel more disaffected from the political process than residents of provinces to their east or west: Ontarians have lower efficacy than do Prairie residents and rate government honesty lower than do residents of most other provinces.... Rather than being centrist and efficacious, Ontario is found to be disaffected and somewhat left of centre."[9]

This is a far cry from Wilson's 1980 assessment of Ontarians as "ascriptive" and "cautious."

But another interpretation is that the basic Ontario political culture of the twentieth century has endured into the twenty-first. While governing parties have come and gone, there may still be core values that have remained consistent.

Sid Noel argued in 1997 that the Ontario political culture has "five operative norms": the imperative pursuit of economic success, the assumption of pre-eminence in the Canadian federation, the requirement of managerial efficiency in government, the expectation of reciprocity in political relationships, and the balancing of interests.[10] In the old campaign adage that "parties don't win elections; governments lose them," changes in government can be seen as occurring when governments have *not* stayed in tune with these operative norms and the prevailing Ontario political culture of moderation, economic growth, and stability. Collier also notes that Ontario's political culture traits and assumptions seem to continue regardless of the province's actual economic fortunes and status in Confederation: "the appearance and presumption of pre-eminence remains strong (and lingering) even if the reality doesn't always align with this view."[11]

This argument – that the underlying managerial Ontario political culture remains intact – explains that the province unexpectedly elected the NDP to power in 1990 because of the arrogance of the then-governing Liberals, which violated the cautious tenets of Ontario political culture. Voters in 1995 then turned to the Ontario PCs when the NDP showed itself unprepared to manage government, again not fitting the political culture. As noted, the 1995 Ontario PCs came to power with an aggressive agenda, the "Common Sense Revolution." Yet Wilson wrote in 1997 that "it does appear to be the same old Ontario."[12] In this interpretation, the Harris Conservatives were not reshaping the province so much as bringing it back to equilibrium after the Liberal and New Democrat detours, especially the principle of "managerial efficiency," which the well-organized 1995 Conservatives were indeed very good at.[13] The underlying political culture – the core values of Ontario politics – remained consistent.

This interpretation was bolstered in 2003 when the PCs ran out of energy and ideas, and were replaced by the Liberals under Dalton McGuinty, a moderate who governed in a style not unlike Bill Davis. In power from 2003 to 2013, McGuinty was nicknamed "Premier Dad" for his well-meaning but sometimes condescending manner, and his government followed a progressive but still cautious direction. This certainly resembled the old PC dynasty, especially when the party was able to transfer power to Kathleen Wynne, who won her own re-election in 2014 despite unfavourable polls. But the Wynne government arguably moved too far to the left while accumulating further scandals. The province thus sought another reset, supplied by the PCs under Doug Ford. And while the Ford government moved aggressively, similar to its 1995 predecessor, Ford himself displays a paternalistic style not unlike some of his predecessors, albeit a far less polished version. The successful 2022 PC re-election slogan – "Get It Done" – fits perfectly with Wilson's and Noel's observations a quarter century earlier that "managerial efficiency" is the key to the Ontario political culture.[14]

Either of these interpretations are plausible. And there is merit in debating them because it brings us back to the core question: what is Ontario? Does it have a distinct and consistent political culture? Is there a consistent key, a sweet spot, to winning power and governing Ontario? Or is Ontario politics an unpredictable rollercoaster, reflecting a lack of underlying provincial consensus and identity? These are key questions to be explored in *The Politics of Ontario*.

ONTARIO AS A PLACE OF CHANGE

One thing Ontario is not is static. It is a changing, growing province – rarely radical change, but certainly continual evolution in its population, economy, and politics. Perhaps this is why it is difficult to nail down any one identity for the province. There is always something new or different or additional about Ontario. This may be what is most distinctive about the province – it is not any one thing, and it does not stand still. Unlike many provinces and societies, it does not struggle to move beyond well-worn narratives and confining expectations of what is and is not Ontarian. Its bland profile provides a blank script, an opportunity for Ontarians to go in many directions and perhaps to grow as they wish.

While vestiges of its British Protestant past remain, including the parliamentary system of government that it shares with the rest of Canada, Ontario has come a long way from the insular colonial identity of a century ago. It is a much more diverse, outward-looking society. Yet there is also much more to go.

In an earlier edition of *The Politics of Ontario*, Graham White noted the tremendous social changes in Ontario since 1950, but asked whether the scale of social change was matched by a similar scale of change politically.¹⁵ This remains a compelling question. Perhaps most importantly, the increasing diversity of Ontario is not reflected in its political class. The province has had a single woman premier (Kathleen Wynne), and only three other women have led its political parties (Lyn McLeod, Liberal leader from 1992 to 1996, and Andrea Horvath and Marit Stiles, the most recent two NDP leaders). No party has had a racialized minority leader. And despite being majority racialized for some time, Toronto only saw its first racialized mayor elected in 2023 with Olivia Chow.

Similarly, the unequal prosperity of twenty-first-century Ontario is concerning, especially the growing unaffordability of homes and the divergence between well-paid and precarious labour – often with racialized patterns. New immigrants struggle to succeed in the same way as previous newcomers. These trends are not unique to the province. But they go against the historic image of a prosperous Ontario in which life was good and affordable, and all boats rose together. While its cities struggle with sprawl and the demands of growth, smaller towns and northern and rural areas often face depopulation and struggle to maintain schools and services. Finally, we can repeat that the Indigenous reality of Ontario and its specific challenges are often muted and overlooked, especially in Southern Ontario.

Ontario is both a place of change and in need of further change. This makes its politics interesting and dynamic. There is no simple response to the question of what is Ontario, but there are plenty of competing answers. Politics is about the authoritative allocation of values, and so Ontario's political struggles are about the values that should be pursued in Ontario government and public policy. Ultimately, the question of what Ontario is sits at the heart of the politics of Ontario.

NOTES

1 A.M. Lower, "Ontario – Does It Exist?," *Ontario History* 15, no. 2 (June 1968): 65–9.
2 All figures from Statistics Canada, *2021 Census of Population*, https://www12.statcan.gc.ca/census-recensement/2021/dp-pd/prof/search-recherche/lst/results-resultats.cfm?Lang=E&GEOCODE=35.
3 "Indigenous Peoples in Ontario," Government of Ontario, last modified May 2, 2022, https://www.ontario.ca/document/spirit-reconciliation-ministry-indigenous-relations-and-reconciliation-first-10-years/indigenous-peoples-ontario.

4 Desmond Morton, "Introduction: People and Politics of Ontario," in *Government and Politics of Ontario*, ed. Donald C. MacDonald (Toronto: Macmillan, 1975), 5.
5 Peter Woolstencroft, "Political Culture in Ontario: Old and New," in *The Politics of Ontario*, ed. Cheryl N. Collier and Jonathan Malloy (Toronto: University of Toronto Press, 2017), 73.
6 John Wilson, "The Red Tory Province: Reflections on the Ontario Political Culture," in *The Government and Politics of Ontario*, rev. ed., ed. Donald C. MacDonald (Toronto: Van Nostrand Reinhold, 1980), 225.
7 Wilson, "The Red Tory Province," 214.
8 Sid Noel, "The Ontario Political Culture: An Interpretation," in *The Government and Politics of Ontario*, 5th ed., ed. Graham White (Toronto: University of Toronto Press, 1997), 60–1.
9 David McGrane and Loleen Berdahl, "'Small Worlds' No More: Reconsidering Provincial Political Cultures in Canada," *Regional & Federal Studies* 23, no. 4 (2013): 486, https://doi.org/10.1080/13597566.2013.794415.
10 Noel, "The Ontario Political Culture," 53.
11 Cheryl N. Collier, "Ontario's New Identity? Assessing Ontario's Political Culture and Place in Confederation under Open Federalism," in *Open Federalism Revisited: Regional and Federal Dynamics in the Harper Era*, ed. Julie M. Simmons and James H. Farney (Toronto: University of Toronto Press, 2022), 48.
12 John Wilson, "The Ontario Political Culture at the End of the Century," in *Revolution at Queen's Park: Essays on Governing Ontario*, ed. Sid Noel (Toronto: James Lorimer, 1997), 71.
13 The 1995 Ontario PC takeover has been recognized as an unusually well-organized and highly professional operation that melded well with the existing public service. See David Cameron and Graham White, *Cycling into Saigon: The Conservative Transition in Ontario* (Vancouver: UBC Press, 1999).
14 Jonathan Malloy, "Ontario Election: Doug Ford's Victory Shows He's Not the Polarizing Figure He Once Was," *The Conversation*, June 2, 2022, https://theconversation.com/ontario-election-doug-fords-victory-shows-hes-not-the-polarizing-figure-he-once-was-183885.
15 Graham White, "Ontario Then and Now," in *The Politics of Ontario*, ed. Cheryl N. Collier and Jonathan Malloy (Toronto: University of Toronto Press, 2017), 3.

The Political Economy of Ontario: How Did Ontario Get So Rich? And Why Are There So Many Poor Ontarians?

Peter Graefe

Every day, people get out of bed, produce and reproduce the world, and engage in relationships with other people. Societies have organized this production in many ways over human history, and even in the contemporary world there are important differences between societies in how this work is organized in and between families, communities, firms, and governments. The premise of political economy is that the organization of the work, and of the power relationships bound up in this organization, provides insight into political conflicts and outcomes.

There are many different approaches to studying political economy,[1] but each, in its own way, insists that the study of the economy and the political system cannot be divorced from each other. A wealthy society can generate resources for the state to invest in social policies. A society with highly concentrated wealth may face greater political instability as the wealthy try to keep the poor out of political power. The industrial structure also affects politics. A resource economy with boom-and-bust swings will adopt different approaches to planning and budgeting than a diversified economy. Gig workers look for different labour market policies than workers in stable long-term jobs. In other words, the way that a society organizes its economy has political consequences. This was particularly visible during the COVID-19 pandemic, as one's placement in the economy affected the likelihood of losing one's job or being deemed an "essential worker" who was expected to risk infection at the workplace. Those at the edges of the labour market were both more likely to lose work or be required to perform in-person work, and this showed up in the disproportionate burden of impacts borne by racialized and low-income Ontarians.[2] And since the economy affects people's livelihoods and distributes resources unevenly, people often contest how it is organized.

This chapter provides an overview of Ontario's political economy, paying attention to the political conflicts that can be traced back to relationships in the daily production of the world. The chapter begins by explaining how Ontario became the industrial heartland of Canada and one of the world's richest societies through the twentieth century. This, nevertheless, was partly based on unequal relationships with Indigenous Peoples and Canadians from other provinces and territories, producing conflicts that continue to animate Ontario politics to this day. The second section of this chapter considers the province's loss of economic competitiveness, especially in manufacturing, in the past fifty years. The third section turns to the transition in the provincial economy, represented by the shift to the service economy. With the decline of manufacturing since the turn of the millennium, high-wage financial services have grown in importance at the same time as low-wage personal services. The fourth section considers some of the implications of that shift in terms of current politics around poverty and racialization.

HOW DID YOU GET SO RICH?

If one were to describe Ontario's current economy in one word, "capitalist" would be the most accurate descriptor. While an important share of economic activity is channelled through the state to provide social policies, and while families and non-profit organizations offer large amounts of caring and support on a non-market basis, these economies ultimately depend on and are geared to wealth creation by private corporations operating in the capitalist market economy. The centrality of capitalism to defining Ontario's political economy reaches back to at least Confederation (1867). From a longer-term perspective, however, capitalism is a new political economic framework for governing the space of present-day Ontario. The pre-existing Indigenous societies organized themselves based on different political economies than capitalism. While these varied, they tended to be more relational and less anthropocentric than individualist capitalism, stressing the importance of maintaining good relations with other living beings and the land.[3]

These political economies were displaced through waves of treaty-making between the Treaty of Niagara of 1764 and Confederation, starting with lands along the Great Lakes and major waterways and spreading outward up to and including the near north. After Confederation, the remaining lands that now make up Ontario's north and northwest were covered as part of the negotiation of the numbered treaties. While the Indigenous signatories understood these agreements to signal a sharing of the land, commit to mutual assistance, and allow each community to continue to govern themselves according to their own laws and customs, the Europeans considered these to be land cessions, and believed that Indigenous Peoples were destined to fall under the paternalistic governance of the Canadian State and its *Indian Act*. As Canada now enters a period of reconciliation, one challenge for Ontarians is to reconcile the capitalist premises of its economic organization with treaty commitments that contain distinctly non-capitalist premises about the proper organization of society. While land acknowledgements are now commonplace before public events, most Ontarians have no knowledge of their treaty responsibilities. Still, if we were to ask, "how did Ontario get so rich," a first part of the answer comes from this story of the dispossession of the lands that produced Ontario's nineteenth-century agricultural wealth and its twentieth- and twenty-first-century mineral and forest wealth.

A second part of the answer comes from the purposes of Canadian Confederation. The coalition in Upper and Lower Canada in support of Confederation came together behind a project of western expansion controlled and directed by the financial and industrial interests in Montreal and Toronto. Prime Minister John A. Macdonald's policy of building a pan-continental railroad and displacing the Indigenous Peoples of the plains with European settlers had obvious benefits for the railway companies, banks, grain companies, and agricultural implement manufacturers of Southern Ontario. Toronto and Montreal could thereby appropriate an important economic surplus from this expanding agricultural economy.

The ability to seize this surplus nevertheless required cutting out competition from the more advanced British and American economies. The decision to impose tariffs as part of the National Policy was crucial to this end, making it too expensive to import foreign manufactured goods. The tariff spurred the development of a Canadian manufacturing economy, centred in Ontario.[4] Unlike other later developing societies that used a tariff wall to shield the development of domestic technological advantages or a locally-based capitalist class, the Canadian one seemed designed to encourage American firms to "jump over the wall" and set up Canadian subsidiaries. Ontario thereby stood to benefit from an influx of American know-how and investment, yet also developed a form of dependency – a successful manufacturing sector would require continued imports of American investment and technological innovation. In sum, a second part of the answer about "how Ontario got so rich" is that the project of creating Canada was intimately related to central Canadian economic interests. It is no surprise that western Canadian farmers' movements after the First World War developed a critique that was both populist (counterposing the powerless farmer to powerful banks, railways, and grain companies) and regionalist (emphasizing how the West was exploited by Central Canada).

Nevertheless, if one were to compare late nineteenth-century Ontario to the neighbouring United States, it would appear as a poor backwater. In 1896, America's GDP per capita was 70 per cent greater than that of Canada.[5] Using the tariff to encourage American investment was one thing, but in the absence of purchasing power, there was not a lot of incentive to serve the Canadian market. What really turned the switch on Ontario's development was the ability to piggyback on the development of the mass production methods developed in the United States in the first decades of the twentieth century,[6] particularly as the wheat boom finally produced the wealth necessary to sustain domestic manufacturing. While Ontario firms continued to lag the United States in innovation and productivity, by borrowing these new techniques and importing the related technologies, they managed to close the gap and jump ahead of many European societies. For instance, by 1913, Canadian productivity had risen to 87 per cent of American productivity, placing it ahead of Great Britain, the previous industrial powerhouse, which was at 84 per cent of American productivity. By 1929, the United States' GDP per capita was only 31 per cent above Canada's.[7]

GETTING LESS RICH

The relative strength of Ontario's manufacturing sector brought generalized prosperity to the province. Profitability in mass production relies in part on mass consumption – there is no profit to be made in unsold goods – and so the productivity gains of this period were paid out not only in high profits but in higher wages. The mechanism for raising wages was the legal recognition of collective bargaining, won by the unions through a wave of strikes after the Second World War. This allowed unions in leading manufacturing industries to set wage expectations that would then shape wage demands in the rest of the economy.[8] Worker power produced an inclusive growth model, in the sense that it extended middle-class standards of living well into the working class.[9] True, this prosperity was also built on a particular gender order. Access to well-paid manufacturing jobs was limited to the male workforce. Women were expected to do unpaid work in families and to be supported by a male wage. Female-dominated sectors such as retail and clerical work were marked by low wages and higher rates of non-standard work, on the convenient premise that this work was a supplement to the male wage.[10] Still, as Ontario moved into the 1970s and 1980s, the women's movement generally made demands to be included equally in this shared prosperity, rather than seeking to change the growth model itself.

The prosperity of these years was reflected in the growth of the state, as the province had to respond to economic and population growth, as well as the increasing complexity of production, by building supportive energy and transportation infrastructure, as well as expanded health, educational and post-secondary systems.[11] The building of the Ontario welfare state nevertheless followed a liberal, as opposed to a social democratic course, reflecting the dominance of the pro-business Conservative party: protection from the risks of modern society (old age, unemployment, injury, ill health) would mainly flow from insurance tied to employment, with meagre benefits for those outside of the paid workforce, while care work for young children and the elderly was mainly a private responsibility to be provided in the family or purchased on the market.[12]

The advantage of the early adoption of the American production model was nevertheless fated to fade as other countries adopted it, especially after the Second World War. This normal loss of productive advantage was nevertheless heightened in Ontario due to the nature of the province's industrial sector.[13] The reliance on American branch plant firms had several ramifications for competitiveness. First, it meant that the research and development and innovation activities for many leading firms in the manufacturing sector were being completed in the United States. New advances were most likely to be piloted and implemented there, creating a lag in their adoption north of the border. Given that Ontario plants were used to service the smaller Canadian market, they often also were less efficient as they had shorter production runs or had to change-over between products more frequently.

Despite these factors undermining Ontario's productivity advantage, the province's industrial strategy in the post–Second World War years remained one of encouraging private sector investment, be it foreign or domestic, through the provision of infrastructure and ensuring a stable investment climate of orderly industrial relations and competitive regulation.[14] While tariffs and international trade barriers slowly came down over the period, Ontario remained Canada's manufacturing heartland. It benefitted from the growing prosperity of the other provinces as it supplied the vast majority of major consumer goods.[15] The manufacturing economy received a further boost with the negotiation of the Auto Pact in 1965, a managed trade agreement with the United States that guaranteed that the American automakers would make a car in Canada for every car they sold in Canada. This ensured that Ontario would benefit from ongoing automotive investment and so remain an important manufacturing hub.[16]

The future of the province's manufacturing economy came to a head in the debate over the free trade agreement with the United States in the late 1980s. Opponents of free trade argued that the branch plant nature of the Ontario manufacturing sector, and the related lower levels of innovation and productivity, would result in American owners shuttering Ontario plants as they would consolidate their operations in more productive American plants and export tariff-free to Canada. Proponents of free trade, including most of corporate Canada, argued that the only way to improve Ontario's lagging productivity was through strengthened competition, as Ontario plants would compete for global product mandates. In the end, neither side was terribly prescient. There was a spate of high-profile branch plant closures, which was accentuated by the early 1990s recession that finished off Canadian manufacturing in the clothing, home appliance, small consumer goods (televisions, radios), and furniture sectors. At the same time, there was also a spate of new firm openings, usually with smaller plants and located outside more traditional industrial areas. These plants were also less likely to be unionized, had a lower salary structure than before, and served as an important point of labour market entry for racialized workers,[17] who are overrepresented in this sector compared to their population share.[18]

Compared to the trend in the Global North of manufacturing employment shrinking in absolute terms through the 1990s, Ontario stood out in its ability to increase manufacturing employment. This could be attributed to the low Canadian dollar, which made Ontario's exports to the United States cost competitive. Public health care also increased Ontario's cost competitiveness,

Table 2.1. Share of Gross Domestic Product by Industry, 1997–2021

Industry	1997	2007	2017	2021
Finance and insurance	7.5	9	9.3	9.7
Manufacturing	21.7	16	12.0	10.9
Public administration	6.4	6.6	7.4	7.6
Health care and social assistance	6.2	6.5	7.0	7.0
Wholesale trade	5.9	6.2	6.4	6.5
Educational services	5.4	5.5	5.8	5.8
Professional, scientific, and technical services	4.6	6.2	7.1	7.8
Retail trade	4.7	5.1	4.7	4.6
Construction	4.6	6	6.9	8.0
Transportation and warehousing	4.1	3.7	4.1	3.7
Information and cultural industries	3.2	3.7	3.8	3.9
Administrative support, waste management, and remediation services	2.3	3.4	3.3	3.3
Utilities	3.3	2	1.8	1.9
Other services (except public administration)	1.9	2	2.0	1.8
Accommodation and food services	1.8	1.8	2.1	1.3
Mining and oil and gas extraction	0.9	1.4	1.0	1.0
Agriculture, forestry, fishing, and hunting	0.9	0.8	1.0	1.1
Arts, entertainment, and recreation	0.9	0.8	0.8	0.6
Real estate and rental and leasing	13.1	12.3	13.0	13.7

Source: Statistics Canada, "Table 36-10-0400-01: Gross Domestic Product (GDP) at Basic Prices, by Industry, Provinces and Territories, Percentage," https://doi.org/10.25318/3610040001-eng. Contains information licensed under the Open Government Licence – Canada.

as manufacturing employers did not have to pay health insurance benefits for their employees.[19] Nevertheless, the weakening of branch-plant linkages did not spur increases in productivity and innovation, but indeed the opposite. In the mid- to late 1990s, as American manufacturing integrated new information and communication technologies to spur productivity, Canadian manufacturers instead relied on cost-competitiveness,[20] and the Canadian high-tech sector showed little vitality outside of a couple of giant firms, the

Table 2.2. Share of Employment by Industry, 1997–2021

Industry	1997	2007	2017	2021
Goods-producing industries	24.6	20.4	17.5	17.8
Forestry, logging, and support	0.2	0.1	0.1	0.1
Mining, quarrying, and oil and gas extraction	0.5	0.4	0.4	0.4
Utilities	0.9	0.8	0.8	0.8
Construction	3.5	4.7	5.5	6.0
Manufacturing	19.5	14.4	10.8	10.6
Service-producing industries	75.4	79.6	82.5	82
Trade	17.4	17.5	17.1	16.8
Transportation and warehousing	4.5	4.4	4.2	4.6
Information and cultural industries	2.8	2.4	2.6	2.5
Finance and insurance	–	5.1	5.5	5.7
Real estate and rental and leasing	–	1.9	1.9	1.7
Professional, scientific, and technical services	4.5	5.6	6.2	7.3
Management of companies and enterprises	0.5	0.8	0.6	0.7
Administrative and support, waste management and remediation services	4.1	6.5	5.7	5.8
Educational services	7.3	7.5	7.8	8.0
Health care and social assistance	9.6	9.6	11.4	12.1
Arts, entertainment, and recreation	1.6	1.7	1.9	1.3
Accommodation and food services	6.8	6.6	7.8	5.9
Other services (except public administration)	3.8	3.3	3.2	2.8
Public administration	5.8	6.7	6.6	7.0
Unclassified businesses	–	1.4	2.0	1.8

Source: Statistics Canada, "Table 14-10-0202-01: Employment by Industry, Annual," https://doi.org/10.25318/1410020201-eng. Contains information licensed under the Open Government Licence – Canada.

largest of which (Nortel) failed in the early 2000s and was sold off in pieces to global competitors.[21]

Ontario therefore prospered as a low-cost manufacturing platform with highly educated labour serving the American market with less specialized products. This kind of cost competitiveness is nevertheless fleeting if a more dynamic competitiveness based on productivity improvements and innovation is weak, as it has long been in Ontario. Once the Canadian dollar increased in value in the early 2000s on the strength of the Alberta (and Saskatchewan and Newfoundland) oil boom, the manufacturing shake out was swift and brutal.

Table 2.3. Ontario Share of Canadian GDP by Industry

Industry	1997	2019	Change (2019–1997)
All industries	39.90%	37.80%	–2.10
Accommodation and food services	35.90%	35.70%	–0.20
AWMR	47.50%	45.50%	–2.00
Agriculture, forestry, fishing, and hunting	18.70%	20.80%	2.10
Arts, entertainment, and recreation	41.90%	40.50%	–1.40
Construction	36.50%	36.60%	0.10
Educational services	39.70%	40.90%	1.20
Finance, insurance, and real estate	44.80%	53.70%	8.90
Health care and social assistance	37.70%	36.20%	–1.50
Information and cultural industries	41.70%	46.30%	4.60
Manufacturing	51.80%	44.30%	–7.50
Mining and oil and gas extraction	5.50%	4.70%	–0.80
Other services (except public administration)	38.40%	36.20%	–2.20
Retail trade	38.70%	36.70%	–2.00
Professional, scientific, and technical services	46.20%	45.00%	–1.20
Public administration	38.00%	40.00%	2.00
Transportation and warehousing	34.70%	33.00%	–1.70
Utilities	32.10%	31.80%	–0.30
Wholesale trade	42.30%	47.60%	5.30

Source: Statistics Canada, "Table 36-10-0434-02: Gross Domestic Product (GDP) at Basic Prices, by Industry, Monthly, Growth Rates (× 1,000,000)," https://doi.org/10.25318/3610043401-eng. Contains information licensed under the Open Government Licence – Canada.

The decline in manufacturing can be seen in tables 2.1 through 2.3. Table 2.1 shows the contribution of different industrial sectors to the provincial Gross Domestic Product. From 1997 to 2021, manufacturing's contribution declined by about half, from just under 22 per cent of economic output to just under 11 per cent. Table 2.2 lists the employment shares in different industrial sectors. From 1997 to 2017, the share of manufacturing jobs in total employment was cut almost in half, as the total number of manufacturing jobs shrank from a late 1990s peak of about 900,000 jobs to 670,000, even as employment grew in the service sector (from 3.4 million jobs in 1997 to 5.1 million jobs in 2017). Table 2.3 is a sector-by-sector breakdown of Ontario's share of Canada's gross domestic product. The figure for all industries indicates that Ontario's economic activity represents 37.8 per cent of the country's total output. Sectors with numbers higher than that therefore indicate areas of Ontario's economic specialization compared to other provinces. Here we can see that Ontario continues to specialize in manufacturing, but that specialization has eroded over the past quarter century, from representing over half of the country's manufacturing to now representing 44.3 per cent. Another way of looking at this is to say that Ontario has been deindustrializing more quickly than the rest of the country over the past twenty years.

SERVICE SECTOR: GROWTH AND POLARIZATION

As noted in the last paragraph, the decline of a quarter million manufacturing jobs over the past quarter century has been masked by the addition of two million service jobs. While no industry has fully absorbed manufacturing's share, tables 2.1 and 2.2 give some sense of which industrial sectors have been particularly dynamic. The biggest increases in GDP share from 1997 to 2021 have come in professional, scientific, and technical services (+3.2% of GDP), construction (+3.1%) and finance and insurance (+2.5%). The biggest increases in employment shares have likewise been in professional, scientific, and technical services and construction, followed by health care and social assistance.

The shift to the service sector holds some benefits for Ontario compared to other provinces and territories due to the lingering effects of the National Policy. Financial and transportation services were concentrated in Toronto and Montreal in 1867, and Toronto has increased its centrality as Canada's financial and business services hub, especially as Montreal became more specialized in serving Quebec's francophone business community. With the growth of the financial services sector across the Global North in the past forty years as part of a broader economic trend of financialization, Ontario, and particularly Toronto, has benefitted.[22] It now ranks as the second-largest financial centre in North America, behind New York and ahead of Chicago. The success of this sector shows up in our tables. Table 2.3 shows the growing concentration of Canadian financial activities in Ontario, with its share of the finance, insurance, and real estate sector growing from 44.8 per cent in 1997 to 53.7 per cent in 2019, and where information and cultural industries have also seen strong growth. Greg Albo is therefore apt to characterize Ontario as a "low-cost production zone within the North American economy anchored by an elaborate financial and producer services sector."[23]

This financialized economy produces different politics than the postwar manufacturing-centred one. While financial services create many high-paying jobs, there are also many less well-paid clerical and customer service roles. Moreover, policy changes supporting the financialization of the economy can have perverse effects. An example would be in housing, where policy changes in the 1990s allowed for the creation of Real Estate Investment Trusts (REITs), which now own a substantial share of multi-residential rental properties in Ontario, and whose business model is built on pushing up rents and renovating affordable rentals into more luxury (and expensive) units.[24] In this manner, the health of the financial sector and investors is directly related to the social crisis of housing unaffordability in Toronto and across urban Ontario.

Ontario is not alone in this story of deindustrialization and financialization. All countries in the Global North have become "post-industrial," as the share of the economy related to manufacturing declines, and as the growth of manufacturing productivity means goods can be produced with fewer and fewer people. Employment comes to be concentrated in the service sector. Service sector employment can nevertheless take many different forms, ranging from highly paid financial services professionals to public school teachers to fast food employees and cleaners. Ontario shows a strong tendency to "service sector dualization," with the creation of well-paid "good jobs" and of poorly-paid "bad jobs," with few job ladders to allow workers in bad jobs to move into better ones.[25] This reflects the strength of employers in convincing governments to only lightly regulate wages and working conditions and to maintain a lean public sector.

This polarized dynamic shows up in studies of changing labour markets. In one study, Tom Zizys disaggregated the labour market into entry-level jobs (requiring no previous work experience and a high-school education), middle jobs (requiring several years of experience or some pre-acquired demonstrable skill), and knowledge jobs (requiring a high level of skills and almost always a college or university degree). He found that nearly all the employment growth since 1991 was either in knowledge work or entry-level jobs. Whereas Ontario had a similar number of middle jobs as knowledge jobs in 1991, by 2006, the proportion of employment in knowledge work was about 50 per cent larger than middle jobs. While Ontario as a whole did well in adding more knowledge worker jobs (about 715,000) than entry-level jobs (about 575,000), there was a clear division between Toronto, where there were 1.3 knowledge jobs for every entry-level job, and the rest of Ontario, where there were 1.3 entry-level jobs for every knowledge job.

In a similar vein, Amy Cervenan broke service employment into a "creative class,"[26] defined by occupations providing workers greater autonomy, and a "service class," defined by lower autonomy and pay (such as cashiers, janitors, personal attendants, security guards, and food service workers). While the latter professions represented the largest employment group in the Ontario population (at over 40% versus just over 30% in the creative class), the average annual income for service-class workers is only 60% of the level of creative-class workers. Cervenan found that service-class employment was more heavily part-time (29%), and that women were overrepresented in its workforce (over 60%).[27] Moreover, recent immigrants and Indigenous peoples were the least well-paid groups within those jobs, earning just 65% and 67% of the already low average income.

These dynamics have produced a more polarized Ontario along several dimensions. Whereas the gap in incomes between the top 10% and bottom 10% of Ontario families raising children long tracked the national average, since the mid-1990s it has grown significantly faster, as top incomes rose, while low incomes stagnated.[28] On this last point, Ontario's labour market continues to produce jobs that make it difficult to sustain livelihoods. About a third of the labour force is in part-time or temporary work or is self-employed without employees. One in eleven Ontarians earns the minimum wage, and indeed Ontario accounts for more than half of the minimum wage jobs in the country.[29] The upshot of this is a long-run secular increase in the poverty rate (measured by the after-tax low-income measure) since the 1980s. From a rate of just under 10 per cent during the 1990s recession, it increased to over 10 per cent into the early 2000s, peaking at 14.5 per cent in 2012 likely due to the twin impact of the 2008 financial crisis and the loss of manufacturing jobs.[30] It then slowly trended down to 12.2 per cent in 2019.

Luxton and McDermott interviewed young Torontonians working close to the poverty line who were unable to escape underemployment in lower-wage service work.[31] They found systematic stories about being hampered by debt, being unable to look after their eyes and teeth, and not wanting to talk about their dreams for the future because they seemed out of reach. Surveys of workers by the Poverty and Precarity in Southern Ontario (2021) project likewise revealed that employment precarity reaches well into middle income brackets, where uncertain scheduling and job tenures, as well as weak training and employment benefits, prevent people from making long-term plans, from investing in community engagement, or even from creating friendships.

These labour market trends map onto other inequalities, as groups that have historically been marginalized in the labour market, such as women, newcomers, and racialized groups, tend to find themselves over-represented

Table 2.4. Average Income in 2015 Dollars by Racialized Status, Toronto and Region, 1980–2015

Region	1980	2000	2015	Percentage Change in 35 years
City of Toronto				
Racialized	38,700	35,200	39,200	1.3%
White	47,100	59,600	75,200	59.6%
Peel Region				
Racialized	45,000	41,700	40,300	−10.4%
White	51,000	57,000	58,300	14.3%
York Region				
Racialized	50,400	45,300	44,800	−11.1%
White	52,600	62,700	67,900	29.0%

Source: Adapted from United Way Greater Toronto, *Rebalancing the Opportunity Equation* (Toronto: United Way Greater Toronto, 2019), https://www.unitedwaygt.org/wp-content/uploads/2021/10/2019_OE_fullreport_FINAL-1.pdf, table 11, with permission of Alan Walks and Dylan Simone.

in the "bad jobs" segment of the service economy. Block and Galabuzi argue that Ontario has a "colour-coded labour market," where, despite important differences between groups, racialized workers face higher unemployment, work in lower-quality jobs, and receive lower wages.[32] As the United Way Greater Toronto's (2019) *Rebalancing the Opportunity Equation* report shows (see table 2.4), the income gains of the past three decades in the Greater Toronto Area have in aggregate almost all gone to whites, while incomes for racialized Torontonians have stagnated or regressed.[33]

POLITICAL ECONOMIC CLEAVAGES

A society's political economy produces politics. The unequal relationships that emerge from a society's economic organization often become the stuff of politics, as "winners" seek to maintain the policies that advantage them while the "losers" organize for change. There is nothing automatic in this process, as social actors must make sense of these relationships and develop political programs and campaigns to contest them. For instance, Northern Ontarians have long contested how the region's wealth is extracted by interests from Southern Ontario, with very little returned to those living there. At times, this sense of regional inequality remains at the level of shared grievance in the community. At other times, this has led to decisions to vote for a particular political party, found regionalist political parties (such as the current Northern Ontario Party), or to rally around local workers striking against large mining companies.

Some of the political economic trends discussed above, such as poor innovation performance, have produced politics in the past, but not so much recently. Others, such as labour market insecurity and poverty, have affected politics over the past two decades and are likely to continue to do so. Finally, some, such as racialized inequality, are starting to affect politics, but with some uncertainty as to the form they will take. Let us look at each of these in turn.

One might assume that the province's declining economic performance would produce potent politics. Whether it is decades of corporate sector failure to invest in productivity enhancement and innovation, or the loss of 400,000 manufacturing jobs in half a decade in the early 2000s, one might expect political parties to make policies to improve competitiveness a central plank of their platforms. In the 1980s and 1990s, the Liberal and NDP governments tried to address this issue by creating a Premier's Council on competitiveness and collaborative industrial policies. These nevertheless remained marginal as businesses wished to preserve their autonomy, and the post-1995 Conservative government responded by returning to an updated version of the old formula of leaving economic development to the private sector with the provincial government providing supporting infrastructure.[34] The post-2003 McGuinty Liberals looked poised to try a new industrial strategy based on supporting green industries, but stepped back when the policy was challenged at the World Trade Organization. This was a more aggressive industrial strategy than had been seen since the 1990s, although it relied on attracting global firms (such as Samsung) and their know-how more than on fostering domestic innovation, a well-worn Ontario tradition.

In the absence of an active industrial policy, Ontario governments over the past two decades have fallen back on another well-worn Ontario tradition of providing the infrastructure needed for growth. For instance, poor land-use planning and underinvestment in public transit produced large productivity losses due to congestion, especially in the Greater Toronto and Hamilton area, already estimated at 7.5 to 11 billion dollars per year in 2013.[35] This helps explain why the McGuinty government tried to improve land-use planning with the *Places to Grow Act* and why the McGuinty-Wynne and subsequent Ford governments have invested in rapid transit and highway construction. There has also been a rhetorical emphasis on investing in education and training, although here the investment has not followed as Ontario boasts high tuition fees and the lowest per-student funding of any Canadian province.

The one exception to this "hands-off" approach to economic performance is the auto sector, where provincial governments of all stripes have provided subsidies to major auto manufacturers in return for large-scale investments in updating their assembly plants. While the 1995–2003 Conservative government took an ideologically consistent position and refused to subsidize these firms, this meant Ontario missed out on a generation of new investments and saw assembly plants close in communities like St. Catharines, St. Thomas, Chatham, and Woodstock.[36] The Ford Conservatives have followed the lead of the 2003–18 Liberal government in providing incentives to these firms, most recently announcing support for Honda to start assembling hybrid cars in Alliston, as well as a large-scale electric battery plant in Windsor. This support nevertheless generally reproduces Ontario's position as a place that assembles cars for firms located elsewhere, not one which innovates new products and technologies.

The lack of political urgency around the province's economic underperformance, which has been a non-issue in provincial elections, including the latest one, is surprising as it is an issue with major ramifications on the life chances of Ontarians in the present and future. In line with Malloy's introduction in chapter 1, this may reflect a political culture of cautious incrementalism. However, the scholars he refers to point to citizen expectations of competent economic governance and of Canadian economic leadership, expectations that have been dashed by deindustrialization and creeping poverty within Ontario and by Alberta's economic predominance through the oil boom. Students of Ontario's industrial policy have a slightly different cultural explanation: Ontario's first-past-the-post electoral system creates large left-right swings, with new governments inevitably throwing out the industrial policy of the previous government. Successful innovation policy, by contrast, requires a more patient politics that allows affected economic actors to develop trust in each other and to make investments in the knowledge that supportive policies are unlikely to change rapidly.[37] A third explanation is that actors that once advanced more ambitious public-led industrial policies, such as the Canadian Autoworkers Union/Unifor, have been weakened by deindustrialization and now rally around Liberal and Conservative policies of providing incentives to auto firms.[38]

Ontario's economic underperformance has not produced much politics lately, but the dualization of labour markets certainly has. As noted earlier,

Ontario has mostly followed a liberal approach to the welfare state, emphasizing the value of paid work as the best way of looking after oneself. However, when full-time work still produces poverty wages, citizens begin to argue that the social contract is breaking down. Moreover, given that poverty runs down the human capital of workers, and that child poverty has long-term developmental consequences, some employers may see the need to lobby governments to reduce poverty. Finally, workers in precarious jobs have lobbied for stronger workplace employment standards, be it paid sick days, higher minimum wages, regulating employment agencies, and better enforcement of regulations around pay and scheduling. These concerns have shown up in competing approaches to dealing with poverty.[39] In the first McGuinty Liberal government, the NDP won by-elections in York South-Weston (2007) and Parkdale-High Park (2006) with promises to raise the minimum wage. The Liberals, recognizing the risk of raising wages in an economy that competed on its lower wages, responded with a Poverty Reduction Strategy and a new Ontario Child Benefit with the aim of reducing child poverty by 25 per cent by 2013.

In the fifteen years since the launch of the Poverty Reduction Strategy, labour market poverty and insecurity have witnessed a back-and-forth between two strategies. On the one hand, labour organizations like the Workers' Action Centre, Justice For Workers, and the NDP have tended to emphasize direct interventions in the workplace in the form of higher minimum wages and more stringent employment protections for workers. The Liberal and Conservative governments have generally shied away from doing so, no doubt fearing a backlash from small businesses, but also the potential for job losses in private services and cost-sensitive manufacturing. Instead, they have preferred to address child poverty, where interventions take place in schools or via the benefit system rather than in workplaces. The exception to this trend was in the final two years of the Wynne government (2017–18), where minimum wages were placed on a rapid upward ascent to reach $15 per hour and several new employment protections, including two paid sick days, were implemented. The Ford government promptly repealed most of these changes, but the popularity of the wage issue was such that the government later saw a benefit in promising to raise the minimum wage to $15.50 and to index it to inflation.

To turn briefly to a third example, racialized inequality is a growing concern in Ontario politics, but it is not yet clear what policy responses will follow. Under the McGuinty and Wynne Liberal governments, a lot of emphasis was placed on policing, particularly carding or street checks. In 2016 and 2017, the government created the Anti-Racism Directorate and released an Anti-Racism Strategic Plan that the Conservative government has continued to implement and monitor. The strategy was mostly focused on addressing disparities in the policing, education, and child welfare systems. While anti-racism measures in these fields are important, their impact on highly unequal labour market outcomes promises to be, at best, well into the future. Measures to combat racism in the labour market, or to reduce labour market inequality generally, are just beginning to enter the margins of the policy conversation. As with economic underperformance and labour market policy, Ontario governments seem happier to act in their existing sphere (e.g., through providing infrastructure or changing how they manage schools and child welfare) than to intervene in employer decisions about wages, working conditions, or innovation strategies.

CONCLUSION

All told, this chapter paints a sombre portrait of Ontario's future. Ontario remains one of the richest societies in the world, yet both low-paid service workers unable to afford dental fillings and young professionals priced out of the housing market may find little solace in that fact. While Ontario took advantage of an undervalued dollar in the 1990s to position itself as a high-quality/low-cost manufacturing platform in North America, the rise of the dollar caused a rapid deindustrialization over the past twenty years. Given the province's long-standing low innovation and low productivity profile, it is hard to foresee a bounce back. The province continues to benefit from Toronto's role as Canada's financial centre (and business services centre more broadly) to draw surpluses from the other provinces. This economic activity nevertheless comes with its own challenges of creating labour market dualisms between high- and low-paid service work, and between Toronto and the rest of the province. In a situation where upward mobility in the service economy is highly constrained, this has knock-on effects of perpetuating labour market inequalities, which is seen most clearly in racialized inequalities in Ontario's "colour-coded labour markets."

A society's economy is a dense web of relationships built on a complex infrastructure of past private and public investments. It is not something that governments can change quickly. As such, the re-election of the Ford

Conservative government in the 2022 provincial election is unlikely to upset the trends discussed in this chapter. One should expect a government whose industrial strategy is largely to keep auto jobs in Ontario, to provide new transit infrastructure in the Greater Toronto Area, and to otherwise maintain a lean and inexpensive state. There is little in its budgets to date to suggest that the government will take anything but a hands-off role in dealing with the province's weak performance in productivity and innovation.

There are also few signs that the government sees the job insecurity, poverty, and racialization related to the current manner of organizing the province's political economy as pressing issues requiring public responses. It has promised to index the minimum wage to the rate of inflation, which will prevent a further loss of its value but not change the fact that it is not enough to allow full-time work to provide a livable income in Ontario's cities. One counter-note to this trend is the government's decision to sign onto the federal government's Canada-wide child care initiative, indicating some awareness of the need for greater state involvement in some social policy fields, if only to enable greater labour force participation by parents.

Could Ontario do better? Other provinces and territories, starting from less advantageous positions, have made different decisions. The most obvious example is neighbouring Quebec, which has followed a higher taxation/higher spending path for the past half century. In that time, it has narrowed the wealth gap with Ontario at the same time as it moved from having a higher poverty rate than Ontario to having a considerably lower one. Quebecers also show very high rates of self-reported happiness, while Ontarians' happiness has declined in recent years.[40] These decisions in Quebec were nevertheless tied to a context of nationalist politics that produced less pronounced partisan swings between governments, providing the time to develop sustained economic and social policy innovations.[41] Ontario sits in a different context, but ultimately Ontarians do have some cards to play in their choices about whether to accept the status quo or expect governments to intervene more aggressively to address an economic structure that is losing competitiveness and that produces low wages and insecurity for many.

ACKNOWLEDGEMENTS

Nicole Fiorillo provided valuable assistance with the data tables, while Cheryl Collier and Jonathan Malloy improved this chapter with their comments.

DISCUSSION QUESTIONS

1 How did Ontario become such a wealthy society? Did Ontario's path to economic development leave your generation with particular political or economic challenges?
2 This chapter discusses the trends of deindustrialization and of the dualization of work in the service sector. Can you find examples of these trends when you think about the city where you live or the work experiences of friends and family? Are there examples that go against this trend?
3 Looking at the issues of economic underperformance, poverty, and racialized inequality, how can we explain the limited policy responses to date? Describe what interests are served by maintaining the status quo, and explain how more extensive policy changes would threaten these interests.

NOTES

1 Examples of different approaches to the study of Ontario's political economy include Keith Brownsey and Michael Howlett, eds., *The Provincial State: Politics in Canada's Provinces and Territories* (Mississauga: Copp Clark Pitman, 1992); Thomas Courchene and Colin Telmar, *From Heartland to North American Region State* (Toronto: University of Toronto, Faculty of Management, 1998); Bryan Evans and Charles W. Smith, eds., *The Transformation of Provincial Politics: The Political Economy of Canada's Provinces and Territories in a Neoliberal Era* (Toronto: University of Toronto Press, 2015); and Greg Albo, "Divided Province: Democracy and the Politics of State Restructuring in Ontario," in *Divided Province: Ontario Politics in the Age of Neoliberalism*, ed. Greg Albo and Bryan M. Evans (Montreal: McGill-Queen's University Press, 2018), 3–42.
2 See Angela Alook, Sheila Block, and Grace-Edward Galabuzi, *A Disproportionate Burden: COVID-19 Labour Market Impacts on Indigenous and Racialized Workers in Canada* (Toronto: Canadian Centre for Policy Alternatives, 2021).
3 For a fuller discussion of these political economies, see Hayden King, "Treaty Making and Breaking in Settler Colonial Canada," in *Contemporary Inequalities and Social Justice in Canada*, ed. Janine Brodie (Toronto: University of Toronto Press, 2018), 107–23; Aaron Mills, "What is a Treaty? On Contract and Mutual Aid," in *The Right Relationship: Reimagining the Implementation of Historical Treaties*, ed. Michael Coyle and John Borrows (Toronto: University of Toronto Press, 2017), 208–47.
4 Albo, "Divided Province."

5 Morris Altman, "Staple Theory and Export-Led Growth: Constructing Differential Growth," *Australian Economic History Review* 43, no. 3 (November 2003): 249–50, https://doi.org/10.1046/j.1467-8446.2003.00053.x.
6 While the result of a number of changes, important features included the further division of labour and the application of electricity to production, allowing for the moving assembly line. These changes were part of a new era of capitalism called "Fordism" – Henry Ford famously provided a high enough wage that the production workers at his plant might aspire to buy the cars they were making.
7 Bruce Smardon, "Rethinking Canadian Economic Development: The Political Economy of Canadian Fordism, 1880–1914," *Studies in Political Economy* 85, no. 1 (March 2010): 191–2, https://doi.org/10.1080/19187033.2010.11675039.
8 Bruce Smardon, "Shifting Terrains of Accumulation: Canadian Industry in Three Eras of Development," *Studies in Political Economy* 87, no. 1 (March 2011): 143–72, https://doi.org/10.1080/19187033.2011.11675023.
9 John Peters, "The Ontario Growth Model: The 'End of the Road' or a 'New Economy,'" in Albo and Evans, *Divided Province*, 43–76.
10 See Smardon, "Shifting Terrains of Accumulation," 156.
11 See Brownsey and Howlett, *The Provincial State*; Bryan M. Evans and Charles Smith, "The Transformation of Ontario Politics: The Long Ascent of Neoliberalism," in *Transforming Provincial Politics: The Political Economy of Canada's Provinces and Territories in a Neoliberal Era*, ed. Bryan M. Evans and Charles W. Smith (Toronto: University of Toronto Press, 2015), 162–93.
12 Rianne Mahon, "Varieties of Liberalism: Canadian Social Policy from the 'Golden Age' to the Present," *Social Policy and Administration* 42, no. 4 (August 2008): 342–61, https://doi.org/10.1111/j.1467-9515.2008.00608.x.
13 Smardon, "Shifting Terrains of Accumulation," 156–7.
14 Brownsey and Howlett, *The Provincial State*, 156–7.
15 Anecdotally, when I dredge up artifacts from my late 1970s/1980s childhood, I am constantly surprised at how things that are now mostly imported, such as toys, board games, or winter boots, came from places like Don Mills, Etobicoke, London, and Hamilton.
16 See Dimitry Anastakis, "A Neoliberal Pause? The Auto and Manufacturing Sectors in Ontario since Free Trade," in Albo and Evans, *Divided Province*, 103–29.
17 Charlotte Yates and Belinda Leach, "Industrial Work in a Post-Industrial Age," in *Work in Tumultuous Times: Critical Perspectives*, ed. Vivian Shalla and Wallace Clement (Montreal: McGill-Queen's University Press, 2007), 163–91.
18 See Tom Zizys, *An Economy Out of Shape: Changing the Hourglass* (Toronto: Toronto Workforce Innovation Group), archived May 4, 2012, at the Wayback Machine, https://web.archive.org/web/20120514212914/http:/www.workforceinnovation.ca/sites/workforceinnovation.ca/files/AnEconomyOutofShape.pdf.
19 See Albo, "Divided Province"; Anastakis, "A Neoliberal Pause?," 116.

20 See Matthias Oschinski, Katherine Chen, with Liza Kobrinsky, *Ontario Made: Rethinking Manufacturing in the 21st Century* (Toronto: Mowat Institute, 2014), 26–7, https://tspace.library.utoronto.ca/bitstream/1807/99262/1/Oschinski_Chan_Kobrinsky_2014_Ontario_Made_Full_Report.pdf.
21 Smardon, "Shifting Terrains of Accumulation," 162–3.
22 Albo, "Divided Province"; Peters, "The Ontario Growth Model," 58–60.
23 Albo, 17.
24 Martine August and Alan Walks, "Gentrification, Suburban Decline, and the Financialization of Multi-family Rental Housing: The Case of Toronto," *Geoforum* 89 (February 2018): 124–36, https://doi.org/10.1016/j.geoforum.2017.04.011.
25 Steven Tufts, "The Geography of the Ontario Service Economy," in Albo and Evans, *Divided Province*, 77–102.
26 Amy Cervenan, *Service Class Prosperity in Ontario* (Toronto: Martin Prosperity Institute, 2018), http://www-2.rotman.utoronto.ca/mpi/wp-content/uploads/2009/02/Service_Class_Prosperity-ACervenan.pdf.
27 Cervenan, *Service Class Prosperity in Ontario*, 24–5, 35, 44.
28 Armine Yalnizyan, *Ontario's Growing Gap: Time for Leadership* (Toronto: Canadian Centre for Policy Alternatives, 2007), https://policyalternatives.ca/sites/default/files/uploads/publications/Ontario_Office_Pubs/2007/ontariogrowinggap.pdf.
29 Diane Galarneau and Eric Fecteau, *The Ups and Downs of Minimum Wage* (Ottawa: Statistics Canada, 2014), https://publications.gc.ca/collections/collection_2015/statcan/75-006-x/75-006-2014001-6-eng.pdf.
30 See Peter Graefe and Carol-Anne Hudson, "Poverty and Policy in Ontario: You Can't Eat Good Intentions," in Albo and Evans, *Divided Province*, 309–33.
31 Meg Luxton and Patricia McDermott, "Getting By but Dreaming of Normal: Low-Wage Employment, Living in Toronto, and the Crisis of Social Reproduction," in *Rising Up: The Fight for Living Wage Work in Canada*, ed. Bryan Evans, Carlo Fanelli, and Tom McDowell (Vancouver: UBC Press, 2021), 115–33.
32 Sheila Block and Grace-Edward Galabuzi, *Ontario's Colour-Coded Labour Market* (Toronto: Canadian Centre for Policy Alternatives, 2018), https://policyalternatives.ca/sites/default/files/uploads/publications/OntarioOffice/2018/12/Persistentinequality.pdf.
33 Some care is needed with these numbers as the composition of the "white" and "racialized" groups has changed in important ways over that time period. There are also important differences within groups based on gender, age, immigration status, and employment type.
34 See Neil Bradford, "Public-Private Partnership? Shifting Paradigms of Economic Governance in Ontario," *Canadian Journal of Political Science* 36, no. 5 (December 2003): 1005–33, https://doi.org/10.1017/S0008423903778949; Rodney Haddow, *Comparing Quebec and Ontario: Political Economy and Public Policy at the Turn of the Millennium* (Toronto: University of Toronto Press, 2015).

35 Benjamin Duchis, *Cars, Congestion and Costs: A New Approach to Evaluating Government Infrastructure Investment,* commentary no. 385 (Toronto: C.D. Howe Institute, 2013), 29, https://www.cdhowe.org/sites/default/files/attachments/research_papers/mixed/Commentary_385_0.pdf.
36 Anastakis, "A Neoliberal Pause?," 118–19.
37 See Haddow, *Comparing Quebec and Ontario.*
38 Scott Aquanno and Toba Bryant, "Workplace Restructuring and Institutional Change: GM Oshawa from 1994 to 2019," *Studies in Political Economy* 102, no. 1 (January 2021): 25–50, https://doi.org/10.1080/07078552.2021.1901012.
39 See Graefe and Hudson, "Poverty and Policy in Ontario."
40 Alain Noël, "Quebec's New Politics of Redistribution Meets Austerity," in *Federalism and the Welfare State in a Multicultural World*, ed. Elizabeth Goodyear-Grant, Richard Johnston, and Will Kymlicka (Montreal: McGill-Queen's University Press, 2019), 91–2.
41 Haddow, *Comparing Quebec and Ontario,* 10, 53.

3

"Business as Usual": The Relationship Vacuum between Ontario and Indigenous Peoples

Rebecca Major

The province of Ontario is a founding constitutional partner in Canada within the colonial construct of the current state. The province immediately assumed responsibility for lands and resources when joining Confederation. This has important implications for the relationship between the province and Indigenous Peoples because it creates a complicated relationship with Indigenous Peoples' primary relationship, that being with the federal government. Building on these land policies in the modern context, some provinces have official mechanisms and tripartite relationships among federal and provincial governments and Indigenous Peoples, such as Treaty Land Entitlement Framework Agreements (TLEFAs). In Ontario, comparatively, there has been historical neglect with few relationship mechanisms between the provincial government and Indigenous communities. The official policy is to direct municipalities to develop relationships with Indigenous communities. While this is an excellent direction to encourage local relationships, Ontario off-loading Indigenous-provincial relationships onto municipalities creates a relationship vacuum.

Why is this important? It is important because it means there is an impact to study at the municipal level, which, due to Ontario off-loading relationship-building responsibility, has produced a void in the relationship, maintained through "business as usual." The municipal materials available show how *some* municipalities are making efforts, but this is not always the case. Suppose you are in Windsor, Ontario, where there has been minimal local relationship or policy with Indigenous Peoples, and the province rarely or never engages. In that case, you have areas where Indigenous communities are left on the sidelines. Over the years, the lack of policy engagement has contributed to persistently poor relationships between the Ontario government and Indigenous communities.

The following chapter explores the Indigenous relationship with the province of Ontario regarding policy, contact, and engagement, focusing on this "relationship vacuum." The Ontario government's relationship with Indigenous communities was poor prior to the deadly 1995 shooting of Dudley George at Ipperwash, an important moment in Ontario-Indigenous relations under the Harris PC government. The subsequent McGuinty Liberal government called an enquiry into the Ipperwash incident, which provided recommendations for mechanisms to improve Indigenous-Ontario relationships, especially concerning land. Yet the Ontario government continued "business as usual" with Indigenous relationships, demonstrated through Provincial Policy Statements (PPSs) and their engagement on Indigenous issues such as the cancellation of educational curriculum updates, conversations and efforts around the National Day for Truth and Reconciliation, or the recognition of the United Nations Declaration of the Rights of Indigenous Peoples (UNDRIP). In the following discussion, the importance of Ipperwash as context assists in demonstrating the need for provincial relationships and how the Provincial Policy Statements do not fill that need, contributing to the trend of "business as usual" regardless the governing party.

BACKGROUND

Two government orders are recognized in Canada's constitutional fabric: the federal government, with responsibilities under section 91 of the *Constitution Act, 1867*, and provincial entities under section 92. This framework includes the recognition of constitutionally protected peoples, including Indigenous Peoples, in section 91(24).[1] Recognizing Indigenous Peoples, the de facto responsibility for maintaining good relations rests with the Crown and the federal branch of public government. The setting of the relationship exists in the "Honour of the Crown."[2] The Supreme Court of Canada enforces these relationships and can expand the federal government's fiduciary duty – which has occurred in one case, *Daniels v. Canada*, 2016. In this case, the courts ruled Métis and non-status Indians (non-registered under the Indian Act) were the duty and care of the federal government.[3] Noteworthy about this discussion are the jurisdictional roles. The specificity of the constitutional jurisdictions can create relationship vacuums where provinces are relatively silent and minimal in their contact with Indigenous communities and Peoples. It appears that Ontario takes a reductionist approach to its relationship with Indigenous communities with the division of powers laid out this way. The pattern of behaviour (path-dependence) of the province leads to "business as usual" as the status quo.

TWENTIETH-CENTURY TENSIONS – IPPERWASH

When thinking of the Indigenous-provincial relationship in Ontario in the twentieth century, one event that comes to mind is the 1995 confrontation at Ipperwash and the deadly shooting of Dudley George. The notoriety of Premier Mike Harris' tenure exists through the enquiry about his government's actions in Ipperwash and their responsibility in the tragic event. Although Harris was premier from 1995 to 2002, the twentieth-century Indigenous-Crown relationship between the Annishinaabeg Communities of Stoney Point and Kettle Point and the Ontario government centred around the surrender of land to the provincial government in the 1940s, which turned it into Ipperwash Provincial Park. In this process, community members indicated burial grounds existed that required protection, with nothing being done on the part of the provincial government. The lack of engagement and lack of effort by the provincial government with the communities ultimately led to armed confrontation with the Ontario Provincial Police, which resulted in the shooting death of Dudley George.[4]

The land in the area of Kettle Point and Stoney Point holds relational history for local Annishinaabeg and the Neutrals.[5] The area was also historically known for the flint beds and became a settlement area for Indigenous communities following the War of 1812 through treaty making.[6] During the Second World War, the Canadian government took the Stoney Point land through the *War Measures Act* for a military training base, forcibly relocating families to Kettle Point. Moving Stoney Point people to Kettle Point also reduced land for Kettle Point people.[7] After generations of former landowners fought to return to their community, a group of the former landowners moved onto an unused portion of the base in 1993, and some moved into barracks in 1995.[8] Among the occupiers was Dudley George, a man killed by Ontario Provincial Police (OPP) Acting Sergeant Kenneth Deane.[9]

The responsibility and the role that the Ontario government played in the death of Dudley George was assessed in an official *Ipperwash Inquiry*, which released its report in 2007 and included one hundred recommendations.[10] The incoming Liberal government called the enquiry in 2003 under *The Public Inquiries Act* "to inquire and report on events surrounding the death of Dudley George, who was shot in 1995 during a protest by First Nations representatives at Ipperwash Provincial Park and later died."[11] The enquiry also served the purpose of proposing recommendations to prevent such events from occurring in the future. While some movement on the recommendations exists, one fundamental recommendation continues to be ignored: the recommendation to have an Ontario Treaty Commission with a Treaty Commissioner.[12] The significance of this is that it would be instrumental in advancing provincial-Indigenous relationships and is seen as a necessary piece to move forward. Calling for this development speaks to a current lack of relationships. The century-long events with little follow-up represent the long-standing neglect and limited attention to Indigenous Peoples and Indigenous-provincial engagement in Ontario, as discussed in chapter 1.

PROVINCIAL POLICY STATEMENTS: 2014 AND 2020

In Ontario, Indigenous relationships with the government are significantly guided by the Provincial Policy Statement (PPS). The Ontario government established the PPS in 1996 to direct growth and expansion of land use and updates it from time to time.[13] According to the province, the role of the PPS is a policy instrument that sets land use and planning rules, and "municipalities are the primary decision-makers for local communities."[14] The idea that municipalities are primary decision-makers for local communities is particularly interesting, while the position of Indigenous communities as inherent rights-holders or relationship partners is absent. Explained by the Northern Policy Institute, it is a policy piece that went through revisions over the years, becoming stronger in language in 2005.[15] The statement went through two more revisions since: 2014 and, most recently, 2020. The 2020 PPS is the result of consultation with Ontario residents.[16] Notably, in the consultations, Indigenous communities and organizations submitted feedback indicating that the proposed change required more Indigenous community engagement.[17] The proposed policy change was to "support rural, northern and Indigenous communities"[18] with specific policy targets. The policy targets were specific to water and sewer, municipal engagement, and agriculture and food production pieces. Yet throughout all the policy renewal processes from the time of its creation, the province's role in relationships with Indigenous communities is minimally discussed in the PPS.

On the surface, it looks like relationship development with Indigenous Peoples is an agenda item for the province; however, the agenda item is really about off-loading relationships to a non-constitutional actor: municipalities. Ontario policy documents show that the province acknowledges its role as "the Crown" but essentially puts the onus on the municipality to engage Indigenous communities. While the delegation is important for relationship building as local communities are impacted by Indigenous rights and what the municipality can do with land, municipalities also impact Indigenous rights because they have delegated authority to create by-laws and collect taxes. The off-load of the responsibility to municipalities to develop relationships with Indigenous communities is part of a "business as usual" in side-stepping, or even erasing, relationships and knowledge. The PPS falls under the *Planning Act* (1990), which coordinates provincial and municipal planning, while municipal planning falls under the *Municipal Act* implemented in 2001.[19] The *Municipal Act* went through changes empowering municipalities over the years; it was amended in 2007 with Bill 130, which included sweeping changes, containing the ability to delegate powers and responsibilities per the *Planning Act*.[20] Various modifications are available through the schedule of amendments.[21] All these changes encouraged relationships between Indigenous communities and municipalities. The relationship vacuum between the Ontario government and Indigenous communities is widening, though, as the province pushes municipalities into that space.

When the province off-loads relationships to the municipalities, not all municipalities create local relationships. Some larger municipalities that have sufficient infrastructure establish relationship channels. Examples are efforts made since the Truth and Reconciliation Commission (TRC) final report in 2015. Cities such as Toronto and Ottawa have departments within their municipal offices for the explicit purpose of relationships.[22] Other cities, such as Windsor, fall short in relationships and engagement to the point where it is not even on their radar. For example, Windsor has yet to develop and properly implement a land acknowledgement, years after the TRC reported. Windsor is not unique – the City of Kawartha Lakes only adopted a land acknowledgement in April 2021 after consulting with communities in that same year.[23] The next section of this chapter further explores varied municipal-Indigenous relations. While a policy and noticeable consultation speak to relationships with Indigenous communities, the call for stronger relationships as part of the PPS consultation process demonstrates a weakness within all the layers of policy and land planning.[24] These calls for change were from the 2019 consultations for the 2020 update to the PPS – this time matters because it means there is persistent neglect of engagement by the Crown.

MUNICIPAL-INDIGENOUS RELATIONS

While it is understudied by academics and practitioners, there is nonetheless an acknowledgement by some scholars of the importance of examining the state of relationships between Indigenous communities and municipalities.[25] The importance of these relationships should not reduce the relationship between other levels of government that represent the Crown and Indigenous communities. Alcantara and Nelles address the shortcomings of Indigenous-municipal relations by looking at different geographic locations for examples of cooperation and what type of things may influence opportunities for cooperation or partnerships.[26] One thing is evident from their research: "business as usual" – lack of institutional coordination or relationship – is the norm in Ontario.[27] Their research examines the types of relationships and how the strength of those relationships influences the kind of partnerships developing between Indigenous communities and municipalities.[28] While exploring case studies, Alcantara and Nelles looked for places where at least a minimal relationship existed and was not wholly absent. When they do find an Ontario example of an Indigenous-municipal relationship, it's a "business as usual" relationship, where the bare minimum exists.[29] This approach is not surprising given the provincial policies encouraging municipalities to do the heavy lifting in relationship building.

Constitutional differences are significant because, when the province offloads and encourages Indigenous relationships, it is with non-constitutional entities. So, while the relationship is encouraged and coached at the municipal level by the Ontario government, very uneven relationships exist that lack continuity. Some municipalities developed relationships, while others have not.[30] In the twenty-first century, the Ontario Ministry of Municipal

Affairs and Housing policy presents municipal engagement with Indigenous communities as opportunities.[31] A 2014 comprehensive study concluded that Ontario's continued inequity in relationships between municipalities and Indigenous communities persists despite policy development.[32] The research attempted to address the needs of both provincial and municipal planners while examining the response to the *Report of the Ipperwash Inquiry*.[33] Ontario is not the only geopolitical jurisdiction that uses these policy planning approaches; but comparatively, the policy instruments used in New Zealand produced more dynamic and constructive relationships.[34] Continuing on the work by Heritz and others, Noelle Bouvier and Ryan Walker explore Indigenization in urban centres and identify the continued need to "develop relational approaches to planning and governance with Indigenous communities," which need to move beyond conditional inclusion.[35] While municipal relationships with Indigenous communities are important, provincial governments should not see this as an opportunity to off-load relationship building.

CANCELLATION OF CURRICULUM

Aside from continuing to off-load Indigenous community relationships to the municipal level, the Ford government has cancelled many developments in other policy areas. Approximately one month after Ford's election on June 7, 2018, his government opted to cancel the Indigenization of the kindergarten to grade twelve provincial curriculum.[36] Plans for updating the curriculum were cancelled only the Friday before writing sessions were set to begin on Monday, July 9, 2018.[37] According to a CBC article, the email communication from the Ministry of Education stated it was a cost-saving measure as part of the commitment to running a more efficient government.[38] But this was highly criticized by multiple commentators. Updating the curriculum was an opportunity to align the education system with the recommendations from the Truth and Reconciliation final report.[39] Cancellation was interpreted as sending a message to Indigenous educators.[40] Through much of the later part of the twentieth century and into the twenty-first century before the TRC, the Ontario government made piecemeal attempts to update the curriculum based on multiculturalism and provided "Aboriginal perspectives" tool kits that may or may not be used.[41] When the newly elected Ford government cancelled the planned work to genuinely revisit the curriculum, the action sent a message of a lack of concern for Indigenous Peoples and issues and a message of continuing the dominant political culture in the education system.

After facing much criticism, the Ford government changed in attitude and declared a commitment to address the current gap. The new commitment wants to address what they call "the current gap" by 2023 as a response to the TRC's Calls to Action. Interestingly, the announcement for curriculum development was for Grades 1–3; while necessary, it is a continuation of piecemeal educational development.[42] Under the previous Liberal government, there were advancements made in the curriculum in other grades, but not to the level that would be considered modern or culturally competent in a comprehensive way. It was for this reason a complete revision was prepared. The irony is that the purpose of the cancelled work in 2018 became the same reason to return to the cancelled work: implementing TRC recommendations. The Ontario government opted for path-dependence and finishing an old Liberal project rather than returning to the more culturally responsive plan that includes the TRC's recommended revisions.[43] Unfortunately, this is a baby step forward for Ontario compared to where education could be if the 2018 work had not been cancelled. This education announcement only came when the Ontario government faced criticism for another missed opportunity for reconciliation with Indigenous Peoples and communities.

Shortly after announcing the above changes in September 2021 and winning the 2022 provincial election, the Ford government returned to "business as usual." Continuing a reduction in the role of Indigenous relationships and Indigenous epistemology, in July 2022, the Ontario government announced the removal of the Indigenous science framework from the curriculum. This change is an active effort and not done purely through negligence, as a level of effort is required to remove the Indigenous content. According to the *Globe and Mail*, nine hundred pages were reviewed to erase the Indigenous content from the curriculum.[44] The reasoning provided by a spokesperson for the government was grounded in economics: "we remain focused on ensuring Ontario's students excel at the foundations of math, science, and reading, so they can pursue good-paying jobs."[45] Indigenous knowledge is perceived as an obstacle through this message. While there was a short time in 2021 when the Ontario government demonstrated a change in commitment to Indigenous knowledge, this recent move exemplifies that the 2021 commitment was short-lived. It did not take long to see a backslide. This change was poignant because it was more than just a failure to act and move forward; an effort to eradicate content took place.

SEPTEMBER 30 – THE NATIONAL DAY FOR TRUTH AND RECONCILIATION

The Ontario government faced mixed reactions to their approach to a new national holiday in honour of Indigenous Peoples. September 30, 2021, marked Canada's first National Day for Truth and Reconciliation as a federal statutory holiday.[46] Also recognized on this day is the grassroots-organized Orange Shirt Day. Both days are meant to honour children who attended residential schools. The establishment of the Truth and Reconciliation Commission (TRC) was part of the Indian Residential Schools (IRS) Settlement, which produced ninety-four Calls to Action.[47] It is in the Calls to Action where the federal government is called upon to create a statutory holiday:

> 80. We call upon the federal government, in collaboration with Aboriginal peoples, to establish, as a statutory holiday, a National Day for Truth and Reconciliation to honour Survivors, their families, and communities, and ensure that public commemoration of the history and legacy of residential schools remains a vital component of the reconciliation process.[48]

While the responsibility is put on the federal government, some other provincial jurisdictions either marked it as a day of commemoration or formally recognized the day as a holiday.[49] Ontario took the position of treating the day like Remembrance Day by not creating a statutory holiday, but at the same time, took the opportunity to off-load the day's status onto industry and recommend it be part of collective agreements moving forward.[50] While the Ontario government stated that its position is based on ongoing conversations with Indigenous communities and leaders, it will be the actions moving forward that will illustrate whether those conversations ever took place.

UNDRIP

The United Nations Declaration on the Rights of Indigenous Peoples (UNDRIP) was a contentious issue for Canada. The federal government did not initially sign the document with some other nations.[51] A few points of the document caused tension, including definitions around identity, particularly "free, prior, and informed consent." Tension and division regarding perspectives of UNDRIP were evident in the 2019 federal election debate, where Conservative leader Andrew Scheer clarified his opposition, grounding his perspective in economic value.[52] While opposition to the document came from non-Indigenous parties, especially during election times, the opposition also comes from Indigenous Peoples about how the document does not go far enough because of the final clause, Article 46.2. Article 46.2 allows states to limit rights within the declaration. Considering the opposition from Indigenous Peoples is key because it means that signing onto the declaration is more symbolic than structural. The federal government passed their federal legislation, *The United Nations Declaration on the Rights of Indigenous Peoples Act*, on June 21, 2021.[53] How the federal government observes this commitment moving forward will undoubtedly require attention.

As part of the symbolic act of recognizing UNDRIP, provinces in Canada saw the introduction of legislation. Some provinces, like British Columbia, passed UNDRIP legislation, while others, like Ontario, could not complete the process. In Ontario, Sol Mamakwa introduced Bill 76, *United Nations Declaration on the Rights of Indigenous Peoples Act, 2019*.[54] The bill had an action plan built into it: "The Government of Ontario shall, in consultation and cooperation with indigenous peoples in Ontario, develop and implement a provincial plan to achieve the objectives of the United Nations Declaration on the Rights of the Rights of Indigenous Peoples."[55] This action plan provided a commitment to work cooperatively. However, the bill expired with the dissolution of the Legislative Assembly for the 2022 election, and it is yet to be seen if Ontario will see UNDRIP legislation passed or even reintroduced.

DISCUSSION

Chapter 1 of this textbook asks whether the political culture has changed in Ontario. When examining from an Indigenous lens, the answer is a blunt no. As indicated in chapter 1, consider that while the parties may change, the politics do not. Indicators of change include advancements in policy and responses to these advancements. For example, in the *Report for the Ipperwash Inquiry*, a recommendation was the creation of an Office of the Treaty Commission to help facilitate relationships.[56] While some recommendations led to responses from the Ontario government, fundamental recommendations for relationship building were not implemented. The failed implementation could be why there is minimal engagement with Indigenous Peoples by the Ontario government in the twenty-first century, as there was in the twentieth century. The *Report* is where scholars turn to see how Ontario uses the *Inquiry* as a catalyst for change.[57] The lack of relationship structure produced uneven relationships and ongoing marginalization of Indigenous communities in land and local planning. As research explores municipal relationships with Indigenous communities, recommendations continue for the development of relationship structures at the provincial level.[58] The repeat calls illustrate that real change and development haven't happened despite changes in political leadership – "business as usual." Until relationships develop, moving forward is next to impossible because change must include Indigenous voices.

Regardless of changes in party leadership, a policy area where the Ontario government continues a trajectory of off-loading responsibility of relationships with Indigenous communities is through Provincial Policy Statements. Policy development produced direction and enhancement for municipalities to follow, creating an off-load of relationships for land and planning. The political culture is path-dependent. Responses to Indigenous policy opportunities, such as thoughtful comments on the new statutory holiday or commitment to UNDRIP, demonstrate a continuation of "do-nothing."[59] Duty to Consult (DTC) processes are increasing in many areas of industry, which is a relationship-building exercise. Still, it should not come at the cost of an absence of a relationship between Indigenous Peoples and levels of government that serve as the Crown, such as the federal government, provincial governments, or territorial governments.

Efforts to Indigenize curriculum illustrate the Ford government's reductionist approach to Indigenous topics, issues, or policies. The discussion throughout this chapter explored "business as usual," which appears to be a do-nothing approach. Under the previous Liberal administration, plans were set to do a complete overview even though the previous Indigenization plans were incomplete. When the Ford government was elected in 2018, as discussed, they cancelled the curriculum update. When they reinstated Indigenization, they returned to a previous path that had been abandoned for the complete review about to take place in 2018. The Conservative government returning to past incomplete Liberal practices ultimately illustrates no change in Ontario's political culture despite leadership changes. Further, extra steps taken most recently in removing content from curriculum reinforce the perceived lack of importance of Indigenous populations by the provincial government.

CONCLUSION

The off-loading of responsibility for relationship-building between the Ontario government and Indigenous communities has left calls for mechanisms to fill the relationship vacuum and to honour recommendations from the *Report for the Ipperwash Inquiry*. This off-loading is important because it left a void where Indigenous communities are not engaged in land and planning as collective entities with constitutional protections and entitlements as First Peoples of Turtle Island. When Ontario became part of Confederation and the Canadian state in 1867, it immediately controlled land and resources, which developed a culture of "business as usual" and subsequently allowed development on land without much consultation (if any). Following the patriation of the Constitution in 1982, an increase of Indigenous case law grew exponentially because the law became the mechanism for defining Indigenous rights legally and exercising them.[60] The case law and Duty to Consult affected all provinces, but not all branches of government were adequately educated, which created the relationship vacuum that endures presently in Ontario in some respects.

Mechanisms, such as Treaty Commissions, or instruments, like policies and agreements, do not create relationships; those require human effort and political will. But these instruments certainly assist. Political will enforces whether a political institution takes action, but when means and methods reduce barriers, the likelihood of a co-production relationship increases.[61] There are many pieces involved in relationship-building, just like there are many pieces to the principle of the Duty to Consult with Indigenous communities. Still, nothing will move forward productively unless meaningful relationships are developed and not just out of convenience. That piece is important because it makes the difference in whether the relationship is based on respect. Failure to respond to calls to action or establish mechanisms produces calls for further action or attention – pointing out shortcomings or lack of engagement. Developing the recommended policy instruments can assist in moving away from "business as usual" and reducing the relationship vacuum that currently exists. Only when there is a fundamental shift to co-production between the Government of Ontario and Indigenous communities, as well as at the municipal level, will there be a real political culture change.

DISCUSSION QUESTIONS

1 What steps should be considered in reducing the relationship vacuum between the provincial government and Indigenous communities?
2 Considering the concept of "business as usual," what policy instruments could be implemented to create political will to change?
3 Why do you suppose some municipalities engage Indigenous communities and some don't?
4 Where are other areas in politics or policy you see the province off-load responsibility?

NOTES

1 *Constitution Act, 1867* (U.K.), 30 & 31 Vict., c. 3, reprinted in R.S.C. 1985, App. II, No. 5.
2 Isabelle Brideau, *The Duty to Consult Indigenous Peoples – Background Paper*, Parliament of Canada Research Publications, pub. no. 2019-17-E, June 12, 2019, https://lop.parl.ca/sites/PublicWebsite/default/en_CA/ResearchPublications/201917E#.
3 *Daniels v. Canada*, 2016 SCC 12, 1 S.C.R. 99 (Indian Affairs and Northern Development 2016).
4 The Honorable Sidney B. Linden, Commissioner, "Conclusion," *Report of the Ipperwash Inquiry* (Toronto: Publications Ontario, 2007), 674–5.
5 Shelly E. Bressette, "The Truth about Us: Living in the Aftermath of the Ipperwash Crisis," in *Strong Women Stories*, ed. Kim Anderson and Bonita Lawrence (Toronto: Sumach Press, 2003), 229–30.
6 Bressette, "The Truth about Us," 230.
7 Bressette, 230.
8 Bressette, "The Truth about Us," 233; Peter Edwards, *One Dead Indian: The Premier, The Police, and The Ipperwash Crisis* (Toronto: McClelland & Stewart, 2006), 61.
9 Edwards, *One Dead Indian*, 124.
10 Government of Ontario, *The Ipperwash Inquiry Report*, accessed June 12, 2022, https://www.ontario.ca/page/ipperwash-inquiry-report.
11 Government of Ontario, "About the Inquiry," *The Ipperwash Inquiry*, archived December 8, 2021, at Archive-It (Archives of Ontario), accessed June 16, 2022, https://wayback.archive-it.org/16312/20211208090646/https://www.attorneygeneral.jus.gov.on.ca/inquiries/ipperwash/mandate/index.html.
12 Shari Narine, "What Happened to the Treaty Commission of Ontario after Ipperwash Inquiry Recommendation?," *Windspeaker*, September 3, 2020, https://windspeaker.com/news/windspeaker-news/what-happened-treaty-commission-ontario-after-ipperwash-inquiry.

13 Neptis Foundation, "Simcoe County in the Toronto-Related Region: A Provincial Planning System in Flux," *Simcoe County*, accessed June 12, 2022, https://neptis.org/publications/chapters/provincial-planning-system-flux.
14 Government of Ontario, Ministry of Municipal Affairs and Housing, *Provincial Policy Statement, 2020* (Ottawa: Queen's Printer, 2020), https://www.ontario.ca/page/provincial-policy-statement-2020.
15 *The Provincial Policy Statement: Local Diversity Beyond the Rhetoric* (Northern Policy Institute, 2016), accessed June 12, 2022, https://www.northernpolicy.ca/article/the-provincial-policy-statement-local-diversity-beyond-the-rhetoric-21234.asp.
16 Government of Ontario, Ministry of Municipal Affairs and Housing, *Provincial Policy Statement Review – Proposed Policies*, February 28, 2020, https://ero.ontario.ca/notice/019-0279.
17 Government of Ontario, Ministry of Municipal Affairs and Housing, *Provincial Policy Statement Review*.
18 Government of Ontario, Ministry of Municipal Affairs and Housing, *Provincial Policy Statement Review*.
19 Government of Ontario, *Planning Act*, R.S.O. 1990, c. P.13, 1.1. Purposes, https://www.ontario.ca/laws/statute/90p13.
20 Constance Lanteigne, "Power to Delegate Far Reaching for Ontario Municipalities," Weir Foulds LLP, June 1, 2007, https://www.weirfoulds.com/power-to-delegate-far-reaching-for-ontario-municipalities.
21 Legislative Assembly of Ontario, Minister of Municipal Affairs and Housing, *Bill 130, Municipal Statute Law Amendment Act, 2006*, https://www.ola.org/en/legislative-business/bills/parliament-38/session-2/bill-130.
22 Ahn Lam, "Indigenous Self-Determination Rights and the Role of Municipality" (master's thesis, University of Windsor, 2021), https://scholar.uwindsor.ca/major-papers/193/.
23 "First Nations Land Acknowledgment," *Living Here: First Nations*, City of Kawartha Lakes, accessed June 12, 2022, https://www.kawarthalakes.ca/en/living-here/first-nations.aspx.
24 Government of Ontario, *Provincial Policy Statement Review – Proposed Policies*, decision posted February 28, 2020, https://ero.ontario.ca/notice/019-0279.
25 Joanne Heritz, "Municipal-Indigenous Relations in Ontario: Initiatives in Brantford, Hamilton, and Niagara," *Journal of Canadian Studies* 55, no. 3 (Fall 2021): 541–63, https://doi.org/10.3138/jcs-2019-0042; Christopher Alcantara and Jen Nelles, *A Quiet Evolution: The Emergence of Indigenous-Local Intergovernmental Partnerships in Canada* (Toronto: University of Toronto Press, 2018), 10.
26 Alcantara and Nelles, *A Quiet Evolution*, 135.
27 Alcantara and Nelles, 53–72.
28 Alcantara and Nelles, 50.
29 Alcantara and Nelles, 55, 135.
30 Alcantara and Nelles, 62.
31 Alia Hanif, Ruth Melady, Donna Simmonds, and Ralph Walton, "Municipal-Aboriginal Relations: An Ontario Perspective," *Commonwealth Journal of Local Governance*, no. 3 (May 2009): 121–2, https://doi.org/10.5130/cjlg.v0i0.1101.

32 Fraser McLeod, Leela Viswanathan, Graham S. Whitelaw, Jared Macbeth, Carolyn King, Daniel D. McCarthy, and Erin Alexiuk, "Finding Common Ground: A Critical Review of Land Use and Resource Management Policies in Ontario, Canada and Their Intersection with First Nations," *International Indigenous Policy Journal* 6, no. 1 (January 2015): 18, https://doi.org/10.18584/iipj.2015.6.1.3.

33 McLeod et al., "Finding Common Ground," 17.

34 Fraser McLeod, Leela Viswanathan, Jared Macbeth, and Graham S. Whitelaw, "Getting to Common Ground: A Comparison of Ontario, Canada's Provincial Policy Statement and the Auckland Council Regional Policy Statement with Respect to Indigenous Peoples," *Urban Planning* 2, no. 1 (2017): 84, https://doi.org/10.17645/up.v2i1.850.

35 Noelle Bouvier and Ryan Walker, "Indigenous Planning and Municipal Governance: Lessons from the Transformative Frontier," *Canadian Public Administration* 61, no. 1 (March 2018): 133, https://doi.org/10.1111/capa.12249.

36 Justin Brake, "Ontario Government Cancels Summer Work Updating K-12 Indigenous Curricula," *APTN National News*, July 9, 2018, https://www.aptnnews.ca/national-news/ontario-government-cancels-summer-work-updating-k-12-indigenous-curricula/.

37 Mike Crawley, "Ontario Cancels Curriculum Rewrite that Would Boost Indigenous Content," *CBC News*, July 9, 2018, https://www.cbc.ca/news/canada/toronto/ontario-education-truth-and-reconciliation-commission-trc-1.4739297.

38 Crawley, "Ontario Cancels Curriculum Rewrite."

39 Theodore Christou, "Why Cutting Indigenous Revisions to Ontario's Curriculum Is a Travesty," *Maclean's*, July 18, 2018, https://www.macleans.ca/news/canada/why-cutting-indigenous-revisions-to-ontarios-curriculum-is-a-travesty/.

40 Rhiannon Johnson, "Indigenous Educators Puzzled, Disappointed After Ontario Cancels TRC Curriculum Writing Sessions," *CBC News*, July 9, 2018, https://www.cbc.ca/news/indigenous/ontario-indigenous-curriculum-writing-cancellation-1.4739691.

41 Evan Habkirk, "A Year of Inaction: Ontario Education and the TRC," *Active History*, November 6, 2019, https://activehistory.ca/2019/11/ontario-education-and-the-trc/.

42 Katherine LeClerq, "Ontario Makes Indigenous Curriculum Mandatory for Grades 1 to 3," *CP24*, September 29, 2021, https://www.cp24.com/news/ontario-makes-indigenous-curriculum-mandatory-for-grades-1-to-3-1.5605160.

43 Shallima Maharaj, "Ontario Education Ministry Scrutinized over Cancelled Truth and Reconciliation Curriculum Sessions," *Global News*, July 9, 2018, https://globalnews.ca/news/4321726/ontario-education-ministry-truth-and-reconciliation-curriculum/.

44 Caroline Alphonso, "Indigenous Science Framework Removed from Ontario Elementary School Curriculum," *Globe and Mail*, July 2, 2022, https://www.theglobeandmail.com/canada/article-indigenous-science-framework-removed-from-ontario-elementary-school/.

45 Alphonso, "Indigenous Science Framework."

46 Government of Canada, "National Day for Truth and Reconciliation," *Canadian Heritage*, September 29, 2021, https://www.canada.ca/en/canadian-heritage/campaigns/national-day-truth-reconciliation.html.
47 "Indian Residential Schools Settlement Agreement," Crown-Indigenous Relations and Northern Affairs Canada, Government of Canada, last modified June 9, 2021, https://www.rcaanc-cirnac.gc.ca/eng/1100100015576/1571581687074.
48 Truth and Reconciliation Commission of Canada, *Truth & Reconciliation: Calls to Action* (Winnipeg: Truth and Reconciliation Commission of Canada, 2015): 9, https://publications.gc.ca/collections/collection_2015/trc/IR4-8-2015-eng.pdf.
49 Megan Devlin, "Here Are the Provinces Observing Truth and Reconciliation Day, and Those That Aren't," *Daily Hive News*, September 23, 2021, https://dailyhive.com/vancouver/who-gets-september-30-truth-reconciliation-off-work.
50 Sean Davidson, "Sept. 30 Will Not Be a Provincial Statutory Holiday in Ontario, Government Confirms," *CTV News Toronto*, September 8, 2021, https://toronto.ctvnews.ca/sept-30-will-not-be-a-provincial-statutory-holiday-in-ontario-government-confirms-1.5578174.
51 CBC News, "Canada Votes 'No' as UN Native Rights Declaration Passes," *CBC News*, September 13, 2007, https://www.cbc.ca/news/canada/canada-votes-no-as-un-native-rights-declaration-passes-1.632160.
52 Justin Brake, "Federal Leaders' Debate Indigenous Rights, Divided on UNDRIP," *APTN National News*, September 13, 2019, https://www.aptnnews.ca/national-news/federal-leaders-debate-indigenous-rights-divided-on-undrip/.
53 Government of Canada, *Implementing the United Nations Declaration on the Rights of Indigenous Peoples Act*, June 21, 2021, last updated June 8, 2022, https://www.justice.gc.ca/eng/declaration/index.html.
54 Legislative Assembly of Ontario, Sol Mamakwa, *Bill 76, United Nations Declaration on the Rights of Indigenous Peoples Act, 2019*, https://www.ola.org/en/legislative-business/bills/parliament-42/session-1/bill-76.
55 Legislative Assembly of Ontario, *Bill 76*.
56 This was the second recommendation, the first being the creation of an independent body for overseeing land settlements and claims. Ipperwash Inquiry (Ont.) and Sidney B. Linden, *Report of the Ipperwash Inquiry* (Toronto: Ministry of the Attorney General, Queen's Printer for Ontario, 2007).
57 McLeod et al., "Finding Common Ground," 1, 18.
58 McLeod et al., 84.
59 During the 2022 provincial election, there was little coverage of Indigenous issues, and very little coverage of UNDRIP. See Jack Hauen, "Chiefs of Ontario Grill Opposition Candidates," *iPolitics – News*, April 27, 2022, archived September 19, 2022, at the Wayback Machine, https://web.archive.org/web/20220919194451/https://www.ipolitics.ca/queens-park/chiefs-of-ontario-grill-opposition-candidates.
60 Rebecca Major and Cynthia Stirbys, "Using the Master's Institutional Instruments to Dismantle the Master's Goal of Indigenous-Rights Certainty," in *Constitutional Crossroads: Reflections on Charter Rights, Reconciliation, and Change*, ed. Kate Puddister and Emmett Macfarlane (Vancouver: UBC Press, 2022), 379.
61 Alcantara and Nelles, *A Quiet Evolution*, 135.

4

A Brief History of the Procedure at the Ontario Legislature

Tom McDowell

INTRODUCTION

Modern parliamentary democracies operate according to the principle of *responsible government*, or the notion that parliament's raison d'être should be to ensure that its members are held accountable to, and reflect the will of, the electorate. Parliament serves as a physical meeting place where the competing objectives and interests of the legislative and executive branches are brought into an immediate relationship.

This fusion of powers, bringing the executive and legislative branches together in a single institutional forum, constitutes the essential character of responsible government in a parliamentary system. Parliamentary democracies are determined by the fact that the executive is directly accountable to, and derives its authority from, the legislature. Members are elected to parliament through periodic elections, after which they serve as representatives of the geographic region that selected them.

In the legislature, ministers of the Crown, who are *both* part of the executive while also retaining a seat in the legislative body, are directly answerable and accountable to other elected members in the house. Additionally, the executive council must continually renew the confidence of the legislature to remain in power. This differs from presidential systems, found in places such as the United States and Mexico, which are characterized by a single executive model, wherein the president and cabinet members are not directly accountable to the legislature, and are subject to fixed term limits.

The exercise of parliamentary democracy requires that the legislature balance dual and contradictory roles. While on the one hand, the executive attempts to have its agenda ratified by the Legislative Assembly of representative members, on the other, the legislature is also responsible for holding the executive to account by scrutinizing its activities to ensure they are aligned with the public interest. The essence of parliamentary democracy, then, involves the mediation between the executive's privilege to have its agenda passed by the legislature, and the legislature's right to interfere with and delay proceedings to exercise scrutiny of the government.

This chapter interrogates the evolution of parliamentary procedure at the *Legislative Assembly of Ontario,* also known as Queen's Park, between 1867 and 2023 to trace the qualitative movement of the executive-legislative dynamic over the course of its history, and to interrogate whether and to what extent the Ontario legislature has ever approached what Pilon has called an "actually existing democracy."[1] Its chief claim is that while a period of legislative reform in the late twentieth century led to variety of important changes, which helped to democratize the legislature, recent decades have witnessed a counter-reformist effort by the executive branch that has rolled back many of these gains.

Thus, while much of the recent literature has focused on the democratization of the legislature in the 1970s and 1980s, the argument made in this chapter is that *for the majority of its history,* the Ontario legislature has been characterized by the existence of a dominant executive and a weak legislature, which has at times functioned as little more than "an appendage of the premier's office."[2] The democratic reforms of the late twentieth century have proven to be the exception rather than the rule – a relatively short, passing moment in the legislature's 155-year history. Although the nature of modern executive dominance is more formal than it was in the early twentieth century, its impacts – including the marginalization of parliamentary scrutiny – have been similar.

To trace the outlines of this process, the following sections detail the historical evolution of parliamentary procedure at the Ontario legislature from Confederation in three phases: (a) The Classical Era (1867–1967); (b) The Reformist Era (1967–92); (c) The Counter-Reformist Era (1992–2023).

RESPONSIBLE GOVERNMENT IN ONTARIO: BALANCING THE EXECUTIVE-LEGISLATIVE DYNAMIC

The idea of responsible government holds that supreme political power should be concentrated in the hands of representatives who are *responsible*, through periodic elections, to the public, rather than the aristocracy or monarchy. Responsible government in Ontario has its origins in Lord Durham's Report, issued after the Rebellions of 1837 in Upper and Lower Canada. Durham recommended, among other things, granting parliament the power to exercise accountability against the coalition of elite families known as the Family Compact, who held considerable political, economic, and administrative influence.[3]

Although the Report offered a template for improving the accountability of the executive, it "did not go far enough," allowing the executive to find new ways to consolidate its power.[4] Thus, the highly centralized and executive-dominant colonial political apparatus that existed in the early nineteenth century was largely replicated internal to the "responsible" legislature by granting the executive control over the programming and scheduling of the house.

Since prior to Confederation, the executive has been responsible for the organization and scheduling of house business. It determines not only which bills will be brought before the house, but the timing, how much time is allocated for debate, which business takes precedent, as well as the duration and timing of house sittings.

The rules of procedure in a parliamentary system are established in two ways: first, through the *Standing Orders*, a set of formal rules drawn up by the legislature, which establish its procedures and processes; second, by way of a series of unwritten norms that, like the common law, guide its activities based upon its own past precedents and those of other Commonwealth assemblies. Once precedents have been established, they come to form part of the substantive history of the assembly, allowing future governments to utilize these same approaches without having to relitigate their legitimacy.

Since the time available to governments is subject to absolute limits by the election cycle, the executive-legislative dynamic is often expressed as a struggle over the use of the *parliamentary time* devoted to debating and scrutinizing contentious or divisive legislation.[5] The right to temporarily obstruct the proceedings of the house is the only procedural instrument granted to the Opposition outside of non-confidence motions to effectively resist government initiatives by delaying their passage and requesting more time for debate. At the same time, since no political assembly could operate if subject to continual delays, the executive also retains the right to bring forward a *motion of closure*, which allows a government to bring an end to debate and a vote on any matter and at any time.

The maintenance of the equilibrium between the executive and legislative, then, constitutes the essence of parliamentary governance. An ideal balance in parliamentary democracy is one in which the government can functionally operate, but its activities are subjected to perpetual and effective parliamentary scrutiny. While the parliamentary majority must tolerate and acknowledge the right of the executive to govern, at the same time, the executive must also respect the right and responsibility of private members to oppose and hold it to account.

In other words, disputes about parliament's rules are also, critically, questions about the nature of this dynamic and the extent to which the legislature's right of accountability should be balanced against the executive's right to govern. The sections to follow explore the nature of this process at the Ontario legislature.

THE CLASSICAL ERA: 1867–1967

The Ontario legislature was established by Section 69 of the *British North America Act*, at Confederation in 1867, which conferred to it authority as the primary law-making body for the newly established province of Ontario. Procedurally, the Ontario legislature adopted the structure of the formal rules that had governed the Legislative Assembly of Canada, while also observing the precedents of the British House of Commons at Westminster. This meant that from its earliest origins, the Ontario legislature absorbed, and was initiated into, the executive-dominant, colonial parliamentary model that governed Canada and preserved the dominance of the Family Compact during the pre-Confederation period.

The first "complete reappraisal" of the *Standing Orders* took place in 1875 when a select committee was appointed to examine updates to the rules of the assembly, which were adopted without amendment by the house.[6] The only revision from the 1875 reforms to have a noteworthy impact on the structure of house proceedings was to establish a limit on the length of time a member could speak on a motion or debate to adjourn the house.[7]

It was not until 1929, more than fifty years after they had last been reformed, that the *Standing Orders* were reassessed. Among these reforms included a provision to allow the Speaker to draw upon precedents from the Ontario legislature rather than the British House of Commons. This was an important moment of maturity and independence for the legislature, since it asserted that the Ontario legislature was an assembly with its own history and right to govern itself.

Another reassessment of the rules occurred in 1939, largely affirming and strengthening many of the 1929 reforms by granting additional powers to the Speaker. These changes also included a provision allowing any member to move adjournment of the house for a special debate, a right that persisted until the 1980s, when it was removed.[8] After 1939, no changes were made to the *Standing Orders* until the late 1960s.

In concrete terms, the Ontario legislature's *Standing Orders* provided considerable leverage to the Opposition to protest the government's agenda through obstructionist approaches. Until the 1990s, there were no restrictions on how long a member could speak in the legislature, and while the early history of the legislature saw few major attempts by the Opposition to obstruct legislative proceedings, this was a right that it did on occasion avail itself of.

The most significant instance of obstruction occurred in 1923 when the Opposition members used "every conceivable variety of the filibuster technique, including long excerpts from *Alice in Wonderland*" to hold up the proceedings of the house for several days.[9] For reasons lost to history, Premier Ernest Drury refused to invoke closure to end the debate, instead calling an election in which his party was defeated.[10]

The lack of formal restrictions on members' rights, however, should not be taken to mean that the legislature served as an example of a "democratic ideal."[11] Rather, in terms of its informal powers, up until the mid-twentieth century, the executive, particularly the premier, exercised a dominant presence over the affairs of the legislature, often flagrantly violating the *Standing Orders* to exert their influence over house scheduling.

During the legislature's early period, it was common for the premier of the house to call items of business regardless of their location on the Order Paper, which designated a strict process for bringing matters forward. Additionally, oral questions were not permitted, and standing committees designed to examine public spending, such as the Estimates and the Public Accounts Committees, were "so large and poorly organized as to be quite unwieldy."[12] This problem was exacerbated by the fact that it was common for the premier to also serve as treasurer, giving him complete control over public finances with little scrutiny.

Thus, more than a century after its creation, the Ontario legislature was "still governed by the mid-nineteenth century rules it adopted in 1867" as the executive continued to exercise remarkable control over the affairs of the legislature.[13] The Premier's Office and cabinet officer included only a few employees, while members of the assembly were granted very little in the way of financial support, making it possible for the premier of the day to cast a long shadow over the entire operations of government.[14]

The premier's grip on the legislature was particularly acute during the reign of "the patriarch," Leslie Frost, from 1949 to 1961.[15] As both premier and treasurer, Frost devoted virtually all the legislature's time to government business, while reducing the total number of days the legislature was in session to fit into the rhythms of rural life "between ploughing in the fall and seeding in the spring."[16]

There were arguably three primary reasons for the preservation of a dominant executive in Ontario until the late twentieth century. First, long periods of single-party rule tended to undermine the competitive dynamic, causing parties to become petrified into their respective roles as the government and the Opposition. This led many backbench members to focus on their tasks as "social workers" in their constituencies, "to the detriment of their responsibilities as legislators."[17]

Second, funding for members was "ludicrously inadequate" as they received neither offices nor staff to complete their legislative responsibilities as the role of the legislator was viewed as a part-time role.[18] Third, a culture of "loose administration" emerged at Queen's Park, in which the informal practices of the assembly proved highly deferential the Premier's Office and the sitting government. This milieu was nurtured by Roderick Lewis, clerk of the Legislative Assembly from 1953 to 1986, while also acting as the province's chief electoral officer. Lewis was highly deferential to the government, and thereby strengthened the grip of the premier over the house by titling the interpretation of the rules in the government's favour.[19]

By the early 1970s, however, it had become apparent that "change was in the air" and it was only a matter of time before major reforms to democratize the legislature were instituted.[20] The section to follow explores the modernization of procedure in the Ontario legislature towards the latter half of the twentieth century.

THE REFORMIST ERA: 1967–92

The period following the Second World War in Ontario was largely concerned with the "adaptation of nineteenth-century public institutions to the new postwar society of the mid to late twentieth century."[21] The expansion of the state's role in the 1950s and 1960s in areas of provincial responsibility such as health care and education, led to a dramatic increase in the size and scope of the provincial government's activities. While the civil service had 7,500 employees at the end of the war, the number had grown to approximately 70,000 by the end of the 1960s.[22]

It was under these circumstances that, beginning the in late 1960s, "a slow and undramatic but real improvement in the relative position of the legislature," occurred, as a series of reforms to the practices of the assembly were instituted.[23] Changes included reductions to the size of standing committees, the inclusion of oral questions, as well as the improvement of working conditions for members, who were each eventually afforded their own offices.

At the same time, however, the government placed time limits on the Committee of Supply – to ninety sittings, or 225 hours.

This "modest regeneration" of the legislature's rules was further actualized in 1969 with the establishment of a parliamentary committee to review the role of the legislature and, with it, a new set of *Standing Orders*, which formalized many of the gains made during the decade.[24] The province also appointed an independent Commission of the Legislature, colloquially known as the Camp Commission, which by 1975 had produced five reports.

The first report made broad recommendations surrounding compensation and financing for members to ensure that they had the time and resources to act like proper parliamentarians. Nearly all its suggestions were adopted by the government, which including a doubling of members' compensation, grants for travel, and a small severance for non-returning members.[25]

In its second report, the Camp Commission continued with its recommendations to improve the independence of the legislature, suggesting that the Speaker's Office take more direct control over the entire legislative precinct and that permanent offices, such as the Clerk, Speaker, and legislative library, receive additional staff, to improve their capacity to support members. Additionally, members should receive more revenue for staff and caucus research funding, as well as offices and the physical infrastructure necessary to carry out their tasks as legislators.

The Camp Commission's Fourth Report focused on improvements to the capacity of the legislature to hold the executive accountable. While its recommendations were general in nature, they included improving members' ability to participate in oral questions and to call for information, allowing the house to determine whether a bill would be considered in committee, a restructured committee system, and a more thorough process for the consideration of private members' bills. The commission also issued two other reports of less significance to the discussion here.

The reality of a minority government after the 1975 election led to another innovation that considerably improved the capacity of the Opposition to scrutinize the executive: the establishment of an informal House Leaders' Committee in which the house leaders of all three parties met regularly to discuss house scheduling. This committee granted a degree of informal influence to the Opposition, which could use its right to hold up the government's agenda to extract more opportunities for debate or committee time from the government, leading to a "more efficient and acceptable management of House business" and led to the development of "a more mature attitude towards the legislature."[26]

In 1975, a select committee under the leadership of former Speaker and Progressive Conservative member of provincial parliament (MPP) Donald Morrow was created to determine which of the recommendations from the Fourth and Fifth Reports should be adopted by the house. The establishment of the "Morrow Committee" allowed Opposition members a significant role in crafting the new rules through "interparty negotiation." [27]

Through these "trade-offs" between the government and the Opposition, a series of compromise solutions were arrived that resulted in meaningful improvements to house scheduling, additional time for oral questions in the house, and formalized procedures for private members' bills. After a two-year pilot, the committee's findings were permanently adopted into the *Standing Orders* in 1978, completing a decade of reform that culminated in substantial changes to the operation of the legislature.

While the reforms to the legislature "had much in common with patterns of structural change appearing in other jurisdictions," they nevertheless led to real improvement in conditions for members and their capacity to hold the government accountable.[28] By the end of the 1970s, members and party leaders had staffed offices, the committee system was considerably improved and functioned as a more effective counterforce against the executive, oral questions had become a regular element of daily proceedings at the legislature, the informal administration and house scheduling of the pastoral era had been greatly improved through the establishment of formal standards for scheduling, and the legislature's control over its own affairs was strengthened through the expansion of the Clerk and Speaker's Offices.

Although the legislative agenda continued to be almost completely controlled by the government, the Opposition gradually began to take its role as a meaningful counterweight to the power of the executive more seriously. In 1982, the New Democrats refused to allow the Bill Davis majority government to pass the *Inflation Restraint Act*, causing the government to bring forward a motion of *time allocation* for the first time in the legislature's history to break the impasse. Time allocation, sometimes referred to as a guillotine motion, because it brings about the cessation of parliamentary debate in a manner similar to closure, allowing the government to place formal time limitations on committee and house debate, would become a common occurrence at Queen's Park in the years to follow.[29]

This changing legislative culture was revealed again during the 1985 election, which returned a Progressive Conservative minority government. Although the legislature had recent experience with Progressive Conservative-led minorities from 1975 to 1981, on this occasion the NDP, which held the balance of power after the election, indicated that it would engage in dialogue with the Liberals and Progressive Conservatives to determine which party should form the next government.

After several weeks of intense interparty negotiations, the NDP and Liberals arrived at an arrangement in which the Liberals agreed to enact a progressive agenda in exchange for a promise not to move or vote for a non-confidence motion for two years. So it was that on June 18, 1985, the forty-two-year Progressive Conservative reign came to an end, as the Liberals, who, with the support of the New Democrats, formed a new government under the premiership of David Peterson.

The Liberal-NDP Accord symbolized the emergence of a new competitive dynamic at Queen's Park in which all three parties held a realistic chance of forming government and began to behave more competitively. The "clubby style" that had characterized the legislature's culture throughout much of the postwar period had given way to a much more partisan and adversarial environment.[30]

The decade that followed would be something of a "golden age" for the Opposition as the interaction of expanded backbench rights and a more hyper-partisan environment led to a more assertive Opposition willing to use the tools at their disposal to assert their will and interfere with the government's agenda. Although the Assembly under the first Peterson government from 1985 to 1987 was reasonably undisruptive because of the Accord, the second Peterson term from 1988 to 1990 was also characterized by several incidents of resistance from the official Opposition New Democrats, which delayed the government's agenda for several weeks.

For instance, on April 14, 1988, NDP members began reading petitions onto the record, refusing to stand down, and thus obstructing the house from moving to the Introduction of Bills or the Orders of the Day in protest of legislation to allow retail shopping on Sundays. Every day for the next week the NDP read petitions continuously until the end of the sessional day, brining the rest of the house schedule to halt. Due to the protest, for the first time in the province's history, the minister of finance was unable to the deliver the budget speech in the legislature.[31]

The use of creative opposition tactics to obstruct continued into the early years of the NDP government from 1990 to 1995 under the premiership of Bob Rae. In 1991, Progressive Conservative leader Mike Harris used the fact that there were no restrictions on the length of titles for legislation to bring forward a private members' bill, Bill 95, the *Zebra Mussels Act*, with the name of every lake, river, and stream in the province. This required each of the members, the Clerk, and the Speaker to read to the title, in its entirety, onto the record, interfering with the passage of the NDP's budget.[32]

The era that began with reforms to modernize the legislature had by the 1990s given rise to a house that was plagued by regular gridlock. Given these untenable circumstances, it would only be a matter of time before the executive would begin to turn back some of the democratic reforms it granted to the legislature.

THE COUNTER-REFORMIST ERA: 1992–2023

While opposition obstruction in the late 1980s and early 1990s sowed the seeds for the establishment of more formal restrictions to the rules, the scale and extent of this counter-reformist movement by the legislature outpaced anything that might have been reasonably anticipated at the turn of the 1980s. Recognizing that it would be impossible to restore the informal culture of executive dominance from the classical period, and facing political pressures to implement neo-liberal state restructuring plans rapidly, by the early 1990s, the executive began to impose formal restrictions on rights afforded to the Opposition.

In this sense, the counter-reform movement differed from the shape of executive dominance in the early twentieth century since it involved the establishment of concrete restrictions on the legislature, rather than a culture of deference to the executive. Since the early 1990s, restrictive reforms to procedure have been actualized through changes to the *Standing Orders* and the introduction of new practices, such as time allocation and omnibus legislation, to circumvent the house, and pass legislation quickly.

Omnibus legislation involves the packaging of usually unrelated reforms under the heading of a single piece of legislation. This has the distinct advantage to the executive of passing several bills in the time allotted for a single bill. While omnibus legislation has long been used as a housekeeping measure, its utilization as an instrument of accountability circumvention is a relatively new phenomenon in Ontario.[33]

With hindsight, it is possible to point to the NDP government's 1992 reforms to the *Standing Orders* – by far the most restrictive in the province's history to that point – under the premiership of Bob Rae, as the approximate moment at which the Counter-Reformist Era can be said to have begun. The new *Standing Orders* formalized time allocation in the legislative rules and established a time limit of thirty minutes for the Introduction of Bills and all speeches in the house. The reforms granted the government full control over the proceedings of the house by ensuring that each bill would pass within the new time limitations.[34]

After the house passed the new rules in 1992, the government brought forward time allocation on three occasions. However, in 1993 it began to use time allocation as a regular course of action, applying it an unprecedented eight times. Plagued by low polling numbers, the NDP's final year in office saw the legislature sit for only twenty days, as the government passed three more motions of time allocation before adjourning the house. As table 4.1 demonstrates, the NDP institutionalized the use of time allocation at Queen's Park, applying it to 21.6 per cent of the total government bills that received royal assent during its mandate.

When the Progressive Conservatives, led by Mike Harris, were elected to a majority government in 1995 on a promise to implement a radical state restructuring agenda, they encountered the reality that the slow and deliberate nature of parliamentary institutions would make it difficult to carry out their ambitious neo-liberal restructuring reforms. However, the 1992 *Standing*

Orders offered the Harris government a legislative design *in principle* that they could use to secure the implementation of their agenda. The Progressive Conservatives would apply these restrictive approaches at an extent and scale never witnessed at Queen's Park – or most other Commonwealth parliamentary assemblies, for that matter – to implement their ambitious austerity agenda as quickly as possible.

The government's first and most aggressive effort to restructure the state administration was Bill 26, the *Savings and Restructuring Act*, a massive omnibus bill, which amended or repealed dozens of other pieces of legislation. Omnibus bills became central to the Progressive Conservatives' legislative implementation strategy, allowing them to save time by packaging numerous reforms together. The government also made prodigious use of omnibus legislation to carry out a variety of major reforms in short order, including what it called "red tape reduction" legislation, bringing a hodgepodge of issues under single pieces of legislation on the grounds that they all involved streamlining the public administration.[35]

In addition to omnibus legislation, the Progressive Conservatives also made unprecedented use of time allocation. Beginning with Bill 26, the Harris government brought forward time allocation on most of their signature articles of legislation, commonly ramming initiatives through the house before the Opposition had time to galvanize popular opposition against them or even properly understand their implications. As table 4.1 shows, the Progressive Conservatives used time allocation on approximately 30 per cent of the government legislation passed during its first term from 1995 to 1999, but in its second it resorted to it more than an unprecedented 60 per cent of the time.

An NDP filibuster that required the legislature to sit day and night for eight days led the Harris government to make another major reform of the *Standing Orders* in 1997. The changes cut debate time nearly in half for legislation and set clear time limitations for house speeches. They also eliminated nearly every conceivable opportunity for the Opposition to hold up the proceedings of the legislature, thus strengthening the executive's grip over the house by removing the Opposition's most important leverage.[36]

Political resistance was not merely limited to parliament, however. There also was a major social mobilization in response to the Harris government's austerity program. The Days of Action saw hundreds of thousands of Ontarians protest the government in cities across the province between 1995 and 1998. The largest event occurred at Queen's Park in 1996, when approximately 250,000 people showed up to protest on the front lawn of the legislature one afternoon.[37] Although important symbolically, the demonstrations had little concrete effect on government policy, as the Harris government charged ahead with their agenda, despite these strong political headwinds.

When the Progressive Conservative's second mandate ended in 2003, they left the legislature a fundamentally different place than they found it. Their changes to the *Standing Orders* and the precedents they set for the use of time allocation and omnibus legislation meant that the legislature's rules were once again highly deferential to the executive, and clearly insufficient to act as a counterforce against a future radical government.

There was initially some hope that when the Liberals, led by Dalton McGuinty, were elected to a majority government that they might reverse some of the changes made by the Progressive Conservatives. However, after some promising first steps early in its first term, the Liberal regime ultimately consolidated and extended the procedural reforms implemented during the Harris years, making almost no meaningful changes to the *Standing Orders*.

Although it did not resort to the use of omnibus legislation at anywhere approaching the rate of the Harris government, omnibus bills nevertheless played an important role in the Liberal legislative strategy. The Liberals adopted the Harris government's strategy of packaging reforms to reduce regulations under the heading of "red tape reduction" bills and used it brazenly during the minority 40th Parliament to wedge numerous reforms, but it was unable to pass through the regular bill-making process, into budget legislation that was subject to a non-confidence motion.[38]

They also used time allocation at a rate approaching that of the Progressive Conservatives before them. As table 4.1 shows, by their second term in office, the Liberal government applied time allocation to more than 40 per cent of government bills passed by the house, percentages rivalled only by the Progressive Conservatives' second term from 1999 to 2003. Although the minority 40th Parliament saw a relaxation in time allocation motions as the government required the support of the Opposition to pass them, they returned to using them routinely after Liberal premier Kathleen Wynne was elected to a majority government in 2014, bringing it forward on more than 40 per cent of government bills, a rate comparable to its second term from 2007 to 2011.

Thus, when the Progressive Conservatives returned to office in 2018 under the leadership of Doug Ford, promising a return to the austerity politics of the Harris era, they found a legislature that was already organized to accommodate the implementation of a radical political agenda in a relatively short

Table 4.1. Time Allocation at the Ontario Legislature, 1981–2023

Parliament	Date	Number of Government Bills Passed	Number of Time Allocation Motions	Percentage of Time Allocation Motions to Government Bills Passed %
32nd Parliament PC	1981–5	292	3	1.0
33rd Parliament LIB	1987–90	183	3	1.7
35th Parliament LIB	1990–5	97	21	21.6
36th Parliament PC	1995–9	118	35	29.7
37th Parliament PC	1999–2003	111	67	60.4
38th Parliament LIB	2003–7	109	28	25.7
39th Parliament LIB	2007–11	94	41	43.6
40th Parliament LIB	2011–14	25	4	16.0
41st Parliament LIB	2014–18	93	39	41.9
42nd Parliament PC	2018–21	89	50	56.2
43rd Parliament PC	2022–3	24	5	20.8

Source: Adapted from Tom McDowell, *Neoliberal Parliamentarism* (Toronto: University of Toronto Press, 2021), table 10.1.

period. This meant they were able to move forward with an aggressive agenda without having to change any of the legislature's rules, since they were already organized to accommodate the policy whims of a dominant executive.

During its first years in office, the Ford government also embraced a highly antagonistic attitude towards parliamentary debate and scrutiny, sometimes referring to it as a wasteful expense of taxpayer money. Its approach to parliament was complemented by a right-wing populist rhetoric that has been used to rationalize transcending accountability measures on the grounds that so doing is necessary to deliver for their constituents, broadly defined as "the pure people," to whom the premier claimed to have a direct line.[39]

This approach divides society into *protagonists*, typically identified by signifiers such as "taxpayers," "middle-class," and "entrepreneurs," and *antagonists*, which included a medley of left-wing "elite" interests, including cyclists, public sector workers, academics, labour unions, LGBTQ+, anti-racist, and anti-poverty activists.[40] Ford's approach to populism weaponized these manufactured divisions by claiming that the left-wing antagonists were ideologically motivated to obstruct growth and prosperity, thus making the case that the premier should be empowered to circumvent the rules of parliament to get results for "the people."[41]

Consistent with its adversarial approach towards the legislature, during its first two years in office, the Ford government applied time allocation to nearly every government bill the house passed, a rate never seen before at Queen's Park. However, with the onset of the COVID-19 pandemic in March 2020, the government's disposition towards the legislature changed markedly, eschewing its publicly hostile attitude towards parliamentary processes. As the reality of the health emergency brought about by the pandemic became apparent, the government reached out to the Opposition to work collaboratively to pass its emergency legislation on an agreed upon timetable. This compromise with the Opposition facilitated an armistice, as the government and the Opposition worked collaboratively to set house scheduling throughout the pandemic.

These developments led to dramatic decline in the use of time allocation as the government applied it to only about one-third of government legislation passed by the house during the final months of the First Session of the 42nd Parliament. Even more significantly, as table 4.2 demonstrates, in the Second Session, the government applied time allocation to just one of the fourteen government bills passed, a marked departure from customary practices at Queen's Park in the post-Harris era. The time allocation figures from the Ford government's second term (July 2022 to August 2023), however, must be viewed in the context of an unprecedented increase in the use of closure, as discussed below.

This climate of relative reciprocity in the legislature during the pandemic, however, was balanced by an increase in the use of executive instruments. As Migone demonstrates in chapter 5 of this collection, although the quantity of the Ford government's use of Orders in Council was generally consistent with their application in the pre-COVID-19 period, it relied more often upon the use of long-term emergency orders, several of which were in effect for more than two years.[42] This gave the government the capacity to manage

Table 4.2. Time Allocation under the Ford Government, 2018–2023

Parliament	Date	Number of Government Bills Passed	Number of Time Allocation Motions	Percentage of Time Allocation Motions to Government Bills Passed %
42nd Parliament, First Session *Before* March 2020	July 2018– March 2020	38	36	95
42nd Parliament, First Session *After* March 2020	March 2020– September 2021	37	13	35
42nd Parliament, Second Session	October 2021–May 2022	14	1	7
43rd Parliament, First Session	July 2022– August 2023	24	5	21

Source: Adapted and updated from Tom McDowell, *Neoliberal Parliamentarism* (Toronto: University of Toronto Press, 2021), 193.

much of the crisis through enabling legislation, without having to regularly seek approval from parliament.

Shortly after winning its second majority, however, the Ford government returned to a more restrictive and adversarial approach towards the legislature. To secure the passage of several contentious policy reforms by the house, it began to use closure with a regularity that had never been witnessed before at Queen's Park.[43] From July 2022 to August 2023 the government used closure on *both* second and third readings of ten of twenty-four – or nearly half – of the total government bills passed by the legislature. This included its most controversial legislation, such as Bill 3, the *Strong Mayors, Building Homes Act*; Bill 39, the *Better Municipal Governance Act*; and Bill 60, *Your Health Act*.

Compared to time allocation motions, closure has two distinct advantages for the Ford government. First, closure does not require that the government devote legislative time to debate the merits of its invocation, as is the case with time allocation motions. Second, it also enables the government to bring an end to debate at a time of its choosing, without having to satisfy any anterior commitments to debate, giving it maximal latitude over the scheduling of house proceedings.

These developments raise the question as to whether the regularity with which the Ford government has resorted to the use of closure has established a new precedent in which closure will usurp time allocation as a routine method for securing the passage of contentious legislation. If this is indeed the beginning of a lasting trend, it will signify a further tightening of executive control over the affairs of the legislature.

CONCLUSION

The history of parliamentary procedure in Ontario has taken something of a circuitous route during its 155 years of existence. For the first one hundred years or so, the legislature was exceptionally weak by Westminster parliamentary standards in the shadow of a dominant executive. During this time, the Ontario legislature has rarely met the standard of what might be called an "actually existing democracy."[44] While its Reformist Era did witness important changes that significantly enhanced the legislature's capabilities to act as a counterforce against the executive, the reforms during the Counter-Reformist Era undermined many of those changes.

The shape of executive dominance differed from the Classical to the Counter-Reformist Era, but its effect was similar – to subordinate the legislature and circumvent its accountability functions. While the Classical Era had fewer formal restrictions on the activities of the legislature – for instance, there were no limits on speeches or debate – its informal culture was largely deferential to the executive. Meanwhile, the Counter-Reformist Era was, in many ways, a *response* to the fact that parliamentarians had more resources and opportunities for accountability and were thus able to scrutinize the executive more effectively. Ultimately, the Ontario legislature saw a relatively short period of perhaps a decade and a half from the 1970s to the early 1990s in which it enjoyed meaningful authority to hold the executive accountable.

Today, legislative procedure at Queen's Park remains configured by the essential structure of the rules and precedents put in place by the Harris government in the 1990s during their radical overhaul of the province. This means that they are characterized by a strong executive that affords certain rights to the Opposition, but ultimately holds the authority to arbitrarily pass major reforms through the house in a relatively short period – as little as a day if so motivated. The Opposition today has little recourse available to it to resist or delay the proceedings of the house to request more time for debate.

DISCUSSION QUESTIONS

1 What is the importance of the control over *time* in parliamentary systems?
2 What are omnibus bills, and how does their abuse undermine parliamentary scrutiny?
3 Which government do you think has been most responsible for the decline of the legislature during the "counter-reformist" period?
4 Why do you think governments sought to turn back many of the changes made to democratize the Ontario legislature during the 1970s and 1980s?

NOTES

1 Dennis Pilon, "The Struggle over Actually Existing Democracy," *Socialist Register* 54 (2018): 1.
2 Donald C. MacDonald, *The Happy Warrior: Political Memoirs* (Toronto: Dundurn Press, 1998), 298.
3 Chester W. New, *Lord Durham: A Biography of John George Lambton, 1st Earl of Durham* (London: Oxford University Press, 1929).
4 New, *Lord Durham*, 111.
5 Herbert Döring, "Time as a Scarce Resource: Government Control of the Agenda," in *Parliaments and Majority Rule in Western Europe*, ed. Herbert Döring (Mannheim, Germany: Mannheim Centre for European Social Research, 1995), 223–46.
6 Frederick F. Schindeler, *Responsible Government in Ontario* (Toronto: University of Toronto Press, 1969), 136.
7 Schindeler, *Responsible Government in Ontario*.
8 Schindeler, 139.
9 Schindeler, 151.
10 Schindeler, 151.
11 Pilon, "Actually Existing Democracy," 2.
12 Kenneth Bryden, "Executive and Legislature in Ontario: A Case Study on Governmental Reform," *Canadian Public Administration* 18, no. 2 (June 1975): 248, https://doi.org/10.1111/j.1754-7121.1975.tb01939.x.
13 Schindeler, *Responsible Government in Ontario*, 143.
14 Graham White, "Change in the Ontario State 1952–2002," paper prepared for the Role of Government Panel (October 2002).
15 MacDonald, *The Happy Warrior*, 298.
16 MacDonald, 316.
17 MacDonald, 319.
18 MacDonald, 317.
19 MacDonald, 323.

20 Graham White, "Teaching the Mongrel Dog New Tricks: Sources and Directions of Reform in the Ontario Legislature," *Journal of Canadian Studies* 14, no. 2 (May 1979): 120, https://doi.org/10.3138/jcs.14.2.117.
21 Randall White, *Ontario, 1610–1985: A Political and Economic History*, vol. 1 (Toronto: Dundurn Press, 1985), 261.
22 White, *Ontario, 1610–1985*, 287.
23 Bryden, "Executive and Legislature," 248.
24 Bryden, 249.
25 Graham White, "The Life and Times of the Camp Commission," *Canadian Journal of Political Science* 13, no. 2 (June 1980): 365, https://doi.org/10.1017/S0008423900033060.
26 Graham White, "Teaching the Mongrel Dog New Tricks," 121.
27 White, "Life and Times," 373.
28 Bryden, "Executive and Legislature," 241.
29 Bryden, 241; Government of Canada, House of Commons, "14. The Curtailment of Debate," in *House of Commons Procedure and Practice*, 2nd ed., ed. Audrey O'Brien and Marc Bosc (Ottawa: Parliament of Canada, 2009), https://www.ourcommons.ca/procedure-book-livre/document.aspx?sbdid=68a2776a-f2a5-4dc3-a6ce-6f0d88b0cf66&sbpidx=4.
30 Tracey Raney, Sasha Tregebov, and Gregory J. Inwood, *Democratizing the Ontario Legislature* (The Canadian Study of Parliament Group, 2013), 13.
31 Tom McDowell, *Neoliberal Parliamentarism: The Decline of Parliament at the Ontario Legislature* (Toronto: University of Toronto Press, 2021), 82–3.
32 McDowell, *Neoliberal Parliamentarism*, 107.
33 Government of Canada, House of Commons, "Forms of Bills," in O'Brien and Bosc, *House of Commons Procedure*, https://www.ourcommons.ca/procedure-book-livre/Document.aspx?Mode=1&sbdid=DA2AC62F-BB39-4E5F-9F7D-90BA3496D0A6&sbpid=1E3A6719-B291-4B7D-B13B-52819E50CE14.
34 McDowell, *Neoliberal Parliamentarism*, 109–10.
35 McDowell, 133–5.
36 Todd Decker, "Ontario Legislative Reports," *Canadian Parliamentary Review*, 20, no. 4 (1997), http://www.revparl.ca/english/issue.asp?param=65&art=83.
37 Dan Darrah, "Ontario's Days of Action Offer a Lesson for Canadian Workers," *Jacobin Magazine*, November 30, 2020, https://jacobin.com/2020/11/ontario-days-of-action-canada-workers-unions-strike-mike-harris.
38 McDowell, *Neoliberal Parliamentarism*, 160.
39 Brian Budd, "The People's Champ: Doug Ford and Neoliberal Right-Wing Populism in the 2018 Ontario Provincial Election," *Politics and Governance* 8, no. 1 (2020): 172, https://doi.org/10.17645/pag.v8i1.2468.
40 Budd, "The People's Champ," 176.
41 McDowell, *Neoliberal Parliamentarism*.
42 Andrea Migone, "The Ontario Executive," in *The Politics of Ontario*, 2nd ed., ed. Cheryl N. Collier and Jonathan Malloy (Toronto: University of Toronto Press, 2023), 72–90.
43 McDowell, *Neoliberal Parliamentarism*.
44 Pilon, "Actually Existing Democracy," 1.

5

The Ontario Executive

Andrea Migone

INTRODUCTION

This chapter tackles the role and history of the executive in the province of Ontario. Where necessary, it also makes brief excursions into federal and local politics, since Canadian provinces occupy an important intermediate space between these jurisdictions.

The concept of the executive is multi-dimensional: on the one hand, there is its parliamentary side, which complements the legislative power and is composed of the monarch's representative (the governor general at the federal level and the lieutenant general at the provincial one), the head of government (prime minister or premiers), and the cabinet. However, a strong argument can be made that in modern states the core administrative machinery, comprising key units like the Treasury Board and the Ministry of Finance, but also high-ranking officials throughout the organization, belong in the executive because they are necessary to the smooth implementation of political platforms by interfacing with politicians.

In Westminster systems, the executive has always been very powerful, and its analysis has a long history in Canada[1] and abroad,[2] usually showing that this concentration of power has causes. Leaders are seen as ensuring their party's electoral success, while the first-past-the-post electoral system favours accountability over representation, leading to a structure where those responsible for either success or failure are clearly identifiable. Naturally, even charismatic political figures could not advance their agenda without relying on the support of the "core executive,"[3] which includes not just the cabinet and the central agencies that manage key financial and policy files, but also a complex cast of both political advisors and top administrators like deputy ministers, who ensure the alignment of government and administration during the policy-making process. Much of the literature about this power concentration has focused on the prime minister: whether in describing its origins,[4] analyzing its structure,[5] discussing its supposed autocratic nature,[6] or examining individual prime ministers' approaches.[7] The particularly relevant role of government executives has been central in the discussion of federal arrangements in Canada.[8] Partially, this is because the federal government, which controls much of the taxation power, has a very considerable edge in many key policy fields in terms of capacity and resources, and can often influence all but the larger and richer provinces. To some extent, broader managerial and political trends have also shaped the role and structure of the public sector in Canada and abroad, like New Public Management (NPM) and the emergence of digital governance.[9] Provincial executives have also played an important role in Canadian policy-making, at times working in unison with Ottawa and other provinces, while in other cases, they had a more adversarial position. It is within the context of this layered history that we look at the nature of Ontario's provincial executive.

This chapter is structured in three sections. After this introduction, we frame historically the political and administrative executive in Ontario while referencing some of the broader Canadian landscape and discussing some of its evolution. The following section tackles how the Ontario executive operates, especially in terms of using executive tools, and explores its uptick in populism. Here, populism is understood as a "thin-centred" ideology,[10] which means that its ideological core is rather small and can be blended with various other ideological currents as leaders see fit. The notion itself of the "people" to which populism refers can be vague and often is replaced with an equally nebulous "heartland." This "thinness" of populism is confirmed in a recent analysis of the People's Party of Canada and Ford Nation, which provides interesting insights into how these groups are distinct ideologically but have very similar populist narratives.[11] Finally, any discussion of the executive is closely correlated to the provincial legislature that, as McDowell shows in the previous chapter, excepting the fifteen years between the late 1970s and early

1990s, seldom had any real capacity to counter the premier's executive dominance. That ability was ended by the reforms of the 1990s, reforms that – should be noted – every government since carefully retained because they weakened the Opposition.

THE EXECUTIVE IN ONTARIO

The public sector is composed of different segments, which are connected by being accountable to the Government of Ontario, with very diverse roles (see table 5.1). The focus here is on the provincial public administration, the Ontario Public Service (OPS), which excludes education and health care workers, and only represents a fraction of the broader public sector. In the past twenty years, the overall number of public sector employees increased, but consider that in 2001 Ontario was home to 11,897,534 people according to Statistics Canada. In 2021, it was estimated to have a population of 14,826,276. Hence, the public service only moved fractionally up when measured against population increases, whereas all other segments experienced much broader growth.[12]

Providing policies and services to over 14 million people, the OPS is second only to the federal administration in terms of employees and spending. In 2023, it had twenty-nine ministries, including both line ministries (tasked with delivering a government's programs) and central agencies, like the Treasury Board Secretariat, which instead ensure the effective functioning of each ministry and remain key players in the province, not just enabling, but also framing the boundaries of political action. Leading each of these units is a deputy minister (DM), who manages the interface between the political system and the administrative one, coordinates the ministry's activities with the rest of the administration and ensures that it operates effectively and efficiently. Notwithstanding the growth in the numbers and reach of the agencies, boards, committees, and Crown corporations over the past three decades,[13] which were designed to make the administration more agile, most line ministries still have a recognizable Weberian pyramidal structure. Each DM is supported by assistant deputy ministers handling operational tasks within specific divisions, usually tied to either regional or functional criteria.

A key figure in the Ontario deputy ministers' group is the secretary of the cabinet (also called the Clerk), who heads the administrative machinery of

Table 5.1. The Composition of the Ontario Public Sector, Select Years

Year	Ontario Public Sector	Provincial Public Administration Workers	Elementary and Secondary Schools	Universities, Community Colleges, and C.E.G.E.P.s	Hospital Workers
2001	549,705	64,251	213,576	106,019	165,859
2005	623,993	70,874	243,147	124,651	185,321
2010	688,041	77,638	262,074	148,400	199,929
2015	716,256	75,039	282,858	147,548	210,811
2021	775,920	81,001	285,859	172,476	236,584

Source: Statistics Canada, "Table 14-10-0202-01: Employment by Industry, Annual," https://doi.org/10.25318/1410020201-eng. Contains information licensed under the Open Government Licence – Canada.

Ontario. The Clerk's job has three major facets: the first is being deputy minister to the premier, which implies providing advice on policies, appointments and the like. Second, the Clerk leads and manages all of the OPS's activities, and finally – through the Executive Council – the position serves as an interface between the political and administrative worlds by aligning cabinet agendas to government priorities and by communicating cabinet decisions to the ministries.

On the political side, the premier represents the main interlocutor of the Clerk and relies on cabinet as the political executive body. Of the twenty-six premiers elected since 1867, only Ernest Drury (United Farmers) and Bob Rae (NDP) broke the Conservative-Liberal seesaw. Nor were premiers a diverse group: all of them have been white, and it was only in 2013 that the first woman and openly LGBTQ+ person – Kathleen Wynne – was elected.[14] Like all first ministers, Ontario premiers loom large over provincial political and administrative decisions.[15] They are in charge – through the largely formal mediation of the lieutenant general – of key decisions like dissolving the Legislative Assembly, and appointing Ontario's top political and administrative leadership. They essentially direct government policy by controlling both the agenda of the cabinet and its composition. This power extends effectively to the institutional sphere since the Ontario premier can change the structure of the provincial bureaucracy at will by creating, fusing, splitting, or eliminating ministries and can even reach into the local government sphere. Hence, it makes sense that some of Ontario's premiers turned out to be larger-than-life figures[16] whose personalities drove much of the agenda.[17]

While executive dominance in Canada is a powerful force, it is not unchecked: first ministers need the support of their ministers without whom the political process would be much diminished and, when the law prescribes it, the minister must be able to act without interference from the premier. The latter also need the support of – at the very least – the central agencies to ensure the smooth implementation of political agendas.

As Evans noted, the core power for the Ontario premier resides in the ability to command the resources of two key units: the Office of the Premier of Ontario and the Cabinet Office.[18] The former is the premier's political arm, the latter the bureaucratic one. Both have seen increased levels of staffing over the past thirty years, likely related to the increased complexity and interconnectedness of many policy issues, but also because of an increased politicization of the system. Both have historically provided strong internal support for the policy phase of the process of decision-making. Today, this is reflected in the presence of both a deputy minister assigned to Policy and Delivery in the Cabinet Office and a policy function reporting to the deputy chief of staff within the Office of the Premier.

The Cabinet Office is an important mechanism in Westminster governance and has long played a key role in both Canadian politics and administration,[19] particularly by supporting a variety of committees, which include standing policy committees, policy and priorities committees, and the Treasury Board. In Canada, it has quite unique characteristics, including a strong political tone.[20] Historically, Ontario retained a departmentalized cabinet until the late 1960s, which allowed for the premier and a handful of ministers in charge of largely siloed, and therefore mostly independent, committees within the cabinet to manage policy within a system and that discouraged the level of cooperation and interaction that is so common today,[21] and that fostered close connections between political and administrative actors.[22] This structure became increasingly problematic during the 1960s, both because citizens expected more transparency and because the increased complexity of the policy landscape demanded more coordinated action. Hence, in 1969, Premier Roberts created the Committee on Government Productivity (COGP), which kickstarted both the effective separation of policy formulation and policy implementation[23] and a realignment of the relationship between the top public service as the loyal, professional implementers and both elected politicians and political advisors who direct policy. By at least the 1970s, the Ontario Cabinet Office, while influenced by the personality of the premier, was focused on process and structure.[24] The political and administrative advice to the premier was still blended in one single person, but in 1985, Premier Peterson began the practice of separating the post of secretary to cabinet, which became the precinct of career administrators, from that of deputy to the premier, which was to be politically-oriented. Over time, the increased complexity of OPS programs has been a key driver in the increased complexity and size of this office.

The Office of the Premier had a complex trajectory, with a long history of experimentation and an incompletely defined political-administrative divide, which varied often based on the political cycle, the premier of the day, and the capacity of both the administrators and political advisors.[25] While one of its key goals was to communicate to the electorate what the premiers intended to do, rather than to influence unduly the administration,[26] the number of political advisors in government, including here, has steadily increased,[27] matching the general trend towards a higher degree of politicization in most Westminster models.[28] Premiers can influence how the top layer of the administrative system functions. For example, Mike Harris used his Common Sense Revolution mandate to change the size and approach of the cabinet over his tenure (1995–2002) according to what he believed was necessary, but also to what he felt was expedient to his political goals.[29] Furthermore, Cooper[30] has shown that in Canada since 1980, newly elected first ministers have measurably correlated with increased mobility of deputy ministers, an important measure of power centralization.

To cap our discussion, we should reiterate that a relevant role is played by central agencies in the Westminster model. Usually identified in Ontario as the Cabinet Office, the Ministry of Finance and the Treasury Board Secretariat, these units represent the backbone of administrative and political power in the province in that they organize, coordinate, implement, and evaluate the many public policies that both keeps the province running and shape its political direction. While the perfectly balanced, technocratic (some would say somewhat dull) model of cabinet government described by Stewart in the late 1980s may have been in part replaced by a more politicized and diverse crowd of consultants, academics, and policy advisors, the role of these agencies remains critical.[31]

To summarize, when speaking of the executive in Ontario, we are discussing a dynamic equilibrium between the administrative and political sides, which interact in multiple ways. Each embedded in complex relationships with one another and the stakeholders, following dynamics partially framed by the Westminster tradition, but also affected by changing economic, social, demographic, and political challenges and opportunities. Furthermore, the degree of centralization/decentralization of the system is determined by a coming together of the disposition and intent of the premier, the capacity and effectiveness of the administrative structure, and the level of trust between political and administrative actors.

Ontario premiers can (and always could) rely on strong executive powers. A power that is built on their political "weight," in their access to key decision-making tools, and in the capacity of the second-largest public service in the country. The recent wave of populism has surely highlighted and perhaps accelerated this dynamic, but it has not created it.

THE POWER OF THE EXECUTIVE

Ontario premiers, relying on advice from the top political and administrative actors, set the course for the province and enjoy remarkable latitude in deciding how to do so. We now turn to the policies that Ontario premiers are enmeshed in, beginning with a general discussion of their role within the Canadian system and then looking at how the executive managed recent events, often dealing with increasing populism, and looking at the use of the powerful executive tool of Orders in Council (OIC) during the COVID-19 pandemic.

The power of first ministers deeply affects Canadian federalism, which in turn is a key driver for the entire political system. In particular, the notion of executive federalism, which Watts defined as "the processes of intergovernmental negotiation that are dominated by the executives of the different governments within the federal system,"[32] is connected to the ability of first ministers to direct policy and implement change throughout the administrative and political systems and therefore to their capacity to manage these challenges through elite accommodation. While executive federalism is sometimes considered a possible gateway to presidentialism, especially when the prime minister is concerned,[33] it has also been an important factor in managing political relations in Canada that cannot be easily dismissed as undemocratic.[34]

Canadian federalism has its roots in the *British North America Act*, which superimposed decentralized federalism onto the British parliamentary system and slowly joined together provinces and territories in the Canadian federation.[35] This approach used elite accommodation to coordinate and align policy goals, while concurrently generating rival nationalisms and regionalisms within the country, and it required shared decision-making to function.[36] Hence, Canadian elites developed a set of "coordinating discourses" that enabled all perspectives to be considered. This institutional balancing act deeply affects policy-making by influencing decisions across the policy spectrum, often generating "institutionalized ambivalence" where cooperation among actors can be very difficult to individuate.[37] This dynamic balance is embodied in the shifting nature of the power relationship at the core of Canadian federalism,[38] which oscillates between centralization and decentralization among federal and regional authorities. Recently, provincial autonomy increased,[39] favouring jurisdictions like Ontario that can harness substantial demographic, industrial, and economic resources. Nonetheless, recall that provincial autonomy is highly dependent on which policy area is being discussed and that even recent significant autonomist pushes like that of Quebec's premier François Legault are only partially mirrored in Ontario, where increased funding in key areas like health care, subjected to less conditionality, has traditionally been the focus.

Not only has the relationship between the legislative and the executive branches in Canada traditionally favoured the latter,[40] but recently, executive creep – progressively marginalizing backbenchers and concentrating power in the executive – has increased in all provinces,[41] and the executive has strengthened its reach. As McDowell notes in chapter 4 of this volume, since the Harris government's reforms, the Ontario legislature has returned to a largely supporting role, and the Opposition has little capacity to hold governments to account. Ontario premiers have extensive capacity, and past attempts at controlling it generally had limited success,[42] partially because of the close connection between caucus and top executive levels. In fact, in 2019, almost all caucus members held some type of executive position.[43] But how is this executive power practically applied?

The political scenarios of the past twenty-five years have been marked by the spread of populism,[44] a series of global crises – including 9/11, the 2008 global recession, climate change, civil war across the Middle and Near East, the COVID-19 pandemic, and the Russian invasion of Ukraine – and by an increased number of challenges to the paradigm of globalization,[45] which until recently had appeared fluid but robust. These events affected all jurisdictions, including Ontario. Some of these effects have been direct ones, like the arrival of refugees or economic downturns. Others touched our polity more obliquely but just as deeply. Recently, all provinces faced two major complex issues: the rise of populism, and the response to long-term, crisis-like emergencies – the most impactful being the COVID-19 pandemic. Next, the chapter examines how the executive in Ontario related to these challenges.

The argument that populism, especially during periods of emergency, inclines towards executive dominance has been made before.[46] However, by highlighting the failure of more problematic candidates,[47] the narrative surrounding Canadian populism stressed its being somewhat less extreme than what emerged elsewhere, especially considering the absence of a competitive anti-immigration party,[48] even in an environment where disciplinary elements still frame Canadian immigration policy.[49] Since the 1990s, Ontario politics has been referencing neo-liberal paradigms independently of whether a Conservative or Liberal premier sat at Queen's Park,[50] and while the 2018 provincial elections may have been more about punishing the previous Liberal government that a truly populist wave,[51] there are signs that a populist approach was in place at least since the Rob Ford years as mayor of Toronto,[52] and that this narrative may resonate with many industrial workers who feel left behind.[53] Populist governments in countries as different as the UK[54] and the Philippines[55] have been linked to the increased use of executive dominance. This has been particularly evident during emergency crises like the COVID-19 pandemic and has had an especially relevant impact upon the legislative role of parliaments in both Europe[56] and Canada.[57] It may be easier for populist politicians to invoke and use broader and less restricted powers given the "thin" ideological premise they rely on and the focus on an "adversary" as a way to focus their political approaches.

Once elected, the Doug Ford government appeared quite happy to implement policies with a strong populist flavour in areas like employment standards[58] or school curricula,[59] and in dealing rather softly with widespread protests against COVID-19 mandates in 2022, such as the occupation of Ottawa by the so-called Freedom Convoy and the blocking of the Ambassador Bridge, a key infrastructural bottleneck in US-Canadian trade. Hence, populism seems to have certainly emerged in Ontario.

Provincial politics in Ontario has been connected to many important challenges that have tested the capacity and political will of its executives: the Walkerton water crisis of 2000, the COVID-19 pandemic, the occupation of Ottawa by anti-vaccine protesters, and climate change, among others. Managing these challenges is often complex, and in Ontario, as late as the 1950s, the system hinged on civil defence to do so. Over time, it evolved, adding strong elements of prevention, community preparedness, and capacity building,

Table 5.2. Orders in Council – Ontario

Orders	2016	2017	2018	2019	2020	2021	2022
All	880	2450	1485	1954	1796	1873	1862
Premier and President of the Council	69	347	201	205	293	289	263
Percentage	7.84%	14.16%	13.54%	10.49%	16.31%	15.43%	14.10.%

Source: Compiled by author from the Government of Ontario, "Orders in Council," https://www.ontario.ca/search/orders-in-council.

but essentially remained often a "policy without a public" in the hands of experts.[60] However, with some of the more recent events, like Walkerton and the COVID-19 pandemic, politics has become a much more central element, demanding responses from the premiers, which may offer particularly interesting opportunities for populist governments. Crises are also an important test of federal systems: they can either divide or bring institutional actors closer. In Canada, war and national emergencies have historically tended to justify an increased role for Ottawa under the guise of "crisis centralism" or "emergency federalism,"[61] even if generally Canada's policy style supports elite cooperation but has a harder time producing unified top-down approaches.[62]

For example, during the COVID-19 pandemic, in a field where federal and provincial dominance in emergency management largely sidelines cities,[63] policy choices were influenced by how dangerous the pandemic was perceived to be and by tensions between the political and scientific framing of pandemic management. But, by the end of summer 2020, when the provinces could demonstrate that they had "flattened the curve," and ensured the continued viability of the medical system, they retook the lead in policy-making with little if any pushback from Ottawa. Competitive intergovernmental dynamics and specific regional policy mixes re-emerged as provinces and territories reopened their economies, which most jurisdictions saw as their key policy challenge.

If current Ontario politics is more populist than during previous periods, does this correlate with an increased level of executive control, especially during the COVID-19 emergency? While this question cannot be answered in detail here, there are some interesting hints in table 5.2. For example, when looking at the number of Orders in Council, the most effective executive tool available to the government, it is evident that they were used fairly extensively in recent years independently of the COVID-19 pandemic, but that the percentage of those signed by the premier and not by a minister rose during the pandemic.

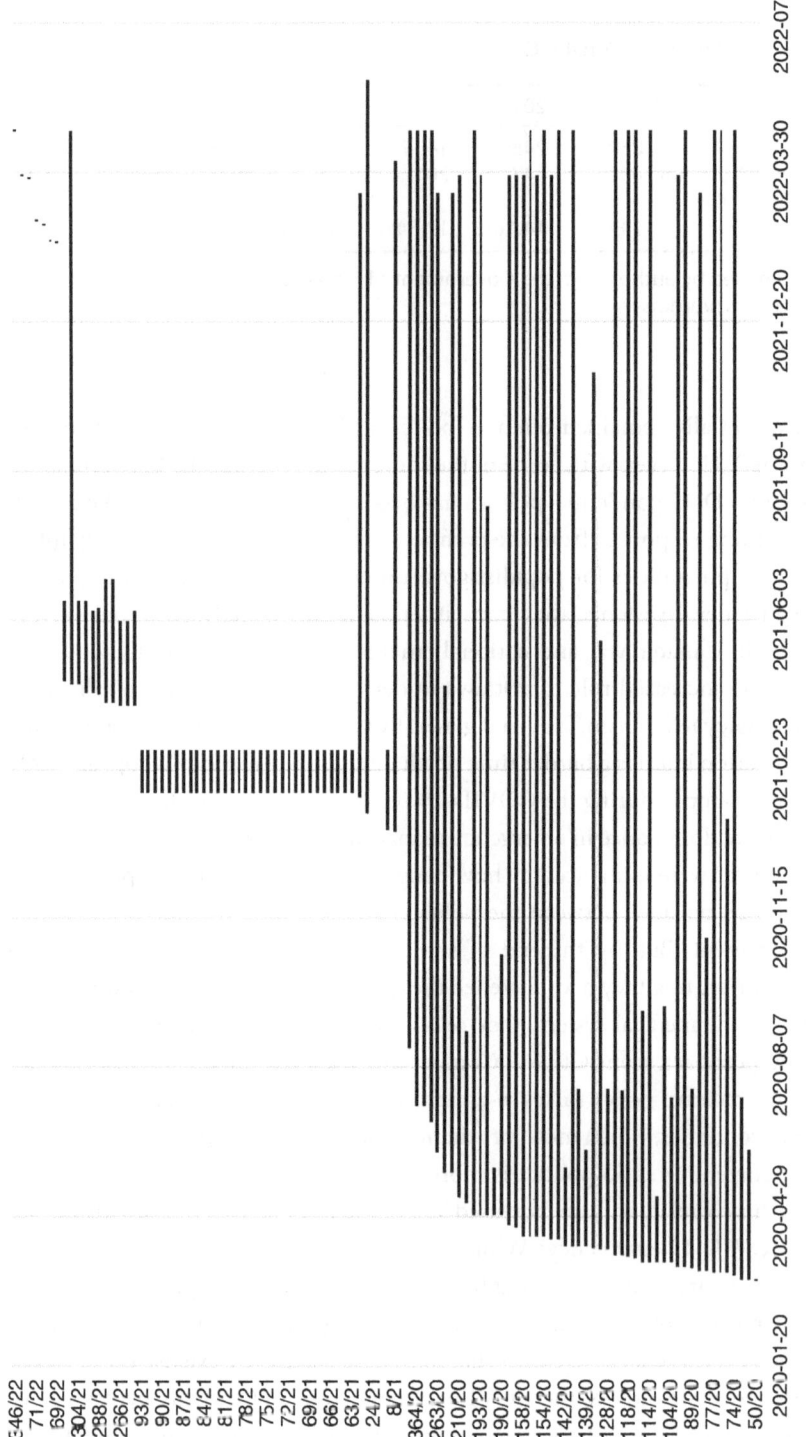

Figure 5.1. Ontario Emergency Orders
Source: Compiled by author from the Government of Ontario, "Emergency Information," accessed August 1, 2023, https://www.ontario.ca/page/emergency-information#emergencyorders.

Likely the Ford government found it expedient to use these tools more than usual. Another indicator is the pattern followed by Ontario emergency orders (see figure 5.1), which also speaks to the use of central executive authority, since 2019. The overwhelming majority of these are related to the COVID-19 pandemic. There are three major periods of executive activity: the initial one between mid-March and early May 2020, when the largest percentage of emergency orders were signed and which includes some of the longest standing orders. The second grouping is a series of month-long stay-at-home orders signed on February 8, 2021, and the third is a set of relatively short emergency orders signed in April 2021. Much of the final set of orders in 2022, which appear punctuated here because they do not have time periods attached to them, enact the reopening of the province, which was effectively completed by the end of April 2022.

Overall, there were 106 OICs during the pandemic and while most lasted less than three months (fifty-eight) there were twenty-nine that lasted over twenty-four months. These generally involved either work deployment measures for long-term care or health facilities or were framing ones like 98/20 (*Prohibiting unfair pricing on necessary goods*). Overall, the province has shown a characteristically Canadian propension for the use of executive tools during the pandemic, but that is not unlike what one would expect. A broader question remains as to whether the use of enabling legislation and generally the trend for populist governments to reduce the capacity of the legislative is occurring in Ontario. While there is no doubt that populist governments often see the Opposition as the "opponent" rather than a partner in parliamentary democracy, it is also clear that the relationship between populism and constitutionalism is varied and complex.[64] Furthermore, the trend in the province towards a more insulated – and to some extent insular – government has been on the march since the early 1990s and independently of emergencies.

These trends did not harm the Ontario Progressive Conservatives at the polls. The June 2, 2022 provincial election returned the party and Doug Ford to Queen's Park, adding 7 seats to their majority for a total of 83 out of 124 and delivering massive blows to both the Liberal party and the NDP. The latter lost 9 of the 40 seats it won in 2018, and the former added just one to their 7 and therefore faced another term without official party status, even if in July 2023 they were able to take the Kanata-Carleton riding in a by-election. Both party leaders resigned on election night. The Ontario legislature is completed by one Green Party representative and one independent. An important corollary to the election has been the plummeting electoral turnout, which at

43.5 per cent was not only 13.5 percentage points lower than in 2018, but also marked the nadir in the province's history. While multiple factors were involved, from the uninspired campaigns the opposition parties ran, to the role of the media and the barrage of polls that since the early days projected a comfortable PC majority, to the effects of the first-past-the-post electoral system, what seems certain is that Ontario voters decided that Ford's style of politics was acceptable. Neither the mishandling of the early pandemic phase, nor his signal absence during the occupation of the nation's capital by the "Freedom Convoy" seem to have helped the Opposition.

The Ford government surely represents a populist model but not an extreme one like Viktor Orbán's in Hungary. Nor is it emerging out of thin air. In fact, throughout Ontario's history, provincial governments have been very – perhaps too – comfortable with sidelining the Opposition whenever they could. It is perhaps because of this that the Ford Nation brand of populism has done little to "extract the people from the people" as of yet[65] – mostly supporting groups opposing vaccines and occupying Ottawa by omission. Nor is it clear that this turn represents a direct challenge to democratic values,[66] or a new response to democratic questions.[67] What seems evident, however, is the lack of effectiveness from the opposition parties in either mounting an effective electoral response, or even an interest in changing some of the executive and legislative premises that have enabled this type of approach. If all parties seem very much comfortable with restricted opportunities for the Opposition to attend its role of counterbalance and oversight, and if increased executive dominance is welcome, from where should a counter to this strategy come?

DISCUSSION QUESTIONS

1 In your opinion, is the strength of the executive – and especially of the premier – in the Ontario context an advantage or a disadvantage for the province? Use some examples to support your perspective.
2 Considering the historical evolution of the executive in Ontario, what are the key trends that you can identify?
3 The executive in Ontario has complex relations not just with the legislative branch, but also with the local and federal jurisdictional levels. By utilizing content from other chapters, try to build a comprehensive image of those relations.

NOTES

1 A.D.P. Heeney, "Cabinet Government in Canada: Some Recent Developments in the Machinery of the Central Executive," *Canadian Journal of Economics and Political Science* 12, no. 3 (August 1946): 282, https://doi.org/10.2307/137283; Thomas A. Hockin, *Apex of Power: The Prime Minister and Political Leadership in Canada* (Scarborough, ON: Prentice-Hall of Canada, 1977); Richard Loreto and Graham White, "The Premier and the Cabinet," in *The Government and Politics of Ontario*, 4th ed., ed. Graham White (Toronto: University of Toronto Press, 1990); Donald Savoie, *Governing from the Centre: The Concentration of Power in Canadian Politics* (Toronto: University of Toronto Press, 1999); Graham White, *Cabinets and First Ministers* (Vancouver: UBC Press, 2005).

2 Richard Heffernan, "Prime Ministerial Predominance? Core Executive Politics in the UK," *British Journal of Politics and International Relations* 5, no. 3 (August 2003): 347–72, https://doi.org/10.1111/1467-856X.00110; Peter Aucoin, "New Political Governance in Westminster Systems: Impartial Public Administration and Management Performance at Risk," *Governance* 25, no. 2 (April 2012): 177–99, https://doi.org/10.1111/j.1468-0491.2012.01569.x.

3 White, *Cabinets and First Ministers*.

4 Patrice Dutil, *Prime Ministerial Power in Canada: Its Origins under Macdonald, Laurier and Borden* (Vancouver: UBC Press, 2017).

5 Christopher Dunn, "The Central Executive in Canadian Government: Searching for the Holy Grail," in *The Handbook of Canadian Public Administration*, 3rd ed., ed. Christopher Dunn (Oxford: Oxford University Press, 2016), 315–62; Heeney, "Cabinet Government in Canada"; Loreto and White, "The Premier and the Cabinet."

6 Herman Bakvis, "Prime Minister and Cabinet in Canada: An Autocracy in Need of Reform?," *Journal of Canadian Studies* 35, no. 4 (Winter 2000): 60–79, https://doi.org/10.3138/jcs.35.4.60.

7 Lawrence Martin, *Harperland: The Politics of Control* (Toronto: Penguin Canada, 2011).

8 Aaron Ames, "Executive Federalism in Canada: Competition or Collaboration?," *Public Policy and Governance Review* 7, no. 1 (Fall 2015): 33–48; Dupré, "The Workability of Executive Federalism in Canada"; Thomas O. Hueglin, *Federalism in Canada: Contested Concepts and Uneasy Balances* (Toronto: University of Toronto Press, 2021); Clement Akwasi Botchway, "The Need for Executive Federalism in Federal-Provincial Relations: The Canadian Example," *Journal of Public Administration and Policy Research* 9, no. 5 (December 2017): 68–75, https://doi.org/10.5897/JPAPR2017.0390.

9 Bryan Evans, "The Politics of Public Administration: Constructing the Neoliberal State," in *Canadian Political Economy*, ed. Heather Whiteside (Toronto: University of Toronto Press, 2020), 123–44; Patrick Dunleavy, Helen Margetts, Simon Bastow, and Jane Tinkler, "New Public Management Is Dead – Long Live Digital-Era Governance," *Journal of Public Administration Research and Theory* 16, no. 3 (July 2006): 467–94, https://doi.org/10.1093/jopart/mui057; Jacques

Bourgault and Karolien Van Dorpe, "Managerial Reforms, Public Service Bargains and Top Civil Servant Identity," *International Review of Administrative Sciences* 79, no. 1 (March 2013): 49–70, https://doi.org/10.1177/0020852312467739.

10 Michael Freeden, "Is Nationalism a Distinct Ideology?," *Political Studies* 46, no. 4 (September 1998): 748–65, https://doi.org/10.1111/1467-9248.00165; Cas Mudde, "The Populist Zeitgeist," *Government and Opposition* 39, no. 4 (2004): 541–63, https://doi.org/10.1111/j.1477-7053.2004.00135.x.

11 Chris Erl, "The People and The Nation: The 'Thick' and the 'Thin' of Right-Wing Populism in Canada," *Social Science Quarterly* 102, no. 1 (January 2021): 107–24, https://doi.org/10.1111/ssqu.12889.

12 In fact, you can somewhat roughly and imprecisely measure this by looking at the number of public service employees per 100,000 Ontarians: in 2001 there were 540, today they are 546.

13 Patrice Dutil, "Infrastructure Ontario: The Agencification of Public Works in a Canadian Province," in *Public Enterprises Today: Missions, Performance and Governance – Learning from Fifteen Cases*, ed. Luc Bernier (Brussels: P.I.E. Peter Lang, 2015), 303–33.

14 Much the same applies to secretaries to cabinet: since 1948, nineteen Caucasians held the post, only three among them were women, the first being appointed in 1995.

15 White, *Cabinets and First Ministers*; Herman Bakvis and Steven Wolinetz, "Canada: Executive Dominance and Presidentialization," in *The Presidentialization of Politics*, ed. Thomas Poguntke and Paul Webb (Oxford: Oxford University Press, 2005), 199–220.

16 Steve Paikin, *Paikin and the Premiers: Personal Reflections on a Half Century of Ontario Leaders* (Toronto: Dundurn, 2013); James Maurice Stockford Careless, *The Pre-Confederation Premiers: Ontario Government Leaders, 1841–1867* (Toronto: University of Toronto Press, 1980).

17 Edward E. Stewart, *Cabinet Government in Ontario: A View from Inside* (Halifax: Institute for Research on Public Policy, 1989).

18 Bryan Evans, "The Commanding Heights of Power and Politics in Ontario," in *The Politics of Ontario*, ed. Cheryl N. Collier and Jonathan Malloy (Toronto: University of Toronto Press, 2017), 100–17.

19 James R. Mallory, "Cabinet Government in the Provinces of Canada," *McGill Law Journal* 3, no. 2 (Spring 1957): 195–202.

20 Graham White, "Adapting the Westminster Model: Provincial and Territorial Cabinets in Canada," *Public Money and Management* 21, no. 2 (April 2001): 17–24, https://doi.org/10.1111/1467-9302.00255.

21 Michael Howlett, Luc Bernier, Keith Brownsey, and Christopher Dunn, "Modern Canadian Governance: Political-Administrative Styles and Executive Organization in Canada," in *Executive Styles in Canada*, ed. Luc Bernier, Keith Brownsey, and Michael Howlett (Toronto: University of Toronto Press, 2005), 3–14, https://doi.org/10.3138/9781442674707-004.

22 Evans, "The Commanding Heights."
23 Evans, "The Commanding Heights."
24 Stewart, *Cabinet Government in Ontario*.
25 Patrice Dutil and Peter Constantinou, "The Office of Premier of Ontario 1945–2010: Who Really Advises?," *Canadian Parliamentary Review* 36, no. 1 (Spring 2013): 43–50.
26 Dutil and Constantinou, "The Office of Premier."
27 Evans, "The Commanding Heights."
28 Jonathan Craft and John Halligan, *Advising Governments in the Westminster Tradition: Policy Advisory Systems in Australia, Britain, Canada and New Zealand*, 1st ed. (Cambridge: Cambridge University Press, 2020), https://doi.org/10.1017/9781108377133.
29 Ted Glenn, "Politics, Personality, and History in Ontario's Administrative Style," in *Executive Styles in Canada: Cabinet Structures and Leadership Practices in Canadian Government*, ed. Luc Bernier, Keith Brownsey, and Michael Howlett (Toronto: University of Toronto Press, 2005), 170–85.
30 Christopher A. Cooper, "The Rise of Court Government? Testing the Centralisation of Power Thesis with Longitudinal Data from Canada," *Parliamentary Affairs* 70, no. 3 (July 2017): 589–610, https://doi.org/10.1093/pa/gsx003.
31 Stewart, *Cabinet Government in Ontario*.
32 Ronald Watts, *Executive Federalism: A Comparative Analysis* (Kingston: Institute of Intergovernmental Relations, Queen's University, 1989), 3.
33 Herman Bakvis and Steven Wolinetz, "Canada: Executive Dominance and Presidentialization," in *The Presidentialization of Politics*, ed. Thomas Poguntke and Paul Webb (Oxford: Oxford University Press, 2005), 199–220.
34 Botchway, "The Need for Executive Federalism."
35 Samuel V. LaSelva, *The Moral Foundations of Canadian Federalism: Paradoxes, Achievements, and Tragedies of Nationhood* (Montreal: McGill-Queen's University Press, 1996).
36 Edwin R. Black, *Divided Loyalties: Canadian Concepts of Federalism* (Montreal: McGill-Queen's University Press, 1975), https://doi.org/10.2307/j.ctt1w0df2t; Donald V. Smiley, "Public Administration and Canadian Federalism," *Canadian Public Administration/Administration publique du Canada* 7, no. 3 (September 1964): 371–88, https://doi.org/10.1111/j.1754-7121.1964.tb00165.x.
37 Carolyn Tuohy, *Policy and Politics in Canada: Institutionalized Ambivalence* (Philadelphia: Temple University Press, 1992).
38 Canadian federalism has been traditionally divided in various stages based on the historical valence of the system: Confederation (1867–83); Dual Federalism (1883–1910); Cooperative Federalism (1910–60); Executive Federalism (1960–93) – itself often broken down into Competitive Federalism (late 1960s–early 1980s) and Constitutional Federalism (1980s–early 1990s) – Collaborative Federalism (1993–2005) and Open Federalism (2005–present).

39 Adam Harmes, "The Political Economy of Open Federalism," *Canadian Journal of Political Science* 40, no. 2 (June 2007): 417–37, https://doi.org/10.1017/S0008423907070114; Richard Simeon, Ian Robinson, and Jennifer Wallner, "The Dynamics of Canadian Federalism," in *Canadian Politics*, 6th ed., James Bickerton and Alain-G. Gagnon (Toronto: University of Toronto Press, 2014), 65–91; Matt Wilder and Michael Howlett, "Bringing the Provinces Back in: Re-Evaluating the Relevance of Province-Building to Theories of Canadian Federalism and Multi-level Governance," *Canadian Political Science Review* 9, no. 3 (November 2015): 1–34, https://doi.org/10.24124/c677/20151282.
40 Jonathan Malloy, "The Executive and Parliament in Canada," *The Journal of Legislative Studies* 10, nos. 2–3 (June 2004): 206–17, https://doi.org/10.1080/1357233042000322319.
41 Paul E.J. Thomas and J.P. Lewis, "Executive Creep in Canadian Provincial Legislatures," *Canadian Journal of Political Science* 52, no. 2 (June 2019): 363–83, https://doi.org/10.1017/S0008423918000781.
42 Kenneth Bryden, "Executive and Legislature in Ontario: A Case Study on Governmental Reform," *Canadian Public Administration* 18, no. 2 (June 1975): 235–52, https://doi.org/10.1111/j.1754-7121.1975.tb01939.x.
43 Thomas and Lewis, "Executive Creep in Canadian Provincial Legislatures," 375.
44 Benjamin Moffitt, *The Global Rise of Populism: Performance, Political Style, and Representation* (Stanford: Stanford University Press, 2016), https://doi.org/10.1515/9780804799331.
45 Patrick Diamond, *The Crisis of Globalization: Democracy, Capitalism and Inequality in the Twenty-First Century* (London: I.B. Tauris, 2019) ProQuest EBook Central.
46 Nicole Bolleyer and Orsolya Salát, "Parliaments in Times of Crisis: COVID-19, Populism and Executive Dominance," *West European Politics* 44, nos. 5–6 (September 2021): 1103–28, https://doi.org/10.1080/01402382.2021.1930733.
47 Brian Budd, "The Populist Radical Right Goes Canadian: An Analysis of Kellie Leitch's Failed 2016–2017 Conservative Party of Canada Leadership Campaign," in *Populism and World Politics*, ed. Frank A. Stengel, David B. MacDonald, and Dirk Nabers (Cham: Springer, 2019), 137–63, https://doi.org/10.1007/978-3-030-04621-7_6.
48 Joshua Gordon, Sanjay Jeram, and Clifton Linden, "The Two Solitudes of Canadian Nativism: Explaining the Absence of a Competitive Anti-immigration Party in Canada," *Nations and Nationalism* 26, no. 4 (October 2020): 902–22, https://doi.org/10.1111/nana.12570.
49 John Carlaw, "Authoritarian Populism and Canada's Conservative Decade (2006–2015) in Citizenship and Immigration: The Politics and Practices of Kenneyism and Neo-Conservative Multiculturalism," *Journal of Canadian Studies* 51, no. 3 (Fall 2018): 782–816, https://doi.org/10.3138/jcs.2017-0054.
50 Greg Albo and Bryan M. Evans, eds., *Divided Province: Ontario Politics in the Age of Neoliberalism* (Montreal: McGill-Queen's Press, 2018).
51 Andrea Perrella, Simon J. Kiss, and Barry J. Kay, "Conservative Populism, or Unpopular Liberalism? Review of the 2018 Ontario Provincial Election,"

Canadian Political Science Review 14, no. 1 (June 2020): 118–46, https://doi.org/10.24124/c677/20201790.

52 Daniel Silver, Zack Taylor, and Fernando Calderón-Figueroa, "Populism in the City: The Case of Ford Nation," *International Journal of Politics, Culture, and Society* 33, no. 1 (March 2020): 1–21, https://doi.org/10.1007/s10767-018-9310-1.

53 Adam D.K. King, "Right-Wing Populism, Organized Labor, and White Workers in Sudbury, Ontario: A Cautionary Tale from the 2018 Ontario Election," *Journal of Labor and Society* 23, no. 4 (December 2020): 485–501, https://doi.org/10.1111/wusa.12489.

54 Joseph Ward and Bradley Ward, "From Brexit to COVID-19: The Johnson Government, Executive Centralisation and Authoritarian Populism," *Political Studies*, 71, no. 3 (December 2023), 1171–89, https://doi.org/10.1177/00323217211063730.

55 Maria Ela L. Atienza, "The Philippines under Lockdown: Continuing Executive Dominance and an Unclear Pandemic Response," in *Routledge Handbook of Law and the COVID-19 Pandemic*, ed. Joelle Grogan and Alice Donald (London: Routledge, 2022), 445–56.

56 Bolleyer and Salát, "Parliaments in Times of Crisis."

57 Kathy Brock, "Executive-Parliamentary Relations in Canada: Moving Forward from the Pandemic," *Canadian Public Administration* 65, no. 3 (September 2022): 497–515, https://doi.org/10.1111/capa.12489.

58 Mark P. Thomas, "For the People? Regulating Employment Standards in an Era of Right-Wing Populism," *Studies in Political Economy* 101, no. 2 (May 2020): 135–54, https://doi.org/10.1080/07078552.2020.1802834.

59 Lauren Bialystok, Jessica Wright, Taylor Berzins, Caileigh Guy, and Em Osborne, "The Appropriation of Sex Education by Conservative Populism," *Curriculum Inquiry* 50, no. 4 (August 2020): 330–51, https://doi.org/10.1080/03626784.2020.1809967.

60 Daniel Henstra, "The Dynamics of Policy Change: A Longitudinal Analysis of Emergency Management in Ontario, 1950–2010," *Journal of Policy History* 23, no. 3 (July 2011): 399–428, https://doi.org/10.1017/S0898030611000169.

61 James R. Mallory, "The Five Faces of Federalism," in *The Future of Canadian Federalism/L'Avenir du federalisme canadien*, ed. Paul-André Crepeau and Crawford Brough Macpherson (Toronto: University of Toronto Press, 1965), 3–15; Edwin R. Black, *Divided Loyalties: Canadian Concepts of Federalism* (Montreal: McGill-Queen's University Press, 1975), https://doi.org/10.2307/j.ctt1w0df2t.

62 Andrea Migone, "Trust, but Customize: Federalism's Impact on the Canadian COVID-19 Response," *Policy and Society* 39, no. 3 (September 2020): 382–402, https://doi.org/10.1080/14494035.2020.1783788.

63 Luc Juillet and Junichiro Koji, "Reforming the Multilevel Governance of Emergencies: Municipalities and the Discursive Politics of Canada' Emergency Management Policy," in *Canada in Cities*, ed. Katherine A.H. Graham, and Caroline Andrew (Montreal: McGill-Queen's University Press, 2014), 39–74.

64 Andrew Arato and Jean L. Cohen, "Populism and Constitutionalism," in *Populism and Civil Society: The Challenge to Constitutional Democracy*, ed. Andrew Arato and Jean L. Cohen (Oxford: Oxford University Press, 2021), 153–84, https://doi.org/10.1093/oso/9780197526583.003.0004.
65 Müller, "The People Must Be Extracted."
66 Giorgos Katsambekis, "The Populist Surge in Post-Democratic Times: Theoretical and Political Challenges," *The Political Quarterly* 88, no. 2 (April–June 2017): 202–10, https://doi.org/10.1111/1467-923X.12317.
67 Cristóbal Rovira Kaltwasser, "The Responses of Populism to Dahl's Democratic Dilemmas," *Political Studies* 62, no. 3 (October 2014): 470–87, https://doi.org/10.1111/1467-9248.12038.

6

Local Government and Politics in Ontario

Zachary Spicer

INTRODUCTION

It is hard to imagine governing a province the size of Ontario without local governments. As Ontarians go about their day, they encounter municipal services at every turn – water, wastewater, garbage disposal, public transpiration, police and fire protection, roads and highways, parks and recreation centres, social services, licensing, public health, and libraries, among others. The list of services delivered locally is long and vital to the health, safety, and prosperity of Ontarians. Why couldn't the provincial government provide these services? One main reason is efficiency. Certain services are best delivered locally, where the scope and scale of servicing can be optimized for the community, allowing for public input and control over the quality and quantity of certain services. Provincial governments could simply not adequately manage or deliver a range of local services, such as waste removal or public transportation, centrally. Having the provincial government run all community services would create far too much uniformity. While we may appreciate uniformity and province-wide service standards in some policy areas, such as health care and education, this is likely not needed in service areas like waste management. Local government, therefore, allows for choice and efficiency, providing communities with the ability to adapt (where permissible under provincial legislation) to local servicing preferences.

The term "local government" refers to both municipalities and special-purpose bodies, such as school or library boards. Municipalities are elected governments, meaning that they are key sites of democratic activity across Ontario and provide residents with the chance to decide how services are delivered and financed. These decisions, however, are subject to parameters outlined by the provincial government, which tightly regulates the shape, size, and decisions made by local governments throughout Ontario. This chapter explores this relationship, discussing the role and responsibilities of local governments in relation to the provincial government. We discuss how decisions about local policies and services are made, the role of those who make them and the way in which local governments and services are financed. Throughout the chapter you will gain an understanding of the role of local government in your community and an appreciation of the challenge of delivering services under tremendous resource and capacity constraints.

THE SHAPE AND STRUCTURE OF LOCAL GOVERNMENT IN ONTARIO

As mentioned, the term "local government" refers to both municipalities and special-purpose bodies. There are 444 municipal governments in Ontario, with tremendous variation in population size and geography. The city of Toronto is Ontario's largest municipality, with close to 2.8 million residents according to the 2021 census. It is very much an outlier, however, with the average municipality in Ontario having under 50,000 residents.[1] Our smallest municipality, Cockburn Island, has only sixteen permanent residents. Despite substantial variation in size, there is remarkably little difference in the power and authority provided to Ontario's smallest and largest municipalities, with most responsible for delivering similar services and operating under very similar legal authority.

Municipalities in Canada are often referred to as "creatures of the provinces" in that they are a responsibility assigned to provincial governments in the *Constitution Act, 1867*. This status has been reaffirmed by the Supreme Court of Canada, which in 2001 asserted that "Municipal governments and special-purpose municipal institutions, such as school boards, are creatures of the provincial governments ... these institutions have no constitutional status or independent autonomy and the province has absolute and unfettered legal power to do with them as it wills."[2] Most provinces exercise roughly similar control over municipalities within their jurisdiction. Every province has a dedicated minister responsible for municipal affairs and at least one statute that articulates the basic purpose, structure, and responsibilities of municipalities. In Ontario, that statute is the *Municipal Act, 2001*, which consolidated much of the province's past legislation addressing municipalities and now governs the extent of powers and duties, internal organization, and structure of municipal government in Ontario. Specifically, the act establishes the framework for how municipalities operate, the composition of their council, the officer roles required, such as a clerk or building official, the process for passing bylaws, conducting council meetings, fiscal and budgetary requirements, parameters for making decisions about local improvements, community grants and financial investments, and the enforcement of bylaws.[3] The province also has a handful of other Acts that address specific municipal policy areas, such as the *Municipal Elections Act*, which sets the parameters for local elections.[4]

Given the important role that the provincial government plays in the life of municipalities, it will come as no surprise how provincial decision makers have shaped the structure of municipal government over time. The provincial government can consolidate or even eliminate municipal governments, if it so desires. The most notable spat of consolidations occurred in the late 1990s and early 2000s, when the amount of municipalities in Ontario was reduced from 850 to the 444 we see today. While the provincial government at the time argued that wide-scale consolidation would create efficiencies and cost savings that could be passed along to taxpayers, few studies have found much support for this notion.[5] In fact, very few cost savings have been found, with most studies showing that servicing costs generally increased after amalgamation in Ontario.[6] In Toronto, the transition from Metropolitan Toronto to the new City of Toronto cost $275 million.[7] While 2,700 positions in Toronto were initially eliminated after amalgamation, 3,600 additional positions were added over time.[8]

Ontario's remaining 444 municipalities can be classified as being either single-tier or part of a two-tier structure, such as a regional or county government. About 40 per cent of municipalities in Ontario are single-tier units, meaning that they are solely responsible for the provision of services within their geographic area.[9] However, most municipalities in Ontario are in a two-tier structure, be it a regional or county government. In two-tier governments, service delivery is divided between the lower- and upper-tier governments. The responsibility between each tier varies, but the system is designed to balance regional interests with economies of scale, meaning that services best delivered locally, such as fire protection or recreation, would be normally delivered by lower-tier municipalities, and those best delivered on a regional scale, such as public transportation or arterial roads, would be handled by the upper tier.[10]

Layered on top of these municipal structures are thirty-six Consolidated Municipal Service Managers (CMSM) in Southern Ontario and eleven District Social Service Administration Boards (DSSAB) in the North. Each are responsible for delivering Ontario Works, social services (child care, public housing, preventative health problems), and land ambulance services.[11] The DSSABs operate in much the same fashion, but also provide services to unorganized municipalities, which have no formal local government.[12]

Special-purpose bodies are local governments that have responsibility for only one function, as opposed to municipalities that have responsibility for a variety of functions and services. While the role of municipalities is generally well defined, the same cannot be said for special-purpose bodies. Some, such as school boards, have elected representatives that guide the operation of the board. Others, such as library boards, have an appointment process where citizens can express interest and possibly serve on the board for a defined period. The authority of special-purpose bodies also varies significantly. For instance, school boards have control over physical assets (i.e., schools) and usually a large amount of land in the communities they serve, making them among the strongest special-purpose bodies in Ontario. School boards in Ontario have gone through considerable change over the past twenty years, however. Changes to the education system in 1998 significantly altered how school boards were financed. Before 1998, school boards in Ontario would set local education property tax rates, and municipalities would collect and remit these taxes on the boards' behalf. This system, however, was largely considered inequitable given that school boards with large property tax bases were able to raise more money than smaller boards, which affected the resources available to students.[13] School boards in Ontario no longer have the authority to determine education tax rates. Rather, the provincial government sets a uniform rate, municipalities collect the education portion of property tax, and the Ministry of Education determines each board's overall allocation.

In comparison, most other special-purpose bodies can be considered quite weak. Most are filled by appointment, and many include some combination of municipal councillors and residents. Occasionally, the provincial government has the ability to appoint a certain number of representatives. The boards are often reliant upon municipal councils for funding, but generally have considerable freedom to set policy on non-financial matters.[14] Examples of local boards include library boards, parks and recreation boards, and public transit boards.

Special mention should be made of police services boards. Police officers are granted a certain degree of independence from local politicians, largely to avoid the perception of political interference in their daily operations.[15] As a result, no municipal council in Ontario has direct control over a police service.[16] However, most police service boards have municipal representation, often members of council, along with provincially appointed members.[17] These boards often scrutinize the operations and planning of the local police service.[18]

Layered on top of local special-purpose bodies are a variety of provincial and federal special-purpose bodies, such as airport authorities, port authorities, conservation authorities, and supra-regional transit boards, such as Metrolinx. While these special-purpose bodies have a similar purpose, they fall under federal and provincial legislation and draw funding and authority from their respective governments. Given that authorities still operate locally, they often find themselves interfacing with municipal councillors and other decision-makers. Conflict can occasionally arise, such as in cases where property or finances are in dispute.

GOVERNING MUNICIPALITIES IN ONTARIO

Municipalities in Ontario operate much differently than the provincial legislature. There is no official "government" nor an official Opposition in local government. The mayor does not exercise powers akin to the premier. Nor do they have a cabinet.[19] Officially, in the *Municipal Act*, the mayor is referred to as the head of council. In a county government, the head of council is often referred to as a warden, and in a regional government, they are commonly referred to as a chair. Section 225(a) of the *Municipal Act* mentions that the role of the head of council is to "act as the chief executive officer of the municipality," but the powers vested in the mayor are very different than what one might expect of a private sector CEO. While the introduction of "strong mayor" powers (discussed later) has changed some of the responsibilities of many big-city mayors, most mayors in Ontario do not have any direct control over the municipality's administrative apparatus.[20] Instead, council appoints a chief administrative officer (CAO) to handle the administrative aspects of the organization. The CAO is the head of the administrative apparatus of the municipality and would also report directly to council, not to the mayor alone. In this sense, they serve as head of the local public service and – at least theoretically – create an important division between the policy-making role of the municipality (mayor and council) and policy implementation (staff).[21]

The size of municipal councils varies across the province. The *Municipal Act* states that a council must have a minimum of five members, of which one must be the head of council. Across Ontario, 195 municipalities have a council of this minimum size.[22] Municipalities routinely conduct council composition reviews and may opt to increase their size, meaning that the size of councils across Ontario are periodically adjusted based on changing population figures, workload, and other changes to the composition of the community. However, councils in Ontario tend to remain small, with only fifty-three municipalities having councils with more than ten members.[23]

Municipal elections in Ontario occur on four-year cycles. In 2018, 6,658 candidates competed for 2,864 elected positions.[24] Of these, only 27.2% were women[25] and 33.9% were incumbents.[26] Acclimations in Ontario local politics are also rather high, with 474 positions going uncontested in the 2018 municipal election.[27] Voter turnout in the 2018 municipal election was 38.29% – the lowest since 1982.[28] In 2022, voter turnout declined to 33%.[29] The number of candidates also declined (6,325), although the number of female candidates did increase (32%).[30]

In Ontario, local elections are governed by the *Municipal Elections Act*, which sets out guidelines that municipal clerks enforce, including stipulations on the length of the campaign, the eligibility to seek office the raising of campaign funds. Candidates for mayor and council in Ontario run independently without parties. The *Municipal Elections Act* provides a great deal of flexibility in how an election can be conducted. Section 42(3) of the Act provides for the use of alternative voting methods during municipal elections if the council of the municipality has approved the use of such methods. This opens to door to substantial adoption of internet voting. Along with Estonia and Switzerland, Ontario has one of the longest-standing deployments of online voting in the world. The use of online voting in binding elections in Canada began in 2003, when twelve municipalities in Ontario adopted the technology. Since then, use of online voting has grown steadily across municipalities in Ontario.[31]

In the 2018 Ontario municipal elections, 177 municipalities offered online voting, accounting for about 45 per cent of cities and towns and 29 per cent of the 9.4 million voters in the province, while 217 municipalities in Ontario used internet voting in the 2022 municipal election.[32]

The flexibility in vote method, however, does not extend to vote systems and choice. In 2016, the previous Liberal government allowed municipalities to switch from a first-past-the-post electoral system to rank ballots with the introduction of the *Municipal Election Modernization Act*. Under a ranked ballot system, electors are asked to rank their choice of candidates. On election night, everyone's first choice is added up and if any candidate fails to win over 50 per cent of the vote, the last placed candidate is eliminated, and their votes are redistributed based upon the second choice listed on the ballot. Only London adopted a ranked ballot system and used it during the 2018 election, which was by all accounts successful.[33] However, in the fall of 2020, the newly elected Progressive Conservative government introduced legislation that eliminated the ability of municipalities to use ranked ballots, with a spokesperson for the Ministry of Municipal Affairs and Housing arguing that "our government is maintaining predictability, and consistency to municipal elections, while better respecting taxpayers' dollars ... now is not the time for municipalities to experiment with costly changes to how municipal elections are conducted."[34] In response, the City of London argued it deserved compensation, given the ranked ballot election cost $515,000 to execute. The province eventually provided London with $51,000 in compensation to support the move back to a first-past-the-post system for the 2022 municipal election.[35]

FINANCING LOCAL GOVERNMENT

The provincial presence looms large over municipal finance in Ontario as well. The province sets out strict rules determining how municipalities can raise revenues, assess and levy a tax on property, and borrow to meet capital requirements.[36] The province also restricts the ability of municipalities to incur deficits in their operating budgets.[37] The *Municipal Act* allows municipalities to impose taxes on property and user fees and permits municipalities to also collect some licensing fees revenues for business-improvement areas and fines from bylaw infractions. However, the Act also prohibits municipalities from imposing income taxes, poll taxes, sales taxes, fuel taxes, and resource extraction taxes.

Property taxes are, therefore, the primary revenue source for municipalities in Ontario. A property tax is a levy based on the assessed value of property. In Ontario, property taxes are calculated using the current value assessment of a property, as determined by the Municipal Property Assessment Corporation. In 2020, municipalities in Ontario collected more than $25 billion in property taxes.[38] Municipalities also charge user fees for certain services, such as public transportation or recreation services. User fees are intended to have those directly benefiting from a service bear the cost of producing it.[39] The costs of these fees range, depending on the quantity or quality of the service or whether the municipal government seeks full or partial cost recovery for the service.[40] In 2020, user fees made up about $10 billion of municipal revenue across the province.[41] A full listing of revenue sources for 2020 is available in figure 6.1.

Development charges are another major (and in some cases growing) source of revenue. A development charge is a one-time levy imposed on new developments to finance growth-related capital costs, such as transportation or water and wastewater infrastructure.[42] The underlying logic behind development charges is that new growth should pay for itself, rather than charging existing residents for the costs of new construction. As many municipalities around Ontario – particularly Southern Ontario and the Greater Toronto Area – expand rapidly, development charges have become an increasingly large revenue source for some municipalities.[43] However, this is not without controversy, as development charges can add as much as $90,000 to the cost of a new home in some parts of the Greater Toronto Area, leading some to argue that we should consider reverting to a past practice where municipalities paid for the cost of new infrastructure associated with development to reduce the cost of new housing.[44]

Municipalities are also eligible to receive a series of grants from both the federal and provincial governments, as seen in figure 6.1. The main provincial transfer to municipalities is the Ontario Municipal Partnership Fund (OMPF), which is a targeted, unconditional transfer and equalization program for northern and rural municipalities.[45] OMPF funding totals approximately $500 million. Municipalities in Ontario are also eligible to receive a portion of the federal gas tax, which has been a relatively consistent transfer intended for transportation since its inception in 2005. In Ontario, the gas tax funding is distributed by the Association of Municipalities of Ontario and was valued at approximately $375 million for the 2021–2 fiscal year.

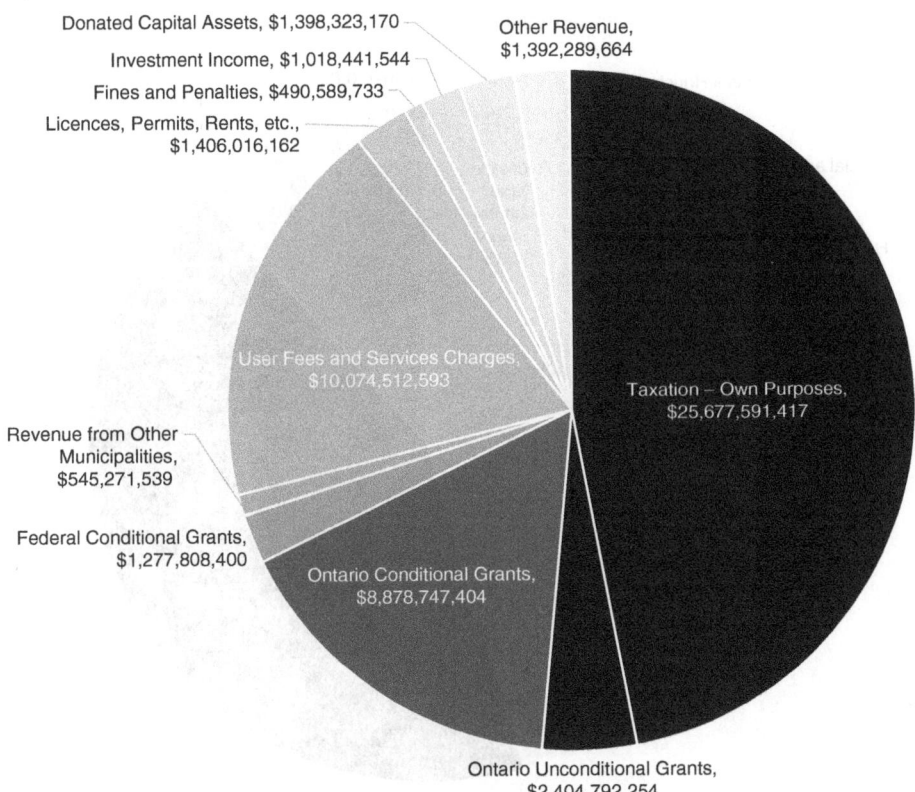

Figure 6.1. Revenue Sources – Ontario Municipalities, 2020
Source: Compiled by author from the Government of Ontario's Municipal Financial Information Returns, https://efis.fma.csc.gov.on.ca/fir/index.php/en/financial-information-return-en/.

Figure 6.2 provides a listing of service expenses as a percentage of total municipal revenue across Ontario. Two large categories immediately stand out: environment and transportation. Environmental services include water, waste water, and waste removal, while transportation services include roads, road maintenance, and public transportation. These two categories account for the bulk of municipal budgets, emphasizing the important role that municipalities play in public health and goods and people movement. The next-largest category is recreation, which is another important service delivered for residents, but which is often not viewed as critical by local decision makers. Other categories, such as

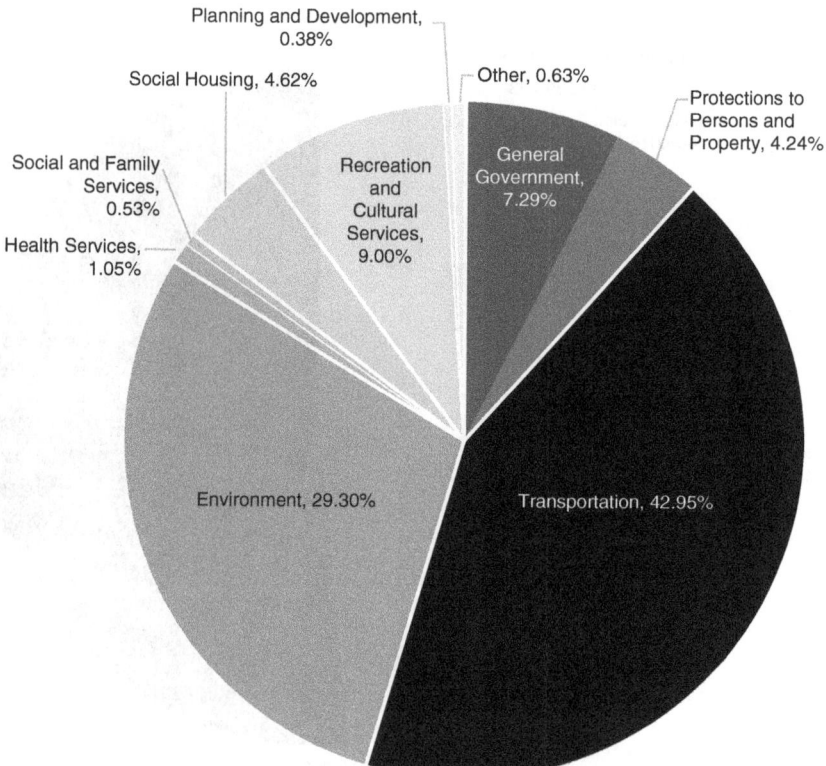

Figure 6.2. Expenditures – Ontario Municipalities, 2020
Source: Compiled by author from the Government of Ontario's Municipal Financial Information Returns, https://efis.fma.csc.gov.on.ca/fir/index.php/en/financial-information-return-en/.

protection and health services, while important, represent significantly less than other categories largely because they are partially financed in conjunction with the provincial government.

Municipal expenditure responsibilities are, of course, not without controversy. Municipal leaders often complain that their governments have an outsized role in service delivery and, when considered alongside some of the revenue constraints that we discussed above, that this creates an untenable financial situation for local governments. These municipal leaders advocate for a larger provincial role in financing these services.

Over the past quarter century, the provincial government and local leaders have tried to sort through some of the main aspects of financing local services. In 1996, the province of Ontario initiated the Who Does What Panel, which was tasked with "disentangling" public service delivery by reducing duplication and inefficiencies and clarifying which services were best delivered and financed locally and provincially.[46] The panel argued that, in general, municipalities should be responsible for "hard" services, such as services to property, such as roads, transit, utilities, police and fire, while the province should be responsible for "soft" services and programs that were redistributive in nature, such as social assistance and public health.[47] As the panel progressed, the provincial government initiated a realignment of services, which saw the province "upload" the full cost of education and "download" services such as roads, transit, and property assessment onto municipalities. Despite the panel arguing that "soft" services be funded and delivered by the province, the provincial government downloaded many onto municipalities, including the full or partial cost of ambulances, public health, and child care, even though many municipal leaders argued they did not have the capacity to cover the costs of these services.[48] Subsequent governments relieved some of these cost pressures, with the provincial cost to public health increasing by 25 per cent in 2007 and a further uploading of costs for the Ontario Drug Benefit, land ambulance, the Ontario Disability Support Program, and Ontario Works. Even with some restoration of provincial contributions, numerous disputes over the funding of services exist, with many municipal leaders regularly questioning the role of provincial funding in many social services areas and rural politicians often criticizing the costs associated with Ontario Provincial Police protection throughout the province.

DOUG FORD: ONTARIO'S MAYOR?

The provincial government looms large over nearly every aspect of municipal life in Ontario. Aside from the *Municipal Act* and other specific municipal legislation, such as the *Municipal Elections Act*, it is estimated that there are seventy pieces of provincial legislation that have implications for the municipal sector[49] and that each municipality is responsible for completing more than 250 separate reports annually to remain in compliance with various provincial acts and mandates.[50] As a result, the provincial government's approach to municipalities is often a source of concern for Ontario's local governments.

Few provincial governments have demonstrated any appetite to dramatically loosen these constraints, although the provincial-local relationship does experience periods of fluctuation, mostly dictated by the whims of the political party governing the province. For instance, in Ontario's recent history, the Progressive Conservative government of Mike Harris dramatically changed the landscape of the municipal sector, consolidating hundreds of municipalities across the province and downloading a slew of traditionally provincially delivered services (addressed in more detail above). In contrast, the Ontario Liberal Party under Dalton McGuinty took a different approach, partially uploading some of the costs that municipal leaders described as irritants and exploring new avenues for municipal autonomy with the *City of Toronto Act*.[51] The current government, however, has taken a much more interventionist position in the governance of Ontario municipalities.

Elected in 2018, Doug Ford came to office with a unique background. Not only was he an executive at his family-owned business, Deco Labels, but he also served a term on the Toronto City Council, alongside his brother Rob who was then mayor. This municipal experience sets Doug Ford apart from his predecessors. In fact, one would have to go back thirty-three years to the premiership of Frank Miller to find a premier who first served in municipal politics before becoming premier.[52] However, Ford did not serve time as a member of the Legislative Assembly prior to becoming premier. His past political experience consisted entirely of municipal politics. Perhaps it is this reason that Ford has spent so much of his first and second terms focused on municipal issues.

Very early in this first mandate, Ford opted to reduce the size of the Toronto City Council from forty-seven wards to twenty-five in the middle of the 2018 municipal election, claiming that such a large council bogged down the city's legislative agenda.[53] At this time, the province also cancelled the first direct election of regional chairs in Peel and York Regions, reverting to the earlier practice of having council appoint the chairs.[54] Around the same time, Ford also announced a sweeping review of regional government across the province. Despite much speculation that certain regional governments would be consolidated or dissolved, very little structural change occurred at this time.[55]

Much of the change to the municipal landscape has occurred in Ford's second term in office. One of the most significant changes in this period was the granting of "strong mayor" powers to the heads of council in both Ottawa and Toronto in 2022 via Bill 3, the *Strong Mayors, Building Homes Act*, and Bill 39, the *Better Municipal Governance Act*. Combined, the legislation provided mayors in both cities veto powers over bylaws that conflict with provincial priorities, as well as responsibility for preparing and tabling the annual budget, and it allows the mayor to appoint a CAO and various other department heads and reorganize certain sections of the municipality.[56] These new powers were linked to the province's housing agenda, specifying two provincial priorities where the powers could be exercised: (1) building 1.5 million new residential units by 2031, and (2) the construction and maintenance of infrastructure to support accelerated support and availability of housing.[57] Bill 3, in particular, provided the mayor with the ability to put into effect a bylaw that may be opposed by as many as two-thirds of council, provided that doing so advances a provincial interest.

In July 2023, the province extended "strong mayor" powers to twenty-six other municipalities across the province – mostly large cities in fast-growing regions, such as Hamilton, London, Windsor, Burlington, and Oakville – that had signed the province's "housing pledge" to prioritize housing construction.[58] For instance, the mayor of Newmarket, a municipality that is part of the fast-growing York Region, did not receive additional powers because the Town's council did not sign the province's housing pledge.[59] Municipalities cannot opt out of Bill 3 or 39, but the mayor is not compelled to use these powers. In fact, several Ontario mayors have transferred or pledged not to use the powers all. For instance, the mayor of Kingston Brian Patterson transferred the ability to determine the city's organizational structure, along with hiring and firing division leads, to the CAO.[60] He further transferred to council the power to appoint or dismiss the CAO, establish or dissolve committees, and appoint committee chairs.[61]

Ford's interest in a smaller, more compact council and a stronger institutional role for mayors is long documented and stems from his experience serving on the Toronto City Council alongside his late brother Rob. In the wake of Rob Ford's death in 2016, Doug Ford published a book entitled *Ford Nation*. In it, he explains how much of a priority enacting "strong mayor" legislation was for him and his brother. Recounting the concerns both Fords had with the slowing, at times, of their collective agenda at Toronto City Hall, Doug Ford notes mayors "deserve" stronger powers and that a veto system similar to that in New York, Chicago, and Los Angeles would be the "first thing" he would do if elected provincially.[62]

Bill 39 also set the groundwork for future interventions in Ontario's regional government. While very little came of the 2018 regional government review, upon the release of Bill 39, the province announced it would appoint facilitators to assess the governance structures of the regional municipalities of

Durham, Halton, Niagara, Peel, Waterloo, and York. The Bill also transferred power to select the regional chairs in York, Peel, and Niagara to the minister of municipal affairs and housing.⁶³ More dramatic changes to regional government in Ontario came in June 2023, when the government passed Bill 112, the *Hazel McCallion Act*, which began the process of dissolving Peel Region entirely, making Mississauga, Brampton, and Caledon single-tier municipalities by 2025.⁶⁴ In December 2023, however, the Ford government reversed course citing higher-than-expected costs of dissolution.⁶⁵

Doug Ford has also had a strong and sustained interest in local planning and housing matters. Since becoming premier, Doug Ford, and his minister of municipal affairs and housing, Steve Clark, have frequently used minister's zoning orders (MZOs) to override municipal council decisions on development. Under the *Planning Act*, the minister of municipal affairs can issue an MZO over any property in the province, essentially determining the development plan for the property and overruling any municipal decision or zoning bylaw attached to the land.⁶⁶ During Ford's first term, the minister of municipal affairs and housing issued just over thirty MZOs, while only forty-nine had been issued between 1969 and 2000.⁶⁷ The government also amended the *Conservation Authorities Act* to limit the ability of conservation authorities to resist or set conditions on MZOs.⁶⁸

In fall 2022, Ford's government introduced the *More Homes, Build Faster Act*, which aims to build 1.5 million homes over ten years by reducing municipal control over certain planning matters. The Act would enable the province to override municipal zoning regulations and allow up to three housing units on a single residential lot while also removing the ability of municipal governments to set restrictions on unit sizes or require more than one parking space per unit.⁶⁹ The legislation also assigned housing targets to twenty-nine large municipalities, where each city will need to develop "pledges" outlining how they will meet the targets.⁷⁰ Finally, the *More Homes, Build Faster Act* removed fees, including development charges, parkland dedication levies and community-based charges, for affordable housing, non-profit housing and inclusionary zoning units.⁷¹

While Doug Ford has become heavily involved in the life of municipal governments, there is no guarantee his successors will share this interest. The involvement of the provincial government in local affairs certainly waxes and wanes and will very likely take on a different dimension under a new administration.

CONCLUSION

Local governments provide a range of vital services to Ontarians. Municipalities are also key sites of local democratic control. It is hard to imagine life in Ontario without their presence. This chapter has detailed not only their importance, but also the political dynamics in which they operate. To borrow an old but common phrase, municipalities are "creatures of the province," with no independent constitutional standing. As a result, municipalities are very much exposed to the political direction employed by the government of the day. Different provincial governments have been more or less interested in the operations of local governments, with some engaging in dramatic change to consolidate and change the financing of municipalities, while others have taken a more reactionary approach to emerging local-provincial policy concerns. Few have shown any genuine interest in loosening the ever-present constraints on municipal policy-making, financial administration, or politics. Even with these constraints in place, municipalities exercise a broad spectrum of authority, providing local variation in service delivery and policy creation. The politics and administration of municipal life is, therefore, an important component in the politics and administration of Ontario.

DISCUSSION QUESTIONS

1. Do Ontario municipalities operate in too strict of a legislative framework? What would happen if the provincial government relaxed some provisions in the *Municipal Act*?
2. What concerns do you have about the introduction of "strong mayor" powers in Ontario? Do you think there is room for potential abuse?
3. Should municipalities have access to more revenue tools aside from the property tax? If so, which ones do you feel would be appropriate for municipalities in Ontario?
4. Given the important services they deliver, should special-purpose bodies all have elected representatives? If not, why not?
5. Why is voter turnout so low in local elections in Ontario? What do you think it would take to get turnout as high as provincial and federal elections?

NOTES

1. Colin Macdonald, *2016 Census Rollout – Municipal Implications* (Toronto: Municipal Finance Officers Association, 2017).
2. See *Ontario English Catholic Teachers' Assn v. Ontario (Attorney General*), 2001 SCC 15 [2001] 1 S.C.R. 470, para 58.
3. Zachary Spicer, Joseph Lyons, and Kate Graham, *Local Government in Practice: Cases in Governance, Planning and Policy* (Toronto: Emond, 2019).
4. Of note, the province of Ontario also passed the *Strong City of Toronto for a Stronger Ontario Act* in 2006, which enacted the new *City of Toronto Act*, providing the City with additional powers and resources. Additional information about the Act can be found in chapter 16 of this volume.
5. Adam Found, "Scale Economies in Fire and Police Services," in *IMFG Papers on Municipal Finance and Governance,* no. 13 (Toronto: Institute on Municipal Finance and Governance, 2012); Joseph Kushner and David Siegel, "Are Services Delivered More Efficiently after Municipal Amalgamations?," *Canadian Public Administration* 48, no. 2 (June 2005): 251–67, https://doi.org/10.1111/j.1754-7121.2005.tb02190.x.
6. Enid Slack and Richard Bird, "Merging Municipalities? Is Bigger Better?," in *IMFG Papers on Municipal Finance and Governance,* no. 14 (Toronto: Institute on Municipal Finance and Governance, 2013); Lydia Miljan and Zachary Spicer, *Municipal Amalgamation in Ontario* (Calgary: Fraser Institute, 2015).
7. Harvey Schwartz, "The Relevance of Toronto's New Governmental Structure for the 21st Century" (paper, International Conference on Structural Reform and the Transformation of Organizations and Business, Homerton College, University of Cambridge, September 3–6, 2003).
8. Harvey Schwartz, "The Relevance of Toronto's New Governmental Structure for the 21st Century," *Canadian Journal of Regional Science* 27, no. 1 (Spring 2004): 99–117.
9. Zachary Spicer, "Organizing Canadian Local Government," *Future of Municipal Government Series* vol. 1, May 2022 (Calgary: School of Public Policy).
10. Spicer, "Organizing Canadian Local Government."
11. Zachary Spicer, "Adapting (Municipal) Form to (Provincial) Function: City-County Separation and the Introduction of the Consolidated Municipal Service Manager System in Ontario, Canada," *American Review of Canadian Studies* 45, no. 3 (July 2015): 346–64, https://doi.org/10.1080/02722011.2015.1086396.
12. Richard M. Bird, Enid Slack, and Almos Tassonyi, *A Tale of Two Taxes: Property Tax Reform in Ontario* (Cambridge, MA: Lincoln Institute of Land Policy, 2012).
13. André Côté and Michael Fenn, "Approaching an Inflection Point in Ontario's Provincial-Municipal Relations," in *IMFG Perspectives,* no. 6 (Toronto: Institute on Municipal Finance and Governance, 2014).
14. Andrew Sancton, *Canadian Local Government: An Urban Perspective* (Toronto: Oxford University Press, 2011); Jack Lucas, "Hidden in Plain View: Local

Agencies, Boards and Commissions in Canada," in *IMFG Perspectives*, no. 4 (Toronto: Institute on Municipal Finance and Governance, 2013).
15 Philip Stenning, "Police Chiefs and their Political Bosses: Discussions in Ontario," *Policing: A Journal of Policy and Practice* 15, no. 1 (March 2021): 150–67, https://doi.org/10.1093/police/pay062.
16 Sancton, *Canadian Local Government*.
17 Stenning, "Police Chiefs and their Political Bosses."
18 If a municipal council does not approve the police budget, the board can appeal to the Ontario Civilian Commission on Police Services, which is entitled to make the final determination and allotment of resources. See Sancton, *Canadian Local Government*.
19 The mayor of Toronto has an "executive committee" but is not akin to a cabinet. For more information on the City of Toronto, please see chapter 16 in this volume.
20 Sancton, *Canadian Local Government*.
21 Michael Fenn and David Siegel, "The Evolving Role of City Managers and Chief Administrative Officers," in *IMFG Papers on Municipal Finance and Governance*, no. 31 (Toronto: Institute on Municipal Finance and Governance, 2017).
22 Association of Municipalities of Ontario, *Municipal Election Statistics* (Toronto: Association of Municipalities of Ontario, 2021), https://www.amo.on.ca/municipal-election-statistics.
23 Association of Municipalities of Ontario, *Municipal Election Statistics*.
24 Association of Municipalities of Ontario, *2018 Municipal Election Analysis* (Toronto: Association of Municipalities of Ontario, 2018), https://www.amo.on.ca/2018-municipal-election-analysis.
25 Of note, the Township of Algonquin Highlands and the Town of Spanish elected new councils comprised entirely of women (see Association of Municipalities of Ontario, *2018 Municipal Election Analysis*).
26 Association of Municipalities of Ontario, *2018 Municipal Election Analysis*.
27 Association of Municipalities of Ontario, *2018 Municipal Election Analysis*.
28 Association of Municipalities of Ontario, *2018 Municipal Election Analysis*.
29 Association of Municipalities of Ontario, *2022 Municipal Election Analysis* (Toronto: Association of Municipalities of Ontario, 2022), https://www.amo.on.ca/municipal-election-statistics.
30 Association of Municipalities of Ontario, *2022 Municipal Election Analysis*.
31 The province of Nova Scotia also uses online voting technologies in a majority of its municipalities. In 2020, thirty-nine of the forty-six municipal elections held in Nova Scotia were conducted online. Although there are forty-eight municipalities in Nova Scotia, two municipalities had committed to using online voting, but all races were acclaimed in the 2020 election.
32 Association of Municipalities of Ontario, *2022 Municipal Election Analysis*.
33 Andrew Lupton, "Can Ranked Ballots, First Tried in London, Ontario, Then Axed by Ford, Make a Comeback?," *CBC News*, May 16, 2022, https://www.cbc.ca/news/canada/london/ranked-ballots-london-history-1.6450544.

34 Sofia Rodriguez, "Ontario Moves to Axe Ranked Ballots from Municipal Elections," *CBC News*, October 20, 2020, https://www.cbc.ca/news/canada/london/ontario-moves-to-axe-ranked-ballots-from-municipal-elections-1.5770209.

35 Andrew Lupton, "City's Fight with Province over Ranked Ballots Ends with $50K in Compensation," *CBC News*, January 19, 2021, https://www.cbc.ca/news/canada/london/city-s-fight-with-province-over-ranked-ballots-ends-with-50k-in-compensation-1.5877980.

36 Bird, Slack, and Tassonyi, *A Tale of Two Taxes*.

37 Bird, Slack, and Tassonyi, *A Tale of Two Taxes*.

38 The province of Ontario collects financial information from all municipalities yearly. Statistical information is available for all revenue sources by examining these files.

39 Catherine Althaus and Lindsay Tedds, *User Fees in Canada: A Municipal Design and Implementation Guide* (Toronto: Canadian Tax Foundation, 2016).

40 Almos Tassonyi and Harry Kitchen, "Addressing the Fairness of Municipal User Fee Policy," in *IMFG Papers on Municipal Finance and Governance*, no. 54 (Toronto: Institute on Municipal Finance and Governance, 2021).

41 Calculated using the Government of Ontario's Financial Information Return files.

42 Enid Slack, "Financing Large Cities and Metropolitan Areas," in *IMFG Papers on Municipal Finance and Governance*, no. 3 (Toronto: Institute on Municipal Finance and Governance, 2011).

43 Tess Kalinowski, "Toronto Has $2.6 Billion in Development Charges and Fees Sitting in Reserve, BILD Report Says," *Toronto Star*, December 1, 2021, https://www.thestar.com/news/gta/toronto-has-2-6-billion-in-development-charges-and-fees-sitting-in-reserve-bild-report/article_3ed6e387-ba07-5aa0-ad2b-cac6ccfc09fa.html.

44 Sancton, *Canadian Local Government*.

45 Gabriel Eidelman, Tomas Hachard, and Enid Slack, "In It Together: Clarifying Provincial-Municipal Responsibilities in Ontario" (Toronto: University of Toronto, Munk School of Global Affairs – Ontario 360 Project, 2020).

46 Eidelman, Hachard, and Slack, "In It Together."

47 Eidelman, Hachard, and Slack, "In It Together."

48 Spicer, "Adapting (Municipal) Form to (Provincial) Function."

49 Côté and Fenn, "Approaching an Inflection Point."

50 Côté and Fenn, "Approaching an Inflection Point."

51 While McGuinty campaigned against the Harris-era amalgamations, he took little action to reverse them once in office. For more information, see Miljan and Spicer, *Municipal Amalgamation in Ontario*.

52 This is not to say that other premiers have not served in local government since. Kathleen Wynne served as a school board trustee for three years (2000–3) prior to being elected as MPP for Don Valley West. Mike Harris also served as a school board trustee until being elected in 1981 as the MPP for Nipissing.

53 Peter Zimonjic, "Ford Government Had Right to Cut Number of Toronto Wards during 2018 Election, Supreme Court Rules," *CBC News*, October 1, 2021, https://www.cbc.ca/news/canada/toronto/doug-ford-supreme-court-ward-ruling-1.6194241.

54 Zack Taylor, "Strong(er) Mayors in Ontario – What Difference Will They Make?," in *IMFG Forum*, no. 13 (Toronto: Institute on Municipal Finance and Governance, 2023).
55 Michelle McQuigge, "Ontario Decides Against Changing Province's Municipal Map After Review," *CTV News*, October 25, 2019, https://toronto.ctvnews.ca/ontario-decides-against-changing-province-s-municipal-map-after-review-1.4655415.
56 Taylor, "Strong(er) Mayors in Ontario."
57 Taylor, "Strong(er) Mayors in Ontario."
58 Evan Mitsui, "Ontario Expanding 'Strong Mayor' Powers to Cities Across Province," *CBC News*, June 16, 2023, https://www.cbc.ca/news/canada/toronto/municipal-affairs-meeting-ontario-big-city-mayors-1.6878776.
59 Mitsui, "Ontario Expanding 'Strong Mayor' Powers."
60 Dan Taekema, "Kingston's 'Strong Mayor' Flexes New Powers by Giving Some of Them Away," *CBC News*, July 13, 2023, https://www.cbc.ca/news/canada/ottawa/bryan-paterson-strong-mayor-powers-returned-1.6904950.
61 Taekema, "Kingston's 'Strong Mayor' Flexes."
62 Rob Ford and Doug Ford, *Ford Nation: Two Brothers, One Vision – The True Story of the People's Mayor* (Toronto: HarperCollins, 2016), 85–6.
63 Taylor, "Strong(er) Mayors in Ontario."
64 Katherine DeClerq, "Ontario Government Passes Bill to Dissolve Peel Region," *CTV News*, June 6, 2023, https://toronto.ctvnews.ca/ontario-government-passes-bill-to-dissolve-peel-region-1.6429566.
65 Katherine DeClerq, "Ontario Reversing Decision to Dissolve Peel Region," *CP24*, December 13, 2023, https://www.cp24.com/news/ontario-reversing-decision-to-dissolve-peel-region-1.6685567.
66 Emma McIntosh, "Ford Government Pledges to Protect Land to Compensate for MZOs," *National Observer*, June 16, 2021, https://www.nationalobserver.com/special-reports/zoning-out-doug-fords-special-land-use-orders.
67 Marsha McLeod, "'Poster Child for Destruction': The Fight to Save the Duffins Creek Wetland from Developers," *TVO*, February 4, 2021, https://www.tvo.org/article/poster-child-for-destruction-the-fight-to-save-the-duffins-creek-wetland-from-developers.
68 Max Hartshorn, "Ford Government to Strip Some Powers of Conservation Authorities," *Global News*, December 7, 2020, https://globalnews.ca/news/7505677/ford-government-strip-powers-of-environmental-regulators/.
69 DeClerq, "Ontario Government Passes Bill to Dissolve Peel Region."
70 DeClerq, "Ontario Government Passes Bill to Dissolve Peel Region."
71 DeClerq, "Ontario Government Passes Bill to Dissolve Peel Region."

7

Ontario Federal-Provincial Relations: Still a Responsible Partner in Confederation?

Julie M. Simmons

What does it mean to be Ontarian? What does it mean to be Canadian? If you live in Ontario, you may struggle more with the first of these questions than with the second. You might even find it hard to separate the two questions. You may also be surprised, even confused, by the following events in other provinces in the fall of 2022. After having declared that he wants his province to be a "nation within a nation," Saskatchewan premier Scott Moe introduced the *Saskatchewan First Act*.[1] This act sought to reaffirm the province's autonomy and jurisdiction over natural resources in its borders. According to Saskatchewan justice minister and Attorney General Bronwyn Eyre, "It is time to draw a line and assert our constitutional rights," as such legislation would protect the province's economic growth and prosperity from federal government measures "that encroach upon our legislative sovereignty."[2] Next door in Alberta, Premier Danielle Smith introduced the *Alberta Sovereignty within a United Canada Act*, which promises to give the Alberta legislature power to counter federal legislation it deems "harmful" to Alberta. According to the premier, the Act "send(s) a message to Ottawa that we will vigorously defend our constitutional areas of jurisdiction and they should just butt out."[3] Meanwhile in Quebec, Francois Legault's Coalition Avenir Quebec won its second election, after having passed two controversial bills in its first term, both of which were accompanied by the use of the notwithstanding clause in the *Charter of Rights and Freedoms* to shield them from judicial review. Bill 21, which prohibits someone employed in the provincial public sector (e.g., teachers and police officers) from wearing religious symbols or clothing cannot be struck down for violating the religious freedom protected in the Charter. Bill 96, which strengthens the use of French in the province, is also protected from court challenge. On the campaign trail, Legault defended these two flagship bills of his first term, arguing that "they are what a majority of Quebecers want" and reasoning that "being nationalist means we are going to defend our French language."[4]

Ontario premiers are not known for such bold expressions of regionalist sentiments as these, and historically, the Ontario government has seen its role as one of a statesperson and mediator in federal-provincial relations, promoting harmony rather than dissent and maintaining national political and economic stability. Indeed, many Canadians, both within the province of Ontario and in the provinces mentioned above, perceive Ontario's political and economic interests as interchangeable with those of Ottawa. Ontario's demographic weight (40 per cent of the Canadian population) and its centrality to the economic well-being of the country mean that Ontario is a formidable power in the making of economic, social, fiscal, and any other policy in Ottawa. Ontario has been seen as a key orchestrator and prime beneficiary of Ottawa policies.

As a quid pro quo, Ontario governments have also seen it as their responsibility to share the province's wealth distributed to "have not" provincial governments through the federal Equalization program. As Nelson Wiseman suggests, "Ontario is not known for regional grievances, for feeling ignored, taken for granted, shunted aside or shortchanged.... Ontarians have touted grandness rather than victimization."[5]

This chapter traces the evolution of the role that Ontario has played in federal-provincial relations in Canada and considers how and why Premier Ford's relations with Ottawa and the other provinces both deviate from that role and reinforce it. Ontario's traditional intergovernmental strategy is one of big brother, "play(ing) neither a purely provincial nor purely national role, but ... exist(ing) in the space between the two levels of government."[6] In the postwar period, a strong federal government and a unified Canada benefitted Ontario's economy and Canada in turn. Ontario's economy was the engine of the Canadian economy, primarily by design but partly owing to evolving social, technological, and global trade patterns. During this period, Ontario figured prominently as a broker of interests in federal-provincial constitutional deliberations, and as a willing participant in national programs redistributing wealth from the prosperous "centre" to the less well-off "periphery" of the country. Since the early 1990s, Ontario's traditional "*noblesse oblige* patina" gradually tarnished as east-west trade linkages between Ontario and other provinces gave way to north-south trade and greater North American integration in the post-1988 free trade era.[7] The Ontario economy has undergone transformation as the manufacturing sector declines and a service-based industry has replaced it (see Graefe, this volume). There is a mismatch between current regional economic patterns in Canada and the mechanisms for regional redistribution. Since the early 1990s, this mismatch has motivated premiers to aggressively argue for Ontario's "fair share" of federal revenues when facing burgeoning deficits (under Bob Rae); the federal government balancing its own budget through reduced transfers to the provinces (under Rae and Mike Harris); declining fiscal capacity as a result of the particularly sluggish recovery of the American economy to the global recession of 2008 (under Dalton McGuinty); and as Ontario slipped from its status as a "have" province to a "have not" province, eligible for equalization payments (under Kathleen Wynne). Yet, under Doug Ford, Ontario appears to have played both a combative role in relations with Ottawa, and a conciliatory one more akin to its traditional, "big brother" role. The "fair share" mantra is decidedly muted, with Ford's brand of populism shaping his intergovernmental strategy.

ONTARIO THEN: THE NATIONAL POLICY AND THE POLITICS OF REDISTRIBUTION

John A. Macdonald's National Policy of 1879 is key to understanding Ontario's traditional intergovernmental role. This policy was intended to create a strong manufacturing base in central Canada, so that the country as a whole was on independent footing vis-à-vis the United States. It was a deliberate attempt to resist the forces of north-south trade and prop up east-west trade. With Canadian tariffs placed on most manufactured goods entering Canada, the nascent manufacturing sector located along the St. Lawrence Seaway in the Montreal-Windsor corridor could sell Canadians goods at a price higher than it would obtain if American products could flood the Canadian market. At the same time, the raw materials from other countries required for the manufacturing sector were subject to reduced customs duties, lowering the cost of production in Canada. The creation of the railway linking east to west facilitated the movement of manufactured goods within the country. The Crow's Nest Pass agreement of 1897 (in place until 1983) guaranteed a western Canadian market for the manufacturing sector in central Canada. It distorted the western Canadian economy by reducing eastbound rates on the Canadian Pacific Railway for unprocessed grain products (encouraging farming) but not for processed products (discouraging manufacturing) and reducing westbound rates for certain manufactured goods (benefitting the central Canadian economy). As a result, Ontario's economy became the engine of the country. In the post-Confederation era the economies of Nova Scotia and New Brunswick also declined – owing partly to the change in marine technology from wooden sailing ships to steel steamships. But these provinces also felt the effect of federal freight rates. The nationalization of the banking system and its centralization in Ontario also negatively affected the Maritimes.

By the end of the Second World War, Ontario's economy remained at the centre of the country as a whole but was now considerably diversified, to the point that virtually every federal policy affected it. Is it any wonder that there is a wide perception that Ontario's interests have been one and the same as Ottawa's interests? Is it any wonder that other regions, particularly in the West, might have voiced what an unsympathetic ear might dismiss as regional whining, to end what a sympathetic ear might call the West's "neocolonial" status within the country?

Ontario premiers have traditionally sought to maintain the status quo, rather than venture into new policy directions in intergovernmental relations. This is not to say that there have not been clashes between Ontario and Ottawa. On the contrary, Oliver Mowat, premier from 1872 to 1896, often joined with his Quebec counterpart, Honoré Mercier, in resisting Prime Minister John A. Macdonald's attempts to centralize power in Ottawa. Howard Ferguson (1923–30) and Mitchell Hepburn (1934–42) both had run-ins with Ottawa over which order of government had constitutional jurisdiction to legislate. For example, Ferguson argued in favour of Quebec's right to develop hydroelectricity on the St. Lawrence River. With the Judicial Committee of the Privy Council (then the highest court of appeal) tending to favour a wide interpretation of provincial jurisdiction, and Ontario involved in a great many of these cases, P.E. Bryden reasons that "successive generations of Ontario premiers had some basis for considering themselves equal to the prime minister."[8]

The quid pro quo for the National Policy's centralization of manufacturing wealth in one part of the country has been Ottawa's redistribution of that wealth to other regions of the country through fiscal federalism: the financial arrangements between the federal and provincial governments.[9] This redistribution has been central to the development of the modern welfare state in Canada following the Second World War. In brief, revenues collected by Ottawa fund initiatives in federal jurisdiction (e.g., national defence) and, through transfer payments to provinces, initiatives in areas of provincial jurisdiction. A key fiscal building block of the welfare state is the Equalization program initiated in 1957: the federal government makes payments to select provincial governments so that the latter have "sufficient revenues to provide reasonably comparable levels of public services at reasonably comparable levels of taxation," as enshrined in the *Constitution Act, 1982*. While the funds come from Ottawa, sometimes equalization is characterized as taking funds from one province and giving them to another. Equalization is an unconditional federal grant received by some provinces according to a complex formula which calculates the revenue-generating capacity of each of the provinces. Ontario taxpayers have collectively always been the largest contributors to equalization, by virtue of their demographic weight and the strength of the Ontario economy that results in higher than average incomes in the province. Nevertheless, Ontario governments have generally supported the development of the welfare state across the country because, as Matthew Mendelsohn explains, "forging a stronger, unified Canada was in the interests of the dominant, most prosperous player in the federation."[10]

Other federal funds are transferred to *all* provinces but targeted to specific provincial policy areas (e.g., health care or post-secondary education and social services), or conditional upon provinces designing provincial programs in specified ways. For example, receipt of the Canada Health Transfer is, in theory, conditional upon compliance with the *Canada Health Act*. The amount of funding each province receives, and the nature of the conditions, indeed whether it is even legitimate for the federal government to impose conditions, are issues of intergovernmental debate. While provinces were largely supportive of the development of the modern welfare state following the Second World War, Ontario did frequently side with Quebec resisting fiscal centralization and federal development of social programs like the Canada Pension Plan (1966) and Medicare (1968).[11] In Hugh Segal's words, "while Ontario has been a reliable ally in defence of the legitimacy of the confederal union, it is not, nor has it ever been, a willy-nilly hallelujah chorus for slapdash trigger-happy excess from any federal administration."[12]

Given the centrality of Ontario's manufacturing sector to the National Policy, the province's historical preference for the status quo, and its track record of challenging Ottawa in the early years following Confederation and in the era of the development of the welfare state, it is understandable that Ontario protested the Ottawa Valley line energy policy brought in by the federal Diefenbaker government in 1961. This policy forced those citizens living west of the Ottawa Valley to buy oil from Alberta, rather than on the international market, where oil could be purchased less expensively. This policy had the effect of protecting the budding oil industry with an inflow of cash for further exploration, but at the expense of consumers in Ontario (and the western provinces).[13] At the same time, it is also understandable why Ottawa (with its track record of shaping the contours of the national economy) and Alberta (having experienced the obstacles to manufacturing put in place through the Crow's Nest Pass agreement) would view this policy as entirely justified.

A further example of Ontario's resistance from this period is its dissatisfaction with the 1957 formula for Equalization which was intended to elevate other provinces to the standard of Ontario and British Columbia, then the two wealthiest provinces. Ottawa considered the per capita value of three provincial tax bases (personal, corporate, and inheritance taxes) in those two provinces and made payments to the other provinces such that they would have the same per capita value. From Ontario's perspective, this was too rich an equalization scheme. A major change five years later was to shift to equalizing to a national average (a less generous scheme), and to include 50 per cent of the revenues provinces generate from the sale of their natural resources as a fourth tax base.[14] The latter captured the growing wealth of Alberta and rendered the province ineligible for equalization payments.[15]

Despite this pattern of Ontario's resistance to federal attempts to centralize controls, particularly in the development of the welfare state, Ontario's support for Ottawa's response to the oil crisis of the 1970s feeds the commonly held perception that Ontario is the prime beneficiary of Ottawa's economic policies and a province in favour of a strong central government. John Ibbitson goes so far as to say that under Premier Bill Davis (1971–85), Ontario "ceased to be."[16] When the value of natural resource commodities changes, so too does which provinces are eligible for equalization. When the federal government includes in the national standard of revenue-generating capacity the provinces that are benefitting from high prices for their natural resources (as is the case with a ten-province standard), the national standard rises. This rise requires that the federal government redistribute more funding to bring less well-off provinces to the national standard. However, the federal government itself does not have access to the royalties from the sale of natural resources (as this lies with the provinces) and can find itself in a financially precarious situation. In the late 1970s, when 50 per cent of the value of natural resources was included in the calculation of a province's revenue-generating capacity and the price of oil surged dramatically during the OPEC crisis, the revenue-generating capacity of Alberta was especially high, pushing up the national standard. Ontario, with its economy built on manufacturing, and without Alberta's natural resource wealth, actually found itself eligible to receive equalization from 1977 to 1982, a politically unacceptable circumstance for Ontario, Ottawa, and the rest of the provinces. This effect was contrary to the spirit of equalization and would have been especially costly for the federal government. It is during this period that the best strategy for defending Ontario's interests was aligning with the federal government. While Ontario could not affect oil prices or provincial taxation revenues, it relied on Ottawa to "correct" the disruption to Ontario's privileged economic position in the country. Looking to access the wealth that could be generated from taxing oil, Ottawa introduced the National Energy Program (NEP) in 1980. Deeply unpopular in Alberta, the NEP centralized oil revenues; partially moved energy development into federal hands; sought to increase Canadian ownership of the oil and gas industry; and artificially kept the cost of oil for the domestic market below world prices.[17] Once again, Ottawa's policy levers seemed to have been set to the advantage of Ontario, and to the disadvantage of Alberta.

Ontario's decision not to accept the equalization payments for which it was eligible is in keeping with the National Policy/Equalization bargain. If Ontario, the traditional economic engine of the country, qualified for equalization, it was time to revisit the formula. In 1981, with the support of Ontario's Premier Davis, the federal government amended the formula with the "personal income override" so that any province with per capita personal income regularly above the national average (i.e., Ontario) would not be eligible.[18] A more permanent solution was put in place the following year. With oil revenues still high, Davis's suggestions for reworking the formula were focused on excluding natural resource revenue entirely. In other words, Ottawa would equalize only non-resource revenues across provinces. Alberta's wealth now made the formula too generous, and it would still be federal taxes collected from Ontarians that would be a substantial portion of the cash Ottawa would be distributing to other provinces. Ultimately, however, in 1982, the federal government moved from the ten-province standard to one based on the average of five supposedly representative provinces (British Columbia, Saskatchewan, Manitoba, Ontario, and Quebec), excluding Alberta, in the calculation, thereby ensuring that the wealth of Alberta would have limited direct bearing on equalization payments, and the federal government would not find itself in the somewhat non-sensical situation where Ontario would again qualify for equalization payments. While this was not Ontario's preferred position, it was still in Ontario's interest relative to the status quo.

There might have been some doubt as to the centrality of Ontario's manufacturing industry to the economy of Canada during the 1970s period of prosperity in western Canada. But in the 1980s, such doubt diminished as the world price of oil collapsed, and, benefitting from a weak Canadian dollar vis-à-vis the American dollar, Ontario manufacturers enjoyed an export boom. This period of prosperity for the province postponed any serious confrontations between Ontario and Ottawa on fiscal matters.

Ontario's support of the federal government extended beyond Trudeau's centralizing NEP to constitutional deliberations as well. Following the failed Quebec referendum on sovereignty association in 1980, Trudeau continued his quest to "patriate" the Constitution, including a *Charter of Rights and Freedoms*, with an eye to securing provincial agreement. However, with most provinces concerned about the implications for provincial rights of a *Charter* promoting individual rights, Trudeau eventually unilaterally asserted that provincial consent was unnecessary. Ontario, for its part, lined up with Ottawa on the *Charter of Rights*, the nature of Canada's political community, bilingualism, and economic policy. Along with New Brunswick, it was the only province that did not join the "gang of eight" challenging Trudeau's vision of a strong central government. When the Supreme Court of Canada ruled that a "substantial" provincial consent was required, Trudeau was forced to return to the bargaining table. At that point, Ontario resumed its historical position of neither a strictly provincial nor federal role, mediating among the parties at the table. Unfortunately, and significantly, premiers reached an agreement with the prime minister that excluded Quebec premier René Lévesque. But with Ontario's interests seemingly so closely aligned with Ottawa, both with respect to the NEP and the patriation of the Constitution, it would be fair to say that this era was a departure from Ontario's earlier willingness to challenge Ottawa.

ONTARIO IN THE FREE TRADE ERA

Despite Ontario's economic boom in the 1980s, major changes to Ontario's economy were at play which eventually broke the province's alignment with

Ottawa. They significantly augmented Ontario's willingness to voice its interests vis-à-vis Ottawa and vis-à-vis other provinces. The regional redistribution of national income and wealth, particularly through the federal Equalization program but also through other federal transfers to provinces for various provisions of the welfare state, came under increasing stress as protected markets established through the National Policy were giving way to more globalized ones governed by free trade agreements. Under these trade agreements Ontario's economy has become more integrated with and dependent upon the economy of the United States. For example, in 1965, Canada signed the Auto Pact with the United States, removing tariffs on vehicles and auto parts crossing the border. Whereas before the Auto Pact there were a diversity of cars made by Ontario's auto industry and almost exclusively for the Canadian market, after the Auto Pact the Canadian and American auto industries were integrated, with the Ontario auto industry making fewer models, but with a much larger percentage now destined for the US market. The 1988 Canada-US Free Trade Agreement and the 1994 North American Free Trade Agreement further reoriented the Ontario economy away from an east-west trajectory towards a north-south trajectory. Contrary to the federal government of the day, Ontario's business community, and almost every other province, the Ontario governments did not support the 1988 FTA and the 1994 NAFTA in part because of the economic vulnerability they perceived that the agreements would expose the province to, given the volatility of international markets. Ontario's opposition can be interpreted as an attempt to protect manufacturing jobs that it rightfully feared would migrate from Ontario to countries where workers earn lower wages. But Ontario's opposition can also be viewed as a defence of Ontario's position of economic privilege established by the old National Policy.[19]

In any case, the free trade era reoriented the Ontario economy from east-west to north-south, removing the protected markets constructed through the National Policy. The vulnerability of the free trade environment meant that when a global recession hit in the early 1990s, Ontario's economy, now so entwined with the US economy, experienced a particularly deep recession. This era also coincides with the neo-liberal politics of fiscal restraint: a rising obsession with balancing budgets, eliminating deficits, and paying down debt. Beginning in the 1990s, as a way to balance its own budget, the federal government unilaterally reduced in various ways the overall amount of funding it delivered to provinces. The first major cut was the 1990 cap on Canada Assistance Plan payments (which in part funded provincial social assistance) to the "have" provinces of Ontario, British Columbia, and Alberta. Facing a recession, double-digit unemployment, and an economy that did not rely in the same way as it once did on interprovincial trade, Ontario premier Bob Rae began the practice of calculating what Ontario put into Ottawa versus what it got out. This "balance-sheet federalism" continued through to the Kathleen Wynne years. Ontario also consistently promoted per capita federal transfers outside of the Equalization program. In other words, each province should receive the same entitlement per person from the federal government for immigration settlement, health care, post-secondary education, etc.

On the constitutional front, both premiers David Peterson (1985–90) and Rae resumed the Ontario tradition of presenting itself as playing neither a strictly federal or provincial role, and instead brokering interests, particularly with an eye to accommodating Quebec. In the late 1980s, Peterson exhausted vast political resources defending the Meech Lake Accord – the first major attempt to amend the Constitution to bring Quebec back into the constitutional fold following the patriation of the *Constitution Act, 1982* – even when there was considerable opposition to it among Ontarians.[20] Bob Rae played a leadership role in the Charlottetown negotiations that followed the failure of Meech Lake, advocating for the position of federalists in Quebec, even when, at the outset of the negotiations, Quebec was not a participant. He also pursued the constitutional entrenchment of a "social charter," which would require the federal and provincial governments to provide Medicare and minimum levels of housing, high-quality primary and secondary school education, and other basic social needs.[21]

Even though he was decidedly right of his predecessor on the ideological spectrum, when Mike Harris became premier in 1995, he continued a similar path of "fair shares" federalism and a call for per capita transfers outside of equalization. He continued the Ontario tradition of constructive engagement in intergovernmental negotiation. On the night the "no" side won by a very fine margin in the 1995 Quebec referendum, Harris offered support for continuing change, urging, "We have a collective duty to address how our federation might better serve all Canadians.… (A)long with Quebecers, Ontarians earnestly believe that the way the federation is managed must be substantially changed for the better."[22] However, during the Harris years, Ontario's role in intergovernmental deliberations pertaining to fiscal federalism and social policy shifted from one of working with the federal government to working with other provinces in the absence of any federal leadership.[23] In 1995, the federal government cut by one third the value of the Canada Health and Social

Transfer to provinces, in an effort to balance its own budget, leaving provinces scrambling to provide the same quality and scope of post-secondary education, health care, and social services citizens expected. Ontario played a significant role in the work of the provincial/territorial Ministerial Council on Social Policy Renewal, which ultimately resulted in the Social Union Framework Agreement between the federal government and the provinces. This agreement included, among other things, a commitment by both orders of government to give the other advance notice prior to the implementation of a major change in a social policy or program that would likely significantly affect the other, such as the Canada Health and Social Transfer.

Like Harris, McGuinty sought interprovincial cooperation, particularly on the fiscal federalism front, establishing with his provincial counterparts the 2005 Advisory Panel of the Council of the Federation to make recommendations to equilibrate the "vertical fiscal imbalance." But during this era when all governments, including the federal government, were establishing their positions on the renegotiation of the Equalization formula, Ontario also acted independently, and sometimes found itself isolated.[24] In 2005, Dalton McGuinty launched a campaign to close what his government called the $23 billion gap between what it calculated the province paid into the federation and what it got out, distinguishing in a very public way what it saw as the interests of Ontarians from the fiscal policies of the federal government. In 2008, McGuinty launched a website, fairness.ca, which sought to inform Ontarians, and presumably other Canadians, as well as those inside the federal government, of the billions of dollars Ontario was contributing to the federal equalization scheme. "It's our money," McGuinty was quoted as saying, inviting Canadians in Ontario to identify with their province, and implying that Ontarians, not Canadians as a whole, or the federal government, were the "owners" of this money: "Every once in a while, you've got to look after yourself, and we've got to do that in Ontario."[25] While the federal and provincial governments worked to confront the impact of the global recession through jointly funded infrastructure projects, every Ontario budget included a balance sheet of fiscal federalism, noting how what Ontarians contributed to the federal government through tax, was less than they received in return. Initially a few pages, with titles like "Bringing Fairness to Ontario" and "Ontario Needs a Strong Federal Partner," these sections of the budget grew to be a full chapter by 2012.[26]

From 2009 to 2019, Ontario again found itself eligible for equalization. Unlike Pierre Trudeau, Prime Minister Harper did not, in 2009, re-introduce the "personal income override." The $347 million Ontario received as a "have-not" province in 2009–10 ballooned to $3.2 billion in 2012–13, before falling back to just under $2 billion in 2014–15 and eventually to 0 in 2019–20.[27] Unlike Bill Davis's support of the 1982 adjustment, Premier McGuinty pleaded with the federal government *not* to change the Equalization formula, likening the program to a national insurance scheme where "we are told we are only to be a contributor – and never a recipient." McGuinty argued, "It's our money.... For years, we made investments in other provinces so that they could grow stronger. Now what we're saying is we want to hold on to a bit more of that money."[28] Why did McGuinty take a position so dramatically different from Davis? The answer lies in the remarkable increases in the value of natural resources on the international market, the concentration of the royalties for those natural resources in specific provinces, and the implications of these increases for the calculation of equalization.

While the Equalization formula has undergone many changes since 1957, a significant change took place in 2006. In brief, 50 per cent of the natural resource revenues were put back into the calculation of provincial capacity and the formula was based on an average of the fiscal capacity of all ten provinces, rather than five. In these two respects, the formula is similar to the one that existed when Ontario became eligible for equalization in the Davis era. Also like the Davis era, oil rose in value, with a barrel of oil fetching over $120 on the international market at its 2013 peak. But, by 2009, the distribution of "have" and "have-not" provinces shifted considerably from that period in the early 1980s; provinces like Newfoundland and Labrador now had strong economies, and the west became the economic engine of the country. Saskatchewan, Alberta, and Newfoundland and Labrador were all enjoying increased revenues from the sale of their natural resources at relatively high prices on the international market. Even with the decline in oil prices from 2015–20, all remained ineligible for payments according to the Equalization formula. But another key difference from the Davis era was that there is no National Energy Program allowing the federal government access to the revenues accrued from these natural resources. To pay equalization to the receiving provinces, Ottawa relies primarily on regular tax revenues. Because Ontario's economy is not primarily based on natural resource extraction, and was still strong, relatively speaking, despite the decline in the manufacturing sector, Ontario argued that a disproportionate amount of revenue was collected by Ottawa from Ontario taxpayers to fund the equalization payments to other provinces. Under these circumstances, Ontario's acceptance of equalization payments from Ottawa was one way to recoup some of the revenue exiting the province through federal taxation. It is also true that under these circumstances Ontario was still a net contributor to equalization, putting in more than it received.

By the Kathleen Wynne era, it seemed that the Liberal Ontario and Conservative federal governments diverged intensely and publicly on almost every issue, with each pointing to the other on who was responsible for job losses in Ontario in the previous decade. Each of Wynne's budgets from 2013–18 included a full chapter devoted to intergovernmentalism and a balance sheet of fiscal federalism. Ontario's 2013 fiscal update argued that Ontario's net contribution of $16 billion to the Equalization program was "redistributed to other regions of Canada to subsidize programs and services that Ontarians themselves may not enjoy." In a 2014 *Financial Post* editorial he penned, Wynne's finance minister, Charles Sousa, argued that "the federal government must stop pick pocketing the people of this Province, and instead help invest in and protect the schools, hospitals and public transit that Ontarians expect and deserve."[29] For its part, the federal government stuck to the narrative that the Ontario government had "no one to blame but themselves" for their troubles and that "Ontario's spending mismanagement (was) a problem for the entire country." In part a reflection of these public feuds, or perhaps because of them, then-prime minister Stephen Harper refused to meet with the premier for over a year.

While one might be tempted to point to ideological differences between Wynne and Harper as the main reason the two governments were so frequently at odds, Wynne's tactics were a continuation of the intergovernmental strategy by Ontario premiers of all parties driven not by ideology, but by a fundamentally reoriented north-south economy, and the context of fiscal restraint. To summarize, in the free trade era, Ontario's intergovernmental relations (a) distinguished Ontario's interests from those of Ottawa; (b) emphasized an approach that highlights what, in dollar terms, Ontario put into the federation vs. what it got out; and (c) particularly in the McGuinty/Wynne years, included a call for major changes to the architecture of Canada's arrangements for income redistribution, including the Equalization program.

THE NEW ONTARIO OF INDUSTRIAL RESTRUCTURING AND POPULISM

Canada now has fifteen free trade agreements with fifty-one countries. With goods and capital flowing freely across country borders, many countries' economies, like that of Ontario, have seen a decline in manufacturing and a rise in service industries. As Graefe's contribution to this volume explains, Ontario's financial services industry has actually flourished, with Toronto second only to New York as the largest financial centre in North America. Insurance, real estate, technical services, and construction industries have all grown, and the manufacturing sector endures, even if in long-term decline. But a hollowing out of the middle class and a ballooning of the low-wage service sector has also occurred. In many countries that have deindustrialized, right-wing populist parties have resonated with the disaffected citizens who are not the beneficiaries of decades of neo-liberalism (free trade coupled with fiscal restraint), and who find themselves outside the professional services industries.[30] The same could be said in Ontario, where Doug Ford was elected in 2018, with very few concrete policy positions, but a folksy appeal. As a mere one-term city counsellor, his was the anti-establishment choice (or, as Esselment argues in this volume, the only choice, given the two-party system in Ontario, and voters' Liberal fatigue), and appealed in particular to those working-class voters who saw the NDP as focused on teachers, nurses, and public servants but felt alienated from politics precisely because neo-liberal policies have made the comfort of middle-class life just beyond their grasp. In the 2022 election, he captured seats previously held by the NDP in areas such as Brampton and Hamilton, where residents disproportionately are represented in low-end service positions and blue-collar alienation is palpable.

But if being anti-establishment was a benefit to getting elected, it came with very little awareness of federalism in Canada. Unlike other Ontario premiers in the free trade era, Ford has had little to say about fair shares and equalization. His budgets no longer included a chapter on intergovernmental relations with a balance sheet of fiscal federalism. Even though the National Policy/equalization equation of the 1950s no longer exists, he is not inclined to highlight how Ontario is "short-changed" by the aging financial architecture of the federation. Ottawa even quietly renewed the Equalization formula in 2018 without notice to provinces or the public.[31] Ford did make his views on equalization known in 2019 when he backed then-Alberta premier Jason Kenney's criticism of the formula's effect *on Alberta*. Ford, apparently concerned about the divisiveness in the country following the 2019 federal election, implored the media to "Keep in mind, the people of Alberta are transferring $20 billion to the federal government, and they just feel like they're being ignored. And we have to work together."[32]

Ford's apparent early lack of awareness of the role of the federal government in finances of the province was also evident in his initial approach to balancing the provincial budget through austerity measures rather than calling for increases to the Canada Health Transfer and Canada Social Transfer. He proposed restructuring health care and post-secondary education within the province, cutting social assistance by a billion dollars, and shifting child care and public health costs to municipalities.[33] At his first meeting of first ministers, Ford also exhibited little understanding of how the chess game of federal-provincial diplomacy is played, and threatened to walk out of the meeting over disagreements with the federal government on the nature of the agenda, potentially giving up the opportunity to influence what happened at the table before any leader sat down at it.

In his first year, he also sought to engage the federal government on two issues related to his voter base of working-class Ontarians. He continued a steady campaign accusing Prime Minister Trudeau of failing to defend Canada's manufacturing sector against President Donald Trump's "Buy American" campaign. He also accused Trudeau of doing little to stem the tide of asylum seekers he believed to have crossed the Canada-US border into Ontario after Trudeau tweeted "those fleeing persecution, terror and war, Canadians will welcome you." Ford argued that "this mess was created by the federal government; and the federal government should foot 100 per cent of the bills."[34]

Ford did utilize a familiar Ontario intergovernmental mantra in his battle with the federal government on carbon emissions, arguing that Ontario should not be expected to do more than its "fair share."[35] As Mark Winfield's details in chapter 14, he dismantled the previous provincial government's cap-and-trade climate strategy, and took his battle with Ottawa over carbon pricing to the Supreme Court, where he lost his bid to have a federally imposed carbon tax deemed unconstitutional. Ford elevated the profile of his fight with the federal government, and campaigned for Ontarian's support in this fight, with television commercials and stickers he attempted to make mandatory at all Ontario gas pumps which read, "the federal carbon tax will cost you." (These were deemed unconstitutional by the Superior Court in Ontario).[36]

Ford's seemingly unrelenting criticism of Trudeau may also have been a reflection of the fact that in 2018, Trudeau's closest staff members were those of former Liberal premier of Ontario, Dalton McGuinty, while Ford was initially advised by staffers associated with former Conservative prime minister Stephen Harper. Since a change to Ford's chief of staff in 2019, Ford seemed to get a better handle on the role Ottawa played in the fiscal well-being of the province. Shortly before the pandemic outbreak, he assembled a team of his cabinet ministers, or as he called them, "stormtroopers," to head to Ottawa in a coordinated campaign to secure more funding from the federal government for health, infrastructure, transportation, and economic development in the province.[37] In the absence of a willingness to raise taxes, revenue for the province could be generated through finding places where both the federal and provincial governments could get a "win."

He also began to take positions that suggest Ontario's identity entrenched in the postwar period in constitutional deliberations and the development of the welfare state, as "big brother" of Confederation, or first among equals is intact.[38] The pandemic restructured both federal-provincial relations and interprovincial relations, as a ceaseless stream of weekly premiers' meetings and biweekly meetings with the prime minister took place. In the early days of the pandemic, Ford developed an unlikely friendship with Chrystia Freeland, the Liberal deputy-prime minister. She shared that they "describe one another as each other's therapists." According to Ford, they would "talk for God knows how long at night-time, and discuss every issue you can possibly think of, and we laugh at the end."[39] This friendship played a role in the eventual terms of the child care agreement signed by both governments in 2022. While Ontario was the last holdout among provincial governments who signed agreements with Ottawa as part of Trudeau's $30 billion national child care initiative, the eventual agreement with Ontario included a $3 billion sweetener to build infrastructure for child care in Indigenous communities.[40] Ontario successfully argued that the federal government was creating the expectation among voters that $10/day daycare would shortly come to exist, but the terms of agreement Ottawa reached through federal-provincial agreements signed with other provinces would be insufficient to make that a reality in Ontario.

In contrast to his first intergovernmental meeting, by 2019 Ford was positioning himself as a unifying force. When western premiers criticized the Trudeau government of not doing enough to support the oil and gas industry, in advance of a 2019 meeting of all premiers, Ford agreed in a press conference that "we have to listen to the people out West and listen to their concerns," but he assured those present that the prime minister "wants to support everyone right across the country. And I'm going to support the Prime Minister."[41] When the federal Liberals were shut out of Alberta and Saskatchewan in the 2019 election, Ford explained to his supporters that he had to step up to help unite the country because "What's good for Canada is good for Ontario." Even Toronto mayor John Tory described Ford's actions as

"Playing the role that Ontario premiers must play and have historically played in holding this country together."[42] Ford and Trudeau's close relationship was also evident when, in 2022, they stood together to announce a $3.6 billion investment to re-fit auto plants in Brampton and Windsor so they would produce electric vehicles. In 2022, as the most senior of the premiers around the intergovernmental table, and with the respect of these colleagues, Ford also played a central role in shoring up provincial support for the shared provincial campaign to raise federal funding from 22 per cent of provincial health care costs to 35 per cent. In short, Ford has transformed from largely unaware of federal-provincial intergovernmentalism to a leader within it, but with a disinterest in esoteric equalization debates, and a penchant for taking positions that seem like they might resonate with those struggling in the province to make ends meet in the era of deindustrialization.

It should be noted that Ford also positioned Ontario in opposition to Ottawa during the pandemic when he accused the federal government of failing to protect seniors, and called on the federal government to "put your money where your mouth is … help us out!"[43] Amidst the Pfizer vaccine shortage in January of 2021, and a second preventable crisis in Ontario's long-term care homes, Ford again placed the blame on Trudeau, explaining, "If I was in (Trudeau's) shoes … I'd be on that phone call every single day. I'd be up that guy's yin yang so far with a firecracker he wouldn't know what hit him."[44] These narratives shifted blame to Ottawa and away from the provincial government, but were positioned to resonate with "average" Ontarians, while lacking the punch and petulance of Manitoba premier Brian Pallister, who, in an effort to embarrass the federal government in charge of national vaccine procurement, put a down payment on 200,000 doses of an unapproved vaccine that had only just started clinical trials.

Contrary to the traditional image of a statesman-like Ontario working alongside the federal government, Ford avoided taking sides in the vaccine protests in Ottawa in January 2022. He did not send a representative to the committee set up to coordinate the federal, provincial, and municipal efforts to end the siege, and the province dispatched a good thousand fewer Ontario Provincial Police (OPP) officers than the 1,500 it claimed it sent to Ottawa to assist.[45] Months later, during the commission hearings in Ottawa over the federal government's eventual use of the *Emergencies Act* to end the protest, Ford went so far as to appeal (successfully) to a federal court judge to get immunity from testifying. While these actions stray from the leadership role in the federation Ontario is historically known for taking, they do not seem out of step for a leader who was likely supported in the last election by the very people protesting in Ottawa the so-called vaccine mandate that his government put in place.

Ford's use of the notwithstanding clause also suggests we should not overstate Ontario's leadership role in intergovernmental relations, as it affirms an inward-looking approach. Prior to Ford, no Ontario government had ever resorted to the notwithstanding clause of the *Charter* to override individual rights. Yet, Ford has chosen to "gorge" on it, using it to limit third-party advertising in provincial elections, and blocking education workers' right to strike.[46] While he has not used the notwithstanding clause in the defence of Ontario culture, as it is used in Quebec, his actions demonstrate that Ford is willing to usurp the Canada-wide values enshrined in the country's 1982 Constitution in pursuit of political goals within his own province.

Perhaps it is also fair to say that the "fair shares" argument has been muted in the Ford era because, in the last decades, Ontario's message got through to Ottawa. The Canada Health Transfer and Canada Social Transfer are per-capita transfers, as Ontario campaigned for in the late 1990s. They remain as such even though some of the other provinces would much prefer that these major transfers were needs based. When the global recession hit in 2009, Harper heeded the province's call not to balance his own budget by reducing transfers to provinces. The 2009 federal budget established the Federal Economic Development Agency (FEDDEV) for Southern Ontario, which has distributed billions of dollars to initiatives in Ontario. This agency levelled the playing field, in the sense that Southern Ontario was the only region in the country without such an agency. Ontario's proportion of infrastructure spending coming from Ottawa is now close to 37 per cent, up from 31 per cent owing to a new transit funding formula.

Not surprisingly, Ford's muting of the "fair shares" narrative is actually in line with Ontario public opinion. One commentator observed in 2010 that Ontario's "poor man of Confederation" narrative was "not persuasive to Ontarians, let alone Albertans" as "there is a reason that immigrants flock to (Ontario's) southern metropolises – it's where the largest number of good jobs are found."[47] Currently polling data reinforces Martin Regg Cohn's 2014 observation that "Ontarians are too quintessentially Canadian to hold a grudge against their federal government. Even when we're being pickpocketed, poked in the eye, shortchanged or double-crossed."[48] The political capital Ford might exhaust in pursuing the long-term goal of equalization reform is disproportionate to any short term increases to his popularity a new formula might yield. In 2022, support for the Equalization program as it stands was at 79 per cent in Ontario, a full five points above the average support in non-receiving provinces; and only 27 per cent of Ontarians were actually aware that Ontario does not receive it.[49] When asked, "Does your province have a distinct culture that is often misunderstood by people living in the rest of Canada?" Ontario is the only province where a majority of respondents do not answer affirmatively. Compared to respondents in other provinces, Ontarians are the least likely to identify with their province, rather than the country as a whole (7 per cent) and most likely to say they are "Canadian first."[50]

Intriguingly, while Ford resembles some of his predecessors (such as Mike Harris) in taking on an interprovincial leadership role in the premiers' quest for an unconditional boost to the Canada Health Transfer to bring the federal share to 35 per cent, the survey data commissioned by the premiers themselves suggest he better tread carefully if he wants to stay in step with Ontario voters. The survey commissioned by the premiers themselves to bolster the legitimacy of their position suggests that Ontarians are slightly out of line with other Canadians on this issue. Relative to other provinces, Ontario respondents are less dissatisfied about the current state of health care than about half of the provinces. And Ontarians are the provincial residents least likely to say that the provincial government is the order of government best able to determine health care spending needs (just 56 per cent agree with this statement).[51]

CONCLUSION

In the free trade era, Ontario governments have argued that "fairer treatment" for Ontario is in the interests of the country as a whole because "A strong Ontario means a Strong Canada."[52] Major changes to the economy of the country brought on by the globalization of trade, and the free flow of capital, untethered the east-west trade linkages that were the foundation of much of the postwar fiscal architecture. But, this approach to intergovernmental relations runs the risk of sharpening among other premiers and Canadians outside Ontario the view that Ontario is the "whiner of Confederation,"[53] and the "vampire squid of fiscal federalism," leaving less for other provinces to feed on with every dollar it "sucks from federal veins."[54]

Those Ontarians who gravitated towards Ford's populism at the ballot box are among those who experience the negative consequences of the neoliberal era: low-paying service-sector employment and public services made leaner through decades of austerity measures of the federal and provincial governments. Now a senior leader among premiers, and with a fairly solid relationship with the prime minister, it is still unlikely that Ford will engage his provincial counterparts and the prime minister in a major overhaul of the fiscal architecture underpinning health care in this country. For this reason, and others, such as his use of the notwithstanding clause to attempt to win fights with foes within his own province, and his lack of coordination and leadership on the vaccine protest front, we should not overstate the likelihood that Ford is returning Ontario to its pre-Davis self: playing a leadership role within the federation, asserting an alternative vision to that of Ottawa, all with an eye to the economic well-being of the federation as a whole. We should also not overstate the apparent symmetry between Ontario and Ottawa that some of Ford's actions during the pandemic suggested. The level of collaboration and communication of that time may not be as exceptional as the pandemic itself, but it is no doubt rare, given that the structural underpinnings of the Ontario economy remain out of step with some key pillars of fiscal federalism.

DISCUSSION QUESTIONS

1 How is Ontario traditionally perceived in intergovernmental relations?
2 How has Ontario's tenor in intergovernmental relations changed since the 1990s?
3 Why has the "fair share" argument not been very successful in Ontario?
4 Is there a consistent approach to federal-provincial relations under the Ford government?
5 Can Ontario still play its traditional role as broker of federal and provincial interests *and* pursue its own self interest?

NOTES

1 Cited in Bill Waiser, "Fighting for Autonomy: A Saskatchewan Tradition," *Globe and Mail*, August 21, 2022, O8.
2 Government of Saskatchewan, "Province Introduces the Saskatchewan First Act," news release, November 1, 2022, https://www.saskatchewan.ca/government/news-and-media/2022/november/01/province-introduces-the-saskatchewan-first-act.

3 Abigale Subdhan, "Alberta's Sovereignty Act Has Been Introduced by Premier Danielle Smith. Here's What You Need to Know: The Alberta Sovereignty within a United Canada Act Would Give the Provincial Cabinet Wide-Ranging Powers to Amend Federal Laws Deemed 'Harmful' to the Province. A Primer on Everything You Need to Know," *Globe and Mail*, November 30, 2022, https://www.theglobeandmail.com/canada/alberta/article-alberta-sovereignty-act-danielle-smith/.
4 Philip Authier, "Legault Says He Won't Shy Away from Defending Quebec Language and Culture," *Montreal Gazette*, October 1, 2022, https://montrealgazette.com/news/quebec/legault-says-he-wont-shy-away-from-defending-quebec-language-and-culture.
5 Nelson Wiseman, *In Search of Canadian Political Culture* (Vancouver: UBC Press, 2007), 187.
6 P.E. Bryden, "Ontario Exceptionalism: Old Ideas in the New Ontario," in *Shifting Power: The New Ontario and What it Means for Canada*, ed. Matthew Mendelsohn, Joshua Hjartarson, and James Pearce, Canada the State of the Federation 2010 (Montreal: McGill-Queen's University Press, 2013), 41.
7 Hugh Segal, "The Evolution of Ontario's Confederal Stance in the Nineties: Ideology or Continuity?," in *Canada the State of the Federation 2001: Canadian Political Culture(s) in Transition*, ed. Hamish Telford and Harvey Lazar (Montreal: McGill-Queen's University Press, 2002), 203; "Noblesse Oblige" translates as "Nobility Obliges."
8 Bryden, "Ontario Exceptionalism, "36.
9 Douglas M. Brown, "Fiscal Federalism: Maintaining a Balance?," in *Canadian Federalism: Performance, Effectiveness and Legitimacy*, 3rd ed., ed. Herman Bakvis and Grace Skogstad (Toronto: Oxford University Press, 2012), 118.
10 Matthew Mendelsohn, "Introduction: Accommodation of the New Ontario and Canada's New Narratives," in Mendelsohn, Hjartarson, and Pearce, *Shifting Power*, 5.
11 See P.E. Bryden, *"A Justifiable Obsession": Conservative Ontario's Relations with Ottawa 1943–1985* (Toronto: University of Toronto Press, 2013).
12 Segal, "The Evolution of Ontario's Confederal Stance in the Nineties," 213.
13 Hugh Segal, *The Right Balance: Canada's Conservative Tradition* (Toronto: Douglas and McIntyre, 2011).
14 André Lecours and Daniel Béland, "Federalism and Fiscal Policy: The Politics of Equalization in Canada," *Publius* 40, no. 4 (Fall 2010): 569–96, https://doi.org/10.1093/publius/pjp030.
15 Alberta did, however, continue to receive equalization payments for several years after 1962 under a special guarantee provision.
16 John Ibbitson, *Loyal No More: Ontario's Struggle for a Separate Destiny* (Toronto: HarperCollins, 2001), 101.
17 David Cameron and Richard Simeon, "Ontario in Confederation: The Not-So-Friendly Giant," in *The Government and Politics of Ontario*, 5th ed., ed. Graham White (Toronto: University of Toronto Press, 1997).

18 Thomas J. Courchene. "Fiscalamity! Ontario: From Heartland to Have-Not," *Policy Options*, June 2008, https://policyoptions.irpp.org/wp-content/uploads/sites/2/assets/po/citizenship-and-immigration/courchene.pdf.
19 Cameron and Simeon, "Ontario in Confederation."
20 Cameron and Simeon, "Ontario in Confederation."
21 See David P. Shugarman, "The Social Charter" in *Constitutional Politics: The Canadian Forum Book on Constitutional Proposals 1991–1992*, ed. Duncan Cameron and Miriam Smith (Toronto: James Lorimer, 1992).
22 Cited in Segal, "The Evolution of Ontario's Confederal Stance," 213.
23 On this era of interprovincialism, see Peter Graefe and Julie M. Simmons, "Assessing the Collaboration that was 'Collaborative Federalism' 1996–2006," *Canadian Political Science Review* 7 (August 2013): 25–36, https://doi.org/10.24124/c677/2013433.
24 Matthew Mendelsohn, "Big Brother No More: Ontario's and Canada's Interests Are No Longer Identical," *Literary Review of Canada*, October 2010, http://reviewcanada.ca/magazine/2010/10/big-brother-no-more/.
25 Lee Greenberg, "'Ontario Must Never Be Allowed to Collect Equalization'; Federal Philosophy One of Worst Kept Secrets in Ottawa, McGuinty Says," *Ottawa Citizen*, September 23, 2008, A3.
26 These titles are in the 2008 and 2011 budgets of the Ontario government.
27 Department of Finance Canada, "Major Federal Transfers," Government of Canada, accessed December 7, 2022, https://www.canada.ca/en/department-finance/programs/federal-transfers/major-federal-transfers.html. For pre-2013 data, see Carleigh Busby and Robert Behrend, *Federal Support through Major Transfers to the Provincial and Territorial Governments*, ed. Chris Matier (Toronto: Office of the Parliamentary Budget Officer, 2020), https://qsarchive-archiveqs.pbo-dpb.ca/web/default/files/Documents/Reports/RP-2021-020-S/RP-2021-020-S_en.pdf.
28 Greenberg, "Ontario Must Never Be Allowed."
29 Charles Sousa, "Ontario Expects Fairness, Not Sad Rhetoric from Ottawa," *Financial Post*, July 8, 2014, https://financialpost.com/opinion/ontario-expects-fairness-not-sad-rhetoric-from-ottawa.
30 On the rise of populism and its effect on welfare states more generally, see Gerda Hooijer and Desmond King, "The Critics of Welfare: From Neoliberalism to Populism," in *The Oxford Handbook of the Welfare State*, 2nd ed., ed. Daniel Béland, Stephan Leibfried, Kimberly J. Morgan, Herbert Obinger, and Christopher Pierson (Oxford University Press, 2021; Oxford Academic, online ed., November 9, 2021), accessed December 8, 2021, https://doi.org/10.1093/oxfordhb/9780198828389.001.0001.
31 Don Braid, "Braid: Trudeau Liberals Quietly Rig Equalization for Five More Years," *Calgary Herald*, June 23, 2018, https://calgaryherald.com/news/politics/braid-trudeau-liberals-quietly-rig-equalization-for-five-more-years.
32 Laura Stone, "Ford Aims for Unity at Premiers Meetings; Ontario Premier Says Leaders Will Discuss Areas of Agreement, Such as Health-Care Transfers, at Summit Next Week," *Globe and Mail*, November 29, 2019, A3.

33 Peter Graefe, "A More Inward-Looking Ontario Emerges under Ford," *Policy Options,* June 7, 2019, https://policyoptions.irpp.org/magazines/june-2019/a-more-inward-looking-ontario-emerges-under-ford/.
34 Royce Coop, "Feds Should Pay for Cost of Asylum Seekers," *Winnipeg Free Press*, July 13, 2018, A9.
35 Aaron Wherry, "By Claiming Ontario's Done its 'Fair Share,' Doug Ford Pushes the Climate Burden West," *CBC News*, April 25, 2019, https://www.cbc.ca/news/politics/doug-ford-climate-carbon-tax-emissions-1.5108852.
36 Robert Benzie, "Ontario Government Loses Carbon-Pricing Fight and Now Wants to Work with Ottawa to Battle Climate Change," *Toronto Sun*, March 9, 2020, https://www.thestar.com/politics/provincial/ontario-government-loses-carbon-pricing-fight-and-now-wants-to-work-with-ottawa-to-battle/article_10e17c8e-b4d8-5f07-a754-4f53593575f2.html.
37 Brian Lilley, "Ford to Take Team Ontario to Ottawa to Push for Federal Funding," *Toronto Sun*, March 9, 2020, https://torontosun.com/news/provincial/ford-to-take-team-ontario-to-ottawa-to-push-for-federal-funding.
38 See Bryden, "*A Justifiable Obsession*."
39 Susan Delacourt, "'He's My Therapist': How Chrystia Freeland and Doug Ford Forged an Unlikely Friendship in the COVID-19 Fight," *Toronto Star*, April 4, 2020, IN1.
40 "Ottawa is Looking at Spending Hundreds of Millions More to ... (Derived Headline)," *Toronto Star*, March 25, 2022, A1.
41 Stone, "Ford Aims for Unity."
42 Brian Lilley, "Premiers Look for Unity; But Trudeau's too Busy Catching Big Waves in Tofino," *Winnipeg Sun*, November 5, 2019, A8.
43 "Stop this Blame Game," *Ottawa Citizen*, June 27, 2020, A16.
44 Jorg Broschek, "The Politics of Blame Avoidance," *Hamilton Spectator*, January 11, 2022, A10.
45 Linda McQuaig, "Ford Plays High-Stakes Game of Vaccine Poker," *Toronto Star*, April 6, 2022, https://www.thestar.com/opinion/contributors/ford-plays-high-stakes-game-of-vaccine-poker/article_f7069ed9-a4e1-540e-a745-a8cdb98dea7c.html.
46 "The Madness of Canada's Premiers," *Globe and Mail*, December 3, 2022, O10.
47 Robin V. Sears, "The Next Federal-Provincial Battles: This Time It's Different," *Policy Options*, May 1, 2010, https://policyoptions.irpp.org/fr/magazines/the-fault-lines-of-federalism/the-next-federal-provincial-battles-this-time-its-different/.
48 Martin Regg Cohn, "No Luck in Premier's Plight to Rally against Feds," *Toronto Star*, February 13, 2014, A6.
49 Environics Institute for Survey Research, "Support for Equalization," April 2022, accessed December 8, 2022, https://www.environicsinstitute.org/docs/default-source/default-document-library/cot-report-1_equalization_april-4f.pdf?sfvrsn=a8417201_0.

50 Environics Institute for Survey Research, *Provincial Identity and Autonomy* (Toronto: Environics Institute for Survey Research, 2022), https://www.environicsinstitute.org/docs/default-source/default-document-library/cot-report-2_identity-apr-18_final6519ce9a07a54bc8959cf98a72b05f8d.pdf?sfvrsn=9bbc85df_0.
51 Canada's Premiers, *Report: National Healthcare Survey* (Ottawa: Council of the Federation Secretariat, 2022), https://www.canadaspremiers.ca/wp-content/uploads/2022/02/Rep_COF_NationalHealthcare_25105-001_24Jan2021.pdf.
52 Government of Ontario, Ministry of Finance, "Statement from Minister Dwight Duncan on Finance Ministers' Meeting," news release, May 22, 2009, https://news.ontario.ca/en/release/6303/statement-from-minister-dwight-duncan-on-finance-ministers-meeting.
53 "McGuinty Fumes Over West's Success," *Regina Leader-Post*, March 2, 2012, A10.
54 Konrad Yakabuski, "How Ontario's Squeezing Other Have-nots," *Globe and Mail*, December 18, 2014, A19.

Government-Media Relations in Ontario: Political Communication in the Time of the COVID-19 Pandemic

Tamara A. Small

On March 17, 2020, Premier Doug Ford held a press conference announcing that the Government of Ontario had declared a provincial state of emergency under the *Emergency Management and Civil Protection Act*. This press conference lasted for almost forty minutes and featured a ten-minute speech from Ford followed by questions from journalists to Ford, (then) chief medical officer, Dr. David Williams, the solicitor general, and the ministers of health and finance. The press conference was notable in that journalists were in the room with the officials, and the officials were neither masked nor physically distant. This would change significantly over the hundreds of press conferences held by the Government of Ontario between March 2020 and April 2022 related to the COVID-19 pandemic. While in democratic countries, press conferences have been a routinized feature of politics for many decades,[1] during the COVID-19 pandemic they became one of the most central venues for political communication in Ontario, Canada, and internationally.[2] The World Health Organization, for instance, delivered almost a hundred press conferences and briefings in the first eight months of the pandemic.[3]

This chapter focuses on political communication within the province of Ontario with special attention given to the first two years of the COVID-19 pandemic. Political communication can be thought of as the "role of communication in the political process."[4] Small, Marland, and Giasson describe political communication as a triangular process that includes political actors, the media, and citizens.[5] Political communication is multi-directional between these three groups. More specifically, we focus on the interaction between the Government of Ontario and the news media. It is tempting to assume that in the twenty-first century the news media is passé – that with digital technologies such as social media, governments and citizens can communicate without mediation. This notion certainly has some merit; the Government of Ontario as well as provincial politicians do make use of social media and other digital technologies. However, as will be discussed, the news media still matter; this was especially the case during the COVID-19 pandemic.

This analysis of political communication in Ontario begins broadly by providing support for the notion that the news media still matters. We narrow by focusing in on the news media within the province, exploring Ontario's press gallery. Within Westminster parliamentary systems, the press gallery is a group of accredited journalists that cover the activities of parliament. The Ontario press gallery is "an essential part" of Ontario's political system, and much of what we know about Ontario politics comes from their reporting and commentary.[6] Finally, this chapter explores a case study of government-media interaction during the COVID-19 pandemic by reflecting on the hundreds of press conferences held by the Government of Ontario between March 2020 and April 2022.

Why should we care about these particular press conferences long after the end of the pandemic? First, there is little academic work on press conferences in the Canadian context, and even less specifically on Ontario. This case study provides us an opportunity to see how they work in practice, regardless of the topic. Second, this case study reaffirms the importance of the news media within Ontario politics. The news media, then as now, plays an educative and accountability function within the Ontario political system. We get to see these functions in action through the case study.

THE NEWS MEDIA STILL MATTERS

In thinking about politics and government in Ontario, why should we be concerned with the news media? It is important to remember that, like governments, the news media are political actors in democratic political systems. As McNair points out, the news media "function both as transmitters of political communication which originates outside the media organisation itself, and as senders of political messages constructed by journalists."[7] Today, the news media consist of broadcasting (television and radio), newspapers, and online media outlets. The news media are the watchdogs of the political system, scrutinizing the actions of politicians and policy-makers and requiring them to account for decisions.[8] The democratic importance of the media is entrenched in Section 2 of the *Charter of Rights and Freedoms*, which specifically guarantees "freedom of the press and other media of communication."

The democratic importance of the news media also stems from the fact that most of what citizens know about politics comes from the news media. Few citizens engage directly with politics. Most citizens gain information about politics and form opinions about it by watching television news, listening to the radio, and reading newspapers or online news sources. Gidengil and colleagues have found that the more attention that Canadians pay to the media, irrespective of media type, the more knowledgeable they are about politics.[9] Today, there are a multitude of options when it comes to news consumption. Technological changes, including cable, satellite, and digital technologies, have extended what is available to consumers. Rather than a few sources dominating the media landscape, news audiences are increasingly fragmented. As a result, the news habits of Canadians (and Ontarians) have changed. Data from the 2022 Digital News Report shows that most Canadians get their news from an online source, including social media (77 per cent).[10] Online sources with the biggest reach include CBC/Radio-Canada, CTV, and TVA (in Quebec). Television news remains a popular source of news at 58 per cent. Print is a source of news for only 16 per cent of Canadians. There is evidence that the news media became more essential to Canadians during the COVID-19 pandemic. A report by Kaiser & Partners in late 2020 found that most Canadians (57 per cent) increased their consumption of news media, with 31 per cent reading more online news from established media and 27 per cent returning to broadcast TV news.[11] The report highlights the need for credible sources of information about the pandemic as a factor.

THE ONTARIO PRESS GALLERY

While there is considerable research on the news media at the federal level, there is less at the provincial level. The work of Frederick Fletcher defines our understanding of the media in Ontario politics, especially regarding the press gallery.[12] The Press Gallery of the Legislative Assembly of Ontario is a group of accredited journalists and camera and sound people from newspaper, magazine, broadcast, and online media organizations. The press gallery reports on the activities of not only the legislature and committees but also the premier, cabinet, and the public service. Many cover election campaigns in the province as well. The press gallery operates as an independent organization within the Office of the Legislative Assembly. It is not merely a group of reporters; the press gallery is a formal association with a constitution, elected executive, and accredited membership. Membership provides access to areas of the legislature that are off limits to the general public. Accredited journalists have their own gallery on the south side of the chamber to watch debates. The Legislative Press Gallery is supported by the press gallery coordinator. An employee of the Office of the Legislative Assembly, the press gallery coordinator liaises between politicians and the media. Tasks include sending out emails to members of provincial parliament (MPPs) and gallery members regarding media events, maintaining the Media Studio in Queen's Park, and providing some clerical assistance.

As part of their daily work, members of the gallery watch and report on legislative debates in the chamber when in session including oral question period. According to White, "question period is arguably the most significant proceeding of the Ontario legislature."[13] Question period is held between 10 and 11 a.m. each day when the legislature is sitting. One reason that question period is so essential stems from the principle of responsible government, which requires the government to maintain the support of the legislature to govern. Oral question period permits Opposition MPPs to scrutinize the actions of the executive and provides an accountability mechanism. Additionally, question period attracts considerable attention from the news media, and consequently citizens who regularly watch or read the news.[14] Indeed, it has been estimated that 80 per cent of news stories on Ontario politics originate from question period.[15] Question period, in Ontario and elsewhere, makes for good television.[16] This said, the nature of question period and the amount of coverage it receives are of concern to many who worry about the potentially negative effects it has on citizens who watch their political leaders hurling insults and heckling one another each night on the evening news.

Another important aspect of the gallery's job is to interview political actors in media scrums or press conferences. Scrums, which can be either impromptu or organized in advance, occur when reporters from different media organizations surround a politician and ask questions. Scrums take place at the end of debates in the legislature when politicians leave the chamber to return to

Table 8.1. Queen's Park Press Gallery Membership

Year	No. of Members
1975	40
1979	40
1984	37
1989	50
1995	52
2015	32
2022	43

Sources: Data from Frederick J. Fletcher, "Between Two Stools: News Coverage of Provincial Politics in Ontario," in *Government and Politics of Ontario*, ed. Donald C. MacDonald (Toronto: Macmillan, 1975), 268–9; Frederick. J. Fletcher, "The Crucial and the Trivial: News Coverage of Provincial Politics," in *The Government and Politics of Ontario*, 2nd ed., ed. Donald C. MacDonald (Toronto: Van Nostrand Reinhold, 1980), 249; Frederick J. Fletcher, "The Crucial and the Trivial: News Coverage of Provincial Politics," in *The Government and Politics of Ontario*, 3rd ed., ed. Donald C. MacDonald (Toronto: Nelson Canada, 1985), 195; Frederick J. Fletcher, "The Crucial and the Trivial," in *The Government and Politics of Ontario*, 4th ed., ed. Graham White (Toronto: Nelson Canada, 1990), 191; Frederick J. Fletcher and Rose Sottile, "Spinning Tales: Politics and News in Ontario," in *The Government and Politics of Ontario*, 5th ed., ed. Graham White (Toronto: University of Toronto Press, 1997), 237. Also updated from Tamara A. Small, "Media and Ontario Politics: The Press Gallery in the Twenty-First Century" in *The Politics of Ontario*, ed. Cheryl N. Collier and Jonathan Malloy (Toronto: University of Toronto Press, 2017), table 9.3, 163.

their offices. Key targets include the premier, cabinet ministers, opposition leaders, and the shadow cabinet. For print journalists, scrums may serve as supplementary material for a story. For television reporters, the scrum may provide the image of the day. The gallery also covers scheduled press conferences held by the government and opposition parties. Government or party communication staff will send a "media advisory" to news outlets detailing the upcoming event or news item. Depending on the nature of the press conference, the event might be limited to accredited members of the press gallery. The COVID-19 pandemic affected the functioning of scrums. Fewer scrums with tighter regulations meant that journalists had less access to quotes and sources to use in their stories.[17] As will be discussed, press conferences became the main venue for political communication during the COVID-19 pandemic.

In the previous edition of this volume, we lamented the shrinking size of the Ontario press gallery.[18] However, table 8.1 shows our consternation over

Table 8.2. News Organizations with Active Members in Queen's Park Press Gallery, April 2022

News Organizations	No. of Active Members
Newspapers	12
Canadian Press	2
Toronto Star	4
Globe and Mail	2
Toronto Sun	2
National Post	1
Le Droit	1
Television	12
Global News	2
CTV News	1
CHCH	1
TVO	1
CityNews	3
CP24	3
OMNI News	1
Radio	1
680 News	1
Online	11
QP Briefing	4
Narwhal	2
Queen's Park Observer	1
Queen's Park Today	3
iPolitics/QP Briefing	1

Source: Data compiled by author from communication with the Press Gallery Coordinator.

this decline was perhaps overstated. As of April 2022, there were forty-three active members of the Ontario press gallery representing a total of twenty-one different news organizations.[19] Active members are journalists, photographers, camerapersons, and soundpersons who cover Queen's Park on a full-time basis and have an office at the legislature. There are also twenty associate members, who cover Queen's Park part-time, typically covering special events such as the Speech from the Throne or the budget.

A couple of factors may account for this increase. First, Brin and Charlton note that the Canadian media is doing better economically.[20] Government support programs, increased advertising revenue during the pandemic, new forms of media collaboration, and paywalls are factors. The result has been some modest reinvesting in newsrooms. For instance, CP24, a Toronto-based twenty-four-hour news channel, had no members of the press gallery in 2015; it now has three active members. Second, there has been a change in the makeup of the media organizations in the press gallery. That is, there are more members from online-only media outlets, several of which are focused on Ontario politics (see table 8.2). In the previous edition of this chapter, QP Briefing, a daily subscription-based digital newsletter, was highlighted as a new and notable member of the press gallery. As of 2022, there were several other online media organizations with active members in the press gallery, including iPOLITICS, the Narwhal, Queen's Park Observer, and Queen's Park Today. The latter two are like QP Briefing in that they are subscription-based digital news focused solely on Ontario politics. The growth in online news outlets in the gallery is also evident in the number of associate members of the press gallery, including the National Observer, Metroland Media, and Loonie Politics (not included in table 8.2).

Table 8.2 presents the current composition of the press gallery by medium. The CBC has been given its own category, as their reporters provide content for both radio and television. Several observations can be gleaned from the composition of the Ontario press gallery relating to diversity. Ontario's population is highly diverse. Ontario has the largest francophone population outside of Quebec; French is the first official language of 4.1 per cent of Ontarians according to recent census data.[21] Moreover, about 250 ethnic origins were reported by Ontarians in the 2016 Census, and almost one-third of Ontarians are racialized.[22] Ontario's bilingual diversity is represented in the press gallery. As table 8.2 shows, there are four active members representing French language news media (e.g., LeDroit and Radio Canada). That said, the participation of ethnic media in the press gallery remains low. Canada has long had a robust network of newspapers, television, radio stations and online-only sources that offer ethnically focused content.[23] In 2015, the only ethnic media organization with a full-time member was *Sing Tao Daily*, a Chinese-language newspaper. Since then, *Sing Tao Daily* has become an associate member. OMNI News is now the only active member representing an ethnic media organization. OMNI is Canada's only multilingual and multicultural television broadcaster. Owned by Rogers Media, it is available in more than ten million Canadian households and provides content in twenty languages.[24] Overall, Ontario's ethnic diversity remains under-served by the current composition of the gallery. Finally, the press gallery is very Toronto-centric. CHCH (Hamilton) is the only regional member. Northern Ontario has no representation at all. More than half a million people live in Northern Ontario. Gina S. Comeau argues in chapter 11 that the "most enduring feature of Northern Ontario politics is that it continues to be significantly different from that of Southern Ontario" (196). This is evident by the need for a separate Northern Ontario debate in Ontario elections. The lack of members of the press gallery from Northern Ontario media results in limited attention to the political interest of the more than half a million people who live there.

The interaction between the press gallery and politicians in Ontario has shifted over time. Newsmaking is an ongoing power struggle between politicians and reporters.[25] Politicians seek "the delivery to voters of as full and unchallenged versions of their messages as possible"[26] while reporters seek to control the framing and content of news stories. Until the 1960s, journalists and the Ontario government had a very "cosy relationship,"[27] where gallery members often had partisan ties, and some were even advisors to politicians. This changed, however, by the 1970s.

While federally, the relationship between the gallery and politicians has always been strained, this has not and does not reflect the relations at Queen's Park. From Pierre Trudeau onwards, relations between the (federal) Canadian Parliamentary Press Gallery (CPPG) and Canadian prime ministers have never been overly harmonious. Indeed, shortly after the Conservative Party took office in 2006, relations between the CPPG and the Prime Minister's Office imploded. The communication staff ceased publicizing cabinet and caucus meeting times and also barred the reporters from the corridor outside of the cabinet room, which limited scrums.[28] They also began choosing which reporters could ask questions based on a pre-assigned list at press conferences. Finally, the party moved to using alternative communication channels to circumvent the CPPG.[29] Alex Marland notes that not much has changed under Justin Trudeau. While the Liberals resumed announcing cabinet meetings, they maintained the ban on access to the third floor of the Centre Block.[30] Moreover, renovations of the House of Commons in 2019 allowed MPs to avoid the media by creating areas off limits to journalists, using security concerns as a justification.

While the interaction between the Ontario press gallery and politicians does not appear to be as strained as federally, similar stories do exist. For instance, in 2009, communication staff instituted a "5 feet buffer" during scrums with then-premier Dalton McGuinty. Reporters were asked to stand at least five feet from McGuinty when asking questions. The goal, according to the premier's aides, was to make the scrums "more civilized."[31] Not surprisingly, the gallery was less than impressed with this rule.[32] The McGuinty Liberals held press conferences a long way from Queen's Park, which made it more difficult for the gallery to cover particular events. This said, for the most part, the gallery members accept this as part of the job. There have also been tensions with Premier Doug Ford. For instance, early in the Ford government's tenure, there were stories of reporter questions being intentionally drowned out by the applause of political staffers at events.[33] During the 2022 provincial election, Ford's campaign strategy seemed to include media avoidance. Throughout the campaign, Ford often did not take questions from the media at campaign stops.[34] Despite expected tensions and difficulties, the relationship between the Ontario press gallery and political parties does not seem to feature the same issues that arise federally.

GOVERNMENT-MEDIA RELATIONS IN ACTION: A CASE STUDY OF COVID-19 PRESS CONFERENCES

In this final section, we reflect on the more than six hundred press conferences held by the Government of Ontario related to the COVID-19 pandemic between March 2020 and April 2022 and provide general trends about them. In 2019, a novel coronavirus began spreading in Wuhan, China. This deadly respiratory disease, eventually termed COVID-19, moved across the globe during the first months of 2020. Canada's first "presumptive" case was reported in Toronto in January 2020. The rapid spread of the virus led the World Health Organization to label the outbreak as a pandemic on March 11, 2020. As of June 2022, Ontario has had the largest number of confirmed cases among Canada's provinces and territories; however, Ontario only ranks sixth in the per capita rate. More than 13,000 Ontarians have died of COVID-19. Like jurisdictions worldwide, COVID-19 is the subject of intense public policy, including lockdowns or stay-at-home orders, mask mandates, vaccine distribution, vaccine mandates, and government assistance or recovery programs.

While the COVID-19 pandemic at the very first instance is a global health crisis, it is also a crisis of communication. It not only matters how political and public officials respond to the crisis in terms of public and health policies, but also how they communicate that response. Press conferences were a crucial vehicle for communicating information and decisions about COVID-19 in Ontario and elsewhere. This reflection is based on a review of Ontario press conferences found on "COVID-19 | Ontario" YouTube playlist, which has archived all the COVID-19 press conferences provincially and federally.[35] We also review media advisories about these press conferences from the

Government of Ontario's Newsroom website.³⁶ Deep analysis of the content of the Ontario press conferences is beyond the scope of this chapter; rather, we focus on describing the nature of these conferences and discussing their implications for political communication in Ontario. While the COVID-19 pandemic was a very unique circumstance, this case study provides an opportunity to reflect on how the government and the media interact with one another as part of their daily work.

A press conference is a form of public communication between an organization and the news media. Within politics, political elites initiate a press conference to make policy announcements, and provide updates and explanations for political decisions. They are also initiated to handle challenging events such as crises (e.g., terrorist attacks or environmental disasters), scandals, or held for special occasions such as the visiting of international dignitaries.³⁷ In terms of format, press conferences typically consists of two main parts: politicians (one or more) and/or officials give a prepared speech, followed by a question-and-answer session with journalists. This first part is very much a public relations exercise, where the politicians or public officials seek to set the agenda of the event. The second part of a press conference is crucial for democratic politics in terms of accountability and transparency of political actors. Press conferences provide a forum where the media is able to perform their "watchdog" role by asking challenging and direct questions of politicians and political officials.³⁸ This watchdog function is particularly important in political systems, such as the United States, where the political executive is not subject to formalized questioning from other branches of government. Press conferences are often broadcast live on television and/or live-streamed on the internet. Kumar notes there are two consequences of live press conferences. First, politicians and political officials are not only explaining their policies and actions to reporters but also to the public.³⁹ Second, because they are live, press conferences are a high-risk environment for politicians and political officials, especially during the Q&A portion. As such, communication staff seek to highly manage press conferences as much as possible. This may include reducing the number of questions asked and by whom. For the news media, press conferences are not only important as sources of information for news stories but also for images and video for newspapers, websites, and television programs.

As mentioned, press conferences are a regularized feature of Ontario politics. However, we argue the COVID-19 press conferences in Ontario held between 2020 and 2022 were significantly more important than press conferences held in normal times for several reasons. First, as noted, a public health crisis is also a communication crisis. Communicating a pandemic requires political and public officials to effectively manage and disseminate information, thereby shaping public perception. Coman and colleagues suggest that effective political communication can aid in resolving the crisis, while ineffective communication can prolong or worsen its impact.[40] Looking at the United States, Hatcher argues that President Donald Trump's communication of the pandemic adversely affected the country's response.[41] Second, the operation of Queen's Park changed significantly during the pandemic. The legislative building was closed to the public. Non-essential staff were encouraged to work from home. Unlike other Canadian legislatures, Queen's Park did not opt for virtual chamber sittings.[42] Physical distancing rules were in place in the chamber, and only a limited number of politicians were permitted to attend at any one time, and there were changes to procedures.[43] Taken together, responsible government in Ontario was challenged. That is, the ability of the members of the Legislative Assembly to scrutinize the actions of Premier Ford and the government was limited within the chamber. As such, press conferences became a regular opportunity for members of the press gallery to challenge Ford and other officials on their handling of the pandemic. Third, press conferences appeared to be very central to the governing strategy of Premier Ford. Unlike other premiers, Ford participated in a daily press conference for nearly forty weeks in 2020. Compare this to Alberta's premier Jason Kenney, who was criticized in November 2020 for a two-week period of press conferences where the provincial chief medical officer spoke to the media alone with no member of the government present. CPAC's "COVID-19 | Ontario" YouTube playlist features more than six hundred press conferences for Ontario. The next closest province is Manitoba at around 440; Quebec, the second-largest province, is listed as having 386. Finally, public health crises such as COVID-19 are times when the "public are likely to be dependent on news media for information."[44] The news media have an essential role in simplifying complex scientific issues and detailed public policy of governments to the public. While this is probably true for most public health crises, the COVID-19 pandemic has been described as an "infodemic," where the global spread of the virus has been mirrored by a global spread of misinformation shared on social media.[45] Canadians were clamouring to the traditional media for higher quality information. The CBC describes Ontario's press conferences as "pandemic ritual," where hundreds of thousands of Ontarians regularly watched them in the early months of the pandemic.⁴⁶ This existed in other jurisdictions as well. For instance, Guzek and colleagues' analysis of media use in Poland found that press conferences were a vital source of COVID-19 information for most respondents by "making government messaging more accessible."⁴⁷

Ontario's COVID-19 press conferences generally followed the format discussed earlier, starting with remarks by politicians and followed by journalist questions. The press conferences were live-streamed on many media websites, and sometimes carried live on television stations. The Government of Ontario also live-streamed them on YouTube with English closed captioning and with French interpretation and closed captioning. The latter ensured the province was meeting its obligation to francophone communities. Many journalists also live-tweeted press conferences in real time. Most press conferences lasted around thirty to forty minutes, with the bulk of time dedicated to Q&A. During the Q&A, journalists were limited to one question and one follow-up. Unlike before the pandemic, where journalists would be in the same room as politicians during the event, press conferences were virtual until mid-2021, with journalists participating by teleconference. That is, they would listen and ask questions by telephone. During the stay-at-home orders, teleconferencing could not be avoided. As per media advisories, journalists were asked to sign up by email with a government communication staffer. Some press conferences were limited to accredited media, that is, members of the press gallery. Virtual press conferences meant that political staff had more control over press conferences than normal. With journalists being on the telephone, they could not "interrupt a politician who [was] filibustering or avoiding the question."⁴⁸ Indeed AlHadidi's analysis, based on interviews with members of the press gallery, found that virtual press conferences left "journalists with uniform messaging and limited opportunities to expand on questions to scrutinize government decisions."⁴⁹ It was impossible to see which journalists wanted to ask a question, and whether some journalists were being overlooked. This is not surprising given that political actors are constantly looking for a way to control the message. By mid-2021, press conferences were a mix of virtual, in person, or both. This would be indicated on the media advisory. For in-person press conferences, the media were required to be physically distant and follow provincial health and safety protocols.

Ontario's COVID-19 press conferences were held at a wide variety of locations over the two years. Many of them were held in the Media Studio at Queen's Park. Some were held virtually by video conference. For instance, in June 2021, then-health minister Christine Elliott held a virtual conference regarding financial support for children's mental health initiatives. Throughout the pandemic, Premier Ford travelled to various parts of the province, meeting with local officials and Ontarians. Many press conferences were held on location around the province, including hospitals, vaccination centres, schools, and universities. An example is in August 2020 when Premier Ford held a press conference in Windsor that featured a tractor and other heavy equipment as a backdrop. In order to be inclusive to hearing-impaired communities, press conferences in the Media Studio always featured a sign language interpreter, while some virtual conferences did as well. However, press conferences in far-off locations rarely featured a sign language interpreter. As noted in the previous version of this chapter, politicians often hold "media avails a long way from Queen's Park," which makes it more difficult for journalists to do their work.

According to Laura Kahn, there are two models of political leadership that arise during public health crises: the *politician prominence model* and *expert appointee prominence model*.[50] In the politician prominence model, the politician is the primary decision-maker and public communicator while accepting advice from experts. In the expert appointee prominence model, the politician delegates the primary decision-making and public communication responsibilities to experts while providing political support. Kahn suggests the second model is preferred by most politicians because they recognize the limits of their scientific and medical expertise during a health crisis. While Kahn's work draws heavily on the analysis of American public health crises, she does note that the expert appointee prominence model was evident in Ontario during the 2003 SARS outbreak. The politician prominence model occurs when a politician prefers to dominate the media or has aspirations for higher political office.

If we consider which actor played the primary communicator role (not the decision-making role), Kahn's models are useful in analyzing Ontario's COVID-19 press conferences. We find that both models were present in Ontario. That is, *both* politicians and experts in Ontario regularly communicated public policy and information about the pandemic – but they generally did so in separate press conferences. This can be contrasted with British Columbia, where the BC premier took a backseat to the chief medical officer.[51] Indeed, one reason contributing to the more than six hundred COVID-19 press conferences in Ontario was that there were two of them held many days: one featuring one set of actors followed later in the day by another press conference featuring the other set of actors. This was especially the case in the first eight months of the pandemic. Press conferences featuring both sets of actors happened, but it was not the norm. They generally occurred for big announcements. For instance, the state of emergency press conference, described at the beginning of this chapter, included both Premier Ford and the chief medical officer. Both were in attendance a year later when Ford announced the twenty-eight-day province-wide "shutdown" in 2021.

Politician-prominent COVID-19 press conferences featured the members of the Ontario cabinet. Premier Ford gave almost daily COVID-19 press conferences for much of 2020. That said, Ford was rarely alone; he was often joined by senior cabinet ministers. Chief among them, unsurprisingly, was the minister of health and deputy premier, Christine Elliott. Elliott also gave numerous press conferences without Ford. COVID-19 measures impacted more than just public health; they also affected education, long-term care, justice, workers, and businesses. As such, cabinet ministers such as Stephen Lecce, minister of education, Ontario Solicitor General Sylvia Jones, long-term care ministers Merrilee Fullerton and later Rod Phillips, Monte McNaughton (labour minister), and minister of finance Rod Phillips then Peter Bethlenfalvy were regular participants. Like Elliott, several of these ministers held COVID-19 press conferences without Ford. This is true for Lecce, as school closures, openings, and safety measures were of particular importance to the public. Other cabinet ministers would feature in COVID-19 press conferences if their portfolio dovetailed with the broader announcement. Depending on the purpose of the press conference, all attending ministers would provide remarks. At other times, only Ford would provide remarks and the attending ministers would be available to answer questions related to their portfolio. Press conferences away from Queen's Park often involved municipal politicians and relevant MPPs. For instance, the previously mentioned press conference in Windsor included Ford, the labour minister, the mayor of Windsor, the associate minister of transportation and the MPP for Chatham-Kent–Leamington. Press conferences where Ford was in attendance were live-streamed on the premier's official English and French YouTube channels. Generally, the format and the approach to these press conferences are very similar to press conferences outside of the pandemic.

In the first year of the pandemic, Premier Ford was lauded for his crisis communication. His folksy style of speaking, his tendency to call out the bad behaviour of protestors, youths gathering in parks, hoarders, and/or price-gougers, and the occasional wearing of t-shirts with messages of support appear to resonate. For instance, TVO's Steve Paikin (a member of the Ontario press gallery) has written of Ford:

> But there's something else that's contributed to Ford's COVID-era aura. Do you watch the premier's daily media briefings? They started off sluggishly back in March. The premier looked nervous reading from the Teleprompter. He hadn't yet found his voice. And his message wasn't always clear.
>
> But those sessions have now become Exhibit A in successful media management and political theatre.
>
> The briefings always start with the premier reading the message of the day off the Teleprompter. He's gotten much better at that. Then the appropriate cabinet minister follows up to reinforce the message with more detail. Ford then returns to the microphone and generally gives a shout-out to a group he's met with, bestowing his ultimate compliment on them. "What a group of champions they are!" he'll say.[52]

Another example comes from Seijts and Young Milani, published in the Elsevier Public Health Emergency Collection:

> Doug Ford, the premier of Ontario, Canada, received praise from all political parties for the way he ran the province's daily press conferences during the present pandemic. Observers noted the deep empathy he conveyed for the public he serves, especially when he delivered the grim message that between 3000 and 15,000 Ontarians might die as a result of the pandemic over the next 18 to 24 months. He brought transparency and candor to his briefings, believing that sometimes knowledge is safer to possess than fear.

Though Ford's public approval rating was high in 2020, it precipitously dropped as the pandemic wore on.[53]

The second type of COVID-19 press conference in Ontario was expert prominent. During the pandemic, Canadians across the country were introduced to a cadre of public health experts at the federal, provincial, and municipal levels. Some experts are entrenched in Canadian politics, while others were created specifically for the pandemic. In terms of the former, the chief public health officers (CMOHs) are created by legislation and exist at all three levels. According to Fafard and colleagues, CMOHs are senior public servants who (1) advise governments on public health matters, (2) communicate public health issues to the public, and (3) manage the implementation of government health priorities.[54] During the pandemic, Ontario had two CMOHs. Dr. David Williams served until his retirement in June 2021. He was replaced by the Kingston, Frontenac, Lennox, and Addington CMOH, Dr. Kieran Moore. Pandemic-specific experts included the Ontario COVID-19 Science Advisory Table, a group of scientific experts and health system leaders who evaluate and report on emerging evidence relevant to the pandemic, and the COVID-19 Vaccine Distribution Task Force, led by retired General Rick Hillier, who managed the early phases of the vaccine rollout. Outside of a crisis, the expert prominent press conferences would be an unusual feature in Canadian politics.

In addition to the almost daily Ford press conferences held during the early months of the pandemic, Dr. Williams also held near daily ones. He was often joined by associate chief medical officer of health, Dr. Barbara Yaffe. These press conferences began by discussing provincial case counts, hospitalization, and deaths due to COVID-19. Later, vaccination rates would be included. The CMOH also provided other remarks, including policy announcements. For instance, Dr. Moore announced Ontario's decision to maintain capacity limits in higher-risk settings in December 2021. Williams and Moore, as with other CMOHs, became central actors in communicating the pandemic in Canada and globally. Other experts that were featured in this second type of press conference included Dr. Adalsteinn Brown, co-chair of the Ontario COVID-19 Science Advisory Table. His press conferences focused on presenting COVID-19 modelling data. Members of the COVID-19 Vaccine Distribution Task Force, including General Hillier and Dr. Dirk Huyer, Ontario's chief coroner and coordinator of provincial outbreak response also participated. Expert prominent press conferences did not travel outside of Queen's Park and were held in the Media Studio. That said, Dr. Moore held virtual ones from his office. Expert prominent press conferences were live-streamed on the government's YouTube channels with English closed captioning and French interpretation and closed captioning (as opposed to the premier's channels). Like elected officials, these experts were subject to journalist questions during the latter portion of the press conferences.

Compared to politician-prominent COVID-19 press conferences, the expert-prominent ones are particularly interesting from a political communication perspective. As discussed, politician-prominent press conferences are a routinized feature of democratic politics. The public is used to seeing elected officials on television news broadcasts or hearing about them in newspapers. Consider the leaders' tour during provincial and federal elections, where the main party leaders attend rallies, give speeches, and make policy announcements in a highly orchestrated media spectacle. In contrast, public officials are not household names, and, importantly, they are not expected to be. In public administration, this is described as the "public service bargain." That is, public servants provide "loyal, politically-neutral service to the government of the day" in return for certain benefits, including the security of anonymity that comes from working "away from the media spotlight."[55] However, through press conferences, public health experts in Ontario, as with other jurisdictions, became important sources of information during the pandemic. Indeed, survey research out of Carleton University found that when asked to rank sources based on trustworthiness and credibility, public health officials were the top choice of respondents in 2020.[56] That said, public support for CMOHs with first ministers decreased steadily as the pandemic wore on. Ontarians were quite critical of both Dr. Williams' and Ford's handling of the pandemic; an Angus Reid polls found Williams' approval drop around 30 percentage points over the first year of the pandemic.[57] There were even calls for Williams to resign in 2020. As the *Toronto Sun* notes, the "issues appear to be Dr. Williams' communication style as well as claims of his inability to lead in a crisis."[58]

In their review of CMOHs in parliamentary countries, MacAulay and colleagues note concerns about the autonomy and independence of CMOHs during the pandemic.[59] They highlight Australian state politics, where some leaders were accused of "hiding" behind the advice of their CMOHs. Similar accusations have been made in Ontario. For instance, CTV's Colin D'Mello (a member of Ontario's press gallery) wrote in 2021 that one of the reasons Ford reduced his number of press conferences was because the "Premier's Office has been looking to change the channel on [Doug] Ford's pandemic faults by allowing ministers and public health officials to "wear" the decisions that they make or recommend."[60] Having CMOHs appear regularly in press conferences about the pandemic, where they were not only providing information but also were subject to journalist questions about advice given and decisions made by the government, can blur lines of accountability between elected officials and experts. The pandemic has raised serious questions about the public service bargain during public health crises.

CONCLUSION

We began this discussion by describing political communication as a multi-directional, triangular process that includes political actors, the media, and citizens. It is worth noting, by focusing on the interactions between government and the news media, that this chapter has only shared one side of the political communication story. We would be remiss to not point out that social media has also been an important part of pandemic communication. Research shows that many of Canada's CMOHs were very active on X (Twitter) providing a lot of information and their tweets were often retweeted.[61] Moreover, some CMOHs were more popular on social media than their respective health ministers, though neither Dr. Williams nor Moore had their own X (Twitter) feeds. It is also worth noting that without systemic analysis of the content of the press conferences, this chapter can say little about the quality or effectiveness of the messages provided by Ford, the cabinet, and/or public health experts in Ontario.

As mentioned, the news media are purveyors of information and a key watchdog of the political system. These roles became doubly important during the COVID-19 pandemic. The Ontario press gallery were crucial political actors. Members of the Ontario press gallery were forced to supplement their normal political expertise with scientific and medical knowledge, so they could effectively perform those two roles on behalf of Ontarians. Lilleker and colleagues found that worldwide,

> political communication during the pandemic adopted a highly personalised approach. In most cases, the prime minister or president became chief communicator and figurehead for the nation and its response. In some nations, key ministers or medical experts gained prominence.[62]

We, too, find evidence of this personalized approach in Ontario, but with both Premier Ford and the CMOHs being key communicators. This interaction between the government and the news media, as seen through the hundreds of COVID-19 press conferences, was an important part of the Government of Ontario's strategy in addressing this ongoing pandemic.

This case study of COVID-19 press conferences provides us an opportunity to shine a light on the relationship between government actors and the press. While some of the features were limited to this particular crisis (e.g., virtual press conferences and the prominence of experts), other features (e.g., press conferences in general and attempting to control the message) exist outside of the crisis. While the COVID-19 pandemic is a very unique political circumstance, it helped to reaffirm the democratic role of the news media in Ontario, and elsewhere. It is certainly positive to see growth in the Ontario press gallery after many years of decline. However, it is too early to tell if the current size is an outlier. The inclusion of online-only media in Ontario is an interesting development. That said, these organizations may have a limited impact due to their specialized and subscription-based format. Moreover, limited regional and ethnic participation in the gallery remains a concern. How well regions outside of the Greater Toronto Area, such as Northern Ontario, and ethnic communities are being served by the overall coverage of Queen's Park is still a key question. That said, we continue to argue Ontarians are well-served by a highly professional and dedicated group of journalists and camerapeople at Queen's Park.

DISCUSSION QUESTIONS

1. What is the optimal size of the Press Gallery of Ontario?
2. Does it matter if the press gallery is not representative of Ontario's regional and ethnic diversity?
3. What type of relationship should a press gallery have with politicians?
4. What are the benefits and drawback of virtual press conferences?
5. Does the news media matter in the age of social media?

NOTES

1 Martha Joynt Kumar, "Source Material: Presidential Press Conferences: The Importance and Evolution of an Enduring Forum," *Presidential Studies Quarterly* 35, no. 1 (March 2005): 166–92, https://doi.org/10.1111/j.1741-5705.2004.00241.x; Göran Eriksson and Johan Östman, "Cooperative or Adversarial? Journalists' Enactment of the Watchdog Function in Political News Production," *The International Journal of Press/Politics* 18, no. 3 (July 2013): 304–24, https://doi.org/10.1177/1940161213482493.

2 Heidi Tworek, Ian Beacock, and Eseohe Ojo, *Democratic Health Communications during Covid-19: A RAPID Response* (Vancouver: UBC Centre for the Study of Democratic Institution, 2020), https://democracy2017.sites.olt.ubc.ca

/files/2020/09/Democratic-Health-Communication-during-Covid_FINAL.pdf; Katie Bates and Lore Hayek, "Austria: A Ski Resort as the Virus Slingshot of Europe," in *Political Communication and COVID-19*, ed. Darren Lilleker, Ioana A. Coman, Miloš Gregor, and Edoardo Novelli (New York: Routledge, 2021), 202–12.

3 Darren Lilleker and Gregor Miloš, "World Health Organisation: The Challenges of Providing Global Leadership," in Lilleker et al., *Political Communication and COVID-19*, 19–33.

4 Steven H. Chaffee, *Political Communication: Issues and Strategies for Research*, vol. 4 (Beverly Hills: SAGE Publications, 1975), 15.

5 Tamara A. Small, Alex Marland, and Thierry Giasson, *Political Communication in Canada: Meet the Press and Tweet the Rest* (Vancouver: UBC Press, 2014), 3–23.

6 Frederick J. Fletcher, "The Crucial and the Trivial: News Coverage of Provincial Politics," in *The Government and Politics of Ontario*, 4th ed., ed. Graham White (Toronto: Nelson Canada, 1990), 190.

7 Brian McNair, *An Introduction to Political Communication* (London: Taylor & Francis, 2011), 12.

8 Small, Marland, and Giasson, "The Triangulation of Canadian Political Communication."

9 Elisabeth Gidengil, André Blais, Neil Nevitte, and Richard Nadeau, *Citizens* (Vancouver: UBC Press, 2004), 26.

10 Colette Brin and Sébastien Charlton, *Digital News Report 2022: Country Data Canada* (Oxford: Reuters Institute for the Study of Journalism, 2022), https://reutersinstitute.politics.ox.ac.uk/digital-news-report/2022/canada.

11 Kaiser & Partners, "Canadians Are Relying More on Established News Sources as a Result of the COVID-19 Pandemic," news release, November 2, 2020, https://kaiserpartners.com/press-release-canadians-are-relying-more-on-established-news-sources-as-a-result-of-the-covid-19-pandemic-study/.

12 Frederick J. Fletcher, "Between Two Stools: News Coverage of Provincial Politics in Ontario," in *The Government and Politics of Ontario*, ed. Donald C. MacDonald (Toronto: Macmillan, 1975), 248–69; Frederick J. Fletcher, "The Crucial and the Trivial: News Coverage of Provincial Politics," in *The Government and Politics of Ontario*, 2nd ed., ed. Donald C. MacDonald (Toronto: Van Nostrand Reinhold, 1980), 245–71; Frederick J. Fletcher, "The Crucial and the Trivial: News Coverage of Provincial Politics," in *The Government and Politics of Ontario*, 3rd ed., ed. Donald C. MacDonald (Toronto: Nelson Canada, 1985), 192–218; Fletcher, "The Crucial and the Trivial: News Coverage of Provincial Politics"; Frederick J. Fletcher and Rose Sottile, "Spinning Tales: Politics and News in Ontario," in *The Government and Politics of Ontario*, 5th ed., ed. Graham White (Toronto: University of Toronto Press, 1997).

13 Graham White, *The Ontario Legislature: A Political Analysis* (Toronto: University of Toronto Press, 1989).

14 Michel Bédard, *Question Period in the Canadian Parliament and Other Legislatures*, pub. no.. 2011-88-E (Ottawa: Library of Parliament, 2014), https://publications.gc.ca/collections/collection_2016/bdp-lop/bp/YM32-2-2011-88-1-eng.pdf.

15 White, *The Ontario Legislature*.
16 David Taras, *The Newsmakers: The Media's Influence on Canadian Politics* (Scarborough, ON: Nelson Canada, 1990).
17 Janine AlHadidi, "Scrum Undone: The Evolution of Media Scrums at Queen's Park in a Post-Covid World" (Paper, Canadian Political Science Association Annual Conference 2022, May 31–June 3, 2022).
18 Tamara A. Small, "Media and Ontario Politics: The Press Gallery in the 21st Century," in *The Politics of Ontario*, ed. Cheryl N. Collier and Jonathan Malloy (Toronto: University of Toronto Press, 2017), 157–74.
19 My thanks to the press gallery coordinator for providing this information.
20 Brin and Charlton, "Digital News Report 2022."
21 Office of the Commissioner of Official Languages, "Infographic: The French Presence in Ontario," Government of Canada, last modified September 18, 2020, archived May 21, 2023, at the Wayback Machine archive, https://web.archive.org/web/20230521054351/https://www.clo-ocol.gc.ca/en/statistics/infographics/french-presence-ontario.
22 Ministry of Finance, "Fact Sheet 9: Ethnic Origin and Visible Minorities| 2016 Census Highlights," Government of Ontario, April 8, 2022, http://www.ontario.ca/document/2016-census-highlights/fact-sheet-9-ethnic-origin-and-visible-minorities.
23 Matthew D. Matsaganis, Vikki S. Katz, and Sandra J. Ball-Rokeach, *Understanding Ethnic Media: Producers, Consumers, and Societies* (Thousand Oaks, CA: Sage, 2011).
24 Rogers, "Rogers Media and OMNI Television Proudly Continue to Serve Canada's Multicultural and Multilingual Audiences," news release, May 23, 2019, https://about.rogers.com/news-ideas/rogers-media-omni-television-proudly-continue-serve-canadas-multicultural-multilingual-audiences/.
25 Taras, *The Newsmakers*.
26 Jay G. Blumler and Dennis Kavanagh, "The Third Age of Political Communication: Influences and Features," *Political Communication* 16, no. 3 (July 1999): 209–30, https://doi.org/10.1080/105846099198596.
27 Fletcher and Sottile, "Spinning Tales."
28 Alex Marland, *Whipped: Party Discipline in Canada* (Vancouver: UBC Press, 2020).
29 Ira Basen, "Stephen Harper's Press Gallery Take Down," *rabble.ca*, October 10, 2008, https://rabble.ca/general/stephen-harpers-press-gallery-take-down/.
30 Marland, *Whipped: Party Discipline in Canada*.
31 Robert Benzie, "McGuinty Shuns Media Scrums; Premier Raises Eyebrows with Policy That Reporters Be 'At Least Five Feet' Away for Questions," *Toronto Star*, February 12, 2009, A4.
32 Karen Howlett, "McGuinty to Reporters: I Need My Space," *Globe and Mail*, February 12, 2009, https://www.theglobeandmail.com/news/politics/mcguinty-to-reporters-i-need-my-space/article1148885/.
33 CBC Radio, "'Unprecedented': Staffers Drown out Reporters by Clapping at Doug Ford News Conference," *As It Happens (CBC Radio)*, August 9, 2018, https://www.cbc.ca/radio/asithappens/as-it-happens-thursday

-edition-1.4779154/unprecedented-staffers-drown-out-reporters-by-clapping-at-doug-ford-news-conference-1.4779157.
34 Mike Crawley, "Why Doug Ford's Media Strategy Works for Him," *CBC News*, May 13, 2022, https://www.cbc.ca/news/canada/toronto/ontario-election-doug-ford-media-strategy-1.6450785.
35 CPAC, "COVID-19 | Ontario," *CPAC YouTube*, n.d., https://www.youtube.com/playlist?list=PLdgoQ6C3ckQsPsp5VN_7xlbY5c9Do3DhD.
36 "Ontario Newsroom," Government of Ontario, accessed June 15, 2022, https://news.ontario.ca/en.
37 Mats Ekström and Göran Eriksson, "Press Conferences," in *The Routledge Handbook of Language and Politics* (New York: Routledge, 2017), 342.
38 Eriksson and Östman, "Cooperative or Adversarial? Journalists' Enactment of the Watchdog Function in Political News Production"; Ekström and Eriksson, "Press Conferences."
39 Kumar, "Source Material."
40 Ioana A. Coman, Dalia Elsheikh, Miloš Gregor, Darren Lilleker, and Edoardo Novelli, "Introduction: Political Communication, Governance and Rhetoric in Times of Crisis," in Lilleker et al., *Political Communication and COVID-19*, 1–16.
41 William Hatcher, "A Failure of Political Communication Not a Failure of Bureaucracy: The Danger of Presidential Misinformation During the COVID-19 Pandemic," *American Review of Public Administration* 50, nos. 6–7 (August–October 2020): 614–20, https://doi.org/10.1177/0275074020941734.
42 Erica Rayment and Jason VandenBeukel, "Pandemic Parliaments: Canadian Legislatures in a Time of Crisis," *Canadian Journal of Political Science* 53, no. 2 (2020): 379–84, https://doi.org/10.1017/S0008423920000499.
43 Mike Crawley, "As Question Period Resumes in Ontario, Will MPPs Do Politics Differently?," *CBC News*, May 12, 2020, https://www.cbc.ca/news/canada/toronto/covid19-ontario-question-period-legislature-1.5564559.
44 S. Michelle Driedger, Cynthia G. Jardine, Amanda D. Boyd, and Bhavnita Mistry, "Do the First 10 Days Equal a Year? Comparing Two Canadian Public Health Risk Events Using the National Media," *Health, Risk & Society* 11, no. 1 (February 1, 2009): 44, https://doi.org/10.1080/13698570802537011.
45 Aengus Bridgman, Eric Merkley, Peter John Loewen, Taylor Owen, Derek Ruths, Lisa Teichmann, and Oleg Zhilin, "The Causes and Consequences of COVID-19 Misperceptions: Understanding the Role of News and Social Media," *Harvard Kennedy School Misinformation Review* 1, no. 3 (June 2020), https://doi.org/10.37016/mr-2020-028.
46 Mike Crawley, "Why Doug Ford's Daily COVID-19 News Conferences Have Suddenly Stopped," *CBC News*, December 11, 2020, https://www.cbc.ca/news/canada/toronto/covid-19-ontario-doug-ford-daily-news-briefings-1.5835706.
47 Damian Guzek, Václav Štětka, and Sabina Mihelj, "'I Don't Vote Because I Don't Want to Get Infected': Pandemic, Polarization, and Public Trust during the 2020 Presidential Election in Poland," in *Political Communication in the Time of Coronavirus*, ed. Peter Van Aelst and Jay G. Blumler (New York: Routledge, 2021), 201.

48 Steve Paikin, "How This Era of No-Scrum Journalism Has Made Doug Ford One Lucky Premier," *TVO Today*, August 10, 2020, https://www.tvo.org/article/how-this-era-of-no-scrum-journalism-has-made-doug-ford-one-lucky-premier.
49 AlHadidi, "Scrum Undone," 18.
50 Laura H. Kahn, *Who's in Charge? Leadership during Epidemics, Bioterror Attacks, and Other Public Health Crises,* 2nd ed. (Santa Barbara, CA: Praeger Security International, 2020).
51 Tworek, Beacock, and Ojo, *Democratic Health Communications during Covid-19*.
52 Paikin, "Era of No-Scrum Journalism."
53 "COVID-19: Third Wave Drives Surge of Criticism for Kenney, Ford, and Other Premiers," Angus Reid Institute, April 9, 2021, https://angusreid.org/covid-restrictions-ford-kenney/.
54 Patrick Fafard, Lindsay A. Wilson, Adèle Cassola, and Steven J. Hoffman, "Communication about COVID-19 from Canadian Provincial Chief Medical Officers of Health: A Qualitative Study," *CMAJ Open* 8, no. 3 (2020): E560, https://doi.org/10.9778/cmajo.20200110.
55 Alex Marland and Jared Wesley, *The Public Servant's Guide to Government in Canada* (Toronto: University of Toronto Press, 2018), 22.
56 Newsroom Carleton, "Carleton Researchers Find Canadians Most Trust Public Health Officials on COVID-19," *Carleton Newsroom*, May 22, 2020, https://newsroom.carleton.ca/2020/carleton-researchers-find-canadians-most-trust-public-health-officials-on-covid-19/.
57 Angus Reid Institute, "COVID-19."
58 Liz Braun, "Dr. David Williams Urged by Some to Step Aside before Second Wave," *Toronto Sun*, July 22, 2020, https://torontosun.com/news/local-news/dr-david-williams-urged-by-some-to-step-aside-before-second-wave.
59 Margaret MacAulay, Anna K. Macintyre, Aryati Yashadhana, Adèle Cassola, Patrick Harris, Caroline Woodward, Katherine Smith, Evelyne de Leeuw, Michèle Palkovits, Steven J. Hoffman, and Patrick Fafard, "Under the Spotlight: Understanding the Role of the Chief Medical Officer in a Pandemic," *Journal of Epidemiology and Community Health* 76, no. 1 (January 2022): 100–4, https://doi.org/10.1136/jech-2021-216850.
60 Colin D'Mello, "'Protect the King': Why Ontario Premier Doug Ford Has Taken the Back Seat," *CTV News*, May 12, 2021, https://toronto.ctvnews.ca/protect-the-king-why-ontario-premier-doug-ford-has-taken-the-back-seat-1.5425619.
61 Catherine E. Slavik, Charlotte Buttle, Shelby L. Sturrock, J. Connor Darlington, and Niko Yiannakoulias, "Examining Tweet Content and Engagement of Canadian Public Health Agencies and Decision Makers during COVID-19: Mixed Methods Analysis," *Journal of Medical Internet Research* 23, no. 3 (March 2021): e24883, https://doi.org/10.2196/24883.
62 Darren Lilleker, Ioana Coman, Miloš Gregor, and Edoardo Novelli, "Governance and Rhetoric in Global Comparative Perspective," in Lilleker et al., *Political Communication and COVID-19*, 345.

Ontario's Political Parties and the Party System

Anna Lennox Esselment

INTRODUCTION

Ontario's party system has been characterized as durable and resilient.[1] For over seventy years, three parties – the Progressive Conservatives, the Liberals, and the New Democrats – have remained the dominant players competing for seats in the legislature. While smaller parties have come to the fore every now and then, grander notions of party system change in Ontario are rarely entertained by Canadian party scholars. Instead, the thrill incited by the rise and success of new or newly merged parties must be examined in other provincial settings, such as Alberta, Saskatchewan, and Quebec. Does this make Ontario party politics less exciting? Not at all. Durability and resiliency focuses scholarly attention on the *inter*party system dynamic.[2] Malloy noted that the sheer stability of Ontario's party system is a potential sign of staleness and atrophy.[3] Despite their mostly efficient ways of blocking new entrants to the system, Malloy suggests the main parties are out of ideas, lack innovative thinking, and are failing to engage with Ontarians. This is a serious charge, but if voter turnout in provincial elections is any indication – particularly the historic low engagement in the 2022 election – Malloy may well be right. But over the past twenty years, particularly over the last four, there have been interesting developments in how the province's parties, and its system, are managing tensions wrought by both inward and outward challenges. This chapter will examine the Ontario party system from 2003 to 2023. It takes an interparty system approach, whereby the fortunes of the three traditional parties are examined with regard to how the existing parties shift in terms of their electoral victories from one election to another, the dependability of their vote and legislative seat share, and how they have marginalized the attempts by new parties to penetrate the party system. Intriguing election results, particularly the election of an independent candidate in 2022, and the trend of continued disengagement by Ontario voters, will also be analyzed. The chapter concludes by suggesting that there has been a change to the provincial party system. The adjustment is one towards greater polarization, which makes the Ontario party system today align more closely with those usually found in Canada's western provinces.

THE ONTARIO PARTY SYSTEM: 2003–18

A common observation is that the party system in Ontario has mostly, and closely, mirrored the federal party system.[4] At both levels, the Liberal and Conservative parties tend to oscillate between governing and occupying the Opposition benches, leaving little room for any other party to take power. One measure of interparty system stability is the percentage of elections won.[5] When applied to the forty-three Ontario elections since 1867, the Progressive Conservative party has won twenty-five, or 58 per cent. The Liberal party has won sixteen, or 37 per cent of all elections held. Together this means that either the Progressive Conservative (PC) or Liberal parties have secured victory in 95 per cent of all provincial elections. The Progressive Conservative "dynasty" in Ontario lasted forty-two years (1943–85), giving that party a more deserving moniker of "natural governing party"; this same term is often used to describe the Liberal party at the federal level. Provincially the New Democratic Party (NDP) had a brief stint in power in the early 1990s, but otherwise has played the typical third party role noted by Canadian party system scholars.[6] Since the late 1960s, the NDP has regularly won enough seats in the legislature to have official party status and even on occasion holds the balance of power when the government is in a minority, but the party primarily aims to be an alternative choice for citizens who may tire of the "Tweedledum and Tweedledee" undulation of the Liberal and PC party options.[7] Also like the federal system, the Green Party has contested elections for several decades, but has only recently managed to win legislative seats at Queen's Park. Unlike the party systems of Saskatchewan, Alberta, and at the national level, Ontario has not experienced party mergers – the three main parties have simply been long-standing and singular stalwarts since the 1950s.

Not much has changed in the twenty-first century. The Ontario Liberal party, under the leadership of Dalton McGuinty, won a majority government in 2003 after the Progressive Conservatives, led by Mike Harris and Ernie Eves, respectively, had an eight-year stint in power. After the 2003 election, the Progressive Conservatives formed the official Opposition, and the New Democrats the third party with just seven members, one seat short of official party status. Official party status is important – at its core, it means the party receives funding from the Legislative Assembly of Ontario to assist with hiring political staff for support and research purposes and being allowed to ask regular questions of the government during question period. Party status was granted to the NDP in spring 2004, when the party won a by-election contest in Hamilton that raised their seat count to eight, and the party has since easily exceeded that number of elected members of provincial parliament (MPPs) in subsequent elections.

The Liberal reign continued through three ensuing elections: 2007, 2011, and 2014, resulting in fifteen years in power and no significant change to the party system. Voters delivered a minority legislature in the 2011 election which still favoured the Liberals, but within a year – and after a series of scandals, the most significant of which involved the cancellation of planned gas plants after residents protested their construction – Premier McGuinty announced his plan to resign. The cost of abandoning the contracts, combined with the fact that the ridings were Liberal-held and strategic to the party's electoral fortunes, infuriated the opposition parties and badly tainted McGuinty's premiership. The outgoing leader prorogued the legislature in October 2012 to give the Liberal Party time to mount a leadership race and find a successor.[8]

The outcome of the party leader contest in early 2013 put Kathleen Wynne in the premier's chair, the first woman and openly gay person in Ontario to hold that position. In the 2014 provincial election, she ran against PC leader Tim Hudak and NDP leader Andrea Horwath and secured a majority government for the Liberals with the first election of a female premier in the province. As before, the durability and familiarity of the provincial party system remained unchanged, with the PCs sitting opposite the government and the NDP taking on the third-party role.

By the time the 2018 election approached, it was clear that Ontario voters were looking for change. Abacus Data polling found 63 per cent of voters "definitely wanting a change of government" in the week before the 2018 election.[9] Wynne in particular was unpopular – she had manoeuvred the party away from its usual centrist position on the political spectrum to a spot much further to the left. Popular initiatives such as permitting beer and wine sales in grocery stores and piloting a guaranteed basic income experiment grated against other decisions, such as the privatization of Hydro One, an updated sex education curriculum in public schools (incorporating the teaching of gender identities which was particularly ill-received by more conservative-minded parents),[10] and an elevated minimum wage that angered small businesses. Heading into the campaign, negative impressions of Kathleen Wynne were particularly high, and the Liberal leader never recovered.[11]

2018 ELECTION OUTCOME AND INTERPARTY SYSTEM CHANGE?

The results of the 2018 election shook up Ontario's internal party system. There was a turnover in the governing party from Liberal to Progressive Conservative, a predictable outcome when we consider almost all previous electoral results in Ontario's party history. In fact, the sheer durability of the revolving door between Liberal and PC transitions into power is reinforced when we consider the tumultuous events the PC party faced in the five months *before* the election: sexual misconduct allegations lost the party its leader, Patrick Brown; a leadership race ensued which installed a new leader, Doug Ford, who just barely beat out the second-placed candidate; the previously publicly released party platform was jettisoned, and so Ford campaigned with few policy positions for voters to consider. Against many odds, the party still managed to elect the most MPPs. The feat was a testament to the resiliency of an entrenched party system in which voters were used to electing a legislature that either favoured the PCs or the Liberals as the governing party at the expense of other possibilities.[12] In spite of this dependable outcome, there are three adjustments wrought by the 2018 campaign that are worthy of note.

First was the elevation of the NDP from third party to official Opposition, an accomplishment that has happened only three times in Ontario's history, and not since the 1987 election.[13] The party's federal counterparts experienced something similar after the "Orange Wave" – led by NDP leader

Jack Layton – vaulted the NDP from fourth party to official Opposition in the House of Commons. In 2018, the provincial NDP won nineteen more seats than in the previous election, which gave them a healthy forty MPPs to keep the governing PCs accountable. Like their federal cousins, the hope was that a strong opposition role would better position the party to win power next time around; a larger share of media attention alone would increase the number of Ontarians familiar with the leader and the party, and could potentially expand their support in the province. By squeezing out the Liberals, the Ontario party system also became slightly more polarized than before; similarities with western provincial party systems, where competition is often between a party on the left and a party on the right, were evident.[14]

A second adjustment was the election of Green Party leader and candidate Mike Schreiner in the riding of Guelph. The Green Party of Ontario (GPO) first contested a provincial election in 1985. Throughout the 1980s and 1990s, the party struggled to gain traction with voters, never winning over 1 per cent of the popular vote, and thus posing no threat to the established party system. More Ontarians supported the party after the turn of the millennium, with a popular vote rising to 8 per cent in the 2007 provincial election,[15] but a lack of deep support in any particular riding made electing even a single MPP elusive. The GPO continued to run almost a full slate of candidates in each Ontario election, buoyed in part by legislative seat wins in other provinces and at the national level.

In 2009 Mike Schreiner was elected leader of the GPO; he had stood as a candidate for the Greens in three previous provincial elections (a by-election in Haliburton-Kawartha Lakes-Brock in 2009, Simcoe-Grey in 2011, and then Guelph in 2014) and had lost them all. But there was something unique about the voters in Guelph. In the 2014 election, Schreiner came third with 19 per cent of the popular vote, only 2 per cent behind the second-place PC candidate. No GPO candidate had ever won such a large popular vote share. For the first time, electing a Green Party candidate to Queen's Park became a real possibility. In the 2018 contest, a confluence of factors worked in Schreiner's favour. First, the party poured their resources into the riding,[16] concentrating on it alone as the best chance for electoral success. Second, popular Liberal incumbent Liz Sandals chose not to run for re-election, and no party candidates from 2014 were trying their luck again – name recognition was thus favourable for Schreiner, the only one on the ballot who had previously run in the riding. Third, the Liberals faced an uphill battle to retain many of their seats. The electorate had had enough of Liberal rule; the desire for change was palpable in the polls. Finally, PC leader Doug Ford was a questionable commodity that left a number of Conservative voters casting about for another option. In Guelph, the Green Party became that option. Schreiner was not the typical Green Party candidate that most voters may conjure up in their minds – the tree-hugging, sandal-wearing, save-the-whales type. While Schreiner certainly embraced the core of Green Party values, he was also the owner of several small businesses, and this offered him some credibility among disaffected Liberals and Conservatives. NDP supporters were also open to a candidate who shared many of their values but happened to run under a different party label. In 2018, voters in Guelph took that chance and Mike Schreiner won 45 per cent of the popular vote, a decisive victory that sent him to Queen's Park. While bereft of caucus colleagues, it is significant that, since 1951, Schreiner became the first MPP to win a seat for a party *other* than the three stalwarts. While parties without official party status have far less influence in the provincial legislature as compared to their official party status colleagues, the voters in Guelph have been pleased with their non-traditional party representative. In the 2022 election, Mike Schreiner was returned to the legislature with an even bigger share of the vote.

Schreiner's back-to-back successes in Guelph could be a precursor to the rise of a fourth party in Ontario's system. Even if winning government themselves is elusive, the Greens can aspire to what Giovanni Sartori describes as coalition or blackmail potential for governing parties[17] – holding just enough seats to bargain for concessions. But based on an analysis of provincial election results since 2003, and aside from Schreiner's two wins, the Greens have struggled to move from strength to strength. On average, popular support for the Green Party has been 4.8 per cent. In the first-past-the-post electoral system, the party's vote is not "efficient," which means that in all ridings (excepting Guelph in 2018 and 2022) the party is unable to mobilize deep enough support to win a plurality of ballots cast in any given riding. In other words, there are voters in all ridings who will vote for the Green Party, but not enough Green supporters live in any particular riding in which the party can concentrate. Moreover, studies of partisan identification suggest that the traditional parties have thoroughly penetrated the electorate, which makes it much harder for new parties to emerge and compete with existing parties.[18] There has, however, been a further glimmer of hope for the Green Party. In a 2023 provincial by-election in Kitchener Centre, Green Party candidate Aislinn Clancy was victorious, finishing first among a field of eighteen candidates vying for the seat; Clancy joined Mike Schreiner as the second Green Party MPP at Queen's Park. Notably, Kitchener Centre also has a Green Party MP, making it the first riding in Ontario history to have Green Party representatives in both the federal and provincial legislatures. While the Greens have certainly made gains, becoming a fourth party – or moving the provincial party system from a two and a half to a truly multi-party system – will remain elusive for the foreseeable future.

The most exceptional modification wrought by the 2018 campaign was the sheer devastation of the Ontario Liberal Party. The party had reigned over the province for fifteen years, winning four consecutive elections. From fifty-eight seats in the 2014 election, the collapse four years later left the Liberals with a rump of just seven seats, its worst result in the party's history. Kathleen Wynne hung on to her seat in the riding of Don Valley West, but other long-standing MPPs went down to defeat, including Jim Bradley in St. Catharines who was first elected in 1977 and was the longest-serving MPP at Queen's Park. Even worse for the Liberals was the fact that they had lost official party status. Used to cadres of political staff to help them with research, administrative, and constituency support, the remaining members of the Liberal caucus were mostly left on their own to figure out how best to represent and serve their constituents. The party requested changes to legislative standing orders that would recognize seven seats as enough for party status (instead of eight), but the government refused and, just several months later, raised the bar even higher, requiring twelve seats (or 10 per cent of the Ontario legislature) before a party would be officially recognized.[19] The Liberals soon became resigned to their fate, appointed an interim leader, and made plans for a comeback.

THE 2022 ELECTION: NEW COVID-19 PARTIES AND THE SURPRISE RISE OF AN INDEPENDENT

The advent of a deadly virus circulating the globe was unpredictable, and the PC government had two years in power before its attention focused almost singularly on combatting the threat this posed to public health. Over the last two years of its mandate, Premier Doug Ford and his cabinet alternated between implementing and lifting various restrictions intended to safeguard both the health of Ontarians and the capacity of provincial hospitals to handle an influx of COVID-19 patients who required medical care. While most Ontarians complied with lockdowns, shutdowns, and vaccine mandates, by the time the 2022 election approached a number of Ontarians were challenging the government and other institutions on the need for any further measures. The Ford government had dropped most of its pandemic-related directives before the writs were drawn up, including the provincial mask mandate. In spite of this, fallout from the previous two years had motivated a newer party and sparked the creation of another one to contest the 2022 election.

The Ontario Party and New Blue Party as Pandemic-Related Challengers

While the Green Party has participated in Ontario elections for decades, two newer parties ran province-wide campaigns in 2022, although neither appear to pose a serious threat to the durability of the existing party system. Both have roots in the effects of the COVID-19 pandemic, but in different ways. Their commonalities are establishment by disaffected Conservative members and the underlying motivation to capitalize on voter anger about the various measures implemented by government – such as business and school closures, lockdowns, and vaccine mandates – to contain the virus.

The Ontario Party was founded in May 2018. It rose out of an earlier Ontario Alliance Party created by former members of the Progressive Conservative party members who were unhappy with then PC leader Patrick Brown. Further dissatisfaction *within* the Ontario Alliance then led to the creation of the Ontario Party. The Ontario Party – described as socially and fiscally conservative with a large dose of right-wing populism – managed to field five candidates in the June 2018 provincial election. Not surprisingly, the popular vote share result was less than 1 per cent. A few years later, the Ontario Party received an injection of attention when, in late 2021, former MP Derek Sloan took over as leader of the party. Sloan represented the federal riding of Hastings-Lennox and Addington from 2019 to 2021, but was expelled from the Conservative caucus in 2021 for accepting a donation from someone linked to white supremacist groups.[20] In the subsequent federal election, Sloan ran unsuccessfully as an independent candidate in the Alberta riding of Banff-Airdrie. In the lead up to that election, Sloan became known for his anti-lockdown and anti-vaccine views. He spoke at demonstrations and railed against the restrictive government measures being imposed on Canadians. At the helm of the Ontario Party, Sloan had a vehicle through which he could connect with Ontarians who felt similarly. The election platform was replete with references to freedom, especially religious freedom and the freedom of expression for those who hold a conservative worldview.[21] Other right-wing policies, such as teaching children that there are only two genders, removing "radical curricula" from the education system, and ending "climate alarmism," were also part of the party's proposals. There was certainly reason to expect an appetite for the Ontario Party's populist, anti-government rhetoric. Many Canadians do hold populist attitudes, and in the 2021 federal election, the People's Party of Canada secured 5.5 per cent of the popular vote in Ontario, although this did not translate to winning any seats.[22] More hopeful for the Ontario Party was that it had a representative at Queen's Park. MPP Rick Nicholls, who represented the riding of Chatham-Kent–Leamington, was ousted from the PC caucus by Premier Doug Ford in summer 2021 for refusing to be vaccinated against COVID-19. After sitting as an independent for a few months, Nicholls joined the Ontario Party and became its sole MPP in the legislature. With Nicholls having represented his riding for ten years, the Ontario Party was optimistic that the conservative-leaning riding would remain faithful to a well-known name.

The Ontario Party ran 105 candidates in the 2022 spring election, but struggled to gain real traction. Nicholls, the party's sole MPP, was soundly defeated by his PC opponent,[23] and no other Ontario Party candidate was elected. Popular vote share was just 1.8 per cent, but this was an increase of 1.7 per cent over 2018. What's more, the party attracted over 84,000 votes, a big swing upwards from the 2,316 votes won in 2018. Derek Sloan announced that he would stay on as leader and continue to build the party.

The New Blue is the second party that emerged from unrest and anger regarding pandemic governance. Cambridge PC MPP Belinda Karahalios was, like Rick Nicholls, kicked out of the Progressive Conservative caucus; in July 2020, she was removed for refusing to support a government bill that, in her view, gave the premier and cabinet too much power.[24] Six months later, Karahalios' husband, Jim, founded the New Blue Party. He took on the role of president, and Belinda Karahalios joined and served as its only MPP at Queen's Park. With shades of the Ontario Party's positions, New Blue Party policies also had an aversion to education about different gender identities and the use of critical race theory, but had far less religiosity woven into its core principles. The main motivation of the party was to oppose and end all lockdown and vaccine-related mandates related to the pandemic, but other key issues included ending taxpayer subsidies to political parties, "defunding" the establishment media, growing the economy by reducing electricity prices as associated with wind turbines, and reducing the harmonized sales tax (HST) from 13 per cent to 10 per cent.[25] Unlike the Ontario Party, this was

New Blue's first electoral contest and it did comparatively well. In the span of just sixteen months, the New Blue Party had 123 candidates in place to contest the provincial election.[26] The party's best chance was in Cambridge, where Belinda Karahalios had held the seat since 2018, and arguably had strong name recognition. Her fate, however, took a similar trajectory as her former PC colleague Rick Nicholls. She came in fourth, well behind the PC candidate who won the riding with 37 per cent of the popular vote. But having earned 11 per cent of the popular vote, Karahalios did better than any of the other New Blue Party candidates, including her husband Jim, who secured just under 6 per cent in the riding of Kitchener-Centre. Overall, the party amassed over 127,000 votes, or 2.7 per cent of the popular vote in its first election. To put this in perspective, the Green Party first earned 2.8 per cent of the popular vote at its *sixth* provincial election in 2003.

These two "pandemic" parties, along with the Greens, posed the broadest challenge to Ontario's entrenched party system. Their long-term threat to the system's composition, however, is limited. With no elected candidates and a smaller vote share, the two newest parties must, like the Greens, also contend with an inefficient spread of voter support. Moreover, the disaffection felt by these 211,000 Ontarians who supported either the Ontario or New Blue parties may dissipate as pandemic measures continue to ease up or are abandoned altogether and some degree of normality resumes with regard to everyday life. Finally, the expectation is that the Progressive Conservative party will seek to either regain or win over voters who may have voted for these new, right-wing parties. Public opinion research suggests that voters who were most likely to vote for New Blue had no political affiliation or were voters who liked Doug Ford but did not identify as Progressive Conservative.[27] Co-opting those voters, and squeezing out these new challengers, is what the traditional parties in the Ontario party system do best, and we should not expect the fortunes of either the Ontario or the New Blue parties to rise.

Independent Candidates and the Curious Case of Haldimand-Norfolk

Another unexpected turn in the 2022 election was the election of an independent candidate in the riding of Haldimand-Norfolk. In electoral systems that use plurality voting such as Ontario's first-past-the-post system, success as an independent candidate is rare. Five such independents have been elected to the House of Commons in the twenty-first century.[28]

But provincially? The last independent candidate who ran and won in Ontario was Peter North in 1995; before that, it was in 1934.[29] Since North's 1995 victory, no independent candidate seeking election has won office, although each contest brings out numerous hopefuls. Incumbency is an advantage here, as is name recognition. Often, these two go hand in hand, but the latter is likely to be particularly helpful.

Neither of these two conditions were applicable in Haldimand-Norfolk, a riding nestled in rural Southwestern Ontario. Until 1995, voters in Haldimand-Norfolk had elected MPPs from all three parties.[30] Progressive Conservatives reigned during the better part of the PC dynasty years, but ended early with the election of Liberal candidate Gord Miller in 1975, who served as the riding's MPP until the NDP victory in 1990. Norm Miller was the NDP MPP for the duration of Bob Rae's government, but lost to Toby Barrett during the Common Sense Revolution sweep under Mike Harris. Toby Barrett, a farmer and former teacher, served from 1995 until the 2022 campaign, putting in twenty-seven years as the stalwart member from the rural riding. But leading up to the 2022 election, Barrett indicated he would not be seeking re-election, opting for retirement instead.

Barrett's long time executive assistant and president of the PC riding association, Bobbi Ann Brady, had planned on entering the party's local nomination contest, but instead Premier Doug Ford used his powers of appointment to select Haldimand mayor Ken Hewitt as the new PC candidate.[31] The appointment did not go over well with Conservative supporters in the riding, but Ford was banking on a PC win regardless of having bypassed a nomination race – as a safe PC riding for almost three decades, there was little reason to think otherwise. Moreover, Toby Barrett had been a strong supporter of the premier's; he was one of just two elected MPPs who supported Ford during the tumultuous leadership race in 2018.[32] But the party underestimated the reaction of the voters in the constituency. Perhaps one reason was the use of the appointment power in the first place. The Samara Centre for Democracy has aptly captured the democratic challenges posed by a leader's power of appointment, and in small towns across a rural riding, the act of appointment can invoke a certain amount of bristling.[33] Second, Ken Hewitt was a suspicious choice for Conservative supporters. Fifteen years earlier, Hewitt had run and lost in a nomination race to be the riding's federal Liberal candidate.[34] His "Liberal" background, lack of a PC party membership in the riding, and his refusal to show up at any all-candidates debates during the election did not bode well for what was expected as an easy win for the provincial party.

Third, the fact that outgoing MPP Toby Barrett called Hewitt his "archrival" did little to help the new candidate with inroads to potential supporters.[35] As a consequence, Barrett's long-time assistant, Brady, announced that she would run as an independent, adding the coup de grâce that Barrett would serve as her campaign manager.[36] Between the two of them, they had run the PC Party Association for almost thirty years. They knew every PC supporter, volunteer, donor, and lawn-sign taker that lived within the riding's 3,000 square kilometres. By the time the ballots were counted, Brady managed a feat only two other independent candidates had achieved in the past eighty-eight years – she won the election, and was the first female candidate in Ontario to do so. With 35 per cent of the popular vote, Brady beat out eight other candidates on the ballot. Overall, almost 75 per cent of voters who cast ballots in the riding of Haldimand Norfolk supported right of centre parties, and the independent candidate on the ballot was the victor.

ONTARIO PARTIES AND VOTER TURNOUT

To this point, the durability and resiliency of Ontario's party system is clear. We are reminded of Malloy's assertion that staleness and atrophy can be the result of a party system so engrained that it can resist almost any incursions by other parties.[37] Staleness refers to parties with fewer innovative ideas that galvanize and mobilize voters, particularly beyond just a four-year mandate; atrophy refers to progressive decline due to "underuse or neglect." Arguably, voter turnout could be a proxy for both. Despite a penetration by the traditional parties into the electorate, average turnout over the past six elections has been just 51.7 per cent. Put another way, only one in two eligible voters manages (or bothers) to cast a ballot. Turnout is highest when voters are antsy and change is afoot – 57 per cent in 2003 when Ontarians rejected the Mike Harris/Ernie Eves PC government and ushered in the era of Liberal rule. Likewise, 2018 turnout was 58 per cent when the Liberals were soundly defeated by Doug Ford's Progressive Conservatives. In between – the elections of 2007, 2011, and 2014 – the highest turnout was 52.8 per cent and the lowest was 48 per cent.

But 2022 was historic in the numbers of voters who simply chose to stay home. Despite the pandemic and all that it wrought, the offer of two new parties, a new (if uninspiring) Liberal leader Steven Del Dulca, and the need for a post-COVID-19 plan for the province, only 43 per cent of eligible voters participated in the most sacred of democratic practices. Is this the result of diminished confidence in Ontario's political parties? Of the mind-numbing repetitiveness presented by the province's party system? Criticism varies.

Some observers lashed out at Ontarians themselves, irked by the fact that citizens do not automatically feel a deep sense of duty to their country and the democratic system afforded them – this alone should result in a high level of turnout. Others blamed the parties, whose key role in a liberal democracy is to inspire and mobilize voters; they are supposed to offer a vision that can resonate and set out choices.[38] Still others point out that low voter turnout can also signal satisfaction with the current government.[39]

All these criticisms have merit. A sense of duty (particularly when coupled with an interest in politics) is key to turnout.[40] But citizens share this civic mindedness unevenly, with just half of voters feeling a strong duty to vote.[41] In the case of the 2022 Ontario election, not even the half with a sense of civic responsibility were motivated to vote! So, what other explanations are there? Pandemic fear and fatigue is certainly plausible, and lower voter turnout during the pandemic was the norm in other provincial and territorial elections too, such as British Columbia, Saskatchewan, Newfoundland and Labrador, and Yukon. Only Nova Scotia has done marginally better with turnout than in the previous non-Covid election, and that was only by a 1 per cent margin. But even where turnout declined in the other provinces, none reached the depths of the Ontario case. Perhaps an underlying current here could be the political divisions wrought within families themselves because of pandemic-related measures that meant choices and consequences. According to reports, families in Canada in the wake of the pandemic had never been so divided.[42] Fractures and tensions among family members meant careful navigation of relationships, some of which may never recover because of diverging views on vaccine mandates and what constitutes safe socializing. Parents have children who are not speaking with one another, relatives may be refusing to issue social invites to non-vaccinated family members, young children kept out of sports or other extracurricular activities because they are not vaccinated while their cousins carry on with their league sports games because they have been. Shrinking from the ballot box may be the only way some citizens feel they can cope with their own family dynamics. If true, this behaviour, however well-intentioned and personally focused, is detrimental to our democracy where participation is key and, pandemic aside, where abysmal voter turnout rates are not isolated to the 2022 election. Low voter turnout is becoming the norm in Ontario electoral contests, not the exception.

CONCLUSION: POLARIZATION AS INTERPARTY SYSTEM CHANGE IN ONTARIO

The main characteristics of durability and resiliency of Ontario's party system are still applicable. No party aside from the Liberals or the PCs have governed the province since 1923, and the role of the official Opposition has also stayed within the traditional three parties. The Liberals, PCs, and NDP attract the popular support of most citizens casting a ballot, which has meant the party system continues to keep minor parties at bay, although the success of the Green Party in Guelph and Kitchener Centre, and the independent candidate elected in Haldimand Norfolk, is evidence that Ontario voters can be open to other choices.

When the previous edition of this collection was published, Malloy asserted, "there was little prospect for change on the horizon."[43] Based on recent history, this position can now be questioned. The continued polarization of the party system since 2018 is perhaps the most observable change over the past two elections. The Ontario Liberal Party was unable to mount a persuasive campaign in the 2022 election and the party's seat count in that election increased by just one. At eight seats, the Liberal party remains a shadow of its former self and faces another four years at Queen's Park with no party status.[44] And while the NDP lost seats as well, the party is firmly ensconced as the official Opposition and will continue to garner more earned media as it fulfills that role. The party system has thus embraced a degree of divergence rarely seen before; a party on the right confronts a party on the left, and the usual pull to a more centrist position that is often the result of the interplay between the PCs and the Liberals is, for now, suspended. In some respects, the 2018 election reminds us of what V.O. Key called a "critical election,"[45] where an obvious electoral realignment occurs; that realignment appears to have some durability when we consider that the 2022 contest appears to have reinforced a shift in the provincial party system. Whether this modification characterizes a new era of party politics in Ontario remains to be seen, but it is clear these party system changes have been the most significant in a long time.

DISCUSSION QUESTIONS

1 Is the result of the 2022 Ontario provincial election a reflection of a growing polarized electorate?

2 Are there benefits to electing independent candidates? If so, what are they?
3 What do you think is the most compelling reason for dismal voter turnout in the 2022 provincial election? What can we do about it?
4 New parties have a hard time breaking into the province's party system. Will either the New Blue Party or the Ontario Party be able to elect MPPs in the next election? Why or why not?
5 Do you agree that achieving official party status should be set at 10 per cent of the seats in the legislature? If not, should that bar be higher or lower? Why?

NOTES

1 For an excellent and thorough review of the history of the Ontario party system please see Jonathan Malloy, "Political Parties and the Party System in Ontario," in *The Politics of Ontario*, 1st ed., ed. Cheryl N. Collier and Jonathan Malloy (Toronto: University of Toronto Press, 2017), 192–208.
2 David G. Pfeiffer, "The Measurement of Inter-Party Competition and Systemic Stability," *The American Political Science Review* 61, no. 2 (June 1967): 457–67, https://doi.org/10.2307/1953257.
3 Malloy, "Political Parties," 193.
4 Malloy, "Political Parties," 200; Anna Lennox Esselment, "Fighting Elections: Cross-Level Political Party Integration in Ontario," *Canadian Journal of Political Science* 43, no. 4 (December 2010): 871–92, https://doi.org/10.1017/S0008423910000727.
5 Pfeiffer, "The Measurement of Inter-Party Competition," 457.
6 See R.K. Carty and David Stewart, "Parties and Party Systems," in *Provinces: Canadian Provincial Politics*, ed. Christopher Dunn (Peterborough: Broadview Press), 63–94. For other party system categorizations, see Jean Blondel, "Party Systems and Patterns of Government in Western Democracies," *Canadian Journal of Political Science* 1, no. 2 (June 1968): 180–203, https://doi.org/10.1017/S0008423900036507, and Giovanni Sartori, *Parties and Party Systems: A Framework for Analysis*, vol. 1 (Cambridge: Cambridge University Press, 1976).
7 Dean E. McHenry, "The Impact of the CCF on Canadian Parties and Groups," *The Journal of Politics* 11, no. 2 (May 1949): 365–95, https://doi.org/10.2307/2126282; Nelson Wiseman, "Get Out the Vote-Not: Increasing Effort, Declining Turnout," *Policy Options* 27, no. 2 (2006): 18.
8 CBC News, "Ontario's McGuinty Surprises with Resignation, Prorogation," *CBC News*, posted October 15, 2012, last updated October 16, 2012, https://www.cbc.ca/news/canada/toronto/ontario-s-mcguinty-surprises-with-resignation-prorogation-1.1156014.

9   David Coletto, "Ontario PCs Lead by 13 as They Head Towards Another Majority Government," Abacus Data, June 1, 2022, https://abacusdata.ca/june-1-final-ontario-poll-abacus-data/.
10 The Canadian Press, "Kathleen Wynne Defends Revised Sex Ed Curriculum," *Maclean's*, February 24, 2015, archived April 18, 2023, at the Wayback Machine archive, https://web.archive.org/web/20230418004436/https://www.macleans.ca/news/canada/kathleen-wynne-defends-revised-sex-ed-curriculum/.
11 Joe Castaldo, "Why Kathleen Wynne Is Still So Unpopular," *Maclean's*, March 12, 2018, https://www.macleans.ca/politics/why-kathleen-wynne-is-still-so-unpopular/.
12 Jared J. Wesley and Clare Buckley, "Canadian Provincial Party Systems: An Analytical Typology," *American Review of Canadian Studies* 51, no. 2 (April 2021): 213–36, https://doi.org/10.1080/02722011.2021.1923249.
13 The NDP served as the official Opposition in the 30th Legislative Assembly, from 1975 to 1977 and again in the 34th from 1987 to 1990. They also filled the role from 1943 to 1945.
14 Wesley and Buckley, "Canadian Provincial Party Systems."
15 "Data Explorer, 2007–2010, The Green Party of Ontario, 2007 General Election," Elections Ontario, October 10, 2007, https://results.elections.on.ca/en/data-explorer?fromYear=2007&toYear=2007&partyNames=The%20Green%20Party%20of%20Ontario&electionId=319&levelOfDetail=party.
16 Rob Ferguson, "With a Toehold in the Legislature, Ontario's Green Party Looks to Grow," *Toronto Star*, July 4, 2018, https://www.thestar.com/politics/provincial/with-a-toehold-in-the-legislature-ontario-s-green-party-looks-to-grow/article_1cc58914-91a9-5324-8984-97fbd99933f9.html.
17 Giovanni Sartori, *Parties and Party Systems: A Framework for Analysis* (Cambridge: Cambridge University Press, 1976).
18 Alan Ware, *Political Parties and Party Systems* (Oxford: Oxford University Press, 1996).
19 Paola Loriggio, "Ontario Government to Raise Threshold for Official Party Status," *CTV News*, November 13, 2018, https://www.ctvnews.ca/politics/ontario-government-to-raise-threshold-for-official-party-status-1.4175699.
20 Ryan Patrick Jones, "O'Toole Says He Wants to Eject Derek Sloan from Caucus after Donation from White Nationalist," *CBC News*, January 18, 2021, https://www.cbc.ca/news/politics/white-nationalist-donation-derek-sloan-1.5878070.
21 "The Ontario Party Platform," Ontario Party, accessed July 15, 2022, archived August 9, 2022, at the Wayback Machine archive, https://web.archive.org/web/20220809152654/https://www.ontarioparty.ca/our_platform_en.
22 The People's Party of Canada ran candidates in the 2019 election and the 2021 election. While unsuccessful at winning a seat, the popular vote increased by 3.3 per cent between 2019 (1.6 per cent) and 2021 (4.9 per cent), which observers have attributed to anger at pandemic measures. Elections Canada, https://www.elections.ca/res/rep/off/ovr2021app/home.html.
23 As the PC candidate in 2018, Rick Nicholls won 51.9 per cent of popular support in his electoral district. As the Ontario Party candidate in 2022, he won just 14.8 per cent. The PC candidate in 2022 garnered 47.6 per cent.

24 The Canadian Press, "Ousted Tory Legislator Says New Law Gives Ford too Much Power," *CityNews*, July 22, 2020, https://toronto.citynews.ca/2020/07/22/ford-defends-controversial-emergency-order-law-despite-legislators-removal-from-caucus/.

25 While not specified in the platform, the assumption is that the reduction in the HST would be on the provincial portion of the HST, shrinking the Ontario tax charged from 8 per cent to 5 per cent. See "The New Blueprint," New Blue Party of Ontario, https://www.newblueontario.com/new-blue-print.

26 The Ontario Liberal party had 122, one less than New Blue.

27 "Who Votes New Blue?," Innovative Research Group, May 30, 2022, https://innovativeresearch.ca/who-votes-new-blue/.

28 Government of Canada, House of Commons, "Appendix 10: General Elections Since 1867," in *House of Commons Procedure and Practice*, 3rd ed., ed. Marc Bosc and André Gagnon (Ottawa: Parliament of Canada, 2017), https://www.ourcommons.ca/procedure/procedure-and-practice-3/App10-e.html.

29 See Sidney Noel, *Revolution at Queen's Park: Essays on Governing Ontario* (Toronto: James Lorimer, 1997), https://books.google.com/books?id=Tqduql80FrkC.

30 The riding was called Haldimand-Norfolk-Brant until boundary changes in 2007 meant a renaming to simply Haldimand-Norfolk.

31 Monte Sonnenberg, "PCs Substitute Hewitt for Barrett in Haldimand Norfolk," *Norfolk & Tillsonburg News*, April 20, 2022, https://www.norfolkandtillsonburgnews.com/news/local-news/pcs-substitute-hewitt-for-barrett-in-haldimand-norfolk-3.

32 Tamara Botting and Shawn Smith, "Barrett Returns to Queen's Park as Part of Ford Nation," *Hamilton Spectator*, June 8, 2018, https://www.thespec.com/politics/provincial-elections/barrett-returns-to-queens-park-as-part-of-ford-nation/article_807a99c1-fe52-5153-9a1c-8f6cac2777db.html.

33 Haldimand Press Letter to the Editor, "On Ken Hewitt's Appointment as Haldimand-Norfolk's PC Candidate," *Haldimand Press*, May 12, 2022, https://haldimandpress.com/letter-to-the-editor-on-ken-hewitts-appointment-as-haldimand-norfolks-pc-candidate/.

34 Vincent Ball, "Brady Enters Provincial Election Race," *Simcoe Reformer*, April 27, 2022, https://www.simcoereformer.ca/news/local-news/brady-enters-provincial-race.

35 Tamara Botting, "I'm Disappointed That One of My Arch Rivals Has Just Announced He's Substituting My Place," *Hamilton Spectator*, April 20, 2022, https://www.thespec.com/politics/provincial-elections/we-defied-the-odds-how-bobbi-ann-brady-shocked-the-conservative-party-to-win-haldimand/article_a163d0f0-975c-5419-b0a0-55307adeba35.html.

36 J.P. Antonacci, "'We Defied the Odds': How Bobbi Ann Brady Shocked the Conservative Party to Win Haldimand-Norfolk," *Hamilton Spectator*, June 4, 2022, https://www.thespec.com/politics/provincial-elections/we-defied-the-odds-how-bobbi-ann-brady-shocked-the-conservative-party-to-win-haldimand/article_a163d0f0-975c-5419-b0a0-55307adeba35.html.

37 Malloy, "Political Parties," 206.

38 Toronto Star Editorial Board, "Parties Share a Lot of the Blame for Record Low Turnout in Ontario," *Toronto Star*, June 3, 2022, https://www.thestar.com/opinion

/editorials/parties-share-a-lot-of-the-blame-for-record-low-turnout-in-ontario/article_89b1461e-6154-589f-b8e6-04a318b2ebf3.html.
39 Jill Mahoney and Oliver Moore, "Ontario's Record Low Voter Turnout 'Not a Good Sign for Our Democracy', Political Observers Say," *Globe and Mail*, June 3, 2022, https://www.theglobeandmail.com/politics/article-ontario-election-results-voter-turnout/.
40 André Blais and Jean-François Daoust, *The Motivation to Vote: Explaining Electoral Participation* (Vancouver: UBC Press, 2020).
41 Blais and Daoust, *The Motivation to Vote*.
42 Zosia Bielski, "Families Face Off Over Covid-19 Vaccination Status Amid Hopes of a More Social Summer," *Globe and Mail*, June 14, 2021, https://www.theglobeandmail.com/canada/article-families-face-off-over-covid-19-vaccination-status-amid-hopes-of-a/.
43 Malloy, "Political Parties."
44 Worthy of note is that the Liberal party won 5,038 *more* votes than the NDP, giving them a fractionally higher popular vote, but only one more seat in the legislature. This uneven distribution of voter support was punished by the province's single member plurality electoral system.
45 V.O. Key Jr., "A Theory of Critical Elections," *Journal of Politics* 17, no. 1 (February 1955): 3–18, https://doi.org/10.2307/2126401.

10

Progress Stalled ... Again: Women, Gender, and Party Politics in Ontario

Cheryl N. Collier

The day before International Women's Day in 2020, Patty Coates, president of the Ontario Federation of Labour, wrote an op-ed published in the *Hamilton Spectator* calling on women in the province to rise up against the Doug Ford Progressive Conservative government in the lead up to the 2022 election claiming that, "if you're a woman in Ontario, the PC party is not looking out for you."[1] Citing recent cuts to rape crisis centres, the elimination of the free-standing ministry responsible for the status of women created by the Wynne government, and Bill 124's freeze on public-sector wage increases which disproportionately impacted women workers in the province, Coates warned that "the mobilizing ha[d] already begun" and that "the power of many women voting will defeat [the sitting PC government]."[2] Yet even though the 2022 provincial election showed a strong gender gap with women voters being less likely to prefer the incumbent Progressive Conservatives than male voters, women still preferred the PCs above the NDP and Liberals. Although, if only women voted, the PCs likely would have ended up with a minority government.[3] Instead, this slight edge in support amongst women-identified voters eventually helped the PCs win a second mandate with a stronger share of the seats in the legislature than when they were first elected in 2018.

This result isn't entirely surprising. After achieving some significant gains in both numeric and substantive representation up to 2018, women in the province saw some cuts and rollbacks to key programs alongside some numeric gains and then a stall, as well as some regressions in representational growth. However, the impact of these substantive losses and the overall stall in women's progress towards greater numeric equality in the province was only just beginning to impact the incumbent party's fortunes with women voters as the election neared. This, combined with weaknesses in both opposition parties, meant that it was unlikely a change in government was forthcoming in 2022. Yet, when we compare the state of women, gender, and politics in Canada's most populous province to that under previous regimes, important distinctions in the openness of different Ontario parties in their commitment levels to gender issues are apparent. If these trends continue as expected, the Ford Progressive Conservative government will have a much harder time securing a third mandate in 2026, as the gender gap will grow even deeper with the passage of time.

This chapter will explore these themes and evaluate significant changes and continuities regarding women, gender, and politics in Ontario from the 2000s to the present day. I focus on tracking the numeric (or descriptive) representation of women in elected and appointed political office alongside a consideration of more substantive forms of representation demonstrated through public policy results. Additionally, I apply an intersectional lens to this analysis, noting that women are not monolithic as a group, but differ alongside many axes, including race, ethnicity, class, sexuality, age, etc. As Brenda O'Neill noted in 2006, there are an unlimited amount of ways in which one can compare and assess the state of women between (or within) the provinces.[4] This is compounded by the fact that there are no specific policies that we can tag as specifically "women's policies" or "women's issues" as "few policy areas [if any] do not have gendered effects."[5] However, the link between women's numeric presence in politics and their ability to influence attention to gender equality issues remains persuasive and deserves continued attention, particularly as women struggle towards the ever-elusive goal of gender parity in most representational arenas. I pay particular attention to women's substantive representation through gender equality policy in the areas of pay equity, child care, and violence against women.

ANALYTICAL APPROACH

Celis and Childs remind us of the dominance of research on women's substantive and descriptive/numeric representation inside gender and politics research internationally. The case for increasing the numbers of women in elected and appointed political office is based on the assumption that women will represent "women's issues, needs and wants" even if these are not monolithically homogeneous or, in many cases, easy to identify.[6] Women have worked towards full representational equality via gender parity in legislative assemblies, but this goal has not been reached in jurisdictions like Ontario that do not employ a quota system to ensure 50/50 representation between men and women. Thus, researchers have used lenses such as critical mass theory or critical actor theory to understand the impact of a substantial minority of women legislators on political power structures.[7] However, a sustained lack of progress in the numbers of women in Canadian legislatures has prompted researchers such as Sylvia Bashevkin to question whether women can exercise enough influence when they remain in a token minority position over time or they do not hold positions as critical actors.[8]

Whether or not women have been able to reach a level of critical mass or whether some feminist women (or men) in key positions have been able to effect change as critical actors, is important to consider when evaluating the progress in women's numeric/descriptive representation in Ontario. We must also use an intersectional lens to consider the promotion of diverse women to elected and appointed office as part of the complexity of women's representation in Ontario. Intersectionality as a concept recognizes that women's oppression and interests are shaped by their complex diversity, not just that they are women, and that this diversity impacts them in ways that are "simultaneous and interacting."[9]

Alongside this, the chapter assesses whether or not women have achieved substantive and sustained policy gains from the provincial state. Even though it is difficult to identify specific public policy issues as being "women's issues," the chapter measures provincial policy in three areas often tied to women's goals of greater societal equality: child care, violence against women, and pay equity. In order to assess the level of substantive responses in these policy areas, the chapter briefly analyzes the attention and commitment to these policy areas over the past two decades.

ONTARIO WOMEN'S NUMERIC/DESCRIPTIVE REPRESENTATION IN ELECTED OFFICE

The obvious place to begin is an assessment of how well women have done in gaining access to the Ontario legislature since being awarded the right to stand and hold elected office in 1917. The *Royal Commission on the Status of*

Table 10.1. Women Elected by Each Party, 1945–2022

Election Year	Progressive Conservatives	NDP/CCF	Liberals	Total No. (%)
1945	0*	0	0	0 (0)
1948	0*	1	0	1 (1)
1951	0*	0	0	0 (0)
1955	0*	0	0	0 (0)
1959	0*	0	0	0 (0)
1963	1*	0	0	1 (1)
1967	1*	1	0	2 (2)
1971	1*	0	0	1 (1)
1975	3*	2	1	6 (5)
1977	3*	2	1	6 (5)
1981	4*	1	1	6 (5)
1985	3	3	3*	9 (7)
1987	1	3	16*	20 (15)
1990	3	19*	6	28 (21)
1995	11*	4	4	19 (15)
1999	9*	6	3	18 (17)
2003	3	2	17*	22 (21)
2007	7	3	19*	29 (27)
2011	8	7	15*	30 (28)
2014	6	11	21	38 (35)
2018	25*	20	4	49 (39.5)
2022	24*	19	4	48 (incl. 1 independent) (39)

Note: * indicates governing party.
Sources: Updated from Cheryl N. Collier, "A Path Well-Travelled or Hope on the Horizon? Women, Gender, and Politics in Ontario," in *The Politics of Ontario*, ed. Cheryl N. Collier and Jonathan Malloy (Toronto: University of Toronto Press, 2017), and Kristin Rushowy, "After Setting a Record in 2018, Ontario's Number of Female MPPs Has Dipped," *Toronto Star*, June 20, 2022, https://www.thestar.com/politics/provincial/after-setting-a-record-in-2018-ontario-s-number-of-female-mpps-has-dipped/article_d558d1ec-0f4f-5161-8ea2-fa37813fcd15.html.

Women in the 1960s, the 1984 Toronto-based *Committee for '94*, and more recently, the non-profit multi-partisan Canada-wide group Equal Voice, have worked to achieve gender parity in Canadian and Ontario legislatures, yet as is evident in table 10.1, the goal of 50 per cent representation of women in the Ontario legislature has still not been achieved.

It wasn't until the late 1980s that women were able to reach double digits in representation at Queen's Park, and even though there was progression to the level of 21 per cent in 1990, we see regression in 1995 back to 1987 levels (15 per cent), illustrating that increases in numbers of women certainly do not follow a linear model. Progress did resume in subsequent elections, reaching a new high in Ontario with 39.5 per cent women in the legislature in 2018.

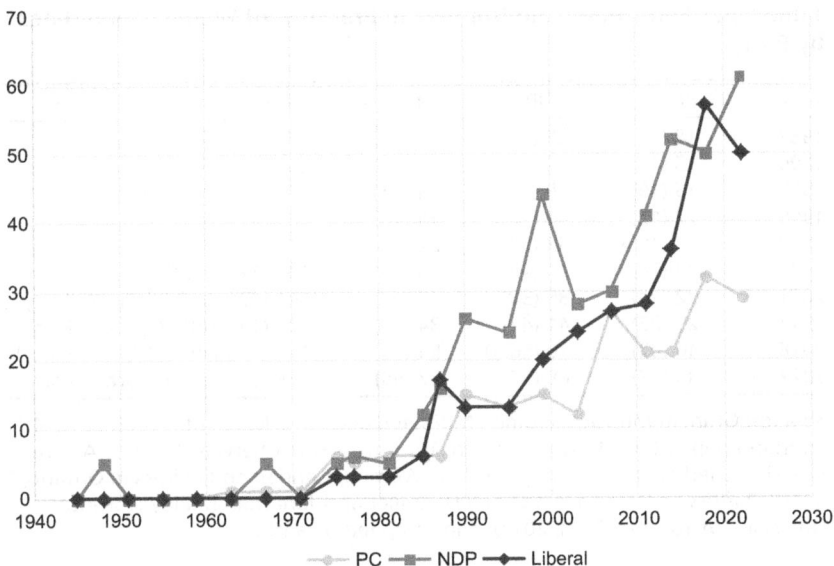

Figure 10.1. Percentage of Women in Party Caucuses, 1945–2022
Source: Updated from Cheryl N. Collier, "Judging Women's Political Success in the 1990s," in *The Government and Politics of Ontario*, 5th ed., ed. Graham White (Toronto: University of Toronto Press, 1997), table 1, and Elections Ontario data.

This was not fully sustained in 2022 with a slight dip to 39 per cent women, and highlights that progression is not guaranteed. Notably, Ontario continues to fall short of gender parity, and the pace of improvement and potential for regression do not suggest parity will be reached any time soon.[10]

When we look even closer at table 10.1, it is apparent that the type of party that wins an election often matters when it comes to the number of women at Queen's Park. Numeric dips below the 20 per cent range since 1990 happened under Progressive Conservative regimes. However, the highest level of representation of women also came in 2018 under the Progressive Conservatives, although no progress was made towards growth in those numbers in 2022, also under the PCs. Since parties are the gatekeepers to elected office in Ontario, including controlling access to the nomination and selection process, it is important to further uncover differences in commitment levels to women's representation amongst the parties and to assess efforts by the parties to increase numbers of women nominees and candidates in turn.

Figure 10.1 shows the number of women in each party in the Ontario legislature by election year as a percentage of the entire party caucus elected that year. As we can see there are stark differences between the parties beginning

Table 10.2. Percentage and Number, in Brackets, of Women Candidates by Party

Year	PCs	NDP	Liberals	Total
1987	18 (23)	35 (45)	21 (27)	95
1990	15 (19)	30 (39)	21 (26)	84
1995	15 (19)	29 (37)	24 (31)	87
1999	17 (18)	31 (32)	18 (19)	69
2003	20 (19.4)	33 (32)	22 (21.4)	75
2007	22 (24)	39 (42)	35 (38)	104 (126 incl Greens)
2011	22 (24)	35 (38)	39 (42)	104 (130 with 26 Green Party)
2014	25 (27)	41 (44)	34 (37)	108 (145 with 37 Green Party)
2018	40 (32)	70 (56.5)	54 (43)	164 (228 with 64 Green Party)
2022	33 (27)	68 (55)	67 (55)	168 (235 with 67 Green Party)

Sources: Graham Murray, "Women MPPs at Queen's Park, 1981 through 2010 (4)" (working paper, G.P. Murray Research, Toronto, 2010); Cheryl N. Collier, "A Path Well-Travelled or Hope on the Horizon? Women, Gender, and Politics in Ontario," in *The Politics of Ontario*, ed. Cheryl N. Collier and Jonathan Malloy (Toronto: University of Toronto Press, 2017); and compiled by author.

in the early 1980s when parties began to implement some programs to assist women's participation in formal politics, in part in response to lobbying from feminist groups. We also see that the NDP consistently has the highest percentages of women inside of its party caucuses than either the Liberals or the PCs, except in 2018 when women made up 57 per cent of the Liberal caucus after it was decimated with only seven elected MPPs. Some of the reasoning behind this is reflected in the data in table 10.2. In this table, we see more distinctions between the parties in the number of women that they run as candidates for election across the province. Again, there is a significant difference between the percentages of women run by the PCs (the highest being in 2018 at 32 per cent) compared to the Liberals and NDP, who have both grown their numbers to over 50 per cent. The NDP was the first to achieve this milestone in 2018 and repeated it in 2022, and the Liberals reached it in 2022. Disturbingly, these gains have also not been linear, with each party showing years when its percentage of women candidates fell compared to the previous election. More recently, however, the Liberals and NDP appear to have embraced a commitment to run more women. Similarly, when we look at the programs put in place to increase the number of women involved in the internal workings of Ontario political parties, we again see a mixed and fleeting effort overall.

The Conservatives are the least committed. In 2007, in response to a challenge to all parties by Equal Voice Canada to increase the number of women candidates, PC leader John Tory pledged that one-third of his candidates would be women, but there was nothing put in place inside the party to facilitate this goal. The PCs encourage two-fifths of the members on internal "Special Party Committees" to be women and two-fifths to be men, however, this is not mandated. The party used to have a PC Women's Association that served as a volunteer arm of the party. That association has since disappeared from the party's online website. It also used to help fund women candidates' campaigns with the national PC Ellen Fairclough Fund that supported women candidates, but this fund was discontinued once the federal Progressive Conservatives joined the Canadian Alliance to form the new Conservative Party of Canada in 2004.

The Ontario Liberal party has an active Women's Liberal Commission (OWLC) with a stated "aim ... to bring equal representation of women in the Ontario legislature by encouraging their active participation in the Liberal party, strengthening women's presence and helping them grow as activists."[11] However, as with the Conservatives, this "policy" does not include any quotas or specific targets. Also in 2007, Liberal premier Dalton McGuinty pledged that 50 per cent of candidates "in ridings not held by Liberal members would be women." In many cases this meant that those ridings were not safe Liberal seats and could be construed as "unwinnable" for a Liberal candidate, thus ensuring that those women had a slim chance of success if nominated. Despite this pledge, which would have added thirty-five women to run alongside the sitting seventeen women Liberal MPPs, the party fell short that year. In 2022, the Liberals earmarked twenty-two ridings as "women-only" nomination contests to increase its candidate pool, but because the Liberals were held to single digit results again, only one of these designated ridings represented a Liberal win. Unlike the PCs, the Liberal party still maintains a special women's fund named after Margaret Campbell, the first Liberal MPP elected in Ontario, to offer financial support to women-identified candidates.

Finally, the Ontario NDP has a similar party-based Women's Committee with a mandate to "encourage women's participation in the political process" and to "break down barriers and dispel stereotypes" related to women.[12] Like the Liberals, the Ontario NDP (ONDP) has a female candidate support fund named after the first woman CCF/NDP MPP (and MP), Agnes Macphail. Additionally, it has an affirmative action nomination policy in its party constitution, which was extended to cover not only women, but also racialized persons, people with disabilities, and Indigenous Peoples' nominations. The party sets a gender parity target for its candidates at each election, but there are no set quotas attached to the target. Despite the lack of quotas, 2018 and 2022 saw women candidates representing more than half of the NDP nominations – although many were in unwinnable ridings.

Women have been able to win the leadership in Ontario in two out of three of the competitive parties. In 1992, the Liberals became the first party to select a female leader: Lyn McLeod. McLeod served as Liberal leader from 1992 to 1996 until she was succeeded by Dalton McGuinty. She led the party in one election in 1995. After McGuinty resigned in late 2012, the Liberal leadership convention held in early 2013 came down to a choice between the two front runners, both women – Kathleen Wynne and Sandra Pupatello – ensuring a woman would be the next party leader and first women premier in the province.

Kathleen Wynne was the eventual victor, which meant that Ontario would also crown its first openly gay premier in 2013. Wynne was also able to successfully defend her position as premier in the 2014 election, bringing the Liberals a majority mandate. The majority win was not predicted by media pundits, and many later credited it more to a failure of the opposition NDP and PC campaigns than as a ringing endorsement of the Liberals. Wynne was much less successful in 2018, where the party saw an historic defeat and loss of official party status in the legislature. Wynne stayed on as an MPP, but resigned as party leader shortly thereafter.

Even though Wynne was immediately replaced by an interim male party leader, the party's most recently elected leader identifies as a woman. Bonnie Crombie, former mayor of Mississauga, won the Liberal party leadership race in December 2023 on the third round of voting. She did not have a seat in the legislature at time of writing.

The NDP is the other party that selected a woman as leader in the province. Andrea Horwath won the job in 2009, replacing long-time leader Howard Hampton. Hampton had just led the NDP to another poor showing in the polls in the 2007 election, and the party was seen as being in a perpetually weak state following the defeat of the Rae NDP in 1995. Horwath was chosen to breathe new life into the NDP and improved the party's fortunes in the 2011 election, nearly doubling its seat total and raising its share of the popular vote to its more traditional 20 per cent. This success demonstrated the potential for a strong female to turn the party around when it was in a weak state. Horwath's NDP wasn't as successful in the 2014 election, but in the 2018 election she oversaw the party's jump to official Opposition status, with the party's best showing since the 1990s. However, Horwath was not able to defeat the Ford government in 2022, and the party actually lost seats, after which she stepped down as leader after four elections, the longest tenure of any Ontario NDP leader since 1967. Horwath was replaced by Marit Stiles who was confirmed as party leader by a majority vote on February 4, 2023. She becomes the second woman leader of the party and was the sole candidate to take on the NDP leadership. In contrast, the Ontario PCs have yet to have a woman leader, even though Christine Elliott ran three times for the leadership in 2009, 2015, and 2018, and three of the four leadership candidates in 2018 were women, yet they were defeated by Doug Ford.

The presence of women leaders in the centre and centre-left Liberal and NDP provincial parties, alongside women's electoral success and institutional party supports in the same parties, demonstrates the openness of those parties to gender equality in leadership compared to the right-wing Progressive Conservatives. It also helps us understand the reason why progress in electoral mirror representation is not linear but instead depends on the party in power at the time. Despite the stated party commitments, however, progress in electoral office remains slow and in the case of women's leadership, arguably fleeting. Also notable is the fact that none of the women Ontario party leaders were racialized minorities. As mentioned, Wynne was the first openly gay premier to be elected in Canada, and she did not hide her sexual orientation during her run for the Liberal leadership. This is a significant milestone in Canadian politics, but it remains to be seen if this is a token recognition or one that truly begins to break down barriers for sexually diverse politicians. The next section examines numeric representation in appointed office to further test these trends.

ONTARIO WOMEN'S NUMERIC/DESCRIPTIVE REPRESENTATION IN APPOINTED OFFICE

Beyond the premier's office, the location of power in Ontario's executive-dominated Westminster legislature is at the cabinet table. To assess how much power and influence women could potentially exert, it is important to examine how many women have been appointed to cabinet posts. Table 10.3 shows the saw-tooth pattern of progress of women as a percentage of cabinet ministers in Ontario since 1970. The high point of representation was in 2018 when

Table 10.3. Women Cabinet Ministers in Ontario, 1970–2022

Year	Party Government	Number	Percentage, %
1970	PC	0/22	0
1972*	PC	1/23	4
1974*	PC	1/24	4
1975*	PC	3/26	11.5
1976*	PC	3/26	11.5
1978*	PC	3/26	11.5
1981	PC	2/26	8
1985	PC	2/28	7
1985	Liberal	2/23	9
1987	Liberal	4/26	15
1990	NDP	11/25	44
1995	PC	4/20	20
1999	PC	5/25	20
2003	Liberal	5/25	20
2007	Liberal	9/28	32
2010	Liberal	11/28	39
2011	Liberal	6/22	27
2013	Liberal	8/27	29
2014	Liberal	8/27	29
2016	Liberal	12/30	40
2018	Liberal	13/28	46
2018	PC	7/21	33
2022	PC	7/30	23

* Years marked with an asterisk is when 100% of women elected to the governing party were promoted to cabinet.
Note: Table 10.3 does not include every cabinet shuffle that occurred, but does include shuffles in which the numbers of women or percentages of women in cabinet changed, along with shuffles that occurred as a result of changes in government.
Source: Data compiled by author and Legislative Assembly of Ontario, "All MPPs," 2018, https://www.ola.org/en/members/all.

Kathleen Wynne shuffled her cabinet, promoting women to 46 per cent of cabinet posts in the lead up to the 2018 election that she would eventually lose spectacularly. Prior to that, it was in 1990 when 44 per cent of the governing NDP cabinet were women. Many of these women, including Evelyn Gigantes, Marion Boyd, and Francis Lankin, were strong feminist activists who had a marked impact on policy results during their time around the cabinet table.[13] Arguably, these substantial minorities, which approached gender parity, were good examples of women constituting a critical mass.

Unfortunately, these milestones were few and far between and certainly not sustained. Table 10.3 shows that after the NDP was defeated, the PCs more than halved women's cabinet representation during its tenure in office to 20 per cent. Similarly, once the Wynne Liberals finally decided to raise women's representation in cabinet during its later years in power, the PC government that replaced them in 2018 pulled that representation down to 33 per cent. And even though they won more seats in 2022, women's cabinet representation sunk again to 23 per cent of an expanded cabinet of thirty. These are representational lows that the province hadn't seen since 2003.

It is also important to assess the numbers of diverse women and men appointed to cabinet where data is available. In 2007, under the Liberal government of Dalton McGuinty, one racialized minority woman (Margarett Best) was promoted to cabinet as a junior minister of health promotion. Best remained in cabinet in 2011 as minister of consumer services but was demoted by Wynne to a parliamentary assistant post in education in 2013.[14] The only other minority woman (representing diversity in sexual orientation) included in cabinet was Wynne herself. She was first promoted to cabinet in 2003 and held the education, chair of cabinet, municipal affairs and housing, Aboriginal Affairs, and agriculture portfolios before becoming premier. In 2013, there were four racialized persons in Wynne's cabinet (14 per cent), all males.[15] In 2015, Wynne increased this number to five, but two of these racialized minority ministers were women, and both held junior posts – Mitzie Hunter, who was the associate finance minister responsible for pensions, and Dipika Damerla, who was the associate minister of health, long-term care and wellness; Hunter was later promoted to minister of education. In 2018, under Doug Ford, no racialized minority women were included in the cabinet. During his second mandate, Ford promoted rookie MPP (and racialized minority) Charmaine Williams to the associate minister of women's and social and economic opportunity portfolio, itself a lesser role than under the previous Wynne regime. Four other racialized minority men were included in the 2022 cabinet, representing 17 per cent of the total.

In 2013 the government had twenty parliamentary assistants, of which six were women (30 per cent). Interestingly, five of these women were racialized minority women. Additionally, there were three racialized minority males, meaning that racialized persons constituted 40 per cent of parliamentary assistants – much higher than in cabinet. In 2015 the number of parliamentary assistants was larger – thirty, reflecting the larger Liberal caucus after the 2014 election – and twelve were women (40 per cent), higher than two years earlier. However, the representation of racialized persons dropped – nine in total, or 30 per cent, with four being racialized minority women. In 2022, there were forty-three parliamentary assistants under the Ford PC government. Only eleven, or 25 per cent, were women and two identified as racialized persons (4 per cent). Overall, eleven out of forty-three were racialized persons (25 per cent) with the majority of these (nine) being men.

SUBSTANTIVE REPRESENTATION OF WOMEN IN ONTARIO

While tracking the number of women appointed to elected and appointed office is an important measurement of women's representation in provincial politics, it is also essential to examine how the provincial state "acts for" women. In this way we can begin to link numbers, or the actions of critical actors, with results and can assess a government's overall commitment levels to women's equality issues. In this section, I examine the bureaucratic department in place to address women's interests and issues – the Ontario Women's Directorate (OWD), which went through a short-lived metamorphosis in 2017 and was eventually reconstituted as the Office of Women's Social and Economic Opportunity. I also assess three areas of public policy that are closely associated with women's equality goals: child care, violence against women, and pay equity.

In 1997, the Mike Harris Conservative government had just eliminated one of two bureaucratic structures put in place to address women's equality – the Ontario Advisory Council on Women's Issues (OACWI). The OACWI had served as an evaluative body that advised the government of the day on ways it could improve public policy to better address women's equality issues. As well, it consulted regularly with women's groups and kept open the lines of communication between the women's movement and the minister responsible for women's issues. In the 1990s, particularly after the Harris Tories took office in 1995, the government was less interested in consulting with women's groups and eliminated the OACWI.[16]

Thus, the role of addressing women's issues inside of government and of advising the minister fell to the lone office for women left in the Ontario bureaucracy at the time – the Ontario Women's Directorate. The OWD was historically more involved in developing women's policy than the OACWI. After the OACWI disappeared, it took on more of an advising and outreach role, although much of its entire mandate suffered as its budget and staff component was cut over time (even after the OACWI was gone). In 1995, the

OWD had a staff of about eighty-five and a budget of about $18 million (down from $24 million under the previous NDP regime). By 1996, the OWD was moving away from a policy role. Instead, gender policy was spread out over many existing departments (Labour, Health, Human Resources) and given less attention.

This did not improve even under the McGuinty Liberals. The OWD took the lead on violence against women policy and implemented the Liberals' Domestic Violence Action Plan and more recent Action Plan to Stop Sexual Violence and Harassment, but it ceased to be an active advisor to the minister responsible for *new* gender equality policy. Notably, its budget continued to be reduced from 1995 levels, reaching a low of $16 million in 2005–6.

When Kathleen Wynne took over as Liberal leader, the OWD saw modest budget increases but did not reach the heights of the NDP era. However, in the lead up to the 2018 provincial election, the Wynne Liberals made a bold move to reconstitute the OWD as a full ministry of the government instead of a department within the Ministry of Community and Social Services and finally brought its budget to a high (not taking into account inflation) of $25 million.[17] In 2017, they created the Ministry of the Status of Women – a standalone ministry dedicated to gender equality policy. Yet, as soon as the Ford Conservatives took power, it eliminated the standalone ministry and downgraded it to an associate minister role of children and women's issues in 2019. Today, it is known as the Office of Women's Social and Economic Opportunity and is located back in the Ministry of Children, Community and Social Services. Its budget was also reduced and in 2021/22 was at $21 million.

SUBSTANTIVE GENDER EQUALITY POLICY

During the 1990s, there was a marked difference between the commitment levels of different Ontario party governments to women's issues such as child care, violence against women, and pay equity. The Bob Rae NDP government, with a strong critical mass of feminist women cabinet ministers has been touted as perhaps the most open to gender equality than any other government in provincial history.[18] By contrast, the Harris Tories and their "Common Sense Revolution" made sustained and deep cuts to women's policy areas, including cuts to child care spaces and child care workers' salaries, elimination of second stage shelter funding for victims of violence against women and abolishing the proxy method of comparison for pay equity cases and capping pay equity payouts.[19] The Harris Tories saw women as "special interests" and strongly resisted calls for improvements in these policy areas, preferring instead to cut back on progress made under the previous NDP government.

On the pay equity file, the SEIU (Service Employees International Union) Local 204 union challenged the Harris pay equity changes in court and, in 1997, these changes were overruled for contravening the *Pay Equity Act* (1987). Even though both Mike Harris and subsequent premier Ernie Eves promised to abide by the court decision and to fully ensure the pay out of retroactive pay equity claims, the government dragged its heels on ensuring subsequent settlements beyond those inside the provincial public service owing for 1995–8. The lack of compliance on the part of the Tory government prompted another court challenge, this one via the *Charter of Rights and Freedoms*, in 2001. The *Charter* challenge was settled in 2003, resulting in payments of $414 million to 100,000 women over three years.

Once the Liberal government took office and the payment of proxy-based claims had been settled in the courts, the issue of proper funding for the Pay Equity Commission (which enforces the *Pay Equity Act*) continued to be a problem. The Harris Tories cut the Pay Equity Commission budget by 46 per cent in the 1997 budget, drastically reducing the effectiveness of the Commission from its previous years under the NDP. When the Liberals took office in 2003, it continued to cut the Pay Equity Commission's budget by a further 20 per cent. In 2006, there were thirty-two employees at the Commission and only fifteen review officers to cover the entire province. By contrast, in 1992, there were eighty-six employees and twenty-eight review officers. In 2014, the Liberal government made an election promise to "develop a wage gap strategy to close Ontario's gender pay gap" which saw women on average earn 31.5 per cent less than men in the province. They subsequently appointed a Gender Wage Gap Steering Committee to examine the issue further. In 2018, the Liberals introduced the *Pay Transparency Act* to require employers to show gendered differences in pay, composition of workforce, and compensation levels. Yet these moves did not substantially move the province towards a fulsome wage gap strategy, and the government continued to appeal unfavourable pay equity rulings by the commission.

The Ford Conservatives did little on the pay equity file except continue to resist pay equity rulings via court challenges and appeals as opposed to working to eliminate pay inequities. In 2020, they appealed a 2018 ruling that would have seen Ontario midwives' salaries increase by 45 per cent to be more in line with similar employment categories in the medical field. They lost the appeal in 2022 in the Superior Court and were weighing options to continue their appeal to the Supreme Court of Canada at the time of writing.

In the areas of child care and violence against women, the approaches of the centre-right versus centre and centre-left governments were even more distinct, with the former being much less willing to improve policy for women in these two key areas. After the Tories left office in 2003, the Liberals reinstated funding and increased government attention to both files in a marked improvement from the Harris years. However, compared to the NDP years, post-2003 was not as fruitful for a child care or violence against women policy. Things deteriorated even further in 2018 when the Ford PC government took office.

The federal government provided child care funding to the provinces in 2000 under the Early Childhood Development Agreement but left the door open to the provinces to decide what to spend the money on. The Harris Tories used it for everything it could associate with "early childhood development" except for increasing child care spaces. In 2003, the federal government announced more targeted funding for early learning and child care for children under six under the Multilateral Agreement on Early Learning and Child Care but still allowed provincial flexibility in using the funds. The McGuinty Liberals directed some of this money to new child care spaces under its Best Start Plan, signifying the first time new money was made available for space creation since the 1990s in the province. The Liberal Best Start plan also included a promise to create and extend full-day junior and senior kindergarten across the province to be rolled out over a five- to six-year period between 2010 and 2015/16.

When the federal government ended its commitment to child care funding in 2009, the Ontario Liberals, in turn, tempered their efforts towards child care space creation. After the McGuinty Liberals won a minority government in 2011 and had to rely on NDP support to pass its budget, this approach to child care again changed. One of the NDP's demands for support was the creation of a child care stabilization fund to address what the industry estimated was a nearly $300 million per year shortfall. The Liberal/NDP budget deal saw just under $250 million earmarked for child care spaces over the next three and a half years. While this was short of the advocacy targets, it was welcomed and demonstrated the distinction amongst the parties once again, with the NDP being more open to increasing government commitment to the child care policy file. By 2012, the Liberals had announced it would change the funding formula for child care and give municipalities more flexibility in how they delivered child care locally. In 2014, the Liberals promised a much-needed one dollar per hour wage enhancement for child care workers in the budget (some made as little as $13 per hour), which was welcomed by advocates but seen as more of a band-aid instead of the desired workplace strategy for the regulated child care sector.[20] In the lead up to the 2018 election, Wynne claimed that her government had created 100,000 new child care spaces during its time in office – a number hotly disputed by advocates as being inflated.

Child care availability and affordability continued to be a key issue for Ontario families leading up to and during the COVID-19 pandemic. This prompted the federal Liberal government to revisit a long-standing promise to create a universal child care system across the country on a $10-a-day model to be in place by 2025. The federal Liberals negotiated agreements with every province and territory in the country prior to inking a deal with the Ford Conservatives, who held out until 2022 (just prior to the provincial election). Critics noted that less than half of child care centres in Toronto alone had joined the program as of July 2022, a mere two months before the deadline to do so. This lack of firm commitment to improved child care in the province followed $50 million in planned provincial cuts in 2019–20 that the Ford government eventually backtracked on after strong lobbying from municipalities, notably from Toronto, who would be short nearly $80 million if these and other related cuts went through.[21]

On violence against women, the Liberals appeared to be more proactive after taking office in 2003, enacting a $60 million Domestic Violence Action Plan at the end of 2004. The plan was supposed to increase funding to shelters and sexual assault centres as well as increase collaboration with anti-violence front-line workers. However, initial funding was provided on a one-time basis instead of for ongoing sustainability, and shelter staff were directed by then-minister responsible for women's issues Sandra Pupatello in 2005 to essentially find their own money thereafter. Even though spending on anti-violence increased over the previous government, the overall percentage of provincial spending remained largely steady through 2007.[22] In 2011, the Liberals launched their Sexual Violence Action Plan to target sexual assault issues more specifically and to encourage better responses from law enforcement agencies. Developed in consultation with provincial sexual assault and anti-violence groups, the Plan committed $15 million over four years for education, prevention, training, and awareness programs.[23] The focus on sexual assault was strengthened in 2015 with the three-year action plan titled "It's

Never Okay," including a public awareness campaign and new funding for sexual assault centres as well as changes to the sexual assault provisions of the *Limitations Act* and a review of provisions in the criminal code to improve the treatment of survivors.[24]

The Ford Conservatives pulled back on violence against women commitments, particularly in protecting feminist anti-violence expertise on the file. In 2018, they immediately disbanded the expert panel to end violence against women that was enacted by the Liberals three years earlier. The PCs did turn attention to campus sexual violence demanding that post-secondary institutions enact anti-sexual violence policies, but most institutions already had processes in place and the intentions and commitment of the PCs were unclear. Funding levels to combat violence against women did not change substantially under the PC regime, despite continued high levels of need, particularly during the pandemic.

CONCLUSION

What has remained constant over many years is the strong impact that provincial parties have on the willingness to see and address gender equality issues. Centre and centre-left parties are more open to gender equality than right-wing ones, with the centre-left NDP performing better in its commitment to affirmative action in numeric representation in elected and appointed office, particularly at the cabinet table. The NDP also continued to positively impact the policy agenda for women through its influence on the minority governing Liberals. The Liberal party's unwillingness to support pay equity enforcement also raises questions about its commitment to gender equality, even under a progressive woman-identified premier who waited to fully embrace a "critical actor role" until very late in her mandate. These moves were not enough to grant Ontario's first lesbian woman premier a second electoral victory, leaving her party decimated with little hope for renewal in 2022. The return of the Progressive Conservatives to power has brought a familiar tone of degendered approaches to key policy areas and to scant attention to the appointment of women to positions of power in cabinet and even parliamentary secretary positions. The immediate future for women in Ontario is not very bright as a result.

As this chapter has shown, it is also extremely difficult to collect data on the intersectionality of women's representation both numerically and substantively. What is apparent in the small amounts of data presented here is that diverse women have an even tougher climb to attain proper representation at Queen's Park. Although they form small pockets of appointed office, diverse men and women are not well-represented at the cabinet table or in policy circles. Even more than gender representation, attention to intersectionality is clearly skewed and marginalized. It remains to be seen whether Ontario parties will be convinced in the years to come to address these representational failures more consistently and systematically than is presently the case. Until then, we are unlikely to see any more "significant breakthroughs" for women, gender, and diversity in Ontario.

DISCUSSION QUESTIONS

1 All three Ontario parties have held power since the 1990s. How open has each been to the promotion of women to elected and appointed office?
2 What's the difference between women's numeric and substantive representation? How easy is it to link both of these concepts together?
3 Do you think Ontario finally has a critical mass of women in elected office, or is the party more determinative in ensuring substantive policy gains for women? What changes do you think will occur as a result of this, if any at all?
4 In your opinion, what has to occur for Ontario women to reach gender parity in appointed and elected office?

NOTES

1 Patty Coates, "This Women's Day, Women Are Mobilizing against Doug Ford's Misogynist Government," *Hamilton Spectator*, March 6, 2020, https://www.thespec.com/opinion/contributors/this-womens-day-women-are-mobilizing-against-doug-fords-misogynist-government/article_c936fb93-0313-55fb-bab1-e8a671427ba2.html.
2 Coates, "This Women's Day."
3 Randy Robinson, "Ontario Election: Where Did 825,000 Swing Voters Go?," *Canadian Dimension*, June 10, 2022, https://canadiandimension.com/articles/view/ontario-election-where-did-825000-swing-voters-go.
4 Brenda O'Neill, "Women's Status Across the Canadian Provinces, 1999–2002: Exploring Differences and Possible Explanations," in *Provinces: Canadian*

Provincial Politics, Second Edition, ed. Christopher Dunn (Toronto: University of Toronto Press, 2006), 467–86.
5 Cheryl N. Collier, "Judging Women's Political Success in the 1990s," in *The Government and Politics of Ontario*, 5th ed. (Toronto: University of Toronto Press, 1997), 468.
6 Karen Celis and Sarah Childs, "The Substantive Representation of Women: What to Do with Conservative Claims?," *Political Studies* 60 (March 2012): 213, https://doi.org/10.1111/j.1467-9248.2011.00904.x.
7 See Drude Dahlerup, "From a Small to a Large Minority: Women in Scandinavian Politics," *Scandinavian Political Studies* 11, no. 4 (December 1988): 283–7, https://doi.org/10.1111/j.1467-9477.1988.tb00372.x. See also Sarah Childs and Mona Lena Krook, "Analyzing Women's Substantive Representation: From Critical Mass to Critical Actors," *Government and Opposition* 44, no. 2 (2009): 125–45, https://doi.org/10.1111/j.1477-7053.2009.01279.x.
8 See Sylvia Bashevkin, "Women's Representation in the House of Commons: A Stalemate?," *Canadian Parliamentary Review* (Spring 2011): 17–22; Sylvia Bashevkin, *Doing Politics Differently? Women Premiers in Canada's Provinces and Territories* (Vancouver: UBC Press, 2019).
9 Leah Bassel, "Intersectional Politics at the Boundaries of the Nation State," *Ethnicities* 10, no. 2 (June 2010): 155, https://doi.org/10.1177/1468796810361818.
10 No historic data is available on the number of racialized minority or other diverse categories of women elected to the Ontario legislature over time.
11 "Commissions," Ontario Liberal Party, accessed August 14, 2015, archived August 25, 2015, at the Wayback Machine, https://web.archive.org/web/20150825193850/http://www.ontarioliberal.ca/OurTeam/WhoWeAre/Commissions.aspx.
12 "Committees," Ontario New Democratic Party, accessed August 14, 2015, http://www.ontariondp.ca/committees.
13 See Collier, "Judging Women's Political Success"; Lesley Byrne, "Making a Difference When the Doors Are Open: Women in the Ontario NDP Cabinet, 1990–95," in *Opening Doors Wider: Women's Political Engagement in Canada*, ed. Sylvia Bashevkin (Vancouver: UBC Press, 2009), 93–107.
14 Best reportedly had health problems and this may help explain the demotion, although this is speculative.
15 No historic data is available on the representation of racialized minorities in cabinet.
16 Collier, "Judging Women's Political Success."
17 Bashevkin, *Doing Politics Differently*, 179.
18 See Collier, "Judging Women's Political Success"; Byrne, "Making a Difference."
19 "History – Ontario," Equal Pay Coalition, accessed August 14, 2015, http://www.equalpaycoalition.org/history/ontario/.
20 Ontario Coalition for Better Child Care, "OCBCC Welcomes Action on Child Care Wages, But Questions Remain ad More Support Needed," *OCBCC Press Releases*, January 20, 2015, http://www.childcareontario.org/ocbcc_welcomes_action_on_child_care_wages_but_question_remain_and_more_support_needed.

21 "Province's Funding Cuts Jeopardize 6,166 Subsidized Child Care Spaces in Toronto, Staff Says," *CBC News*, May 3, 2019, https://www.cbc.ca/news/canada/toronto/child-care-funding-cuts-toronto-budget-1.5121320.

22 Cheryl N. Collier, "Violence against Women or Violence against 'People'? Neoliberalism, 'Post-Neoliberalism' and Anti-Violence Policy in Ontario and British Columbia," in *Women and Public Policy in Canada*, ed. Alexandra Dobrowolsky (Toronto: Oxford University Press, 2009), 175–6.

23 Government of Ontario, *Changing Attitudes, Changing Lives: Ontario's Sexual Violence Action Plan*, March 2011, http://www.women.gov.on.ca/owd/docs/svap.pdf.

24 Government of Ontario, *It's Never Okay: An Action Plan to Combat Sexual Violence and Harassment*, March 2015, http://www.ontario.ca/document/action-plan-stop-sexual-violence-and-harassment.

11

Northern Ontario

Gina S. Comeau

Northern Ontario is geographically vast and sparsely populated. It consists of almost 90 per cent of the province's land area, yet is home to just over 5 per cent of its total population. According to the latest census data in 2021, there are close to 800,000 individuals living in Northern Ontario, with five major population centres located in North Bay, Sault Ste. Marie, Sudbury, Thunder Bay, and Timmins.[1] Recent population trends indicate growth in a few cities but with decreasing numbers in the vast majority of other municipalities. Given its vastness, several authors question whether speaking of Northern Ontario as one region can encompass the diversity of its various parts. While some researchers, such as Beaulieu, prefer to divide the North into five distinct regions,[2] and others prefer to divide it into northwest and northeast, the fact remains that in most substantive terms there is one North. Whether one classifies Northern Ontario as one region or many, one of its unifying features is the heartland-hinterland dynamic, which has persisted since its creation and remains a recurring theme in Northern Ontario literature. While the assumptions that inform the heartland-hinterland dynamic are debatable, few authors would dispute that the politics of Northern Ontario differ from those of its southern neighbours. Any disagreement lies in the perceived degree of the distinction.

This chapter examines the politics and society of Northern Ontario, with particular attention to the elements of continuity and change rather than themes of convergence found in the rest of Ontario, as argued by Malloy (see chapter 1). It is divided into four parts, the first of which provides a brief overview of the region's development by outlining the historical forces that have shaped Northern Ontario's politics and political culture. The second part provides a demographic profile of the region, followed by a third section on political culture and behaviour and, finally a discussion of government policies and institutions. As a whole, this chapter argues that while Northern Ontario has witnessed important changes in the last twenty years, a number of issues and challenges remain that reflect the persistence of the heartland-hinterland dynamic. The most enduring feature of Northern Ontario is that it continues to be significantly different from that of Southern Ontario.

HISTORICAL DEVELOPMENT

The history and politics of Northern Ontario are intrinsically linked to the development and exploitation of its natural resources.[3] It is in large part the extraction of natural resources from the North to serve the needs of the South that created the heartland-hinterland relationship between Northern and Southern Ontario.[4] In the heartland-hinterland relationship, the hinterland region is used to serve the needs of the heartland or metropolis, which in turn influences the hinterland's politics.[5] This theory owes its origins to Innis's seminal work on the history of the Canadian economy. Innis's staples theory argues that the development and exportation of raw materials, such as fur, fish, and lumber, explain the development and settlement patterns of many communities and the regional character of the Canadian economy. The exportation of these raw materials from the hinterland (Canada) to the heartland (Britain) hindered Canada's ability to diversify its economy by creating an overreliance on primary resources and continued dependence on Britain.[6] Many authors have expanded on the heartland-hinterland thesis by applying it to the Canada-US relationship, and to the centre and periphery within Canada, which has led to a political analysis of subregions such as Northern Ontario.[7] For example, Weller builds upon the heartland-hinterland thesis to explain the impact of these development patterns on the politics of Northern Ontario.[8] He argues that the economics and politics of attraction (characterized by the politics of futility and handouts) led to the politics of frustration (radicalism and fringe movements) and the politics of parochialism (the politics of sublimation and dependency). The resulting politics of frustration are still evident today, albeit to a much lesser extent.

The vast majority of Northern Ontario communities can be categorized as resource communities and, like many other resource communities, they experience "boom-and-bust" cycles that reveal their vulnerability to external forces. One such example amongst many is the town of Sturgeon Falls, which was hard hit when its pulp and paper mill was shut down.[9] The North was not originally developed for its natural resources but rather was intended as a transportation route to the western part of Canada. The provincial government subsequently attempted to develop the area first as an agricultural region and a market for the South. As Nelles explains, it took years for the government to realize the futility of its efforts to develop a new agricultural frontier: "Whenever the farmers of the southern part of the province demanded the opening up of more land in the north the lumbermen reminded them of the cold, inhospitable nature of the land and the government the revenues that would be lost if such a course of action were followed. The Shield itself and the economic interests dependent upon it challenged a unitary, agrarian view of the environment."[10] While the terrain proved to be too rugged to flourish as an agricultural region, it was rich in mineral deposits and other natural resources. It was thus only in the early 1900s that the exploitation of the environment through forestry and the mining industry truly became the driving force of economic growth in the region.[11]

Resource companies located outside the region largely undertook the extraction of northern resources. The region's infrastructure was developed to facilitate the exploitation and transportation of resources from north to south, which in turn impacted the development of many communities.[12] Government policies targeting the North were largely intended to encourage the exploitation of the region, referred to as "New Ontario," in order to benefit Southern Ontario.[13]

Weller argues that the politics of extraction and dependency have led to northern alienation and the rise of fringe movements supporting greater autonomy.[14] The quest for greater autonomy has taken various forms throughout the years, with some seeking greater representation at Queen's Park and others calling for provincial status or union with Manitoba. The first of these movements for separation occurred shortly after Confederation in the 1870s and again in the early 1900s, periods when other new provinces were joining Confederation. In the 1940s and the 1950s, Limerick tried to generate support for provincial status with the New Province League. In the 1970s, Diebel championed the movement for separation, and the idea continues to recur in editorials and public discussion from time to time.[15] A 2016 publication released by the Northern Policy Institute argues that Northern Ontario should be treated as a distinct province in order to facilitate economic and statistical analysis and that it should also explore notions of regional governance.[16] While not clear calls for separation, these ideas clearly support greater autonomy for the North. The politics of extraction also plays out in attempts by both regions, Northern and Southern Ontario, to extract benefits from each other. The North seeks "economic and social change" or concessions, often in the form of political handouts, and the southern part of the province attempts to extract resources from the North at the lowest possible cost.[17] This cycle contributes to a sense of alienation and frustration among the residents of Northern Ontario.

In addition to creating a sense of alienation, the politics of extraction significantly influence the demographics of the region, as detailed further in the next section. The exploitation and extraction of natural resources is ever more reliant on heavy machinery rather than intensive labour, with serious consequences in terms of population growth, immigration, age, and population distribution.[18] An economy dependent on natural resources tends to channel the flow of resources and wealth outside the region, limiting the number and diversity of job opportunities for youth and leaving the population highly dependent on external forces. These adverse implications of the politics of extraction are also found in other Canadian hinterlands, creating an increasing divide in employment and population rates.[19] In Northern Ontario and other Canadian hinterland regions, external factors have created conditions that persist today, including unemployment and out-migration, with a devastating impact on resource economies.

While the politics of extraction shape the contemporary moment, they have a long history of producing alienation and discontent in Northern Ontario. Such sentiments were present during the investigatory phase of the provincial Royal Commission on the Northern Environment during the late 1970s and early 1980s. The commission was to examine both the positive and negative impacts of resource development on the environment and the people of Northern Ontario, and the politics of frustration are evident in its report: "beneath the many conflicts over resource development lies a widespread belief amongst northerners that they have precious little influence over the course of development. That belief is well-founded."[20] The importance of consulting northern populations and understanding the differences between Northern and Southern Ontario were key in quelling the evident dissatisfaction among both Indigenous and non-Indigenous communities in Northern Ontario. The Final Report and Recommendations of the Royal Commission on the Northern Environment was submitted in 1985,[21] and it recommended the development of institutional mechanisms to ensure the voices of the North were heard, as well as environmental and land-use guidelines for sustainable development practices. Although it was a provincial commission report, it argued that both federal and provincial policies played a central role in reinforcing feelings of disaffection, and it detailed specific recommendations for both the federal and provincial governments in regard to consultation practices and education, treaty, and environmental negotiations with Northern Indigenous communities. But four decades later, these concerns remain. Beaulieu argues that the provincial and federal policies have often been "adversarial, and steeped in attitudes of colonialism that regional concerns are secondary."[22] Such policy decisions have fuelled the alienation and discontent still prevalent in Northern Ontario, with a particularly devastating impact on many Indigenous communities.

DEMOGRAPHICS

The demographic profile of Northern Ontario starkly differs from other regions in the province in terms of ethnicity, language, economic status, and population density. The most significant difference is population density, measured by calculating the number of individuals living in specific land areas. The 789,519 individuals living in Northern Ontario comprise approximately 5.6 per cent of Ontario's total population living on close to 90 per cent of the province's land mass.[23] The 2021 census data indicates that the population density of Northeastern Ontario is 2 persons per square kilometer in the northeast and 0.5 persons in Northwestern Ontario.[24] This is significantly different from the provincial average of 15.9 persons per square kilometre. There is also a significant difference in urbanization.

Suffice it to say that it is possible to discern a number of distinct demographic trends that differentiate Northern Ontario from the remainder of the province. According to Southcott, these include increasing youth out-migration (which is increasing at a faster rate than in previous decades), an aging population, and slow population growth, and estimates indicate that this trend will continue.[25]

Northerners are more likely than other Ontarians to be employed in natural resource industries such as forestry and mining; there is also a greater reliance on public-sector employment.[26] Further, low levels of education and literacy persist; while these are improving, the regional gap compared to the provincial average is growing rather than shrinking.[27] While some of these tendencies are apparent in other areas of the country, such as Atlantic Canada, when one compares Northern to Southern Ontario, there is an increasing divide and intensifying inequality between the two areas of the province. The North continues to depend on natural resources, rendering it extremely vulnerable to external forces. While other industries, such as manufacturing in Southern Ontario, are also vulnerable to external forces such as trade and globalization, natural resource economies tend to be more volatile and experience more frequent and extreme boom-and-bust cycles.

Of the various demographic trends that shape the politics of Northern Ontario, perhaps the most salient is the continual decrease in its population relative to that of the province as a whole. In 2001, the population of Northern Ontario constituted 7.4 per cent of the provincial population; by 2006, this figure had decreased to 6.6 per cent; by 2011, to 6 per cent, and to 5.6 per cent in the 2021 census.[28] Only four northern areas (Manitoulin, Parry Sound, Nipissing, and Greater Sudbury) experienced growth in the early 2000s but the increases remained below the provincial average of 5.7 per cent and the national average of 5.9 per cent. Twenty years later, in 2021, Greater Sudbury and Parry Sound saw another jump in their populations, a changing trend in the last decade. Smaller increases were also seen in a few cities, such as North Bay.[29] The remaining northern areas witnessed a decrease in population while the southern part of the province has experienced continued growth almost everywhere except some rural and more remote areas, mainly in Eastern Ontario.[30]

Such significant variations between north and south carry over into the realm of language and ethnicity. Northern Ontario has fewer immigrants settling into the region than Southern Ontario, as the majority of immigrants to Ontario opt to settle in larger urban centres. Yet Northern Ontario is home to substantially larger francophone and Indigenous populations. One quarter of the francophone population in the province resides in this region[31] – as does 40 per cent of the Indigenous population. Despite different challenges, both minority populations face shared language and cultural barriers, albeit to varying degrees. Furthermore, they are each bearers of unique constitutional rights according to their recognized status in the Canadian polity. Both groups are also less likely to have a university degree or high school education, and both earn less than the provincial average, with a greater gap in income between northern francophones and Indigenous residents of the province, on the one hand, and their southern counterparts on the other.[32] Little preoccupation was given to either group in recent cuts at Laurentian University, which some have argued were disproportionate for francophone and Indigenous programs, although it should be noted that cuts were severe across all programs with many English programs also affected. While these examples illustrate some similarities between the Indigenous and francophone populations of Northern Ontario, significant differences remain. For example, the Northern Ontario population is generally aging, whereas the Indigenous population is getting younger. The opposite is true of the francophone population, which is older than the provincial average.[33]

Indigenous communities in remote areas often face a number of additional social issues, such as access to clean drinking water, access to affordable and nutritious food, higher suicide rates, and higher chronic and infectious disease rates, to name a few.[34] The majority of these issues are not new. They were noted by the provincial Royal Commission on the Northern Environment in 1985 and the federal Royal Commission on Aboriginal Peoples in 1996 and have been studied repeatedly by numerous experts. The problem with some of these issues, such as food insecurity, is that many solutions are "short-term emergency"-driven solutions rather than long-term ones that address infrastructure issues magnified by COVID-19.[35] The media coverage of such issues provides immediate short-term awareness, but does not necessarily aid the long-term situation.[36] An example was in 2011 over housing conditions found in the Northern Ontario First Nations community of Attawapiskat. The community declared a state of emergency when many residents were found living in makeshift accommodations without water or electricity or in houses in states of serious disrepair. The response of the federal government – which involved a decision to send in emergency shelters and dispatch third-party management – was deemed insufficient by the community, with the courts laying the blame on bureaucratic problems in a subsequent judicial review in 2012.[37] Attawapiskat and many other First Nations communities across Canada have also faced a youth suicide crisis with Attawapiskat declaring another state of emergency over rising youth suicides in 2016.[38] In June 2022, Neskantaga marked the anniversary of the longest boil advisory in Canada, reaching 10,000 days.[39] It is one of nineteen communities in Ontario still facing long-term drinking water advisories. This is the highest number of any Canadian province and these municipalities are all located in the north of the province. To put into perspective, the next highest number of advisories in a province is five communities in Saskatchewan.[40]

While these fall primarily under federal jurisdiction, they illustrate unique challenges faced by isolated Indigenous communities. Authors such as Charania and colleagues have noted that improved collaboration, communication, and interpretation among federal, provincial, and First Nations communities could improve health care delivery in such remote communities when a patient must receive services outside the community.[41] A number of similar results are found in a 2017 study citing a history of discriminatory policies as one of the main reasons for these health discrepancies.[42] As mentioned above, a number of these issues have been iterated by numerous scholars, policy experts, and oversight committees. One such example includes the Auditor General's reports, which have noted deficiencies in health and safety requirements, lack of proper training, and transportation issues in 2017[43] and weaknesses in Indigenous Services Canada's management of its personal protective equipment stockpile and inability to meet the needs of health care personnel in remote communities during the pandemic in its 2021 report.[44] These illustrate the failings – identified by the numerous governmental and societal failings cited by various commissions – mentioned above, of managing when a crisis occurs rather than addressing long-term systemic issues. Scholars have recently pointed to the need for home-grown third-sector institutions in providing care and advocating for their communities.[45]

POLITICAL CULTURE AND POLITICAL BEHAVIOUR

There are ongoing debates regarding the nature of Ontario's political culture, as explored in the first chapter of this collection. Key to such debates are questions as to not only whether Ontario has a distinct political culture, but also whether Northern Ontario, in particular, has its own separate political culture. Wiseman, for example, distinguishes a specific provincial culture for Ontario but does not address the possible existence of regional subcultures.[46] However, authors such as Dyck, Weller, and Martin, among others, have argued that Northern Ontario has its own distinctive regional subculture. For Dyck, the political culture of Northern Ontario is "a culture of alienation, dependence, handouts, and frustration, based on isolated settlements, distance from Toronto, poor communications, and inadequate services."[47] For Martin, the political culture of Northern Ontario is similarly distinguished by its "feelings of dissatisfaction, dependency, and domination, as well as by parochialism and pragmatism."[48]

This distinct political culture manifests itself in what Weller has labelled the "politics of disaffection." The politics of disaffection are a reflection of the profound discontent triggered by neglect at Queen's Park, isolation from and exploitation by Southern Ontario, a lack of political representation, inequalities of wealth, and underfunded basic services such as health and education. The politics of disaffection manifest themselves in a number of ways, including voting patterns. Particularly evident is a tradition of protest voting evident in NDP support; while Liberal and Conservative fortunes may rise and fall considerably, the NDP is regularly a strong presence in northern voting and consistently competitive in almost every northern riding. In the 2022 provincial election, Northern Ontario went decisively for the NDP, which won seven of the eleven seats despite the massive Progressive Conservative majority in the rest of the province. The remaining four seats went Conservative and the Liberals were shut out, a reversal from a decade before when the Liberals regularly won northern seats and the Conservatives did not. These trends can be linked to the politics of dependence and swinging to whatever party holds power at the moment; yet regardless, the NDP remains predominant.[49] There are also signs of a radical undercurrent in strong support for workers' movements. The politics of dissatisfaction are further expressed in minority politics, with both francophones and Indigenous people constituting important segments of the population for whom issues of service and accessibility are magnified. As noted, statistical measurements of levels of employment, income, and education indicate that francophone and Indigenous communities continue to receive inferior services in comparison to the Northern Ontario average, which in turn pales in comparison to Southern Ontario averages. The politics of disaffection for these groups are often expressed in different ways and arenas but constitute an important part of Northern Ontario's politics.

Given such widespread disillusionment, perhaps it is not surprising that there have been regular calls for internal secessions since the late 1800s, as mentioned above, either for separate provincial status or for the northwestern part of the province to join Manitoba. The latter option is principally fuelled by two factors: first, the closer proximity to Manitoba's capital, and second, a greater influence in the smaller legislature. As Di Matteo and colleagues note, using 2006 formulas, the merger of Northwestern Ontario and Manitoba could signify a 16 per cent increase in the number of seats, thereby increasing the weight of the former's voice in the legislature.[50] For many secessionists, the desire to separate is often expressed in a number of recurring themes. Nieguth identifies six themes in the Northern Ontario separatist discourse: "neglect, adverse effects, heartland mentality, distinct identity, representation and self-determination."[51] Many northerners express discontent at their continual battle for services more easily obtained in the southern part of the province. The impacts of these struggles are well illustrated in the health care field, where many have to travel significant distances to obtain services that are easily accessed in the South. Health statistics indicate that Northern Ontarians have shorter lifespans, and many indicate finding it difficult to access primary health care providers.[52] The lack of political power and issues of representation are a continuous struggle given the dwindling population of Northern Ontario. While the North is actually somewhat overrepresented with ten electoral districts federally and eleven provincially, when its share of the Ontario population would only warrant eight,[53] it is still heavily outweighed in provincial politics, comprising less than a tenth of the legislature.

Northern Ontario mirrors the overall stability of the Ontario three-party system but expresses itself somewhat differently than the South in relation to party standings.[54] Historically, there were two voting tendencies in Northern Ontario. While northerners tended to vote for the party in power at both the provincial and federal levels – hoping this would lead to political assistance – there was also a strong undercurrent of radical politics illustrated by solid support for the NDP, as noted above. Weller suggests that the trend to vote with the ruling party was broken in 1995,[55] and recent electoral outcomes seem to support this argument, at least provincially, as the Ontario NDP continues to win more northern seats than any other party despite not forming government. The NDP did lose two northern seats in 2022 amid the smashing Ford re-election victory, including a surprising upset in Timmins. Whether this indicates a permanent shift in provincial voting patterns that have been consistent since 1995 remains to be seen.

Dynamics at the federal level are somewhat different and more volatile, with all three parties rising and falling in popularity. However, the three most recent elections of 2015, 2019, and 2021 indicate a return to past northern voting patterns, mentioned earlier, where residents voted for the party in power in the hopes of gaining favour and political handouts. For these last three elections, six of the nine northern seats remained Liberal despite the shift from a majority to a minority government in 2019. It is perhaps safer to say that at the federal level, Northern Ontarians are left-leaning rather than an indication of seeking political handouts; since the 1990s, Northern Ontarians have voted primarily for either the Liberals or the NDP in all federal elections. A shift towards the NDP occurred in 2008 and 2011, but the region then saw a return in 2015 to a majority of the seats being Liberal. These trends seem to indicate strong support for left of centre-leaning parties, particularly the Liberal party, in the North. However, a recent study by King indicates that an undercurrent of right-wing populism is slowly growing amongst workers who traditionally support left-wing parties,[56] which, if it continues to grow, might have broader implications on future voting patterns.

For years, the source of much discontent in Northern Ontario was the piecemeal approach of both the provincial and federal governments to addressing the problems of the North. These efforts were often criticized for failing to create a long-term strategy rather than ad hoc measures to appease discontent in northern communities. Weller argued that policy development in the North not only failed to incorporate any long-term vision but also lacked coordination among the different levels of government and local organizations.[57] The end result was that development efforts occurred in metaphorical silos. Recent policy initiatives indicate longer-term planning in federal government initiatives which might somewhat appease discontent in the area. However, it is the Government of Ontario – with its jurisdictional responsibility for Northern Ontario's primary industries of mining, forestry, and tourism – that can most significantly alter Northern Ontario's political economy.

At the federal level, some authors argue that significant changes have occurred, with greater foresight in planning and increased communication among governmental agencies and a considerable change in the political context of economic development in Northern Ontario. For decades, authors have noted the need to work collaboratively in the field of economic development by rejecting the silo approach typical of governmental agencies. Recent attempts in the field of economic development reflect a changing multi-level government environment in which actors seek to work cooperatively to coordinate regional development efforts.[58] The Federal Economic Development Initiative for Northern Ontario (FedNor), established in 1987, has come a long way in its attempts to adapt its model of policy implementation to its external environment. The creation of FedNor represented an attempt to develop programs with an inclusive regional focus in a departure from previous top-down approaches.[59] It emphasizes economic development through partnerships between levels of government, First Nations communities, non-governmental organizations, and the private sector.[60]

The field of health care is plagued by many of the same problems that have traditionally faced the field of economic development. Attracting and retaining physicians was a long-standing particular concern.[61] The lack of training opportunities was noted as problematic by many authors, with young Northern Ontarians moving to more central locations for training and then not returning to the North. The creation of a new Northern Ontario School of Medicine (NOSM) in 2005 has helped alleviate the lack of training opportunities in the field of health. In addition, to address the physician shortage in the North, NOSM has also taken a different approach than other schools in Canada by requiring an eight-month community clerkship in Northern Ontario. The Ontario Medical Association recently released a five-point plan that includes prescriptions to tackle some of Ontario's health care issues; they underline the importance of using a multi-stakeholder service to address disparities between north and south.[62] The plan was released prior to the 2022 provincial election to put pressure on political parties. The COVID-19 pandemic also highlighted a number of cracks in an already precarious health care system, particularly in remote communities.

In previous decades, there was also a tendency to develop short-term strategies in an attempt to alleviate the political disaffection of Northern Ontarians. In recent years, however, there has been a shift in government policies, actions, and programs. The 2011 provincial Growth Plan for Northern Ontario established a framework for the next twenty-five years structured around six themes: economy, people, communities, infrastructure, environment, and Indigenous Peoples. While the policy goals included within the plan are quite commendable, there are few indicators developed to assess both the plan and progress to date, and this makes it highly challenging to measure results.[63] Recent mining discoveries also seem to reflect previous patterns that shape the politics of extraction. This is seen in the drawn-out discussions over the Ring of Fire. The Ring of Fire is an area located in Northern Ontario, discovered in 2008 to be rich in chromite, nickel, copper, and platinum and originally estimated to be worth up to $60 billion.[64] From an Indigenous standpoint, there are important jurisdictional and environmental issues that need to be resolved prior to any development, and from a corporate standpoint there are a number of infrastructural issues. The area is approximately 300 kilometres from the nearest railroad or highway and 500 kilometres north of Thunder Bay, which raises a host of questions as to how the minerals will be transported. Current efforts are underway to develop the Northern Road Link project to develop an all-season road; a first step is to undertake an environmental impact study whose terms of reference are developed by local Indigenous communities. The need to include impacted communities in natural resource development projects is crucial to recognizing Indigenous rights. Many First Nations communities view the potential development of the Ring of Fire with mixed feelings. While it could provide employment and a boost to the local economy, there are also environmental and cultural costs. For Northern Ontario as a whole, there is certainly the potential for job creation, but there is also the prospect of the Ring yet again serving as a development hub for the South, thus raising the spectre of a resurgence of the politics of extraction. More recently, estimates of the value of the Ring of Fire have fallen dramatically, though the Ford government continues to pursue its development.[65]

Beyond the Ring of Fire there is little indication that the North is a priority under the leadership of Doug Ford. There has been very little movement on northern projects in recent years such as the Ontario Northland rail and bus network or highway expansions, nor was there much support for Laurentian University, located in Sudbury, as it navigated the *Companies' Creditors Arrangement Act* (CCAA) insolvency process, a process traditionally reserved for the private sector. The Conservatives were frequently criticized in northern media outlets and by many labour groups across the country for its handling of the Laurentian crisis.[66] Rates of homelessness and the opioid crisis have continued to worsen in Northern Ontario, under the leadership of Ford, with little action taken to develop a multi-pronged strategy, a crisis magnified by the COVID-19 pandemic with northern communities leading in terms of homeless populations in comparison to Ontario's larger municipalities.[67] However, the North featured prominently in Ford's 2022 Ontario budget, which was more of a spending platform to kick off the election campaign, and was mentioned in his victory speech on election night. Ford also included four northern members of provincial parliament (MPPs) in his cabinet, all with important portfolios relevant to the North. As with all campaign promises, time will tell whether the North manages to gain traction on social and economic development projects.

Transportation in the North has been a prominent issue under both the Wynne and Ford governments, with progress only seeming to occur when linked to the extraction of resources. For example, the provincial government decided to privatize the Ontario Northland Transportation Commission (ONTC) in 2012. This decision angered many Northerners, as it seemed to confirm perceptions that their concerns were subordinate to those of the province's southern residents. Requests to further investigate the divestment of the ONTC were realized with the provincial auditor's report in 2013. The report held the Liberal government accountable for the misinformation, asserting that it failed to properly communicate the implications of the divestment and citing a lack of communication between the ONTC and the Ministry of Northern Development and Mines.[68] The report's findings did nothing to assuage the perception that regional concerns are secondary. Such government decisions reinforce the politics of disaffection and the idea of services taken for granted in Southern Ontario are not obtained without a fight, a typical pattern in the heartland-hinterland relationship. Ten years later, transportation is still an issue, with many routes cancelled. In the weeks leading up to the 2022 provincial campaign every party included promises to restore Ontario Northland passenger train service. While this could be seen as a way to regain support from the North, one could also argue that these promises, in conjunction with other electoral transportation promises, are consistent with policy decisions relating to the politics of extraction.

The politics of disaffection are also expressed through municipal organizations. The Federation of Northern Ontario Municipalities (FONOM), which represents the northeastern municipalities, has in recent years asked the provincial government to desist from ignoring the concerns of northern municipalities. Two other organizations provide a forum for northern mayors: the coalition of Northern Ontario Large Urban Mayors (NOLUM) and the Northwestern Ontario Municipal Association (NOMA). Recent concerns brought up by FONOM have been the need to address mental health, the opioid crisis, and homelessness, as well as communication issues (such as high-speed connectivity) in the North. They have also been quite vocal in communicating the economic toll of the pandemic in their communities.

CONCLUSION

In the last twenty years, Northern Ontario has witnessed significant structural, political, and economic change. Progress has been made on a number of fronts in the form of improvements to infrastructure, the creation of NOSM, and the instalment of a twenty-five-year growth plan. The majority of these, however, were undertaken in the early 2000s with no recent developments. In addition, the socio-demographic trend remains the same, with a population that is both declining and aging as well as ongoing out-migration characteristic of many hinterland economies. Significant inequality between Northern and Southern Ontario continues to exist in population growth, education, and health services. The federal and provincial governments have attempted to address a number of these issues for decades, some more successfully than others.

The economic cycles of boom and bust persist as the region continues to rely heavily on natural resources. Decisions related to infrastructure are somewhat reminiscent of earlier policies, with government action occurring principally around the exploitation of natural resources. Since the discovery of the Ring of Fire, promises of investment in infrastructure to improve access to resources have been frequent, including Ford's recent election promise to build a $1-billion road to the Ring, which are reminiscent of Wynne's previous campaign promises. Yet the feelings of alienation persist, albeit to a lesser extent than in the previous decade, and while there continues to be discussion of secession or distinct governance mechanisms for Northern Ontario, mobilization efforts are few to non-existent.[69]

The politics of disaffection are still evident in Northern Ontario, with recent trends indicating an increase in protest voting. There are still elements of secessionist discourse, and even if not strong, they point, among other things, to continued discontent with the lack of representatives at both the provincial and federal levels of government. Relatedly, many northern communities feel ignored by key decision-makers, as civil responses to the privatization of the Northland Transportation system reveal. This feeling is magnified in Northern Indigenous communities where long-standing boil water advisories and housing shortages are major priority issues that are often neglected, leaving residents feeling unheard and ignored by the federal and provincial governments.[70]

Recent decades point to some changes in Northern Ontario both in how the politics of disaffection manifest themselves as well as in terms of issues of governance and policy orientation. Even the recent changes in voting patterns, with greater support for the NDP provincially, continue to reflect hinterland politics, and the most significant changes in governance and policy orientation are at the federal level, which has a lesser impact on the dynamics of the heartland-hinterland relationship. The provincial government's requirement to work closely with Indigenous communities and to consider environmental factors in developing the Ring of Fire may help diminish some of the negative aspects traditionally related to the politics of extraction.

One thing that remains certain is that the politics of Northern Ontario continue to distinguish themselves from those of Southern Ontario. Until important structural changes are made to Northern Ontario's political economy, the effects of the heartland-hinterland relationship will continue to manifest themselves, albeit to a lesser extent than in the past, given some of the positive changes in recent decades.

DISCUSSION QUESTIONS

1 Do you agree that Northern Ontario politics are distinct from the rest of the province, and if so, in what ways?
2 How has the heartland-hinterland dynamic shaped Northern Ontario over time, and is it likely to continue in the future?
3 How do the politics of alienation and disaffection shape voting and political activity in Northern Ontario?
4 Is new and expanded economic development the best solution to meet the needs of Indigenous communities in Northern Ontario? Why or why not?
5 Would Northern Ontario be better off becoming a province of its own? Explain.

NOTES

1 Statistics Canada subdivides the population of Northern Ontario into two regions: northeast with a population of 557,220 and northwest with a population of 232,299, for a total of 789,299. Statistics Canada, "Census Profile," 2021 Census of Population, Statistics Canada catalogue no. 98-316-X2021001, released October 26, 2022, https://www12.statcan.gc.ca/census-recensement/2021/dp-pd/prof/index.cfm?Lang=E.
2 Michel S. Beaulieu, "A Historic Overview of Policies Affecting Non-Aboriginal Development in Northwestern Ontario, 1900–1990," in *Governance in Northern Ontario: Economic Development and Policy Making*, ed. Charles Conteh and Bob Segsworth (Toronto: IPAC and University of Toronto Press, 2013), 95–114.
3 Chris Southcott, *The North in Numbers: A Demographic Analysis of Social and Economic Change in Northern Ontario* (Thunder Bay: Centre for Northern Studies, 2007), 4.
4 For a more detailed description of the development of the North as a hinterland and the relevant literature, see Geoffrey R. Weller, "Hinterland Politics: The Case of Northwestern Ontario," *Canadian Journal of Political Science* 10, no. 4 (December 1977): 727–54, https://doi.org/10.1017/S0008423900050873.

5 Weller, "Hinterland Politics," 731.
6 For a more detailed overview of Innis's staples theory see, Harold Innis, *The Fur Trade in Canada* (Toronto: University of Toronto Press, 1999). The original text was published in 1930 but this edition provides a new introduction outlining the impact of Innis's work. The staples theory has fallen into disuse in recent decades but some of the work inspired by this seminal text continues to influence.
7 For example, Kari Levitt, *Silent Surrender* (Toronto: Macmillan, 1970).
8 In this first instance, Weller, "Hinterland Politics," examines Northwestern Ontario but in subsequent studies he examines the politics of Northern Ontario as a whole. In later texts, Weller does not always specifically refer to the metropolis-hinterland relationship. He does continue to argue that the resulting politics continue to influence both the policies and politics of Northern Ontario and its relationship to Southern Ontario. See Geoffrey R. Weller, "Managing Canada's North: The Case of the Provincial North," *Canadian Public Administration* 27, no. 2 (June 1984): 197–209, https://doi.org/10.1111/j.1754-7121.1984.tb00614.x; Geoffrey R. Weller, "Politics and Policy in the North," in *The Government and Politics of Ontario*, 5th ed., ed. Graham White (Toronto: University of Toronto Press, 1997), 284–306.
9 See Steven High's recent study which documents the impact on the community of Sturgeon Falls.
10 H.V. Nelles, *The Politics of Development: Forests, Mines and Hydro-Electric Power in Ontario, 1849-1941*, 2nd ed. (Montreal: McGill-Queen's University Press, 2005), 45.
11 It should be noted that for the first few decades of the twentieth century, there were still intermittent government efforts to develop the North as an agricultural frontier. For a detailed historical development of natural resources in the North, see Nelles, *The Politics of Development*, 45–62.
12 Beaulieu, "A Historical Overview," 97.
13 Beaulieu, 96. See also Tim Nieguth, "We Are Left with No Other Alternative: Legitimating Internal Secession," *Space and Polity* 13, no. 2 (August 2009): 141–57, https://doi.org/10.1080/13562570902999817.
14 Weller, "Hinterland Politics."
15 Weller, "Politics and Policy in the North."
16 David MacKinnon, *Governance in Northern Ontario: Taking Ownership of the Future* (Thunder Bay, ON: Northern Policy Institute, 2016), https://www.northernpolicy.ca/upload/documents/publications/commentaries-new/mackinnon1_governance-in-northern-ontari.pdf.
17 For more information on the history of these movements, see Livio Di Matteo, J.C. Hebert Emery, and Ryan English, "Is It Better to Live in a Basement, an Attic or to Get Your Own Place? Analyzing the Costs and Benefits of Institutional Change for Northwestern Ontario," *Canadian Public Policy/Analyse de politiques* 32, no. 2 (June 2006): 173–96, https://doi.org/10.2307/4128727.
18 See Weller, "Hinterland Politics," 735–7, for a detailed analysis of how the politics of extraction have influenced the demographics of Northern Ontario. Note that

this article specifically deals with Northwestern Ontario but the argument is also applied to a lesser extent to the whole of Northern Ontario in the various editions of Weller, "Politics and Policy in the North."
19 D. Micheal Ray, R.H. Lamarche, and Maurice Beaudin, "Economic Growth and Restructuring in Canada's Heartland and Hinterland: From Shift-Share to Multifactor Partitioning," *Canadian Geographer* 56, no. 3 (Autumn 2012): 296–317, https://doi.org/10.1111/j.1541-0064.2012.00435.x.
20 Government of Ontario, Royal Commission on the Northern Environment, *Final Report and Recommendations* (Toronto: Ontario Ministry of the Attorney General, 1985), 2.
21 Government of Ontario, Royal Commission on the Northern Environment, *Final Report*, 2.
22 Beaulieu, "A Historical Overview," 94.
23 Mercedes Labelle, *Magnetic North: Attraction, Retention, and Welcoming in Ontario's Northern Regions: Magnetic North 2021 Conference Report* (Thunder Bay, ON: Northern Policy Institute, 2022), https://www.northernpolicy.ca/upload/documents/publications/reports-new/magnetic-north-conference-report-jun2021008.pdf.
24 Data from Statistics Canada, "Census Profile," 2021 Census of Population, Statistics Canada catalogue no. 98-316-X2021001, November 15, 2023, https://www12.statcan.gc.ca/census-recensement/2021/dp-pd/prof/details/page.cfm?Lang=E&SearchText=Northwest&DGUIDlist=2021S05003595&GENDERlist=1,2,3&STATISTIClist=1,4&HEADERlist=0.
25 Chris Southcott, "Regional Economic Development and Socio-economic Change in Northern Ontario: Economic Development and Policy Making," in *Governance in Northern Ontario: Economic Development and Policy Making*, ed. Charles Conteh and Robert Segsworth (Toronto: Institute of Public Administration of Canada, 2013), 16–42.
26 Southcott, *The North in Numbers*, 9.
27 For example, Southcott's 2007 study indicated that 44 per cent fewer Northern Ontarians had a university education than Southern Ontarians. Southcott, *The North in Numbers*, 176.
28 OMNDM, *Northern Ontario: A Profile*. Further decline is predicted in the Northern Ontario population; see *Ontario Population Projections Update, 2015–2041* (Toronto: Queen's Printer for Ontario, 2016), www.fin.gov.on.ca/en/economy/demographics/projections/projections2015-2041.pdf.
29 Eric White, "Northern Ontario Grew by 8,647 People in the Last 5 Years According to the 2021 Census," *CBC News,* February 9, 2022, https://www.cbc.ca/news/canada/sudbury/2021-census-population-northeastern-ontario-1.6343586.
30 White, "Northern Ontario Grew."
31 Ministry of Francophone Affairs, "Profile on the Francophone Population in Ontario – 2016," Government of Ontario, published February 5, 2019, https://www.ontario.ca/page/profile-francophone-population-ontario-2016.

32 It should be noted that the trend is shifting; Ministry of Francophone Affairs, "Profile of the Francophone population in Ontario – 2016," Government of Ontario, https://www.ontario.ca/page/profile-francophone-population-ontario-2016.
33 Office of Francophone Affairs, "Inclusive Definition of Francophone."
34 Shinjini Pal, Francois Haman, and Michael A. Robidoux, "The Costs of Local Food Procurement in Two Northern Indigenous Communities in Canada," *Food and Foodways* 21, no. 2 (April 2013): 132–52, https://doi.org/10.1080/07409710.2013.792193.
35 Elisa Levi and Tabitha Robin, *COVID-19 Did Not Cause Food Insecurity in Indigenous Communities but It Will Make It Worse* (Toronto: Yellowhead Institute, 2020), https://yellowheadinstitute.org/2020/04/29/covid19-food-insecurity.
36 These stories also tend to frame Indigenous communities in a negative manner or as problems rather than as communities with rights. For more on the media portrayal of Indigenous communities in Canada, see Angie Fleras, *The Media Gaze: Representation of Diversity in Canada* (Vancouver: UBC Press, 2011).
37 Meagan Fitzpatrick, "Attawapiskat Handed Victory by Federal Court Judicial Review Says 3rd Party Manager Was 'Unreasonable' Fix to Housing Crisis," *CBC News*, August 1, 2012, https://www.cbc.ca/news/politics/attawapiskat-handed-victory-by-federal-court-1.1149282.
38 The Globe and Mail and the Canadian Press, "Attawapiskat: Four Things to Help Understand the Suicide Crisis," *Globe and Mail*, April 11, 2016, https://www.theglobeandmail.com/news/national/attawapiskat-four-things-to-help-understand-the-suicidecrisis/article29583059/.
39 Heather Kitching, "Neskantaga First Nation Surpasses 10,000 Days Under a Drinking Water Advisory," *CBC News*, June 20, 2022, https://www.cbc.ca/news/canada/thunder-bay/neskantaga-water-advisory-anniversary-1.6494213.
40 Indigenous Services Canada, "Remaining Long-Term Drinking Water Advisories," Government of Canada, accessed January 15, 2024, https://www.sac-isc.gc.ca/eng/1614387410146/1614387435325.
41 Nadia A. Charania, Don Wowan, and Leonard J.S. Tsuji, "The Health Care Delivery Remote in Remote Isolated First Nations Communities in Canada," *The International Journal of Technology, Knowledge, and Society* 8, no. 5 (May 2013): 71–80, https://doi.org/10.18848/1832-3669/CGP/v08i05/56328.
42 Health Quality Ontario, *Health in the North: A Report on the Geography and the Health of People in Ontario's Two Northern Regions* (Toronto: Queen's Printer for Ontario, 2017), 7.
43 Office of the Auditor General of Canada, *Report 4: Access to Health Services for Remote First Nations Communities* (Ottawa: Minister of Public Works and Government Services, 2015).
44 Office of the Auditor General of Canada, *Report 11: Health Resources for Indigenous Communities – Indigenous Services Canada* (Ottawa: Minister of Public Works and Government Services, 2021).

45 Frances Abele and Chris Southcott, *Care, Cooperation and Activism in Canada's Northern Social Economy* (Edmonton: University of Alberta Press, 2016).
46 Office of the Auditor General of Canada, *Report 4*.
47 Rand Dyck, *Provincial Politics in Canada: Toward the Turn of the Century* (Scarborough, ON: Prentice-Hall Canada, 1995), 311.
48 Charles Martin, "The Politics of Northern Ontario: An Analysis of the Political Divergences at the Provincial Periphery" (master's thesis, McGill University, 1999).
49 "Ontario Votes," *CBC News*, 2022, https://newsinteractives.cbc.ca/elections/ontario/2022/results/.
50 Di Matteo et al., "Is It Better to Live in a Basement," provides a brief historical overview of these movements and also outlines the various advantages and disadvantages relating to union with Manitoba, provincial status, and regional government options.
51 Nieguth, "We Are Left."
52 Health Quality Ontario, "Health in the North."
53 CBC News, "Northern Ontario Keeps Its 10 Federal Ridings," *CBC News*, October 1, 2013, https://www.cbc.ca/news/canada/sudbury/northern-ontario-keeps-its-10-federal-ridings-1.1874615.
54 See chapter 9 in this volume for an expansion on Ontario's political parties and party system.
55 Weller, "Politics and Policy in the North."
56 Adam D. King, "Right-Wing Populism, Organized Labor, and White Workers in Sudbury, Ontario: A Cautionary Tale to Understand the Appeal of Right-Wing Populism in Northern Ontario," *Journal of Labour and Society* 23, no. 4 (December 2020): 485–501, https://doi.org/10.1111/wusa.12489.
57 Weller, "Politics and Policy in the North."
58 Charles Conteh, "Policy Implementation in Multilevel Environments: Economic Development in Northern Ontario," *Canadian Public Administration* 54, no. 1 (March 2011): 121–42.
59 Conteh, "Policy Implementation in Multilevel Environments." Conteh also outlines the differences in autonomy between FedNor and other federal development agencies.
60 Conteh, "Policy Implementation in Multilevel Environments."
61 Raymond Pong, "Strategies to Overcome Physical Shortages in Northern Ontario: A Study of Implementation over 35 Years," *Human Resources for Health* 6 (2008): article 24, https://doi.org/10.1186/1478-4491-6-24.
62 Ontario Medical Association, *Prescription for Ontario: Doctor's 5-Point Plan for Better Health Care* (Toronto: Ontario Medical Association, 2022).
63 Bob Segsworth provides a number of recommendations to rectify the plan's shortcomings in "Results Measurements and Economic Development in Northern Ontario," in Conteh and Segsworth, *Governance in Northern Ontario*, 58–75.

64 Government of Ontario, "Ontario, First Nations to Work Together on Ring of Fire," Ontario Ministry of Energy, Northern Development and Mines, news release, March 26, 2014, https://news.ontario.ca/en/release/28828/ontario-first-nations-to-work-together-on-ring-of-fire.

65 Nial McGee and Jeff Gray, "The Road to Nowhere: Claims Ontario's Ring of Fire is Worth $60-billion are Nonsense," *Globe and Mail*, October 26, 2019, https://www.theglobeandmail.com/business/article-the-road-to-nowhere-why-everything-youve-heard-about-the-ring-of/.

66 For example, see Sudbury.com Staff, "Tricultural Group Unimpressed by Ford's $53.5M for Laurentian," *sudbury.com*, May 22, 2022, https://www.sudbury.com/local-news/tricultural-group-unimpressed-by-fords-535m-for-laurentian-5418752; or see "Tell Ford to Save Laurentian University," CUPE/SCFP Ontario, accessed April 10, 2024, https://cupe.on.ca/savelaurentian/.

67 Holly Parsons, *Solving the Homelessness, Addiction, and Mental Health Crisis in the North* (Thunder Bay, ON: Northern Policy Institute, 2022).

68 *Divestment of Ontario Northland Transportation Commission: Special Report* (Toronto: Office of the Auditor General of Ontario, 2013).

69 Di Matteo et al., "Is It Better to Live in a Basement," 191.

70 For example, see Logan Turner, "For Ontario's Most Northern Riding, There's a Feeling of Neglect That Residents Are Looking to Change," *CBC News*, May 31, 2022, https://www.cbc.ca/news/canada/thunder-bay/kiiwetinoong-riding-profile-2022-1.6471375.

12

Race and Ontario Politics

Asif Hameed

On June 2, 2020, during a press conference where he was questioned on funding cuts to the province's Anti-Racism Directorate, Premier Ford spoke of his deep commitment to racial equality. "I won't tolerate racism for a second," he mused before affirming that Ontario was "the most multicultural province [and] jurisdiction anywhere in North America."[1] When subsequently pressed for comment on the push for racial equality in the United States by anti-racist activists such as Black Lives Matter, the premier commented that differences between Canada and the United States with regards to racism were "like night and day." He continued by saying "Thank God we're different than the United States. We don't have the systemic, deep roots [of racism]. The difference between the US and Canada is we all get along; we live together; we share communities. Believe me, it's night and day between Canada and the US."[2]

Nearly a year to the day later, on June 6, 2021, on a warm summer night in London, Ontario, Nathaniel Veltman entered his car with the intent to kill any Muslim he could find and was successful in murdering three generations of the Afzaal family in a single stroke, including seventy-four-year-old Talat, forty-six-year-old Salman and his wife Madiha, alongside their fifteen-year-old daughter Yumna. We called them Our London Family. After one more trip around the sun, as the Ford Administration were given their second majority, not a single legislative act had been enacted to address the murder of the Afzaal family, nor the countless incidents of racial animus and bigotry perpetrated against non-white citizens in Ontario in the year since.

Ontario occupies a unique place in the Canadian multicultural project as a kind of city on a hill – a space where racialized others have thrived, and the social and political inclusion of non-white bodies occurs quite unlike anywhere else in Canada. It boasts the largest population of ethnoracial minorities in the country, with over one third of the provincial population being of a visible minority background, according to the most recent census data.[3] It is also home to the Greater Toronto Area, a location widely considered to be the most ethnoracially diverse region on the planet, as well as being home to the largest number of racialized political representatives in Canada.[4]

And yet race – at the best of times – is treated as a political afterthought in Ontario politics. It is used as a political tool or ideological marker when necessary, but is given little consideration as a signifier of power, as are the relations of power within Ontario, and Canada more broadly, that make and perpetuate race. This chapter will explore the fabrication of race in Ontario and interrogate its central – though too often overlooked – role in the broader politics of the province. While a central theme of Ontario politics is the province's place at the centre of diversity and multiculturalism in Canada, this paper will critically evaluate the thinness of this view and instead argue that while non-white bodies are given inclusion into the Ontario body politic, they are denied *belonging* within it. To begin, this chapter will evaluate the central race regime of Canadian, and by extension Ontario, politics – multiculturalism – and the ways in which it both reifies and obscures racial oppression in Ontario. Next, this chapter will explore issues surrounding minority representation in Ontario politics, and dissect the current "unprecedented" level of descriptive representation at Queen's Park, highlighting discrepancies in proportionality and participatory potential. This chapter will then move on to discuss the ways in which non-white substantive representation has been made effectively hollow in Ontario, focusing on institutional norms, political practices, and the inherently discriminatory nature of politics in Ontario. Finally, this chapter will conclude by analyzing the role of race in Ontario's response to the COVID-19 pandemic, alongside some final musings on multiculturalism, belonging, and the minority experience in Ontario.

MULTICULTURALISM: STRENGTHENING DIVERSITY OR RACE WITHOUT RACISM?

Even before the Confederation Debates, diversity and difference were existential concerns for the settler territory that would eventually be christened Canada, and for Ontario, this has been no different. Since the 1960s, the primary lens through which difference has been filtered in Canadian political science – and Canadian politics more broadly – has been that of liberal multiculturalism: a uniquely Canadian mode of diversity management premised on cultural accommodation and the recognition of minority interests.[5] Multiculturalism created a defined area of public policy that extended civil and political rights to minority groups through greater economic support and legal recognition toward potentially emancipatory ends.[6] Through its inclusion in the *Charter of Rights and Freedoms*, it is also a uniquely Canadian constitutional doctrine and governing discourse, and has led to Canada being lauded as a multinational state, a post-national community and even the world's first postmodern state.[7]

However, while the multicultural doctrine would seem to herald Canadian exceptionalism in diversity, inclusion, solidarity, and belonging, the simple truth is multiculturalism is hardly unproblematic in how it also promotes exclusion, fragmentation, and white supremacy just as effectively as cultural pluralism. The core of this issue rests in the continued focus on "culture" as the standard Canadian metric of difference. According to Dhamoon, there is actually no clear definition in liberal multicultural theory as to what culture is, beyond being a broad signifier grounded in nationality, history, and language.[8] This focus on the distinct elements that separate the white settler colonial societies of the "Two Solitudes" as the litmus for identity has the inevitable outcome of privileging particular forms of difference over others. Specifically, it makes differing forms of whiteness the standard for difference in Canada, thereby naturalizing whiteness as "Canadian."[9]

Cultural integration and accommodation, as a result, do not emerge as practices to promote or celebrate difference, but instead are developed as ways to *manage* difference both across the nation and within provinces alike. Thompson rather famously pointed to the ways in which the dogma of "culture" as the Canadian shorthand for difference actively obscures other forms of difference directly tied to dynamics of power, such as gender, sexuality, class, and, most importantly, race.[10] For Thompson, the power dynamics of race are shrouded in the guise of Canadian multiculturalism, a point exemplified by the generalization of non-white/non-Indigenous citizens into the broad, official category of "visible minorities," essentializing not only the individual experiences of members of different racialized communities, but condensing the experiences and differences of *all* non-white and non-Indigenous people into one uniform and static identity.[11]

This is *not* the same as race. *Visible minority* connotes difference based on colour, on the identification of a minority group based predominantly on visible differences stemming from differentiated concentrations of melanin within skin. By extension, it also assumes a natural majority (i.e., whiteness) based on this same litmus, thus rendering whiteness invisible. Race is not just a matter of physical difference, but rather how physical difference is socially constructed as biological fact through forms of knowledge.[12] Hall famously conceptualized race in this regard as a floating signifier that gives meaning and validity to socially and culturally ascribed aspects of racial identity. These signifiers are given weight and meaning through the continued discursive power of debunked forms of racialized pseudoscience, such as eugenics and phrenology.[13] Race as a concept is tied to power; it is inherently concerned with the ways in which non-white bodies are discursively constructed as scientifically *and* socially inferior. *Visible minorities* as a concept does no such thing.

Similarly, race is not ethnicity. While similar as both are categories of difference often tied to dynamics of power, there are important differences between race and ethnicity. Race is linked to the physical, thus it is immutable and ascribed by external imposition. It is constructed as biological: a matter of skin, blood, and bone. Ethnicity, however, is a cultural concept, and as a result, ethnicity is a characteristic that can be hidden or displayed at the discretion of the individual.[14] Simply put, one can choose to display their ethnic identity, but their race – and the various stereotypes and biases associated with it – is imposed onto them. In reality, there are many forms of ethnic identity that can be ascribed to white-passing citizens, but socially and culturally the colour of their skin often determines how our society understands their belonging.

Lastly, while the literature of Canadian political science often conflates racial identity with immigration status, it is important to note that these categories are not identical. This conflation of terms stems in large part from the long-standing availability of statistics and public data on immigration, compared to the complete absence of race-based data in Canada. Immigration status is a matter of formal citizenship, and while in practice immigration status assumes racial difference, the formation of every non-white person in Canada as a recent addition rather than a natural and pre-existing part of Canadian politics presumes a nation of whiteness.

Immigration becomes a way of talking about race without talking about the dynamics of racism and presumes *immigrant* is synonymous with *outsider*, even though the term is rarely applied to white-passing immigrants in Canadian political discourse. The term *immigrants* unearths a very specific understanding of who is being discussed, which effectively constructs non-white people as tolerated guests rather than the reality that non-white people have lived and worked in this country for many generations. As such, race and racial identities are best conceptualized not as matters of the concentration of melanin in skin, culture, or citizen status, but rather as sets of power relations.[15]

DESCRIPTIVE REPRESENTATION: DIGGING BENEATH THE NUMBERS

Race occupies a strange place in Ontario politics, in that it is both present in and absent from it. It is present as a form of difference, but substantively absent as a meaningful and important area of political discourse or policy. This would seem strange given the extraordinary presence of racialized minorities in Ontario and their apparent success at political mobilization. After all, the current Parliament of Ontario is the most diverse in Ontario history, featuring twenty-nine members from minority communities within the 124-seat legislature. While this gives Ontario the image of an exemplar of minority political inclusion, this section will dig into the weeds to interrogate the ways in which the political inclusion of minorities is inherently limited, focusing on issues related to racial proportionality, barriers to participation, and the activity of the province's major political parties.

And again, on paper, Ontario would seem to be an exemplar of minority inclusion in the political process. Ontario, at present, has the largest number of racial minorities within provincial legislatures in the country – in fact, there are presently more minority representatives within Queen's Park than in every other provincial and territorial legislature from the Atlantic Ocean to Saskatchewan *combined*. Further, of the fifty members of parliament at the House of Commons that identify as racial minorities, well over half – a total of twenty-nine representatives – come from ridings in Ontario. Simply put, in terms of descriptive representation, one would be forgiven for viewing Ontario as a bastion of political inclusion given its place as the epicentre of minority representation in Canada.

However, closer interrogation of this data illuminates some troubling trends. The first is in relation to proportionality. According to 2021 census data, Ontario has a population of 14,031,750 people, 34.3 per cent of whom – or 4,817,360 citizens – come from an ethnoracial minority background.[16] When looking at the representation of minorities in the Ontario Legislative Assembly, however, minorities are proportionately underrepresented. Non-white members of provincial parliament (MPPs) make up only 23.7 per cent of the current Ontario Legislative Assembly (OLA); while this only marks a 10.6 per cent distortion in proportionality from the actual population of non-white bodies in Ontario, this discrepancy leads to minority populations being disadvantaged in representation by a factor of 1.5, while representation by demographic weight favours white Ontarians by a factor of 1.2.

Proportional disadvantage is also not equal between groups. In studying the 2018 Ontario provincial election, Passy and Gueye found that Chinese Canadians were the most proportionately underrepresented racialized group in Ontario. By population, there should have been seven Chinese Canadian MPPs at Queen's Park, yet there were only three. In other words, Chinese Canadians were proportionately underrepresented by a factor of 2.3 in the aftermath of the 2018 Ontario Election.[17] The study also found that the *only* ethnoracial minority group overrepresented in the 42nd Ontario legislature was that of Black Canadians, who were overrepresented by a factor of 1.3.[18]

The notion of descriptive representation contends that minority interests are best represented within governing institutions by individuals drawn from their communities in order to develop policy that attends to their specific needs and concerns.[19] Racialized communities in particular face issues of material and economic inequality at disproportionate rates in Ontario, coupled with systemic forms of disadvantage and oppression ranging from unfair hiring practices to increased rates of surveillance, arrest, and targeting as the object of hate crimes.[20] As a result, political representation is all the more paramount for these communities; and yet, even in Canada's most diverse province, that representation is inherently limited in comparison to white citizens and residents. Further, while Ontario is currently in an era of previously unprecedented levels of minority representation, prior to the McGuinty years, fewer than a handful of MPPs from any given parliament were from minority backgrounds in Ontario. In fact, from 1963 – the year Leonard Braithwaite, a

Black Canadian and the first non-white MPP in Ontario, was first elected – to 1999, only seventeen non-white MPPs were elected in Ontario, or roughly 1.26 per cent of *all* MPPs elected during that near four-decade period.

While descriptive representation may have improved in Ontario, progress has been stunted at best, and still places minorities at a systemic disadvantage in terms of representation in the Legislative Assembly. The root causes of parliamentary disadvantage and political (dis)integration more broadly as a product of race have been a matter of concern for researchers within the academy of Canadian political science – though admittedly, much of this research has been centred on the previously discussed political activity of immigrants at the federal level, with some consideration of the role of race. Authors have pointed to issues such as differentiated political opportunity structures of immigrants versus nationalized, white Canadians, their comparable lack of participation within political organizations, and impediments for adapting to the institutional and social norms of their new host country as broad sources for the stunted political incorporation of immigrants into party politics in Canada.[21]

While these issues represent barriers to political integration, they do not necessarily mark barriers to participation. In fact, regarding differing forms of political participation – from interest in politics to various forms of participatory behaviour – immigrant engagement, when other factors are controlled, is comparable to non-immigrants and, in some cases, even exceeds it.[22] But the material and social experiences of immigrants – especially racialized immigrants – are much different than that of white, "old stock" Canadians, and the disproportionate deprivation faced by non-white citizens has unfortunately acted as a systemic impediment on the ability of racialized bodies to fully participate in political life in Ontario. In comparing white and non-white participatory behaviour, Bevelander and Pendakur found that the actual patterns of voting and civic engagement of these two racial categories were incredibly similar when controlling for socio-economic and social capital factors.[23] However, the participatory potential of non-white immigrants was shown to be increasingly vulnerable to the impact of issues like social exclusion, level of education, and economic hardship to a far greater extent than white/non-racialized Canadians, with the authors highlighting that civic engagement has little to do with race specifically, but rather the social, demographic, and material reality that surrounds racialized bodies.[24]

W.E.B. Du Bois would famously contend that the colour line – the discriminatory cleft between white and non-white bodies – was the defining issue of the twentieth century,[25] and with regards to political participation, it remains one of the most prevalent roadblocks to minority political integration in Canada. It is a line made manifest across the gamut of social and economic life in Ontario, from the deep prevalence of racial discrimination in the Canadian job market to the disproportionate lack of home ownership among Black Ontarians in the Greater Toronto Area (GTA), to the complete absence of non-white civil servants from the top thirty of the Ontario Sunshine List.[26] And it continues to limit the ability of non-white citizens to effectively participate in political life in Ontario. While institutional factors may limit the ability of minorities to effectively navigate the body politic, it is this discriminatory cleft that erodes the desire to actively be a part of it.

Political exclusion is not only a function of economic discrimination, but of social discrimination as well. In fact, one of the most prevalent findings within the literature about minority participation in Canada is the ways in which discrimination is a source of demobilization and civic disengagement among non-white citizens.[27] The perception of being excluded, of not being an accepted member of the community, is an every-day part of the minority experience in Canada – it hollows attachment to the broader Canadian community and reduces one's sense of citizenship to mere words and title as opposed to identity. It dissolves one's sense of belonging to the nation.

While the concept of belonging will be discussed in greater depth later in this chapter, political inclusion is a right meant for all citizens of Canada as outlined by Section 3 of the *Charter of Rights and Freedoms*. And while this chapter has, up to this point, discussed informal, non-institutionalized sources that inherently limit minority representation in Ontario, there are notable institutionalized limiters as well. One such concern is that of voter dilution.

While Canada's non-partisan electoral management bodies are often lauded for their lack of politicization, voter dilution marks a "Canadian variant" of American gerrymandering processes like stacking and packing. According to Pal and Chowdry, voter dilution is an outcome of attempts by Canadian electoral management boards at developing constituencies which promote regional representation first and foremost.[28] Deviating from constituency redistribution approaches that are based on population and the concept of "one person-one vote" – the global standards for constituency distribution – the Canadian approach has sought to promote rural representation through allocating a greater number of constituencies to remote areas. The result is a sacrifice of voter parity in favour of regional inclusion, and for Pal and Chowdry, this has had a negative impact on the strength of racialized votes.[29]

As Canada's minorities predominantly live in the country's urban centres, the redistribution process has increasingly weakened the voter strength of Canada's non-white population, and it is a process that is getting worse over time. In 1996, the voter strength of a single non-white vote within urban centres was 0.96 of a vote; by 2001 this would drop to 0.91, while voter strength in rural constituencies rose to 1.22 by 2001. In other words, a non-white urban vote roughly carried two-thirds the strength of a rural vote.[30] By 2014, the cleft between rural and urban votes had jumped from one-third to over 50 per cent, with a single vote in districts with a non-white population under 1 per cent commanding the strength of nearly one and a half votes – or a voter power of 1.49 – while votes in ridings with minority populations over 30 per cent carrying a voter power of 0.9. For non-white voters in Ontario specifically, their voter strength dropped even further, falling to 0.89 as of 2014.[31]

But voter dilution is not the only source of institutionalized discrimination within Ontario's electoral landscape. In fact, in many ways the true depths of voter dilution cannot be fully understood without consideration of the activities of Ontario's political parties. While strategic in their inclusion of minority voices, the activity of the major parties in Ontario is also the source of some of the greatest limitations placed on minority voices as well, offering non-white bodies political representation that is conditional at best. Since the 2003 Ontario election – roughly around the same time the Conservative Party of Canada began a standard of tactically concentrating on minority outreach with its "Bridge Building Committee" – Ontario's major political parties have made a concerted effort to run a greater number of non-white, minority candidates. The 2003 electoral victory of the Ontario Liberal party under Dalton McGuinty was a critical juncture for minority representation in the province, resulting in the election of ten non-white MPPs and marked the start of a steady rise in minority representation that has come to define the past two decades.

These MPPs came from markedly diverse communities in the GTA, such as Markham, Scarborough, Brampton, Mississauga, and Etobicoke – communities that would grow from having significant populations of non-white minorities to becoming majority-minority cities in the years since.[32] And across that period of time, minority representation in Ontario, as reflected by both elected MPPs and candidates run, has almost entirely been *confined* to these communities.

Research by Black and Hicks has shown that minority representation predominantly occurs in majority-minority ridings in Canada, thus the likelihood of the major political parties running non-white candidates in majority-white areas is very low.[33] And nearly two decades later Ontario is no exception to this rule. In fact, of the twenty-eight non-white MPPs elected to Queen's Park in 2018, twenty-one were elected in constituencies with a minority population of over 40 per cent, and nineteen came from constituencies with a non-white population of over 50 per cent.[34] Further, among the six majority-white constituencies where non-white candidates won, three were victorious in ridings where they represented the second-largest ethnoracial group.[35] While it is to be expected that an abundance of non-white candidates would seek nomination in predominantly non-white constituencies, this striking lack of non-white candidates in majority-white constituencies illustrates a defined trend among the political parties in Ontario – and Canada more broadly – of only engaging in minority candidacy as a cynical and exploitative means to electoral success.[36] Parties are all too willing to "play ethnic politics" when advantageous, engaging cultural communities and leaders for their support through candidates who are essentially used as tokens for access.[37] Minority representation thus becomes a calculus, a box to be checked in order to ensure victory in the Greater Toronto Area, instead of a means to better, more representative governance. In the years since the McGuinty government's first victory, the winning party in Ontario provincial elections have consistently been those which can win Ontario's majority-minority constituencies, a fact that hardly signifies inclusion, but rather the successful mobilization of essential "ethnic" blocs throughout the GTA, regardless of party.

This is, of course, problematic for a multitude of reasons, not the least of which includes the exploitative nature of Ontario's party dynamics and the broader uniquely Canadian "brokerage" approach that informs them. Brokerage parties are, in essence, Canadian variants of the "big tent" party, which eschew overtly ideological approaches in favour of building the broadest support base possible.[38] And while they generally do so by employing messages of unity and inclusion – and a vision of the party being the only actor capable of ensuring these ideals – such cosmopolitan veils masquerade the pragmatic, power-driven, majoritarian-focused politic at their core.[39] As such, parties are quick to extol the virtues of diversity, and run non-white candidates in constituencies where they can ensure success, but – as the next section discusses in greater depth – despite that success, they rarely govern for these communities or with their needs in mind.

SUBSTANTIVE REPRESENTATION AND THE QUESTION OF "WHO GOVERNS?"

As mentioned, descriptive representation is the notion that policy is made best through the inclusion of representatives and policy makers from the communities impacted by the policies in question. But as the previous section illustrated, while Ontario stands as a supposed exemplar of ethnoracial inclusion in Canada, that inclusion is inherently hindered by systems of institutionalized exclusion, and material and social realities that reduce the ability and the drive of non-white citizens to fully participate in political life.

But descriptive representation is just one aspect of minority representation – more paramount is the notion of *substantive* representation, or the ability of legislators from marginalized groups to exercise agency and actively pursue the interests of their communities.[40] Or, put differently: that non-white bodies are not only a critical mass in representative democracy, but have the capacity to be critical *actors*.[41]

Unfortunately, parallel to the descriptive inclusion of non-white communities, the substantive clout of non-white voices within the halls of Queen's Park have traditionally rung resoundingly hollow. But this lack of substantive representation is hardly an outcome of chance, but rather is by design. This section will discuss the dynamics of race as they relate to executive authority and the overriding of representation in favour of effectiveness in governance.

As Tom McDowell discusses in chapter 4, Canada is notorious as a global outlier in the centralization of governing power, with the authority of first ministers in Canada being famously described as akin to "an elected dictatorship."[42] In Ontario, the racial dynamics of leadership are quite stark – there has simply never been a non-white leader of a major political party, let alone premier. Further, while cabinet offers an opportunity for minority inclusion into executive deliberation at Queen's Park, Ontario cabinets have almost exclusively comprised white male voices; even now in an era of unprecedented inclusion of non-white voices in Ontario governance, those voices are largely confined to the backbench or are marginalized in a cabinet dominated by, generally, a lone white male premier.

One need only look to the composition of cabinet under Premier Ford to see these issues at play. A rallying call of the Ford campaign during the 2018 Ontario election heralded "Ford Nation is for everyone," yet the twenty-minister cabinet that formed the core of his first administration would boast just *one* non-white minister.[43] And in the years since, little has changed in this regard; while efforts were made to increase cabinet diversity in line with the needs and composition of the electorate for the 43rd Ontario Parliament, racialized minorities within cabinet totalled only seven out of thirty ministerial appointments for a province that is home to over 4 million non-white citizens. Famously, not even the minister of citizenship and multiculturalism portfolio – the ministry most concerned with issues of diversity and race in the province – was given to a member of a racialized community. Rather, it was assigned to a white, rookie MPP that Premier Ford claimed had more experience than "60% of [the Progressive Conservative] caucus": his twenty-eight-year-old nephew, Michael Ford.[44] As long as power is fully centred within the executive, and the executive remains solely in the purview of whiteness in Ontario, substantive representation of minority interests will remain an impossibility. The result isn't just policy devoid of minority voices, but policy that simply cannot conceive of the minority condition. Who governs matters, and who does not govern equally matters.

While such discriminatory institutional practices would seem in contradiction to the logics of representation central to democracy in Ontario and across Canada, they are actually fully in line with the majoritarian institutional makeup of Canadian democracy. This is not meant to be a claim that Canada is somehow not democratic, but rather our democratic institutions are geared towards effective, majoritarian governance over more representative, consensual, or proportional patterns of democracy.[45] As discussed throughout this volume, good governance in Ontario has traditionally been measured not by progress, fairness, or consensus, but by effective management of governing portfolios. As a result, institutional arrangements and practices in Ontario are geared towards effectiveness as the central ethos of governance, rather than democratic norms like egalitarianism or inclusion.

Take for instance the concept of party discipline – the notion that members of a political party should never break rank or diverge from the position of party leadership. Party discipline is as close to an iron law of Canadian governance as is institutionally possible, being more prevalent within the legislatures across the Canadian federation than other Westminster systems.[46] And this is infinitely true for Ontario as well, with deviations from the party line being incredibly rare at Queen's Park. However, such institutionalized discipline runs counter to the agency required for substantive representation to even be possible, and reduces MPPs to mere "members of provincial party" rather than "members of provincial parliament." But as counter to democratic representation as such norms may seem, this view that political representatives are party delegates *first* rather than community agents is fully in line with the logic of effectiveness that filters institutional behaviour in Ontario. As parties are institutions in their own right, they too are subject to the overarching structural trend towards majoritarianism in Ontario's political institutions and the dogmatic rationality of effective governance.

A stark example of this can be seen in the fallout of the murder of the Afzaal family discussed at the start of this chapter. When Liberal MPP Mitzie Hunter attempted to pass an act condemning Islamophobia in the days that followed, members of the Ford government refused to give it their consent.[47] While the administration would cite a lack of advanced text being made available, it was clear that the administration's rejection of the bill – alongside its continued ignorance of the NDP's own Bill 86, the *"Our London Family" Act*, which was formally tabled several months later – had little to do with formality and was largely done as an act of party unity. At the same time, this example also makes clear the depths of racial insensitivity and animus within Ontario governance itself. While the government was quick to take on the rhetoric of "Our London Family" and the premier wasted no time in labelling the attack an act of terror at a vigil in the family's honour, words such as these fall increasingly hollow when they are not followed by efforts to address the ecosystem of Islamophobic, white supremacist groups that are increasingly committing acts of hate against not only Ontario's Muslim population, but all racialized, non-white minority groups.[48] And that deafening silence reveals a dire double-standard in Ontario not only as it relates to the securitization of white versus non-white terrorism, but also between the victims who are worthy of state protection and the others whose murder is deemed acceptable.

COVID-19 AND THE DOCTRINE OF DISCRIMINATION

What should now be evident is that the chasm between white and non-white bodies in Ontario isn't solely a matter of differential quantities of melanin in skin, or even differing patterns of electoral representation, but the occupation of wholly separate political realities. This is neither new nor novel, but has been true and institutionalized since Turtle Island was settled in line with *terra nullius* and its history erased by the "doctrine of discovery." While this chapter has noted improvements to conditions and progress in representation, the simple reality is non-white bodies continue to be subjected to and governed by different rationalities compared to their white, "old stock" counterparts.

This condition of governance isn't just an issue of institutional fallacy or verbal faux pas, but is the product of an approach to race, equality, and justice that is *actively* discriminatory towards non-white minorities, while continually and simultaneously denying the existence of discrimination. The racial dynamics of the COVID-19 pandemic stand as clear examples of these processes. While all Ontario citizens suffered under the weight of the pandemic, the disproportionate impact of COVID-19 on non-white bodies took a myriad of forms. One of the most noteworthy was the increased exposure to infection non-white citizens endured due to their disproportionate placement in low-wage, "essential" workplaces throughout the various waves of the pandemic.[49] While these workers were deemed "essential," they were – and continue to be – denied essential protections, such as paid sick leave or hazard pay, and were instead forced to work throughout the oscillations of lockdowns and reopenings. The outcome was a pandemic in Ontario that affected all, but killed Black and Brown bodies in the province's most diverse areas at a rate three times higher than the provincial average.[50]

Further, the pandemic also saw a wide expanse of racially motivated hate crimes, especially those targeting individuals of East-Asian ethnoracial origin.[51] While official data on the prevalence of racially motivated hate crimes is exceedingly rare in Canada, Statistics Canada recently compiled a scan of hate crime prevalence using data from the Uniform Crime Reporting Survey, noting an 80% spike in racially motivated hate crimes across Canada between 2019 and 2020.[52] While these crimes "only" increased by 35% across Ontario during this period, hate crimes within white-majority cities in the province skyrocketed, with Kitchener-Cambridge-Waterloo experiencing a 253% surge, followed by Peterborough (126%) and Guelph (80%).[53] These are not insignificant numbers; rather, they illustrate an exponential rise in the targeting of non-white bodies within some of Ontario's largest metropolitan areas outside the GTA, in communities where whites are still the majority population. And while racially motivated hate crimes – both violent and non-violent – continue to climb to unprecedented levels in the province, comprehensive anti-racism policies have remained underdeveloped and largely non-existent.

This increased violence is not the only well of discriminatory behaviour in Ontario associated with the pandemic. Throughout the pandemic's various waves, political representatives have also sought to frame non-white bodies as spreaders of disease, using minority communities as scapegoats for national and provincial hardship. In a particularly infamous example of this, following the release of a *Toronto Star* column chastising the South Asian community of Brampton as being responsible for the heightened infection rate in the city, Premier Ford blasted South Asians as COVID-19 super-spreaders, citing culturally essentialist stereotypes such as proclivities towards big weddings, multi-generational homes, and lavish parties.[54] While the premier's comments would be made as a warning against families getting together for Diwali, the relative silence of similar criticisms made towards non-minority families for holidays such as Halloween, Thanksgiving, Christmas, and New Year's Eve – holidays which, in Ontario, resulted in significantly higher spikes in COVID-19 infections when compared to Diwali – illustrates the all-too-familiar double standard in holding whiteness to account for dangerous, socially irresponsible behaviour.[55]

While the dynamics of the COVID-19 pandemic continue to be exceptional in nature, the politics of race at their core are hardly exceptional in the Ontario context. One need only look to the "Common Sense Revolution" of the 1990s to see it at play through the ways in which Black and Brown women were framed as a mass of undeserving poor "welfare queens" to justify social retrenchment.[56] Or to the silence that continues to surround the legacy of segregated education in Ontario, a system that lasted until 1965 – over a decade after *Brown vs. Board of Education* eroded the practice in the Jim Crow American South.[57] Or, more recently, to the Freedom Convoy protests in Ottawa, which saw activists, adorned in symbols of hate and imbricated in the ideology of white supremacy, lay siege to the second-largest city in the province for over two weeks before the Ford Administration called a state of emergency.[58]

These events and countless other examples throughout the history of Ontario illustrate a differential political reality as it relates to non-white bodies in the province; one not defined by full citizenship, but a tenuous, conditional form of belonging that will always remain subject to further review and perpetually out of reach. As previously discussed, whether the condition of being accepted or the feeling of attachment to the larger political community, belonging is a fundamental mediator in the integration of non-white bodies into social and political life. However, as Nira Yuval-Davis has outlined, "place belonging" – or the emotional attachment to a place or location – is a very different beast to the "*politics* of belonging," which is centred on the internal boundaries constructed within a delineated collectivity, or the borders that create the cleft between "us" and "them"; "member" and "other"; "white" and "non-white."[59] And for non-white bodies in Ontario, while they may have citizenship and a place within the province de jure, it does not come with unqualified access to the nation, nor belonging within it.

CONCLUSION

This chapter marks an attempt to illustrate the nature of political exclusion in the province of Ontario and interrogate its sources. And while institutional factors and the deprivation of social and material capital have no doubt played a role, the cleft between white and non-white bodies in Ontario – as should now be quite clear – is chained to something more primal and more fundamental to the Canadian condition.

With regards to Ontario's politics of belonging, the outcome is quite clear for racialized, non-white bodies – despite the virtues of multiculturalism so often extolled by political actors like Premier Ford above, the politics of exclusion, marginalization, and punishment that so disproportionately impact the lives of non-white bodies are not a defect of multiculturalism and Canadian governance, but rather these outcomes are by design. Multiculturalism and its discourses of diversity and inclusion are more than just areas of policy or a constitutional doctrine, but are part of a political project: a project to create a national myth of tolerance and racial harmony while simultaneously reproducing the institutional and normative hegemony of white settler colonial dominance. This myth of tolerance not only seeks to masquerade past and present racism and genocide as events lost to antiquity, but to naturalize the settler society that was built atop the bones of Turtle Island. Ontario occupies a central place in this project – as the hub of diversity in the nation, it in many ways epitomizes the multicultural mosaic in all its forms; but it also epitomizes the fallacies of that myth and the true face of the mosaic. And until we come to terms with the myths we tell ourselves, we will continue to believe that "night and day," as Premier Ford contrasted the American melting pot and the Canadian mosaic, are somehow not part of the same cycle.

DISCUSSION QUESTIONS

1 Many of the chapters in this volume have discussed Doug Ford's unique brand of populism as being somewhat at odds with other right-wing populist politicians across the world, and

this holds true for race politics as well. How is the populism of Ford Nation explicitly "anti-nativist," and how can that be explained by some of the dynamics discussed in this chapter?
2 The COVID-19 pandemic has had a disproportionately severe impact on non-white bodies in Ontario – from greater rates of infection and mortality to the spike in racially motivated hate crimes that coincided with the pandemic. How have these impacts intersected and overlapped with other forms of oppression, such as class, gender, etc.?
3 This chapter presents a critical view of the way multiculturalism obscures other forms of difference beyond culture. Can multiculturalism be adjusted to be more inclusive in how it conceptualizes diversity? What kinds of changes would be required to make multiculturalism "see" more than just culture?

NOTES

1 The Canadian Press, "Doug Ford Says Canada Doesn't Have Same 'Systemic, Deep Roots' of Racism as U.S.," *Toronto Star*, June 2, 2020, https://www.thestar.com/news/canada/doug-ford-says-canada-doesn-t-have-same-systemic-deep-roots-of-racism-as-u/article_d156deeb-f158-59e0-a2b3-85b3505d00d7.html.
2 The Canadian Press, "Doug Ford Says."
3 Statistics Canada, "Census Profile, 2021 Census of Population," Statistics Canada catologue no. 98-316-X2021001, released February 9, 2022, https://www12.statcan.gc.ca/census-recensement/2021/dp-pd/prof/index.cfm?Lang=E.
4 Statistics Canada, "Toronto – A Data Story on Ethnocultural Diversity and Inclusion in Canada," released April 29, 2019, https://www150.statcan.gc.ca/n1/pub/11-631-x/11-631-x2019002-eng.htm; BBC Radio 4, "WS More or Less: The World's Most Diverse City," *BBC*, May 2016, https://www.bbc.co.uk/programmes/p03v1r1p.
5 Will Kymlicka, "Neoliberal Multiculturalism," in *Social Resilience in the Neoliberal Era*, ed. Peter A. Hall and Michèle Lamont (Oxford: Oxford University Press, 2013), 101.
6 Kymlicka, "Neoliberal Multiculturalism," 101–2.
7 Sujit Choudhry, "Does the World Need More Canada? The Politics of the Canadian Model in Constitutional Politics and Political Theory," *International Journal of Constitutional Law* 5, no. 4 (October 2007): 609, https://doi.org/10.1093/icon/mom028; Michel Seymour, "Quebec and Canada at the Crossroads: A Nation Within a Nation," *Nations and Nationalism* 6, no. 2 (April 2000): 239, https://doi.org/10.1111/j.1354-5078.2000.00227.x; Charles Foran, "The Canada Experiment: Is This the World's First 'Post National' Country?," *The*

Guardian, January 4, 2017, https://www.theguardian.com/world/2017/jan/04/the-canada-experiment-is-this-the-worlds-first-postnational-country; Kenneth McRoberts, "Canada and the Multinational State," *Canadian Journal of Political Science* 34, no. 4 (December 2001): 683, https://doi.org/10.1017/S0008423901778055.

8 Rita Dhamoon, *Identity/Difference Politics: How Difference is Produced and Why It Matters* (Vancouver: UBC Press, 2009), 20.

9 Himani Bannerji, *The Ideological Condition: Selected Essays on History, Race and Gender* (Toronto: Brill, 2020), 378; Sunera Thobani, *Exalted Subjects: Studies in the Making of Race and Nation in Canada* (Toronto: University of Toronto Press, 2007), 3–4; Dhamoon, *Identity/Difference Politics*.

10 Debra Thompson, "Is Race Political?," *Canadian Journal of Political Science* 41, no. 3 (September 2008): 528–30, https://doi.org/10.1017/S0008423908080827.

11 Keith Banting and Debra Thompson, "The Puzzling Persistence of Racial Inequality in Canada," *Canadian Journal of Political Science* 54, no. 4 (2021): 875–6.

12 Ian F. Haney López, "The Social Construction of Race," in *Critical Race Theory: The Cutting Edge*, ed. Richard Delgado and Jean Stefancic (Philadelphia: Temple University Press, 2000), 164–5.

13 Stuart Hall, "Race, The Floating Signifier: What More Is There to Say about 'Race'?," in *Selected Writings on Race and Difference*, ed. Paul Gilroy and Ruth Wilson Gilmore (Durham: Duke University Press, 2021), 359–60.

14 Aliya Saperstein, Andrew M. Penner, and Ryan Light, "Racial Formation in Perspective: Connecting Individuals, Institutions, and Power Relations," *Annual Review of Sociology* 39 (July 2013): 365–6, https://doi.org/10.1146/annurev-soc-071312-145639.

15 Charles W. Mills, *The Racial Contract* (Ithaca: Cornell University Press, 2014), 3.

16 Statistics Canada, "Toronto – A Data Story."

17 Pascasie Minani Passy and Abdoulaye Gueye, "Ethnoracial Identities and Political Representation in Ontario and British Columbia," *Canadian Parliamentary Review* 42, no. 4 (Winter 2019): 19.

18 Passy and Gueye, "Ethnoracial Identities and Political Representation," 20.

19 Sara Childs and Mona Lena Krook, "Analyzing Women's Substantive Representation: From Critical Mass to Critical Actors," *Government and Opposition* 44, no. 2 (2009): 125–26, https://doi.org/10.1111/j.1477-7053.2009.01279.x; Jane Mansbridge, "Should Blacks Represent Blacks and Women Represent Women? A Contingent Yes," *The Journal of Politics* 61, no. 3 (August 2009): 629, https://doi.org/10.2307/2647821.

20 Robyn Maynard, *Policing Black Lives: State Violence in Canada from Slavery to the Present* (Halifax: Fernwood, 2017); Rita Dhamoon and Yasmeen Abu-Laban, "Dangerous (Internal) Foreigners and Nation-Building: The Case of Canada," *International Political Science Review* 30, no. 2 (March 2009): 163–83, https://doi.org/10.1177/0192512109102435; Daiva Stasiulis and Yasmeen Abu-Laban, "Unequal Relations and the Struggle for Equality: Race and Ethnicity in Canadian Politics," in *Canadian Politics in the 21st Century*, 6th ed., ed.

Michael Whittington and Glen Williams (Toronto: Thomson Nelson, 2004), 371–97.

21 Jerome H. Black and Bruce M. Hicks, "Visible Minority Candidates in the 2004 Federal Election," *Canadian Parliamentary Review* 29, no. 2 (Summer 2006): 27–9 ; Karen Bird, "Guess Who's Running for Office? Visible Minority Representation in the 2004 Canadian Election," *Canadian Issues* (Summer 2005): 80–3; Elisabeth Gidengil and Jason Roy, "Is There a Racial Divide? Immigrants of Visible Minority Background in Canada," in *Just Ordinary Citizens? Towards a Comparative Portrait of the Political Immigrant*, ed. Antoine Bilodeau (Toronto: University of Toronto Press, 2018), 150–4; Elisabeth Gidengil and Dietlind Stolle, "The Role of Social Networks in Immigrant Women's Political Incorporation," *International Migration Review* 43, no. 4 (December 2009): 728–35, https://doi.org/10.1111/j.1747-7379.2009.00783.x; Jeffrey G. Reitz, Rupa Banerjee, Mai Phan, and Jordan Thompson, "Race, Religion, and the Social Integration of New Immigrant Minorities in Canada," *International Migration Review* 43, no. 4 (December 2009): 697, https://doi.org/10.1111/j.1747-7379.2009.00782.x; Jeffrey G. Reitz and Rupa Banerjee, "Racial Inequality, Social Cohesion and Policy Issues in Canada," in *Belonging? Diversity, Recognition and Shared Citizenship in Canada*, vol. 3, ed. Keith Banting, Thomas J. Courchene and F. Leslie Seidle (Montreal: Institute For Research on Public Policy, 2007): 5–10; Irene Bloemraad, "Becoming a Citizen in the United States and Canada: Structured Mobilization and Immigrant Political Incorporation," *Social Forces* 85, no. 2 (December 2006): 670–4, https://doi.org/10.1353/sof.2007.0002.

22 Antoine Bilodeau, Stephen E. White, Luc Turgeon, and Alisa Henderson, "Feeling Attached and Feeling Accepted: Implications for Political Inclusion among Visible Minority Immigrants in Canada," *International Migration* 58, no. 2 (April 2009): 276–7, https://doi.org/10.1111/imig.12657; Jerome H. Black, "Immigrant and Minority Political Incorporation in Canada: A Review with Some Reflections on Canadian-American Comparison Possibilities," *American Behavioral Scientist* 55, no. 9 (September 2011): 1169–72, https://doi.org/10.1177/0002764211407843; Gidengil and Roy, "Is There a Racial Divide?"

23 Pieter Bevelander and Ravi Pendakur, "Social Capital and Voting Participation of Immigrants and Minorities in Canada," *Ethnic and Racial Studies* 32, no. 8 (October 2009): 1414, https://doi.org/10.1080/01419870802298447.

24 Bevelander and Pendakur, "Social Capital and Voting," 1420.

25 W.E.B. Du Bois, *The Souls of Black Folk: The Unabridged Classic* (New York: Simon and Schuster, 2019): 1.

26 Lincoln Quillian and John J. Lee, "Trends In Racial And Ethnic Discrimination In Hiring In Six Western Countries," *Proceedings of the National Academy of Sciences* 120, no. 6 (February 7, 2023): 1, https://doi.org/10.1073/pnas.2212875120; Rupa Banerjee, Jeffrey G.Reitz, and Phil Oreopoulos, "Do Large Employers Treat Racial Minorities More Fairly? An Analysis of Canadian Field Experiment Data," *Canadian Public Policy/Analyse de politiques* 44, no. 1 (March 2018): 1–12, https://doi.org/10.3138/cpp.2017-033; Lincoln Quillian, Anthony Heath, Devah Pager, Arnfinn H. Midtbøen, Fenella Fleischmann, and

Ole Hexel, "Do Some Countries Discriminate More than Others? Evidence from 97 Field Experiments of Racial Discrimination in Hiring," *Sociological Science* 6 , no. 18 (2019): 467–96, https://doi.org/10.15195/v6.a18; Rachelle Younglai, "Black Canadians Have Some of the Lowest Home Ownership Rates in Canada, StatsCan Says," *Globe and Mail*, November 22, 2021, https://www.theglobeandmail.com/business/article-black-canadians-have-some-of-the-lowest-home-ownership-rates-in-canada/; Joe Darden and Sameh Kamel, "Black and White Differences in Homeownership Rates in the Toronto Census Metropolitan Area: Does Race Matter?," *The Review of Black Political Economy* 28, no. 2 (September 2000): 53–76, https://doi.org/10.1007/s12114-000-1017-6; Amara McLaughlin and Mike Crawley, "Sunshine List So White: Minorities Almost Invisible Among Ontario's Best-Paid Public Servants," *CBC News*, March 27, 2018, https://www.cbc.ca/news/canada/toronto/sunshine-list-so-white-ontario-public-sector-executives-1.4593238.

27 Gidengil and Roy, "Is There a Racial Divide?," 153; Antoine Bilodeau, "Mobilisation or Demobilisation? Perceived Discrimination and Political Engagement among Visible Minorities in Quebec," *Political Science* 69, no. 2 (May 2017): 128–32, https://doi.org/10.1080/00323187.2017.1332955; Reitz and Banerjee, *Racial Inequality, Social Cohesion*, 8–11.
28 Michael Pal and Sujit Choudhry, "Is Every Ballot Equal? Visible Minority Vote Dilution in Canada," *IRPP Choices* 13, no. 1 (January 2007): 3–4.
29 Pal and Choudhry, "Is Every Ballot Equal?," 4; Michael Pal and Sujit Choudhry, "Still Not Equal? Visible Minority Vote Dilution in Canada," *Canadian Political Science Review* 8, no. 1 (August 2014): 85–101, https://doi.org/10.24124/c677/2014470.
30 Pal and Choudhry, "Is Every Ballot Equal?," 6–7.
31 Pal and Choudhry, "Still Not Equal?," 89.
32 Or cities where the majority population is a minority community relative to the national population.
33 Black and Hicks, "Visible Minority Candidates," 27–8.
34 Passy and Gueye, "Ethnoracial Identities," 20.
35 Passy and Gueye, 20.
36 Bird, "Guess Who's Running," 82–3.
37 Erin Tolley, *Framed: Media and the Coverage of Race in Canadian Politics*, (Vancouver: UBC Press, 2015), 11–13.
38 R. Kenneth Carty and William Cross, "Political Parties and the Practice of Brokerage Politics," in *The Oxford Handbook of Canadian Politics*, ed. John C. Courtney and David E. Smith (Oxford: Oxford University Press, 2010), 193.
39 Carty and Cross, "Political Parties," 195.
40 Childs and Krook, "Analyzing Women's Substantive Representation," 128.
41 Substantive representation is not solely the purview of race, but rather is an ideal form of representation for marginalized groups across the intersectional axes of oppression and privilege, including – but not limited to – gender, age, language, location, and sexuality. Though substantive representation often requires a level of descriptive representation, the latter does not ensure the former.

42 Herman Bakvis, "Prime Minister and Cabinet in Canada: An Autocracy in Need of Reform?," *Journal of Canadian Studies* 35, no. 4 (Winter 2000): 60–79, https://doi.org/10.3138/jcs.35.4.60; Donald J. Savoie, *Governing from the Centre: The Concentration of Power in Canadian Politics* (Toronto: University of Toronto Press, 1999).

43 Michelle McQuigge, "Ontario Premier Doug Ford's Cabinet Criticized for Lack of Diversity," *Global News*, June 29, 2018, https://globalnews.ca/news/4306035/doug-ford-ontario-cabinet-diversity.

44 Robert Benzie, "Doug Ford Defends Appointing His Nephew to Cabinet, Arguing Michael Ford Has 'Extensive Experience,'" *Toronto Star*, June 27, 2022, https://www.thestar.com/politics/provincial/doug-ford-defends-appointing-his-nephew-to-cabinet-arguing-michael-ford-has-extensive-experience/article_dcc73b0e-ec02-5429-b2ee-43cc625ada5f.html.

45 Peter Loewen, "Democratic Stability, Representation, And Accountability: A Case for Single-Member Plurality Elections," in *Should We Change How We Vote? Evaluating Canada's Electoral System*, ed. Andrew Potter, Daniel Weinstock, and Peter Loewen (Montreal: McGill-Queen's University Press, 2017), 23–32; Arend Lijphart, *Patterns of Democracy: Government Forms and Performance in Thirty-Six Countries* (New Haven, CT: Yale University Press, 1999), 245–6.

46 Graham White, *Cabinets and First Ministers* (Vancouver: UBC Press, 2011); Savoie, *Governing From the Centre*.

47 Nick Westoll, "Some Ontario Government MPPs Reject Request for Vote on Motion Condemning Islamophobia," *Global News*, June 10, 2021, https://globalnews.ca/news/7940095/ontario-islamophobia-london-attack.

48 Jing Hui Wang and Greg Moreau, "Police-Reported Hate Crime in Canada, 2020," Statistics Canada catalogue no. 85-002-X, March 17, 2022, https://www150.statcan.gc.ca/n1/pub/85-002-x/2022001/article/00005-eng.htm.

49 Sara Mojtehedzadeh and Andres Bailey, "Who is an Essential Worker in the GTA? Millions of Us, Data Shows. This Is Life – Outside Lockdown – In Five Graphs," *Toronto Star*, February 17, 2021, https://www.thestar.com/news/gta/who-is-an-essential-worker-in-the-gta-millions-of-us-data-shows-this-is/article_790ce9ba-ca8a-5af9-bf15-8d4a2eab8d4b.html; Aaron Wherry, "One Country, Two Pandemics: What COVID-19 Reveals about Inequality in Canada," *CBC News*, June 12, 2020, https://www.cbc.ca/news/politics/pandemic-covid-coronavirus-cerb-unemployment-1.5610404; Sabina Vohra-Miller, Amanpreet Brar, and Ananya Tina Banerjee, "'It's Not Diwali, It's Precarious Employment and Less Health Care Resources.' South Asian Medical Experts on Brampton's Rising COVID-19 Cases," *Toronto Star*, November 19, 2020, https://www.thestar.com/opinion/contributors/it-s-not-diwali-it-s-precarious-employment-and-less-health-care-resources-south-asian/article_9acfdcea-3e86-5f5a-8ef0-5a7faa58d187.html.

50 Rajendra Subedi, Lawson Greenberg, and Martin Turcotte, "COVID-19 Mortality Rates in Canada's Ethno-Cultural Neighbourhoods," Statistics Canada catalogue no. 45-28-0001, October 28, 2020, https://www150.statcan.gc.ca/n1/pub/45-28-0001/2020001/article/00079-eng.htm.

51 Stephanie Liu, "Reports of Anti-Asian Hate Crimes are Surging in Canada during the COVID-19 Pandemic," *CTV News*, March 17, 2021, https://www.ctvnews.ca/canada/reports-of-anti-asian-hate-crimes-are-surging-in-canada-during-the-covid-19-pandemic-1.5351481; Chinese Canadian National Council – Toronto Chapter, *A Year of Racist Attacks: Anti-Asian Racism Across Canada, One Year into the Pandemic* (Chinese Canadian National Council, 2020), Finding 2020 Report, accessed April 8, 2021, https://www.covidracism.ca/.
52 Wang and Moreau, "Police-Reported Hate Crime."
53 Wang and Moreau, "Police-Reported Hate Crime."
54 Vohra-Miller, Brar, and Banerjee, "It's Not Diwali."
55 Asif Hameed and Alexandra Wishart, "Mapping the Limits of Multiculturalism and Diversity: COVID-19, Race, and the South Asian State of Exception" (paper presented at the 2021 Canadian Political Science Association Annual Conference: Diversity and the Discipline of Political Science, online, June 11, 2021).
56 Laura Elizabeth Pinto, "Race and Fear of the 'Other' in Common Sense Revolution Reforms," *Critical Education* 4, no. 2 (February 2013): 8–9, https://doi.org/10.14288/ce.v4i2.182344.
57 Funké Aladejebi, "Black History: How Racism in Ontario Schools Today Is Connected to a History of Segregation," *The Conversation*, February 8, 2021, https://theconversation.com/black-history-how-racism-in-ontario-schools-today-is-connected-to-a-history-of-segregation-147633.
58 Taylor Dysart, "Perspective: The Ottawa Trucker Convoy Is Rooted in Canada's Settler Colonial History," *Washington Post*, February 11, 2022, https://www.washingtonpost.com/outlook/2022/02/11/ottawa-trucker-convoy-is-rooted-canadas-settler-colonial-history/; Fiona MacDonald, "The 'Freedom Convoy' Protesters Are a Textbook Case of 'Aggrieved Entitlement,'" *The Conversation*, February 16, 2022, https://theconversation.com/the-freedom-convoy-protesters-are-a-textbook-case-of-aggrieved-entitlement-176791; Jerald Sabin, "Canadian Federalism, Multilevel Politics, and the Occupation of Ottawa," *Canadian Journal of Political Science* 55, no. 3 (September 2022): 751, https://doi.org/10.1017/S0008423922000579.
59 Nira Yuval-Davis, "Belonging and the Politics of Belonging," *Patterns of Prejudice* 40, no. 3 (July 2006): 197–214, https://doi.org/10.1080/00313220600769331.

"Just Want a Regular Life": Race and the Educational Credentials of Black Youth

Carl E. James

A recent (January 18, 2023) Statistics Canada report titled, "A Portrait of Educational Attainment and Occupational Outcomes among Racialized Populations,"[1] shows that this group of Canadians "tend to be highly educated" – particularly, first-generation Canadians[2] – with levels of education significantly above the national average.[3] Specifically, data from the 2021 census indicate that nearly 40% of racialized Canadians aged twenty-five to sixty-four years held a bachelor's degree or higher (the national average was 32.9%), and they made up slightly over one-quarter (27.3%) of the Canadian population. But there are differences among the racialized groups based on ethnicity, gender, and generational status.[4] For instance, more than 50% of Korean, Chinese, South Asian, and West Asian Canadians, and over 40% of Arab, Japanese, and Filipino Canadians, had a bachelor's degree or higher, and many earned their degrees around the age of twenty-five years. In contrast, members of Latin American (37.1%) and Black (32.4%) communities were less likely than Asians, but closer to the national average, to have a bachelor's degree or higher. In the case of the Black population, region of origin and generational differences account for the significant differences in their educational attainment.[5] For instance, over 40% of those who immigrated from Africa (predominantly Nigeria) and 46.3% their children (in other words, first- and second-generation Canadians) held bachelor's degrees and higher; while those of Caribbean origin – 19.4% of those born in the Caribbean, 28.5% of their children, and 15.8% of third generation and more – held similar educational credentials, which they earned at an average age of twenty-nine years. Slightly more than half (50.2%) of this last group of Black Canadians – made up mostly of Jamaican descendants in Ontario and Haitians in Quebec – "had no postsecondary credentials."[6]

So, what is the educational performance and academic attainment of Black youth in Ontario and the Greater Toronto Area (GTA) in particular, where most of them reside, and where the country's largest school boards, post-secondary education institutions, cultural organizations, and economic enterprises are located? In exploring the schooling lives and educational attainment of Ontario students, I first discuss findings presented in Statistics Canada reports; then I employ 2021 census data – referencing the educational credentials of individuals aged twenty-five to twenty-nine by race, gender, province, and generational status – to provide a quantitative profile of this age group of youth. I chose this age group since they are likely to have completed high school and engaged in post–high school educational, professional, and employment activities by this age. I further turn to qualitative data of elementary, middle, and high school students in a GTA school board to learn about their educational experiences; using data from high school students at the same board, I discuss the impact of the COVID-19 pandemic on their studying habits, learning experiences, teacher-student relationships, educational compromises, and post–high school aspirations.

Evidently, the pandemic has and will continue to influence the schooling contexts, and in turn, the experiences and outcomes of young people. It has served, as poet and essayist Dionne Brand writes seven months into the pandemic, to have us question "the normal," noting how the "normal" to which we hope to return is a nostalgia,[7] which should be rejected for it has served to shape and maintain the inequities, injustices, sexism, racism, homophobia, and transphobia that individuals have experienced.

> But, I and many other people hate that normal. Who would one have to be to sit in that normal restfully, to mourn it, or to desire its continuance? We are, in fact, still in that awful normal that is narrativized as minor injustices, or social ills that would get better if some of us waited, if we had the patience to bear it, if we had noticed and were grateful for the miniscule "progress" etc.... Well, yes, this normal, this usual, this ease was predicated on dis-ease.[8]

To understand the impact of the pandemic is to give attention to the social, cultural, and educational context and "the endoskeleton of the world" that the pandemic has exposed, as well as the societal structures, inequitable opportunities, and social dynamics shaped by colonialism and the resulting systemic racisms, xenophobia, and patriarchy that mediate upward social and educational mobility of young people.

Walcott argues that "the catastrophe of COVID-19 resides in an already existing state-derived practice of antiblack racism."[9] In other words, in addition to anti-Black racism,[10] COVID-19 has been one of two pandemics with which Black people struggle. This is the case despite living in a society which for decades has been admired internationally for its Multiculturalism Policy (1971) and Act (1988) which earned it the ranking as "the most inclusive country in the world."[11] Moreover, the *Canadian Human Rights Act* (1977/1985)[12] and the *Employment Equity Act* (1986/1995) were established to prohibit discriminatory practices, and as stated in the Ontario Human Rights Code, "against people based on a protected *ground* in a protected *social area*."[13] And recently, equity, diversity, and inclusion (EDI, 2020s) programs, initiatives, and pledges have served to reinforce Canada's reputation – and by extension its provinces, including Ontario – as an inclusive multicultural society with related discourses in public and private institutional ecosystems. In addition to these legislations and initiatives, Black History Month is officially recognized and celebrated with related events in Canada and its provinces; so too, the United Nation's International Decade for the People of African Descent (2015–24) is acknowledged and since then extended by Prime Minister Trudeau to 2028, which might be seen as further demonstration of Canada's inclusive character. Furthermore, in the wake of the George Floyd murder in the United States in spring 2020 and protests by Black Lives Matter contesting anti-Black racism and calling for racial justice, educational institutions (K–12 schools; colleges and universities) – the responsibility of Ontario government – have put in place initiatives that are expected to address the experiences, needs, interests, expectations, and aspirations of Indigenous and Black students and job seekers.

If EDI initiatives are really going to help increase the number of Black youth attaining bachelor's degrees, then education institutions must live up to their EDI pledges, and to this end, come to a recognition of how racialization and racism (with attention to how they intersect with other systemic structures and identity characteristics) operate systemically as obstacles to the schooling opportunities, academic performance, and educational attainment of students. This idea serves to structure this exploration, and in the following section, before considering Statistics Canada literature, I discuss how giving critical consideration to the inter-relationships of individuals, communities, institutions, and society – informed by colonialism and anti-Black racism – offers indispensable insights that can move us more towards the equitable and inclusive institutions and society in which race does not determine, nor operate as a barrier to, attaining post-secondary education credentials.

COLONIALISM, STRATIFICATION, AND RACE: THE SCAFFOLDS OF BLACK LIFE

Coming to an understanding of the level of education credentials attained by young people requires critical examination of the generally accepted neo-liberal notion that individuals have equal opportunities to freely enrol in school programs of their choice, pursue the education they desire, and follow the path towards a career and employment of their choosing or as expected. In other words, the expectation is that individuals would take responsibility for their social and educational paths and outcomes – including failures.[14] This prevailing framework of neo-liberalism or "transnational political project," as Wacquant refers to it,[15] premised on individualism, meritocracy, competition, entrepreneurship, and freedom of choice, negates the impact of settler colonialism, structural inequity, and racial capitalism that serve as limits to individuals' interests, efforts, and aspirations.[16]

Missed, therefore, is the fact that individuals exist in relation to their parents, family members, friends, peers, mentors, educators, and to cultural and social groups (sometimes identified as clubs or regarded as communities) with which they identify (e.g., ethnic, racial, gendered, disabled) and/or choose to associate (or become members). At another level, the neighbourhoods or communities (physical) in which individuals reside intersect with their family circumstances (income/social class, level of education, employment, etc.) and the social, recreational, cultural, and economic opportunities offered in the area. These intersections influence perceptions of their opportunities and in turn their educational lives and outcomes. Furthermore, institutions such as social service organizations, justice bureaus, media agencies, and schools all intersect and together help to determine individuals' outcome. Schools,[17] primarily K–12, build on individuals' education from daycares and early childhood education (ECE) settings, and serve as a foundation for post–high school – including college and university – program activities and aspirations that would ultimately lead to the university credentials they attain.

Basically, in Canada, individuals, parents, families, communities, and institutions (for this discussion, Ontario K–12 schools and post-secondary institutions) exist in a society where the social, economic, and political systems structure the cultural values, norms, ethics, and traditions that are followed, and largely shaped and sustained, by government – local, regional (or provincial), and national – whose legislations, policies, programs, and initiatives are moulded by colonialism. Growing up and being educated in a schooling system structured by a culture of whiteness – that of colonialism associated with the dominant ethnoracial group of the society, and one into which parents, family members, mentors, teachers, and others have also been socialized – young people develop an awareness of what it takes to live and succeed in the society, which means compliance with cultural expectations. The point is, colonialism as supported by material resources and the cultural norms, values, and ideas of individuals also generates structures, possibilities, aspirations, and defines the future in people's lives. Indeed, these are not static, but ongoing, processes that continue to shape our contemporary world; and unsettling such processes, as De Lissovoy proffers, must start "from the vantage point of those who have been excluded and made invisible."[18]

Maldonado-Torres argues for decoloniality, which entails "breaking hierarchies of difference that dehumanize individuals and communities" and engaging in counterdiscourses and actions that "open up multiple other forms of being in the world."[19] And Mignolo and Walsh write that this work also involves "recognition and undoing of the hierarchical structures of race, gender, heteropatriarchy, and class that continue to control life, knowledge, spirituality, and thought – structures that are clearly intertwined with and constitutive of global capitalism and Western modernity."[20] Furthermore, moving towards establishing the equitable and inclusive society we seek also involves critical self-reflection, or what McDermott and Varenne refer to as "cultural analysis," through which we come to understand our respective roles in creating the structures and traditions that have produced the circumstances which are operating to regulate individuals' lives and their potential.[21] The idea, then, is to conceive of individuals' circumstances not simply as a product of their own making but, more importantly, of societal cultural structures. In this regard, in the following review, the various Canadian census reports provide valuable insights on societal culture.

NATIONAL PORTRAIT OF BLACK YOUTH EDUCATIONAL JOURNEY: A REVIEW OF STATISTICS CANADA REPORTS

In a Statistics Canada report,[22] 2016 census data shows that there were nearly 1.2 million Black people living in Canada, making them some 3.5% of Canada's total population and 15.6% of the racialized population; they tended to be younger than the total Canadian population with the median age being 29.6 years, compared to 40.7 years for the total population; children under fifteen years old represented 26.6% of the Black population and 16.9% of the total Canadian population. Predictions were that the population "will continue to increase and could represent between 5.0% and 5.6% of Canada's population by 2036."[23] The census also showed that the majority of the Black population (52.4%) resided in Ontario (Quebec was the second in terms of population size), with Canada being the birthplace for close to half of them – which, in part, reflects their long history of immigration to this province. Another report by Do, Houle, and Turcotte states that in 2016, "close to 7 in 10 Black adults had a postsecondary diploma,"[24] but there were notable differences in terms of gender and place of birth. For instance, "among the non-immigrant population 18% of Black men had a bachelor's degree or higher ... compared to 31% of Black women (a similar situation in the rest of the population)."[25] And among the immigrant population, 29% of immigrant Black men and 25% of women (about 3% to 7% lower than the general Canadian population) had a bachelor's degree or higher.[26]

In his report on the "Education and Labour Market Integration of Black Youth in Canada," Turcotte writes that compared to other Canadian youth, Black youth aged twenty-three to twenty-seven years in 2016 were just as likely to have "at least a high school diploma," but were less likely "to attain postsecondary qualification."[27] And young Black women were twice as likely as men to have a university degree (34% and 17%, respectively). Besides, "Black men and women are less likely than their counterparts in the rest of the population to have a bachelor's degree or higher." While only 51% of Black young men – compared to 62% of other Canadian young men of similar background – had post-secondary credentials in 2016, 34% of Black young women compared with 41% of other young women did. Hence, with such educational attainment, unemployment rates and lower salaries tended to be higher among Black Canadian adults. Turcotte submits that

> Despite a few nuances, it can be concluded that – regardless of the level of certificate, diploma or degree – Black youth have relatively less favourable outcomes in terms of postsecondary education. Furthermore, neutralizing different socioeconomic factors does not significantly affect the size of the gaps in outcomes between Black youth and other youth, These results suggest that, even if Black youth in this cohort had socioeconomic and family characteristics similar to those of other youth,[28] their postsecondary graduation rates would have been lower on average. This suggests that other factors are associated with the relatively less favourable outcomes of Black youth.[29]

Turcotte goes on to suggest that the educational expectations and aspirations of parents and youth are strongly associated with Black youth's pursuit of and graduation with post-secondary education credentials. But as studies indicate, while Black youth do aspire to achieve bachelor's degrees, their schooling circumstances – such as being disrespected by teachers and administrators, non-responsive and irrelevant curricula, and alienating school environment[30] – mitigates against them attaining their aspirations. As Do, Houle, and Turcotte found, in 2016, "94% of Black youth aged 15 to 25 said that they would like to get a bachelor's degree or higher," but only 60% of them thought that they would be able to – a 34% difference; while for the rest of the population, the difference was about 3% (82% of other Canadian youth having similar aspirations and 79% thinking that it can be attained).[31] This high aspiration of Black youth might be explained by their determination to remain optimistic, and what Do, Houle, and Turcotte refer to as "resilience" – that is, their ability to continue going about their life as they normally would after difficult experiences (41% compared to others 31%).[32]

The general or national representation of the schooling experiences and educational attainments of Black youth suggest that whether they are immigrants (or first-generation Canadians) who have entered Canada with the immigrant dream of "a better life;" are Canadian-born youth; or have ancestral roots that go back generations, as young, racialized men, their race acts upon their gendered privileges to stifle the opportunities they would have had if they were white. And for young women, even though, like other young women, they are academically outperforming their male counterparts and entering post-secondary institutions in increasing numbers, their engagement in the education system is not bringing them the benefits as their other racialized and white counterparts. So, for many Black youth, staying in school and pursuing post-secondary education are not bringing them the benefits – "wider range of labour market opportunities and better-paying jobs, better health and greater social participation" – that Turcotte envisions;[33] and socioeconomic status does not make a difference. The next section uses the census data to delve more into the educational attainment of Ontario students – particularly Black students.

THE EDUCATIONAL ATTAINMENT OF CANADIAN YOUTH AGED 25–9 YEARS: FOCUSING ON ONTARIO

A close examination of the educational attainment of Canadian youth aged 25–9 years (see table 13.1) shows that Canada-wide and in Ontario only about one-quarter of these Black youth (25.2 per cent and 26.4 per cent, respectively) managed to earn a bachelor's degree. And while this was about 3 per cent less than the Canadian and Ontario average, it was far less than their South Asian, Chinese, and Filipino counterparts. And Black youth were more than half as likely as Chinese and South Asian people to have master's and medical degrees. It reveals then, that compared to other Canadians, more Black youth of this age were living with only having their high school diploma. This might be a reflection of their schooling experiences, access to information about post-secondary education, as well as physical access to colleges and universities – that is, in relation to where they reside.

When we look across the provinces (figure 13.1), we observe that Black youth in Quebec, British Columbia, and Nova Scotia (about 36% in each province) attain at least a bachelor's degree, while only 34% in Ontario have similar qualifications. And at 22% – 2% more than the national average – many more Black youth, compared to those in other provinces, have college or non-university diploma as their highest education credential. Alberta (at 34.8%) had the highest percentage of Black youth with a high school diploma as their highest level of education. In all six provinces, the percentage of Black youth with a high school diploma or equivalent certification was higher than the national average of 23.3%. Some provinces even exceeded the national average by as much as 11%.

Studies indicate that, in part, generational status accounts for some – if not a significant amount – of the differences in achievement of individuals of immigrant backgrounds.[34] In this regard, before further discussing the levels of educational attainment of Black youth aged 25–9, we look at what the 2021

Table 13.1. Highest Level of Education by Race, Ages 25–9, 2021

Race	Black	South Asian	Chinese	Filipino	White	National Average
Canada						
High school diploma or equivalency certificate	27.9%	14.3%	11.4%	23.6%	25.7%	23.3%
Apprenticeship or trades certificate or diploma	6.3%	1.7%	1.6%	5.0%	10.5%	8.1%
Bachelor's degree	25.2%	40.7%	50.0%	32.3%	24.1%	28.5%
Medicine, dentistry, veterinary, optometry degree	0.5%	1.9%	1.6%	0.3%	0.6%	0.9%
Master's degree	6.0%	14.6%	15.2%	1.6%	5.2%	7.0%
Ontario						
High school diploma or equivalency certificate	30.8%	12.4%	9.9%	21.3%	26.1%	23.3%
Apprenticeship or trades certificate or diploma	3.6%	1.0%	0.6%	3.2%	4.3%	8.1%
Bachelor's degree	26.4%	43.9%	49.9%	35.0%	27.2%	28.5%
Medicine, dentistry, veterinary, optometry degree	0.4%	1.9%	1.7%	0.3%	0.5%	0.9%
Master's degree	5.5%	15.2%	19.2%	2.4%	6.3%	7.0%

Source: Statistics Canada, "Table 98-10-0429-01: Highest Level of Education by Census Year, Visible Minority and Generation Status: Canada, Provinces and Territories, Census Metropolitan Areas and Census Agglomerations," https://doi.org/10.25318/9810042901-eng. Contains information licensed under the Open Government Licence – Canada.

census – figures 13.2 and 13.3 – shows about these youth by generational status disaggregated by gender and race (Black, other racialized, and white youth).[35]

Figure 13.3 shows that, like their other racialized peers in Canada, a vast majority of both Black young men and women were first-generation Canadians (53.3% and 55.6%, respectively) representing about 12% lower than other racialized (or "visible minority") populations of youth (68% men and 68.5% women). There were more Black young men (39%) and women (37%) – more than their other racialized group members – who identified as second generation. And the percentage of Black young men (8%) and women (7%) were more than double that of other third-generation racialized ("visible

Race and the Educational Credentials of Black Youth   247

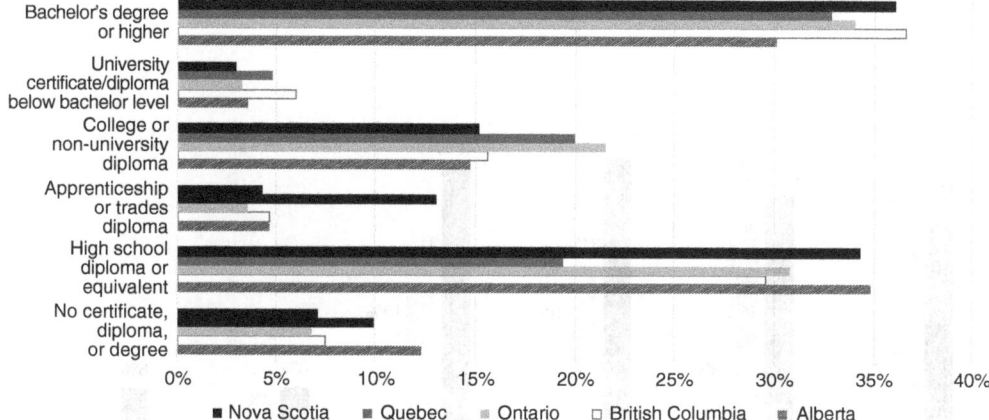

Figure 13.1. **Highest Level of Education of Black Youth, Ages 25–9, 2021**
Source: Statistics Canada, "Table 98-10-0429-01: Highest Level of Education by Census Year, Visible Minority and Generation Status: Canada, Provinces and Territories, Census Metropolitan Areas and Census Agglomerations," https://doi.org/10.25318/9810042901-eng. Contains information licensed under the Open Government Licence – Canada.

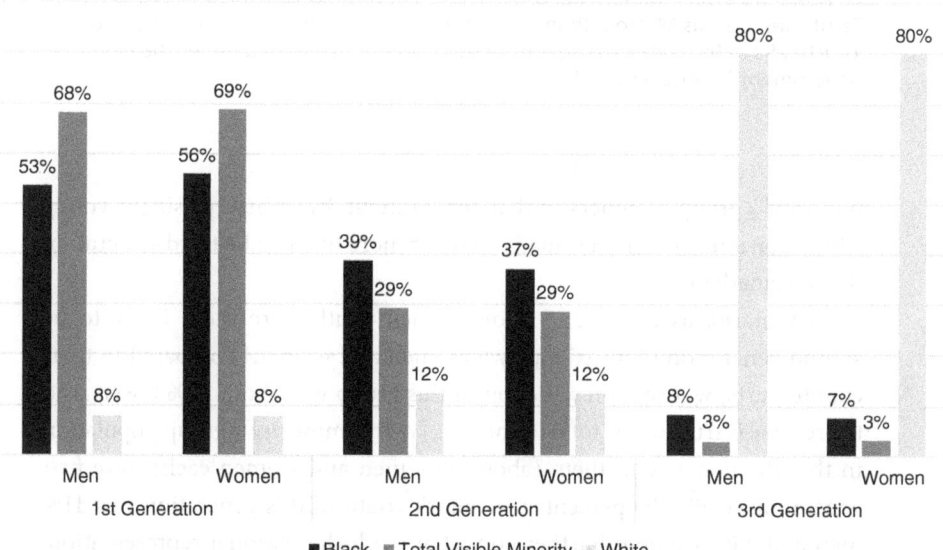

Figure 13.2. **Generational Status by Race and Gender, Ages 25–9, in Canada**
Source: Statistics Canada, "Table 98-10-0429-01: Highest Level of Education by Census Year, Visible Minority and Generation Status: Canada, Provinces and Territories, Census Metropolitan Areas and Census Agglomerations," https://doi.org/10.25318/9810042901-eng. Contains information licensed under the Open Government Licence – Canada.

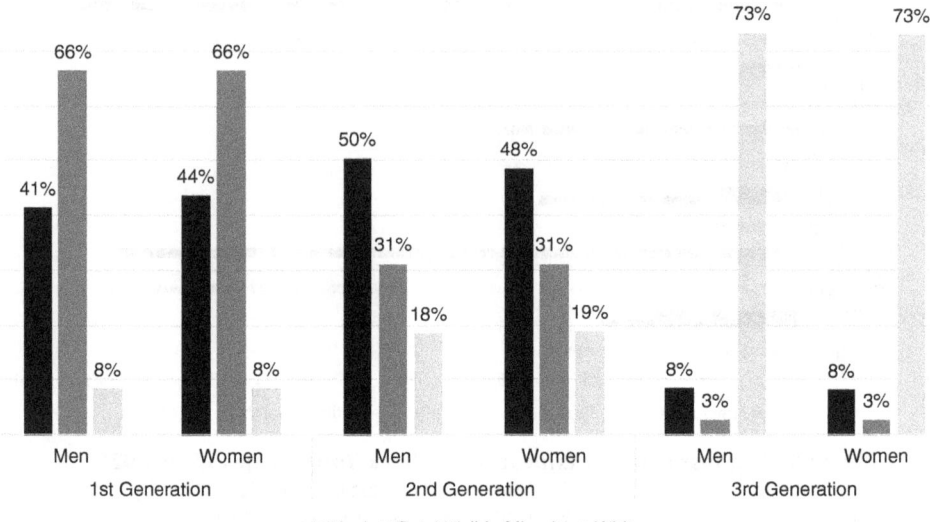

Figure 13.3. Generational Status by Race and Gender, Ages 25–9, in Ontario
Source: Statistics Canada, "Table 98-10-0429-01: Highest Level of Education by Census Year, Visible Minority and Generation Status: Canada, Provinces and Territories, Census Metropolitan Areas and Census Agglomerations," https://doi.org/10.25318/9810042901-eng. Contains information licensed under the Open Government Licence – Canada.

minority") group members of that age – (about 3%). Unsurprisingly, young white men and women in Canada were far more likely to be third-generation (80%) Canadians.

In Ontario, as figure 13.3 shows, Black youth were more likely to be second generation (approximately 50% men and women) compared to their counterparts, whose representation in this group was about 20% lower. And the reverse is true for the total racialized ("visible minority") group population in that the majority of them (about 66% men and women each) were first generation, while the percentage of Black youth in this generation was 41% men and 44% women. Further consistent with the national representation, while only about 8% of Black women and men identified as third generation, this was more than twice that of other racialized (visible minority) group men and women, which was about 3%. Likewise, most white men and women (73%) aged 25–9 years were third generation and far less of them were second (about 18–9%) and first (8%) generation.

Table 13.2. Highest Level of Education of Black Youth, Ages 25–9, by Generational Status and Gender, 2021

	1st Generation		2nd Generation		3rd Generation	
Highest Level of Education	Men	Women	Men	Women	Men	Women
Canada						
High school diploma or equivalency certificate	28.8	19.4	38.8	23.7	45.8	36.8
Apprenticeship or trades certificate or diploma	6.7	6.1	7	5.1	8.8	4.9
Bachelor's degree	24.6	29.8	18.7	30.0	11.1	17.2
Degree in medicine, dentistry, veterinary, or optometry	0.4	0.7	0.3	0.4	0	0.4
Master's degree	7.5	8.9	2.2	4.9	1.2	3.3
Ontario						
High school diploma or equivalency certificate	32.1	21.2	41.5	24.3	47.0	37.4
Apprenticeship or trades certificate or diploma	4.4	3.0	4.3	2.4	5.7	3.1
Bachelor's degree	24.7	32.6	19.9	32.0	12.8	17.3
Degree in medicine, dentistry, veterinary, or optometry	0.5	0.6	0.3	0.5	0	0
Master's degree	7.3	9.1	2.0	5.1	1.2	3.9

Source: Statistics Canada, "Table 98-10-0324-01: Visible Minority and Population Group by Generation Status: Canada, Provinces and Territories, Census Metropolitan Areas and Census Agglomerations with Parts," https://doi.org/10.25318/9810032401-eng. Contains information licensed under the Open Government Licence – Canada.

The profile of these youth can be explained through immigration patterns of various ethnoracial groups and where people chose to settle. The fact is, Ontario, and the GTA in particular, is an area/region where immigrants have long settled, likely drawn here by economic, cultural, employment, educational, and other opportunities, as well as familial connections. Hence, Ontario and the GTA has had a population that has contributed to it becoming not only one of the most populus and racially and ethnically diverse area/region of the country, but an economic hub where educational credentials play a crucial role in individuals' social and economic outcomes.

Table 13.2 shows that in all of Canada, third-generation Black youth were the most likely not to have any certificate, diploma, or degree. Specifically, 12.8% of men and 10% of women ages 25–9 did not have a certificate, diploma, or degree. And while about one-quarter of the second-generation (25.9%) and third-generation (24.2%) Black women had a college or other non-university diploma, for second-generation men it was 20.7% and for third-generation men 17.2%. Only 16% of the men and 18% of the women who are first generation had this credential. In terms of those holding bachelor's degrees or higher, women in general were more likely to do so – more so first-generation women (42%) and somewhat less so for second-generation women (37%). More than one-third (34.8%) of first-generation young men had a bachelor's degree or higher; even fewer second-generation men (22.4%) attained this credential. Only 12.7% of third-generation men, compared to 21.7% of women in this generation, had a bachelor's degree or higher.

The pattern of credential attainment at the provincial level generally mirrors that of the national level; and in all generations, women more than men tend to have the highest education credentials. Specifically, as table 13.2 shows, in Ontario as in Canada, Black men of all three generations were more likely to have a high school diploma or certificate as their highest level of education. This was more the case for third-generation men (45.8%); about one-quarter first-generation men in Canada (24.6%) and Ontario (24.7%%) had bachelor's degrees. More women had bachelor's, master's, and professional degrees (e.g., medicine) as their highest education credentials. Also, women holding bachelor's degrees were first generation (32.6% in Ontario; 29.8% in Canada) and second generation (32% in Ontario; 30% in Canada). Generally, the patterns at the national level and Ontario did not differ much for most of the educational credentials – seemingly, an indication that throughout Canada, Black youth are having similar schooling experiences, educational and career plans, and perceptions of the credentials needed to realize their aspirations, and are confronting similar barriers.

A close look at the early schooling experiences of Black youth offers some helpful insights into understanding the level of educational credentials attained by Black young adults aged 25–9 years – especially those residing in the GTA.

EDUCATIONAL EXPERIENCES AT THE FOUNDATION LEVEL: THE EARLY SCHOOLING YEARS

About a year before the pandemic changed things, forty-four students (twenty-eight young men and sixteen young women) aged 9–18 years participated in four focus groups[36] in which they discussed with me their schooling, academic, and extracurricular (particularly athletic) experiences with teachers, peers, school staff, and administrators. Depending on their grade level, they were asked about the middle school or high schools they planned to attend, as well as their post–high school aspirations. The students were in a school board which, like all others in the GTA, claimed to be addressing the alienating experiences of racialized students and Black students in particular. These are efforts that both Liberal and Conservative governments have signalled they support – evidenced by their "systemic racism" programs related to the *Anti-Racism Act* of 2017, the collection of race-based data, having in place an Educational Equity Secretariat in the Ontario Ministry of Education headed by an assistant deputy minister, and in some of Ontario schools, having graduation coaches who work with Black and Indigenous students supporting them to high school completion. So, what we heard from students about their lives in school, and their thoughts about what needs to be done to address the problems they experienced, are signals of how the early years of education – the foundational level – might not have provided the needed preparation for post–high school credentials and social outcomes.

Quaylan Allen writes that schools

> are powerful but contested sites of cultural reproduction ... that, in addition to contributing to inequitable economic stratification, also reproduce dominant ideologies.... Specifically, schools and their institutional actors draw upon and contribute to dominant ideologies of black male identity by positioning them as culturally deficient, anti-intellectual, deviant, and intimidating.[37]

How then do Black students – to frame Allen's argument as a question – "take up dominant assumptions of their identity or reposition themselves as a way to push back against dominant hegemonic discourses"[38] so that they might attain the educational credentials by which they might realize their aspirations? In exploring this question with the students, I asked them: how does being Black affect your schooling experience?

Many of the students asserted that their identity as a Black student was a constant marker they have had to negotiate with their peers and teachers. For example, in the focus group of middle school students, Jay shared: "It affected my whole life. In grade 8 ... I was the only Black kid in the class for the longest time," and his teacher sat him in the middle of the class – something which heightened his consciousness about himself and his relationship with his peers. Joan added: "I remember when I was in Grade 1 looking around the room and being, like: 'Oh, it's just me;' and then Grade 2: 'Oh, it's just me.' Up until, I think, Grade 7, I was the only Black person. And it was really weird." The idea of not having others in their classes with similar background and who share their experiences was a major issue in their learning, as Jonathan explained referencing his English class. He mentioned that "it's kind of different when ... we are talking about social issues and racist stuff come up. I feel as though some people don't ever have brains for understanding things." To this assertion, Jay rejoined with the fact that he had friends in his class who "are aware; and they try to stay woke – but emphasis on the word 'try.' It's like ... they try to understand when I try to talk about things.... But when someone doesn't understand the full story – like [my] growing up and being the only Black person in the class and how that impacts you – it doesn't help."

The high school students talked about the "racist stereotypes about Black people" that misrepresent Black communities – and hence them. This was something most of them were determined would not define them. As Michael stated: "The main thing wrong with society [is that] ... they see us as gangsters when all of us here, and none of us, want to be in a gang.... We're living proper lives, and just want a regular life; want to have a regular house ... get regular cheques." It is some of these stereotypes that these students perceive to trigger the differential treatment and often the punishment of Black students by teachers. For example, one middle school participant observed that white students were often not reprimanded for poor behaviour in the classroom, while Black students tended to receive more reprimands and oftentimes more severe treatment even for similar behaviours. Kevin shared this example.

> This happened in grade 7. So, I was in French class and I didn't have a pencil. So, I was asking my friend for a pencil and the teacher said: "Why are you interrupting my class and study." And I said: "I wasn't interrupting, I was just asking my friend for a pencil." And she said: "Get up and go sit over there by yourself...." And I said: "I was just asking for a pencil; what did I do? ... Why should I get up and move?" And she's like: "I want you to get up and go sit over there." And I finally got up and went.... And then like 5 minutes later, my White friend did the same thing. But nothing happened to him.

Many students perceived that their schools' recognition or celebration of Black History Month did not make a difference to the education they received.

Some mentioned that during Black History Month, they would have "Black performers and Black artists and people coming" to their schools to "lecture" about how they "could be successful" or talk with them about the "need" for them to "better" themselves. But some students were quite sceptical of their school's staging or *performance* of Black History Month. They saw the special activities at their school during February as just a reminder, as one participant cynically said: "Like, it's Black History Month" – conveying the idea that the activities are just to appease them, but the school has no real commitment to what the month stands for. Other participants expressed concerns with the lack of effort put into planning the month's activities, which often results in a paucity of activities. According to one high school student, Michele, "They will play one song from Bob Marley the whole month and call it Black History Month and then play the same song over and over.... "

That some students would look to Black History Month to have Black presence in Canada and their presence in the classroom recognized could be explained by their absence from the curriculum and learning materials. For instance, in discussing the extent to which the presence and experiences of Black people were reflected in the curriculum and taught by their teachers, as to be expected, some students shared that they have had teachers who would reference or talk of Black leaders like "Martin Luther King and Nelson Mandela." But there were others who would say that they were going by the mandate of the curriculum. As Sophie stated, when they would "bring up" having materials relating to Black people, teachers would respond with "I would teach you that, but the curriculum told me I had to do this." Althea concurred adding, "It gives them a way out." And Michael also pointed out: "It's not like you can change that ... or have a voice.... They're not accountable.... They're not responsible for teaching it to you, because: 'Oh it's not in the curriculum,' so they don't have to." Further speaking to the salient notions that Black knowledges are often left out of school materials, Jerry suggested that teachers were afraid to be "wrong" for they were compelled by a fear of not knowing and consequently a fear of the implications of not knowing.

The discussions with the students point to how much today's schooling environment continues to contribute to a climate which is not contributing to the emotional well-being of students and thus their learning. For these students, it is not simply about their teachers and school administrators being ill-equipped, ill-prepared, or unwilling to address anti-Blackness, but also about feeling unwelcomed in the school and lacking a sense of belonging in the educational spaces. The sense of *un-belonging* is indeed a product of the cultural hierarchy of schools based on the perceived ability, knowledge, worth, and behaviour of some students with whom teachers have built relationships and, as a result, give preferential treatment.[39] Therefore, in response to the question, "How can the school better support you or make you feel more connection to your learning?" students submitted that having educators and an educational system that was culturally responsive to their learning needs, interests, and aspirations would help. Probably, the words of middle schooler Justin best sum up the sentiments of participants: "I just want the teachers to believe in us."

FEELING UNDER-PREPARED: THE COST OF THE PANDEMIC ON LEARNING AND STUDENT ASPIRATIONS

Given the above experiences of Black students, it is worth knowing how such students' learning experiences were exacerbated by COVID-19, and as a consequence, might have made even more difficult their journey through school and their perceptions of realizing their educational aspirations. To find out about this, I engaged in a focus group discussion in spring 2021 with eight Black high school students – six females and two males; five Grade 12s, two Grade 11s, and one Grade 10 – who resided in the GTA. I was particularly interested in how they coped with online (or virtual or hybrid) schooling given having to learn from home where quiet spaces are not always possible, computers are not always available or reliable, and having limited or inadequate access to relevant learning materials – something for which neither they, nor their teachers, were prepared.[40]

Most of the participants expressed dissatisfaction with their schooling experiences. As Cathy said: "It wasn't fun" and their teachers "weren't there" for them. And Ronald inserted: "We missed out on a lot of stuff that we could have potentially received if we were in person – even though we were trying hard to participate." Moreover, Marcella questioned how useful the education that they were receiving was – for teachers were rearranging the curriculum and delivering the lessons in "condensed speed," which meant they had to quickly learn the materials so that they would "regurgitate" them according to Ronald. "But to be honest," as Marcella concluded, "I don't think I can remember half the stuff I learned from any of my classes, because essentially all I did was race to get everything done correctly and how the teacher wanted it done." Given this situation, Heather felt, as other students did, that teachers seemed not to "care about their job.... They care more about giving us the work and having it submitted." In such a context, students became reluctant participants in the teaching-learning process; as Heather put it, "I was there to pass, not to learn. So, unfortunately online school will not be for me...." And while students would routinely attend classes, they did so, as Karen shared, "for my grades" and not because they were engaged in meaningful learning.

Another problem that participants consistently identified was feeling "under-prepared" for the next grade or stage of their education – specifically, for Grades 11, 12, and university. As a consequence, Marcella – who was going into Grade 11 the coming fall semester – explained: "I just feel like I'm going to constantly stress and struggle to catch up with things that come. I have to learn what I should have done in Grade 10." Similarly, Rachel submitted:

> I would say that I have a majority of negative experience when it comes to schooling during the pandemic. Especially going into grade 12, I feel that with some of the courses ... I'm severely under-prepared. I know that especially because we had to do school online.... For me, the classes that I enjoyed ... I was very engaged. But courses that I didn't really enjoy, it was like ... I'm doing it just because they told me that I had to.

Major concerns for many of the participants who planned to enter university that fall semester were feeling that they did not receive the Grade 12 leaning that would prepare them for university and not knowing whether their first semester in university would be a continuation of online learning. Their concern was also premised on the fact that they wished to have personal interactions with their university peers and professors. For instance, Alicia, who loathed online learning and was "about to start my first year" university in the fall, lamented having to miss out on "two years" of learning – having spent "them at home" – and having "to make up for my grade 12 year with my first year" of university. For students like Alicia, the cost of limited access to needed educational materials, minimum in-person learning opportunities, not having physical access to university spaces and hence personal interactions with educators, were astronomical costs – especially when the foundational learnings or educational prerequisites that should have been completed during high school or in the first year of university are added. It is thought that students will likely have to put effort, time (in terms of months or years), and finances into attaining the extra or supplementary educational requirements.

For the most part, for most of these participants, the pandemic, coupled with their alienating schooling experiences before then, contributed to difficulties in seeing promising educational prospects – especially for those students planning to enter university. For students who would be the first in their family to attend university (which was six of the eight participants) not knowing what to expect of university and not having appropriate or adequate family supports to help them navigate the system caused them much stress.[41] Nevertheless, for some participants, despite, and even *because of,* the limitations posed by the delivery of their education and lack of support from teachers, there were some benefits in terms of what they learnt about themselves. Seemingly grateful for the opportunity to navigate learning on their own, some of the participants discovered and developed new capacities and responsibilities. For instance, after admitting that online learning was not "really useful," Marcella went on to say, "But it did teach me a few things, like how to multitask and work effectively." Similarly, Alicia stated, "I guess being online taught me to be a lot more disciplined with myself and to be a lot more responsible because … only you can take care of yourself … online – like it really is only you. So, I guess I could say that I've become a lot more independent." And Munjeera added: "I think this online experience was essential for my development, like when I used to go to school before, I just would go to school and that was it. But when online, I found that I had to push myself – like if the teachers were just giving us the information. But if you wanted to learn, you had to go learn on your own.… I think it was good preparation for university – for me to know how to study. " But ultimately, despite their independence, disciplinary disposition, and responsible behaviour, their success in the society – or attainment of educational credentials – will still be mediated or facilitated by institutional and societal factors.

CONCLUSION

The Ontario government recently (April 2023) announced that it planned "to hire 1,000 new teachers to 'boost' math and literacy skills for students." Education minister Stephen Lecce contends that this move is to ensure that students "reach their full potential" and "master their foundational skills" which would lead "to better outcomes" and "better jobs."[42] The government also announced that it intends to introduce legislation by which it will assume "greater control over school boards" and have "a say in priorities in student achievement, especially in the basics of reading, writing and math, and ensure all 72 publicly funded boards provide information on that progress to parents in a transparent and timely manner, as well as update teacher training at universities."[43] For Black youth and families, such moves by the government would be welcomed and appropriate, if such legislation and related programs and actions speak directly to their experiences thus making it possible for them to realize their educational potential as promised. To this end, schools, colleges, and universities – with the support of governments – must have programs that pay attention to the systemic ways in which race and racialization, structured by vestiges of colonialism, account for the failure of Black youth to attain the educational and career credentials they seek so that they might fully participate and contribute to society. It is quite telling that the longer they have resided in Canadian society – that is, being here for more than two generations in Canada[44] – the less they and/or their proteges will experience educational, economic, and social successes.

DISCUSSION QUESTIONS

1 Resilience is typically used to convey the idea that individuals have the capacity to overcome whatever adversities, barriers, or disadvantages they may have in life. What might account for the differences between Black youth and their counterparts in terms of their thinking about being able to attain a bachelor's degree or higher? Is resilience a factor in the case of Black youth?
2 In addition to the federal *Multicultural Act* (an extension of the 1971 Multicultural Policy) – which has brought Canada worldwide recognition as one of most culturally and racially inclusive societies – Ontario governments have had similar inclusion and equity Acts in place. Yet, research indicates that racialization and racism account for the significant underachievement of Black students. Will the equity, diversity, and inclusion pledges and initiatives introduced since the death of a Black American, George Floyd, make a difference? How so?
3 In their Statistics Canada article, "Canada's Black Population: Education, Labour and Resilience" (2020), Do, Houle, and Turcotte observe that the longer Black people reside in Canada – like being three or more generations in Canada – the lower their educational attainment, which has implications for

their economic and social successes. How might this situation be explained? What accounts for situation?
4 The COVID-19 pandemic is said to exacerbate the schooling and educational situation of students generally, and more so for some racialized students in particular. In the case of Black students, what are some of the things that might have contributed to their educational circumstances and outcomes during the COVID-19 pandemic?
5 In December 1995, the House of Commons officially recognized February as Black History Month in Canada, but is this recognition helping to make a difference in educating *all* Canadians about the history, presence, contributions, and lives of Black people? Is it contributing to Black people having more equitable participation and successful lives in Canadian society? And will the Ontario government's plan to make Black history compulsory learning in Grades 7, 8, and 10 – the first in Canada – by September 2025 help?

NOTES

1 Statistics Canada, "A Portrait of Educational Attainment and Occupational Outcomes among Racialized Populations in 2021," Statistics Canada catalogue no. 98-200-X, January 18, 2023, https://www12.statcan.gc.ca/census-recensement/2021/as-sa/98-200-X/2021011/98-200-X2021011-eng.cfm.
2 This refers to individuals born outside of Canada; second generation refers to individuals with at least one parent born in Canada.
3 Insofar as education is a one of the selection criteria for immigrants to gain entry into Canada, it is understandable that these individuals would have high levels of education, and so would their second-generation children since these parents would likely expect and encourage their children to aspire to attain similar levels of education – and their children are likely to oblige. See Carl E. James and Leanne E. Taylor, *First-Generation Student Experiences in Higher Education: Counterstories* (New York: Routledge, 2023).
4 See Statistics Canada, "A Portrait of Educational Attainment," 10. They note that "Japanese (31%) and Black (5%) populations were the only racialized groups where over 2% of the working-age population were in the third generation of more." They also point out that substantial numbers of immigrants from the Caribbean entered Canada in the late 1960s, whereas immigrants from Africa took place within "the last few decades, when educational requirements for economic immigrants have been very high."
5 Carl E. James, *Colour Matters: Essays on the Experiences, Education, and Pursuit of Black Youth* (Toronto: University of Toronto Press, 2021); Statistics Canada, "A Portrait of Educational Attainment," 8.

6 Statistics Canada, "A Portrait of Educational Attainment."
7 "The repetition of 'when things return to normal' as if that normal," Brand puts it, "was not in contention. Was the violence against women normal? Was the anti-Black and anti-Indigenous racism normal? Was white supremacy normal?" See Dionne Brand, "On Narrative, Reckoning and the Calculus of Living and Dying," *Toronto Star*, July 4, 2020, https://www.thestar.com/entertainment/books/dionne-brand-on-narrative-reckoning-and-the-calculus-of-living-and-dying/article_47884274-07ad-561a-973b-027ef2cbc8fb.html.
8 Brand, "On Narrative, Reckoning."
9 Rinaldo Walcott, "Nothing New Here to See: How COVID-19 and State Violence Converge on Black Life," *Topia: Canadian Journal of Cultural Studies* 41 (Fall 2020): 158, https://doi.org/10.3138/topia-019.
10 I take anti-Black racism to be systemic – the convergence of three inter-related levels of racism – individual, institutional, and societal/structural. So, the racism that Black people experience is not merely based on individuals' attitudes, but is grounded in a social construction (or stereotypes) of Black people in which race as represented by skin colour and other physical features are used to define them – "despite evidence that race is neither a genetic, biological, or physical state of being nor a fixed or stable category. As well, the history of enslavement continues to define Black people and dictate their presence and potential as citizens. Also, race is often the basis upon which a group's presence is affirmed, difference is constructed, status is conferred, social roles are assigned, and agency is attained." See Carl E. James, *Seeing Ourselves: Exploring Race, Ethnicity and Culture* (Toronto: Thompson Educational Publishing, 2010), 285.
11 Derek Thompson, "Canada's Secret to Escaping the 'Liberal Doom Loop,'" *The Atlantic*, July 9, 2018, https://www.theatlantic.com/ideas/archive/2018/07/canadas-secret-to-escaping-the-iberal-doom-loop/564551/.
12 More than a decade earlier, the Ontario Human Rights Code, enacted in 1962, and the Ontario Human Rights Commission (OHRC), launched on March 29, 1961, as an arm's-length agency of government created to administer the Code and accountable to the legislature, were the first in Canada to be established. See Ontario Human Rights Commission, "The Ontario Human Rights Code," https://www.ohrc.on.ca/en/ontario-human-rights-code.
13 "The Ontario Human Rights Code," Ontario Human Rights Commission, accessed January 9, 2024, https://www.ohrc.on.ca/en/room-everyone-human-rights-and-rental-housing-licensing/ontario-human-rights-code-and-licensing.
14 Susan Braedley and Meg Luxton, "Competing Philosophies: Neoliberalism and the Challenges of Everyday Life," in *Neoliberalism and Everyday Life*, ed. Susan Braedley and Meg Luxton (Montreal: McGill-Queen's University Press, 2010), 3–21; James, *Colour Matters*.
15 Loïc Wacquant, *Urban Outcasts: A Comparative Sociology of Advanced Marginality* (Cambridge, UK: Polity Press, 2008).
16 According to Robinson, "the development, organization and expansion of capitalist society pursued essentially racial directions, so too did social ideology," which frame the structures responsible for the uneven life chances that are a product of

racialized historical exploitations. See Cedric J. Robinson, *Black Marxism: The Making of the Black Radical Tradition* (London: Zed Press, 1983), 2.

17 For the most part, the K–12 schools that individuals attend are located in their communities/neighbourhoods, and hence tend to evolve a related reputation which is likely to influence the opportunities, possibilities, and limits to students' educational and social experiences and outcomes.

18 Noah De Lissovoy, "Decoloniality as Inversion: Decentring the West in Emancipatory Theory and Pedagogy," *Globalisation, Societies and Education* 17, no. 4 (August 2019): 426, https://doi.org/10.1080/14767724.2019.1577719.

19 Nelson Maldonado-Torres, "Outline of Ten Theses on Coloniality and Decoloniality," posted on the Caribbean Studies Association website (unpublished manuscript, October 23, 2016, last modified January 30, 2018), 10, https://caribbeanstudies association.org/docs/Maldonado-Torres_Outline_Ten_Theses-10.23.16.pdf.

20 Walter D. Mignolo and Catherine E. Walsh, *On Decoloniality: Concepts, Analytics, Praxis* (Durham, NC: Duke University Press, 2018), 17.

21 Ray McDermott and Hervé Varenne, "Reconstructing Culture in Educational Research," in *Innovations in Educational Ethnography*, ed. George Spindler and Lorie Hammonds (Mahwah, NJ: Lawrence Erlbaum Associates, 2006), 3–31. See also Ray McDermott, Shelley Goldman, and Hervé Varenne, "The Cultural Work of Learning Disabilities," *Educational Researcher* 35, no. 6 (August 2006): 12–17, https://doi.org/10.3102/0013189X035006012.

22 Statistics Canada, "Diversity of the Black Population in Canada: An Overview," *Statistics Canada: Ethnicity, Language and Immigration Thematic Series*, February 27, 2019, https://www150.statcan.gc.ca/n1/pub/89-657-x/89-657-x2019002-eng.htm.

23 Statistics Canada, "Diversity," 4.

24 Generally, since 2001, the proportion of Canadians with a post-secondary education has increased – something that "was more pronounced among women than among men, for both the Black population and the rest of the population." Deniz Do, René Houle, and Martin Turcotte, "Canada's Black Population: Education, Labour and Resilience," *Statistics Canada: Ethnicity, Language and Immigration Thematic Series*, February 25, 2020, 7, https://www150.statcan.gc.ca/n1/pub/89-657-x/89-657-x2020002-eng.htm.

25 Statistics Canada, "Diversity," 6.

26 The authors explain that the post-secondary credentials of immigrant Black men "can be partly explained by immigrant admission categories" in that in the case of immigration from Africa, a higher proportion of Black men tend to be given entry over women based on "their skills and qualifications, such as educational attainment." However, once in Canada, Black immigrants experience worse educational outcomes over every generation, so that third-generation Black Canadians are less likely than their parents and grandparents to graduate from university. See Do, Houle, and Turcotte, "Canada's Black Population," 6.

27 Martin Turcotte, "Education and Labour Market Integration of Black Youth in Canada," Statistics Canada catalogue no. 75-006-X, released February 25, 2020, corrected May 19, 2022, https://www150.statcan.gc.ca/n1/pub/75-006-x/2020001/article/00002-eng.htm.

28 See Turcotte, "Education and Labour Market Integration," 3–4. The author writes that for Black youth these include being "twice as likely as other youth to be in the bottom quintile of family income," less likely to live in a household owned by a family member, and more likely to live with only one parent.
29 Turcotte, "Education and Labour Market Integration."
30 James, *Colour Matters*.
31 Do, Houle, and Turcotte, "Canada's Black Population."
32 Do, Houle, and Turcotte, "Canada's Black Population."
33 Turcotte, "Education and Labour Market Integration," 2.
34 James, *Colour Matters*; Turcotte, "Education and Labour Market Integration"; Statistics Canada, "A Portrait of Educational Attainment."
35 Recall that generational status refers to a person's or their parents' place of birth. First generation applies to individuals who were born outside of Canada and immigrated here, while second generation includes individuals who were born in Canada with at least one parent also born in Canada. Third generation or more includes individuals who were born in Canada with parents and grandparents also born in Canada. This categorization is based on the person's responses to questions about their and their parents' place of birth.
36 The focus groups were conducted by school level. Participating in each group were thirteen elementary, nine middle, and twenty-two (divided into two groups of nine and thirteen each) high school students.
37 Quaylan Allen, "'They Write Me Off and Don't Give Me a Chance to Learn Anything': Positioning, Discipline, and Black Masculinities in School: Black Male Resistance," *Anthropology & Education Quarterly* 48, no. 3 (September 2017): 269, https://doi.org/10.1111/aeq.12199.
38 Allen, "They Write Me Off," 270.
39 Eva Pomeroy, "The Teacher-Student Relationship in Secondary School: Insights from Excluded Students," *British Journal of Sociology of Education* 20, no. 4 (December 1999): 476, https://doi.org/10.1080/01425699995218.
40 Dakshana Bascaramurty and Caroline Alfonso, "How Race, Income and 'Opportunity Hoarding' Will Shape Canada's Back-To-School Season," *Globe and Mail*, September 6, 2020, https://www.theglobeandmail.com/canada/article-how-race-income-and-opportunity-hoarding-will-shape-canadas-back/; Frances Henry and Carl E. James, *Impacts of COVID-19 in Racialized Communities: An RSC Collection of Essays* (Ottawa: Royal Society of Canada, 2021), https://rsc-src.ca/sites/default/files/RC%20PB_EN%20FINAL_0.pdf.
41 See James and Taylor, *First-Generation Student Experiences*.
42 Joanna Lavoie, "Ontario Announces Plan to Hire 1,000 New Teachers to 'Boost' Math and Literacy Skills for Students," *CTV News*, Toronto, April 16, 2023, https://toronto.ctvnews.ca/ontario-announces-plan-to-hire-1-000-new-teachers-to-boost-math-and-literacy-skills-for-students-1.6357615.
43 Kristin Rushowy, "Ford Government Assuming Greater Control over School Boards," *Toronto Star*, April 17, 2023, https://www.thestar.com/politics/provincial/ford-government-says-it-will-take-more-control-of-school-boards-to-refocus-on-what/article_5b3ccc86-8c9a-567b-9c90-2c8dea6a67ff.html.
44 See Do, Houle, and Turcotte, "Canada's Black Population."

14

The Environment, Climate Change, and Market Populist Politics

Mark Winfield

INTRODUCTION

The election of a Progressive Conservative (PC) government led by Premier Doug Ford in June 2018 was followed by an unprecedented break from the trajectories that had defined, with the exception of the 1995–2000 "Common Sense Revolution" period of the Harris government, the province's approach to environmental issues throughout the post–Second World War era.

The 1945–2018 period had been characterized by the development of an increasingly sophisticated legal and institutional framework for managing the environmental challenges facing the province. That process, although at times painfully incremental, had demonstrated a capacity to respond to major new issues like the pollution of the Great Lakes, acid rain, smog, and most recently, a changing climate. These developments were accompanied by a gradual strengthening of mechanisms for public participation, transparency, and accountability in governmental decision making, including the adoption of an *Environmental Assessment Act* in 1975, an *Environmental Bill of Rights* in 1994, major reforms to the land-use planning process in 1995 and again in 2006, and legislation to curb "strategic lawsuits against public participation" (SLAPPs) in 2015.[1] There were also efforts to link responses on the environment and climate change to the wider economic transitions taking place in the province, notably under the NDP government led by Bob Rae (1990–5) and the Liberal McGuinty and Wynne governments (2003–18).[2]

By comparison, the first Ford government (2018–22) was a period of extraordinary retrenchment, affecting virtually every dimension of the province's approach to environmental issues, and turning the institutional and legislative clock back, in some cases, more than seven decades, to the immediate post–Second World War era and beyond. The prospects for progress on the environment and climate change under a re-elected Ford government are, at best, unclear.

The chapter gives an overview of the developments around environmental policy during the first Ford government. Included with this is a contextual discussion of the approaches of the preceding administrations, with a focus on the latter stages of the Liberal government led by Premier Kathleen Wynne. The chapter positions the Ford government's behaviour around environmental issues in the wider context of its overall approaches to governance. It also places the Ford government within the broader historical patterns seen in environmental policy in the province. Earlier work has highlighted the importance of intersections of public salience on environmental issues, and the ideational and discursive orientations of successive governments in understanding their environmental policy choices.[3] The chapter asks whether Ford's "market populism" constitutes a new dimension of political discourse in Ontario,[4] and examines its potential implications for the future of environmental policy in the province.

For the purposes of the chapter, environmental policy is defined broadly. It encompasses not only the traditional dimensions of air and water pollution, and water resource and waste management, but also includes more systemic issues like smog and climate change that require wider linkages to land-use, transportation, resource development, and energy policies. In the context of the more expansive concepts of sustainable development and sustainability,[5] growing attention is being given to the distributional justice aspects of environmental policies, particularly the impacts of pollution and climate change on marginalized communities.[6] Reconciliation with Indigenous Peoples is an increasingly central question in Canada and Ontario, particularly around natural resources development,[7] although it is beyond the scope of this chapter to explore these issues fully.

BACKGROUND AND CONTEXT

As noted in the introduction, the overall direction of environmental policy in Ontario in the post–Second World War period had been one of a (at times painfully) gradual upwards trajectory, beginning with the creation of Conservation Authorities and the Ontario Water Resources Commission in the 1940s and 50s, through the establishment of a provincial Ministry of the Environment in 1971, and the adoption of an *Environmental Assessment Act* in 1975.[8] The pace of change accelerated significantly during the 1985–7 Peterson/Rae Liberal/NDP minority government period, with major strengthening of the province's approach to environmental law enforcement, environmental assessments of major projects, acid rain, municipal waste management, and industrial water pollution.[9] The 1990–5 NDP Rae government saw the adoption of extensive reforms to the land-use planning process, enactment of an *Environmental Bill of Rights*, completion of the Municipal-Industrial Strategy for Abatement (MISA) industrial water pollution regulation program, and major changes to the regulation of mine closure and forest management. The period also witnessed the first formal steps towards a strategy to respond to the emerging issue of climate change.[10]

The first Harris government (1995–9) operating under the auspices of the PC's avowedly neo-liberal "Common Sense Revolution" platform was defined, in contrast, by an unprecedented period of retrenchment. This applied both in terms of the institutional capacity (i.e., budgets) of environmental and natural resource management agencies, and regulatory regimes, especially around land-use planning, mining, and natural resources. Efforts to restructure the electricity sector coincided with major failures within Ontario Hydro's nuclear fleet, leading to a large run-up of coal-fired generation with an accompanying increase in air pollution and smog-related incidents in Southern Ontario.[11] The May 2000 Walkerton drinking water disaster, in which seven residents of the town died and nearly 3,000 became seriously ill as a result of the contamination of the town's drinking water supply from agricultural runoff, was widely seen as the consequence of the government's large-scale budget cuts to environmental agencies and its anti-"red tape" orientation. That conclusion was reinforced by the subsequent judicial enquiry into the disaster.[12]

The Walkerton disaster and enquiry, along with continuing challenges with the electricity sector, marked the beginning of the end for the Harris government, with Harris himself resigning as premier in 2002. Dalton McGuinty arrived as leader of a new majority Liberal government in 2003, in part on the basis of a very strong environmental platform.[13] This included commitments to phase out coal-fired electricity by 2007 (ultimately completed in 2013), and major reforms to the land-use planning process. The planning reforms were largely implemented by the end of 2006, including the creation of the Greater Golden Horseshoe (GGH) Greenbelt and Growth Plans, the latter emphasizing "smart" growth and "complete" communities.[14]

The 2008 global financial crisis would prompt the most significant effort seen so far to integrate environmental and economic strategy in the form of the 2009 *Green Economy and Green Energy Act* (GEA). The act provided for the subsidization, through a feed-in-tariff (FIT) program, and accelerated approval of renewable energy projects. The legislation and a number of other initiatives were successful in prompting a major wave of renewable energy development in the province. Approximately 5400MW of wind and 2600MW of solar photovoltaic (PV) capacity were installed from a starting point of near zero between 2006 and 2018,[15] amounting to more than four times the electricity-generating capacity of the Sir Adam Beck facilities at Niagara Falls. At the same time, these developments became the focus of growing and ultimately politically fatal controversies over rising electricity costs.[16]

Kathleen Wynne succeeded Dalton McGuinty as Liberal Party leader and premier in February 2013. Wynne arrived with a limited environmental platform beyond the completion of the phase out of coal-fired electricity. In response to the growing controversies over electricity costs, the acquisition of new renewable energy projects began to be run down under the GEA. High-cost commitments to refurbish the Bruce and Darlington nuclear facilities, and "life-extend" the Pickering facility, continued, along with an implicit reliance on natural gas–fired generation to make up the required electricity supplies during the nuclear refurbishment period.[17]

Climate change would emerge as the central environmental focus of the Wynne government following its unexpected majority government victory in the 2014 election. The province would adopt a fairly comprehensive Climate Change Action Plan (CCAP) in 2017.[18] This included participation in a greenhouse gas (GHG) emission cap and trade system with Quebec and California. The system required both industrial emitters of GHGs and the distributors of consumer transportation and heating fuels (e.g., gasoline and natural gas) to purchase emission allowances to cover their emissions. The charges on heating and transportation fuels were passed on to consumers, functioning as a de facto carbon price on these products.

Following the model, adoption in Quebec and by the NDP Notley government in Alberta, revenues from the auction of emission permits under the cap-and-trade system were to be invested, among other things, in energy efficiency retrofits for buildings and the electrification of transportation. There was a strong focus on the adoption of electric vehicles and their associated charging infrastructure, and public transit.

In an Ontario context, where industrial emissions had already fallen substantially, largely as a result of economic restructuring, and with the phase out of coal-fired electricity, this overall approach made a great deal of sense. Buildings and transportation were projected to be the largest sources of growth in greenhouse gas emissions in the province. Both sectors involve long-lived investments and infrastructures and are relatively insensitive in the short-term to price signals. They are therefore likely to require substantial public investment to achieve emissions reductions within the timescales envisioned in the CCAP and through Canada's commitments under the 2015 United Nations Paris Climate Change Agreement.[19]

The province's actions on climate change had national significance as well. Ontario is Canada's second-largest source of GHG emissions after Alberta.[20] The province's agreement to move forward with Quebec on a carbon pricing system, along with the existing carbon tax system in British Columbia and the arrival of the Notley government in Alberta in 2015, played central roles in the ability of the new federal government, led by Justin Trudeau, to develop the 2016 Pan-Canadian Framework (PCF) for Climate Change and Green Growth. The PCF had buy-in from all provinces except Saskatchewan. The framework laid the groundwork for a "backstop" federal carbon pricing regime to be applied in provinces that did not develop carbon pricing systems of their own.[21] Ontario would have been exempted from the federal carbon price at the point of its planned introduction on April 1, 2019, by virtue of the existence of its cap and trade regime.

The emerging challenge for the Wynne government was that the climate change issue seemed to play differently with the public at the national and provincial levels. While climate change polled strongly at the national level,[22] reflecting the issue's international profile and the poor performance of the 2006–15 Conservative Harper federal government on the question, it registered weakly with Ontario voters as a provincial issue. By the fall of 2016, only 4 per cent of respondents identified it as the most important provincial concern. What was registering with Ontario voters was the question of rising hydro rates.[23] That development, perhaps more than any other, would prove fatal for the Liberal government.

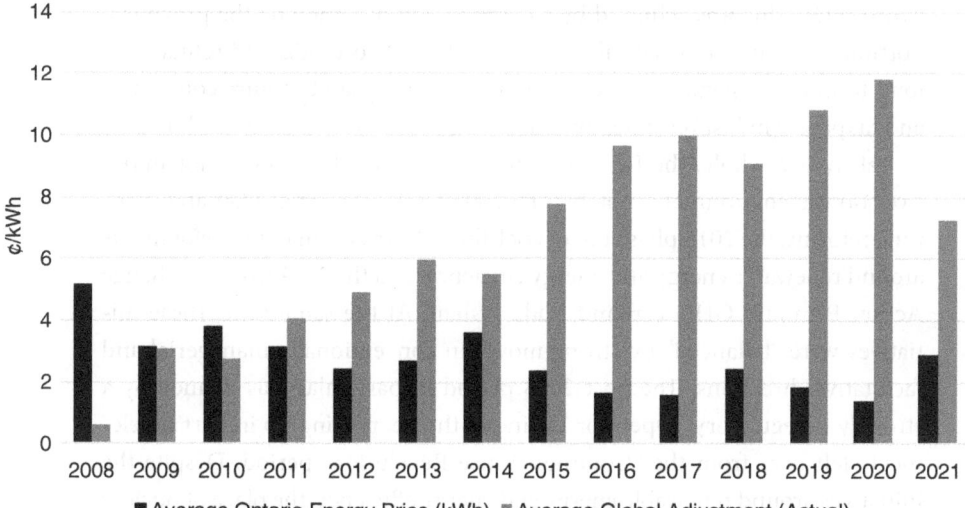

Figure 14.1. Average Global Adjustment vs. Average Market Electricity Price, 2009–19
Data Source: Independent Electricity System Operator (IESO), "Average HOEP Plus Average GA," accessed January 8, 2024, https://ieso.ca/-/media/Files/IESO/Power-Data/price-overview/Average-HOEP-plus-Average-GA.ashx.

Electricity costs had begun to rise in the aftermath of the 2003 election. The situation reflected a realization that after a period of relative neglect during the Harris government's experiments with marketizing the province's hydro system, nearly 80 per cent of the system's generating assets would need to be replaced or refurbished over the following twenty years. As shown in figure 14.1, electricity prices nearly doubled between 2003 and 2017. Although often blamed on the impact of the Green Energy Act FIT program, the increased costs actually reflected the impact of a series of major capital investments in the system. These included the partial refurbishments of the Bruce and Pickering nuclear facilities, the construction of new gas-fired generating facilities to help with the phase-out of coal-fired generation, and the upgrading of electricity transmission and distribution grids, as well as new renewable energy projects under the GEA and other initiatives. The rate increases were particularly acute in rural areas served by the Hydro One transmission and distribution utility.[24]

In response, the Wynne government introduced a "Fair Hydro Plan," in March 2017. The plan was intended to deliver an immediate 25 per cent cut in hydro rates. This was achieved by a combination of removing the provincial portion of the harmonized sales tax (HST) from hydro bills and refinancing long-term investments.[25] The estimated cost of the plan to future consumers and taxpayers in lost revenues and financing costs was placed at $45 billion.[26]

Taken as a whole, the Liberal period was defined by some major initiatives on the environment, notably the 2006 GGH Greenbelt Plan and planning reforms, the 2013 phase out of coal-fired electricity, major developments around renewable energy and energy efficiency, and the 2017 Climate Change Action Plan and GHG cap and trade system. At the same time, these initiatives were "balanced" by strong moves in conventionally managerial and facilitative directions. The post-2008 period in particular was defined by a strongly deregulatory "Open for Business" theme, picking up in part on elements left over from the "Common Sense Revolution" period. Despite the initiatives around renewable energy and energy efficiency, the place of nuclear energy as the dominant component of the province's electricity system was emphatically reaffirmed, and major investments were made in new natural gas-fired generation. The "Ring of Fire" mineral deposit emerged as the centrepiece of the province's development plans for the North, despite its implications for the environment and the interests of Indigenous Peoples. Fiscal restraint remained a central theme, prompting in part the partial sale of the Hydro One electricity transmission and distribution utility.[27]

THE 2018 ELECTION AND THE FORD "REVOLUTION"

Despite its enormous cost, the Fair Hydro Plan made no difference in the outcome of the June 2018 provincial election, which saw the Liberals go down to an historic defeat, replaced by a majority PC government led by Doug Ford. The Ford government arrived on the basis of a relatively thin platform focused on cutting taxes, particularly the carbon "tax," and hydro rates.[28]

What followed was the most significant period of retrenchment in environmental and climate policy of the postwar period. Although in contrast to the "Common Sense Revolution" period, major budget cuts to provincial agencies were avoided, virtually every other dimension of the province's legislative, regulatory, and institutional framework for managing environmental issues was affected.

The government moved to dismantle the previous government's climate change strategy almost immediately upon taking office.[29] The GHG emission cap and trade system was terminated, along with initiatives related to electric vehicles, building retrofits, industry, and climate change adaptation that would have been funded through the estimated $3 billion in revenues the system would have generated over the first three years of its existence.[30] The province then joined with Alberta and Saskatchewan in challenging the constitutional basis of the federal government's "backstop" carbon pricing system. Without a provincial cap and trade regime, that system now applied to Ontario. The provincial challenges ultimately ended in a decisive loss before the Supreme Court of Canada.[31] An attempt to require that gas stations apply stickers to their pumps indicating the impact of the federal carbon price on gasoline prices ended in an embarrassing fiasco. The initiative was ruled to be unconstitutional, and the stickers failed to stay attached to the pumps.[32]

With respect to electricity, the government moved to cancel the final tranche of renewable energy projects under development. This amounted to more than seven hundred projects, most of them small scale and community based. The total cost of the cancellations ultimately exceeded $230 million.[33] The province's largely successful strategy on energy efficiency was terminated the following year,[34] and the requirement that the province develop any long-term energy plans at all quietly ended.[35]

One of the Ford government's most significant areas of activity was with respect to land-use planning. Although the government had to retreat repeatedly in the face of municipal and public opposition to efforts to open the GGH Greenbelt to development, provincial planning rules were extensively rewritten in favour of development interests.[36] The use of ministerial zoning orders (MZOs) and similar instruments to override local planning decisions and rules became commonplace, again almost exclusively in response to industry demands for higher-intensity development.[37] The authority of Conservation Authorities within the planning process was significantly constrained, even in relation to areas subject to flooding or other hazards.[38]

The province's moves with respect to land-use planning were accompanied by an aggressive push for the expansion of the provincial highway network, particularly within the Greater Toronto Area (GTA). Many of these projects, like the Vaughan to Milton 413 Highway and Highway 404 to 400 Bradford Bypass, revived concepts originally proposed under the Harris government, and that had been subsequently rejected as unnecessary and likely to induce additional automobile-dependent urban sprawl.[39] New transit projects were also pushed forward aggressively, although many, like the Ontario line in Toronto, seemed poorly conceived and politically motivated.[40] Protections for endangered species were significantly weakened, particularly with respect to resource development.[41]

On pollution-related issues, the province's toxic use reduction legislation was repealed.[42] The MISA regulatory framework for controlling industrial water pollution, initiated under the Peterson government and completed by Bob Rae's administration, was dismantled. The regime was effectively returned to the 1960s and 70s approach of negotiating discharge limits on a facility-by-facility basis. Rules around agricultural pollution of drinking water sources, particularly nutrients (e.g., fertilizer and manure), which had been a key factor in the Walkerton disaster, were weakened.[43] As a final touch the province's previously independent Environmental Commissioner's office, created through the 1994 *Environmental Bill of Rights*, was folded into that of the Auditor General.[44]

The government's agenda continued, and in many ways accelerated, under the cover of the COVID-19 pandemic and subsequent recovery efforts. One of the government's first moves in response to the pandemic was to suspend the application of the *Environmental Bill of Rights* notice and comment requirements regarding changes to environmental laws, regulations, policies, and approvals.[45] The application of the province's environmental assessment process, mandatory for public-sector projects since its establishment by the Davis government in 1975, was made discretionary, and the content of the assessment process significantly weakened.[46] Broad powers were given to provincial agencies, most notably the provincial transit agency Metrolinx,[47] allowing them to override any potential objections to their projects and effectively giving them the authority to approve their own undertakings. Legislation adopted in the run-up to the 2022 election sought to further marginalize the roles of local governments in planning matters, and to eliminate public consultation requirements in the planning process as "red tape."[48]

A "Made in Ontario" Environment Plan was released at the end of 2018. The plan was motivated in large part by the government's desire to stave off the application of the "backstop" federal carbon price to Ontario.[49] Although relying on an ill-defined incentive system in place of a carbon pricing system, the plan did include a number of interesting elements. These related to climate change adaptation, linkages between land-use planning, transportation and climate change, distributed energy resources (e.g., renewables and energy storage), and community energy and climate change planning. However, virtually nothing was done to implement the plan.[50]

The federal backstop carbon pricing regime was implemented in the province in April 2019. A distribution-level carbon levy applied to heating and transportation fuels, and an output-based pricing system (OBPS) applied to industrial emissions.[51] Ontario was granted an "equivalency" exemption from the OBPS for industrial emissions at the beginning of 2022 on the basis of its own emission standards, although these were widely regarded as substantially weaker than the federal backstop requirements.[52]

In the final months before the 2022 election, the government did begin to take an interest in the "greening" of the steel sector,[53] and in the electric vehicle (EV) and battery supply chains.[54] These developments, likely the products of international developments within the steel and auto industries, seemed to indicate some recognition that a wider global economic shift in the direction of decarbonization had been taking place, and that Ontario was at risk of losing what remained of its manufacturing sector if it didn't respond in some way.

These types of developments however, remained sporadic and reactive. In sectors like mining[55] and hydrogen,[56] the government's initiatives relied heavily on the input of industry lobbyists, with little evidence of external thought or critical analysis. The Critical Minerals Strategy, for example, released in the spring of 2022, was criticized for largely ignoring its implications for Indigenous Peoples and their rights.[57] The potential consequences for climate change of a major industrial development in the province's boreal region, part of one of the world's most significant carbon sinks and storage sites, were also overlooked.[58] There remained no movement in key areas like renewable energy, and certainly no wider vision for Ontario's role in a low-carbon economic transition.

UNDERSTANDING THE FORD GOVERNMENT'S APPROACH TO THE ENVIRONMENT

The Ford government's record on environmental issues is best understood as an extension of its wider approach to governance. It was observed that the government's agendas seemed driven by "instinct more than ideology."[59] The government came to power with little vision for what a provincial government should do other than cut taxes, "red tape," and hydro rates. It struggled when confronted with more complex problems that required the province to play a more active role. The resulting governance model was fundamentally reactive, and grounded in relatively short-term perspectives.[60] The government tended to act once situations reached a crisis stage, rather than identifying potential problems and taking action to prevent them. The pattern was especially evident in the government's hesitant responses to the COVID-19 pandemic.[61] There, it tended to react to the waves of COVID-19 infections rather than anticipating them and taking measures to minimize their impacts,[62] even when given clear and consistent scientific advice to do so.[63]

Issues like the environment and climate change are destined to do poorly under such a governance model. The reports of the Intergovernmental Panel on Climate Change,[64] and federal[65] and provincial environmental commissioners,[66] are constant reminders that these issues require taking action now to avoid more serious problems in the future.

This fundamentally reactive model of governance was combined with a tendency to accept uncritically whatever business lobbyists with the necessary access asked the government to do. This was evident in the province's approaches to COVID-19,[67] housing and infrastructure,[68] mining,[69] gravel pits and quarries,[70] energy,[71] and long-term care.[72] The overall decision-making model that emerged seemed based on connections[73] and political whim.[74] The voices of the public, civil society organizations, and even those of local governments and the provincial public service were aggressively marginalized.

All of this was in sharp contrast to the rules, evidence, and public input-based approaches that the structures that emerged throughout the postwar period, like the *Planning Act*, *Environmental Assessment Act*, and *Environmental Bill of Rights*, were intended to establish. It, in part, explains the government's behaviour towards these frameworks, which has at times bordered on the authoritarian in its approaches to dealing with local governments, particularly around governance,[75] planning, and infrastructure issues.

THE FORD GOVERNMENT AND THE DYNAMICS OF ENVIRONMENTAL POLICY

In previous work around understanding the behaviour of provincial governments in relation to environmental issues, the author found it helpful to employ a modified version of the institutional-ideological policy model used by Bruce Doern and Glen Toner in their landmark 1982 study on the National Energy Program.[76] The approach is based on an analytical framework of four basic categories of variables: the institutional context within which policy is being made; the underlying normative assumptions about both the role of the state in general and the specific policy issues in question; the underlying physical and economic landscape conditions defining the context in which policy debates occur; and the roles of non-state actors and forces, such as interest groups, public opinion, and the media.[77]

Although the institutional framework and economic circumstances within which successive Ontario governments have operated have provided key contextual elements to the narrative, the key drivers in terms of understanding government behaviour in Ontario regarding the environment have generally been found within the other two categories of variables. The first relates to societal factors and forces – specifically, the public salience of environmental issues as apparent in public opinion polling and the level of media and legislative opposition attention given to environmental issues. It has been long recognized that governments increase their levels of activity in the environmental field when public concern is high, and that policy activity is likely to stall or even reverse when concern is low. Levels of public concern for environmental issues have historically tended to be cyclical, characterized by relatively short periods of very high concern, and longer periods of relatively low concern. More recent national polling, from the mid-2010s onwards, has tended to show more consistently high levels of concern, with a particularly strong focus on climate change.[78] However, concern for the environment in Ontario as a provincial issue has consistently polled lower than as seen in national-level polls.[79]

The second key variable relates to the government of the day's normative assumptions about the role of the provincial state. Historically, in Ontario's case, these assumptions could be broadly organized into three categories. Managerial and facilitative governments have tended to focus on measures that they perceive as being necessary to facilitate economic growth and development (understood in conventional terms of industrialization, resource extraction and processing, and urbanization), but have not sought to expand the role of the state beyond these roles unless politically or practically necessary. The managerial/facilitative governance model was exemplified by the long PC "dynasty" and, to a considerable degree, during the McGuinty and Wynne periods as well. Alternatively, activist/progressive governments have envisioned a more directive role for the state in shaping the province's economy and society. Such an approach was evident during the Peterson minority period and the first half of the NDP Rae government. Finally, neo-liberal governments have sought to minimize state interference with the market, as epitomized by the Harris "revolution."

Earlier analyses had concluded that the combination of public salience of environmental issues and the normative orientation of the government of the day provides the strongest predictor of a government's likely behaviour towards environmental issues.[80] As shown in table 14.1, all six potential combinations of public concern and government orientation had been seen in the postwar era in Ontario. At one end of the spectrum, the combination of low public salience and a neo-liberal government produced the major environmental policy retrenchments of the "Common Sense Revolution." At the other end, the combination of high levels of public attention and relatively activist governments resulted in periods of high policy activity and innovation, exemplified by the minority Peterson government and the first half of the Rae administration.

Historically the dominant combination in Ontario has been one of relatively low public salience of environmental issues and facilitative and managerially oriented governments. The result has tended to be patterns of incremental policy progress, with an emphasis on achieving a "balance" between progressive and conventional themes. Such an approach became particularly pronounced under the McGuinty and Wynne governments, with the pursuit of, at times, deeply contradictory directions of transitional strategies around the environment and climate change on one hand, and highly conventional, if not almost neo-liberal, pathways on the other.

The arrival and apparent political success of the Ford government seems to have introduced a new dimension on ideational/discursive spectrum of Ontario politics, one that might be termed "market populism."[81] In practice, this seems to combine a relatively neo-liberal policy approach with a populist focus on reducing costs to consumers (e.g., taxes, hydro rates) in the short term. The approach reframes in populist terms traditionally neo-liberal economic goals such as a reduction in the size of the state and deregulation of the economy. These are then branded as what "real Ontarians" want. Slogans such as "open for business" and "respecting taxpayers" suggest a direct connection between policies that favour minimal government interference and personal economic prosperity. They imply that anything beyond minimal government action is incompatible with respect for voters – something the Liberal governments failed to show.

In the run-up to the 2022 provincial election, the Ford government added a new form of post-pandemic activism to its "market populism." This has

Table 14.1. Discursive Orientation and Public Salience of Environmental Issues

Discursive Orientation	Activist/ Progressive	Managerial/ Facilitative	Neo-Liberal	Market/ Authoritarian Populist
Public Salience of Issue: High	Policy Outputs High policy activity. Exploration of environment-economy relationship. Disruption of traditionally dominant policy relationships. Examples Peterson (accord period) Rae (Part I)	Policy Outputs Bipolar – high-profile environmental initiatives matched with major countervailing moves in conventional directions. Policy driven by political management as opposed to reflection on conventional economic model. Examples Peterson (majority) McGuinty (1st mandate)	Policy Outputs Reactive. High profile but one-off initiatives. Maintenance of core policy path. Examples Harris post-Walkerton Eves	Policy Outputs Reactive. High profile but symbolic one-off initiatives. Responsiveness to some industry pressures for transitions. Maintenance of core policy path. Examples None to date. Likely similar to neo-liberal responses
Public Salience of Issue: Low	Policy Outputs Follow-through on existing initiatives. Few new initiatives. Examples Rae (Part II) Wynne – Climate Change	Policy Outputs Incremental responses to crises (physical or political). Mitigation of impacts of conventional economic development models. Examples The "dynasty" Davis (1975–84) McGuinty (2nd /3rd mandate) Wynne (except climate change)	Policy Outputs Retrenchment. Environment unimportant. Reinforcement of traditionally dominant policy relationships. Examples Miller Harris "Common Sense Revolution" period (1995–2000)	Policy Outputs Extreme Retrenchment. Environment unimportant. Near total reliance on established economic interests for policy input. Exclusion of civil society, local governments, and public service Examples Ford (1st mandate)

Source: Adapted from Mark Winfield, *Blue-Green Province: The Environment and the Political Economy of Ontario* (Vancouver: UBC Press, 2012), 190, figure 8.1.

focused on further cutting red tape and increased spending to "Get it done"[82] in terms of housing, highway, and transit construction. Whether the projects being "done," such as the 413 Highway,[83] actually made sense was a secondary question. At the same time, a populist focus on short-term affordability through moves such as a promised gas-tax cut,[84] and the removal of road tolls[85] and vehicle licencing fees,[86] responded well to public concerns[87] over rising living costs.

In the context of the analytical frame outlined above and shown in table 14.1, the Ford period would be defined by a combination of low to middling public salience of environmental issues and a "market populist" approach to governance. The policy results are similar to those seen with the neo-liberal/low salience combination, although in some ways more extreme – significant retrenchment, and a near total reliance on established economic interests for policy input. Where the government has felt the need to act on environmental issues, this has largely been in response to pressures from the affected industries themselves (e.g., steel and EVs), or in the case of the 2018 Made-in Ontario Environment Plan, the federal initiatives around carbon pricing.

The behaviour of a "market populist" government in response to higher levels of public concern, potentially prompted by climate change–related extreme weather events or another form of environmental or Walkerton-like public health disaster is difficult to predict. High-profile but symbolic gestures are likely, but substantive changes in direction seem unlikely except where there is pressure from the affected industries themselves. The government's responses to the COVID-19 pandemic may be instructive in this sense. There, despite the extremely poor performance of for-profit long-term care facilities in the pandemic, such facilities have emerged as the primary beneficiaries of the government's investments in the sector.[88]

CONCLUSIONS AND PATHS FORWARD

The 2022 provincial election ended with a strengthened PC majority, although on the basis of an historically low voter turnout. All three major opposition parties (NDP, Liberal, and Green) had presented platforms including detailed provisions around the environment and climate change.[89] There was substantial and sustained coverage in the mainstream media of environmental issues through the campaign, particularly the implications of the 413 Highway project[90] and climate change[91] more generally as well. The environment was consistently identified in media commentary as an area of vulnerability for the PC government.[92] The government, in response, presented nothing new on environmental issues, and retained its steadfast commitments to infrastructure, particularly highway construction.

The election outcome, in this context, was deeply distressing to those concerned about the environment and climate change, particularly the apparent failure of these issues to connect with the provincial electorate.[93] Whether the outcome signals a true realignment of the norms in Ontario politics, or is a product of COVID-19-induced political exhaustion on the part of an electorate presented with underwhelming alternatives remains an open question.

That said, one of the defining features of the environment as a public policy issue is its fundamental grounding in biophysical reality. Environmental issues do not go away just because a government chooses to ignore them. In Ontario's case, the province is now on track to see major increases in greenhouse gas emissions, particularly from the electricity sector.[94] The impacts of a changing climate are likely to become more and more apparent in the form of extreme weather events, flooding, forest fires, extended ranges of disease vectors, and cyanobacteria blooms.[95] Long-standing issues related to air and water pollution, and losses of biological diversity, natural heritage, and prime agricultural lands to resource extraction and urban development continue to worsen,[96] and in many cases seem likely to accelerate, as a result of the decisions made by the first Ford government.

The responses of a re-elected Ford government to these kinds of developments remains unknown. As noted earlier, the government's past behaviour does not inspire confidence about its ability to change direction substantively even in the face of obvious policy failures, particularly in dealing with relatively complex issues like the environment and climate change. It has not been a government that sees its role as leading societal transformations in directions like sustainability and decarbonization. Indeed, the government's immediate post-election behaviour was a doubling down on themes evident its first term, particularly its top-down approach to municipal governance[97] and aggressive support of urban land development interests,[98] culminating in the removal of 7,400 acres of land from the GTA Greenbelt at the end of 2022.[99]

An important variable in the post-2022 election environment may be the behaviour of the federal Liberal government towards its Ontario counterpart. As noted earlier, environmental issues, particularly climate change, appear to poll differently in Ontario when seen by voters from a federal[100] as opposed to provincial perspective.[101] This dynamic was reflected in the relative success of parties favouring climate action in Ontario in the September 2021 federal election, where the Liberals, NDP, and Greens obtained 78, 6, and 1 seat(s) respectively, versus 37 for the Conservatives.

So far, the legal battle of carbon pricing notwithstanding, the federal government has been relatively accommodating of the Ford government's behaviour around environmental issues. It has allowed the province an exemption from the federal OBPS for industrial GHG emissions on the basis of a weaker provincial system. It was reluctantly drawn into conducting a federal environmental impact assessment of the 413 Highway project, and declined to conduct a similar review of the Bradford Bypass project.[102] The federal government's draft Clean Electricity Regulations, intended to implement a federal commitment to a net-zero electricity grid by 2035,[103] seemed designed to accommodate the province's increasingly carbon-intense trajectory in the electricity sector. If the federal government has any serious hope of achieving its GHG emission reduction targets, it is likely to have to take a more assertive approach to dealing with Ontario.

As was the case with the Harris government, the consequences of the renewed Ford government's approach to environmental issues may yet to come back to haunt it. A high-profile report by the Auditor General in August 2023 on the December 2022 removals of land from the Greenbelt determined that the process had been "biased" in favour of certain well-connected developers, by-passed normal decision-making processes, and had no basis in evidence.[104] The full scale of the fallout from the episode remains unclear, but it presented the Ford government with the most serious political crisis of its second term, resulting in resignations of two ministers and the reversal of the Greenbelt decision.[105] Whether the experience has been sufficient to compel the government to change its approach to environmental matters or, more broadly its style of governance, remains an open question. The same conclusion applies to the prospects for a healthy and safe environment for Ontario residents in the face of a changing climate, losses of biological diversity, and a range of other growing environmental challenges.

ACKNOWLEDGEMENTS

The author wishes to thank MES/JD students Mikaela Kyle and Peter Hillson for their contributions to the development of this chapter.

DISCUSSION QUESTIONS

1 What do you see as the most important environmental problem facing Ontario?
2 How can advocates of action on the environment and climate change advance these issues with a "market populist" government like that led by Doug Ford?
3 What role should the federal government play in environmental and climate change policy in Ontario?
4 How can the voices of marginalized communities, including Indigenous Peoples, be strengthened in the environmental policy-making process?

NOTES

1 *Protection of Public Participation Act*, 2015, SO 2015, c. 23.
2 See Mark Winfield, *Blue-Green Province: The Environment and the Political Economy of Ontario* (Vancouver: UBC Press, 2012); Mark Winfield, "Environmental Policy: Greening the Province from the Dynasty to Wynne," in *Politics of Ontario*, ed. Cheryl N. Collier and Jonathan Malloy (Toronto: University of Toronto Press, 2017), 251–73; and Mark Winfield and Colleen Kaiser, "Ontario and Climate Change," in *Ontario Since Confederation: A Reader*, ed. James Onusko and Dimitri Anastakis (Toronto: University of Toronto Press, forthcoming).
3 Winfield, *Blue-Green Province*, 9 (figure 1.4), 190 (figure 8.1).
4 Mark Winfield and Peter Hillson, "Understanding Doug Ford's Political Durability," *Policy Options*, May 24, 2022, https://policyoptions.irpp.org/magazines/may-2022/doug-ford-political-durability/.
5 Mark Winfield, Stephen Hill, and James Gaede, "Introduction," in *Sustainable Energy Transitions for Canada*, ed. Mark S. Winfield, Stephen D. Hill, and James R. Gaede (Vancouver: UBC Press, 2023), 3–26.
6 Dayna Nadine Scott, "What is Environmental Justice?," *Osgoode Legal Studies Research Paper Series* 4, no. 72 (2014), https://digitalcommons.osgoode.yorku.ca/olsrps/4.
7 Indigenous Corporate Training, "What Reconciliation Is and What It Is Not," August 18, 2018, https://www.ictinc.ca/blog/what-reconciliation-is-and-what-it-is-not.
8 Winfield, *Blue-Green*, chap. 2.
9 Winfield, chap. 3.
10 Winfield, chap. 4.
11 Winfield, chap. 5.
12 The Hon. Dennis R. O'Connor, *Report of the Walkerton Inquiry*, 2 vols. (Toronto: Queen's Printer, 2002), pt. 1.
13 Ontario Liberal Party, *Growing Strong Communities: The Ontario Liberal Plan for Clean, Safe Communities That Work* (Toronto: Ontario Liberal Party, 2003).

14 See L. Anders Sandberg, Gerda R. Wekerle, and Liette Gilbert, *The Oak Ridges Moraine Battles: Development, Sprawl, and Nature Conservation in the Toronto Region* (Toronto: University of Toronto Press, 2013); Winfield, *Blue-Green Province*, 153–63.
15 Independent Electricity System Operator (IESO), "Supply Mix and Generation," accessed December 23, 2023, https://www.ieso.ca/en/Learn/Ontario-Electricity-Grid/Supply-Mix-and-Generation.
16 Becky MacWhirter and Mark Winfield, "Competing Policy Paradigms and the Search for Sustainability in Ontario Electricity Policy," in *Divided Province: Ontario Politics in the Age of Neoliberalism*, ed. Greg Albo and Bryan M. Evans (Montreal: McGill-Queen's University Press, 2018), 359–93, https://doi.org/10.2307/j.ctvbj7g4v.16.
17 MacWhirter and Winfield, "The Search for Sustainability."
18 Government of Ontario, *Climate Change Action Plan* (Toronto: Queen's Printer, 2017).
19 Winfield and Kaiser, "Ontario and Climate Change."
20 Government of Canada, "Greenhouse Gas Emissions by Territory," last modified June 29, 2023, https://www.canada.ca/en/environment-climate-change/services/environmental-indicators/greenhouse-gas-emissions.html.
21 Douglas Macdonald and Mark Winfield, "Federalism and Canadian Climate Change Policy," in *Canadian Federalism: Performance, Effectiveness, and Legitimacy*, 4th ed., ed. Herman Bakvis and Grace Skogstad (Toronto: University of Toronto Press 2020), 363–92.
22 CBC News, "Vote Compass: Economy and Environment Rate as Top Issues," September 10, 2015, https://www.cbc.ca/news/politics/vote-compass-canada-election-2015-issues-canadians-1.3222945.
23 Nanos Research, "Hydro Rates Are the Top Issue for Ontarians; PCs Lead and Wynne Takes an Image Hit," November 2016, https://nanos.co/wp-content/uploads/2017/07/2016-Ontario-OMNI-Populated-Report-with-tabs-R.pdf.
24 MacWhirter and Winfield, "The Search for Sustainability."
25 Office of the Premier, "Ontario Cutting Electricity Bills by 25 Per Cent: System Restructuring Delivers Lasting Relief to Households across Province," news release, March 2, 2017, https://news.ontario.ca/en/release/43881/ontario-cutting-electricity-bills-by-25-per-cent.
26 Auditor General of Ontario, *Special Report: The Fair Hydro Plan: Concerns about Fiscal Transparency, Accountability and Value for Money* (Toronto: Queen's Printer, 2017).
27 Winfield, "Greening the Province."
28 Progressive Conservative Party of Ontario, *Plan for the People* (Toronto: PC Ontario Party, 2018).
29 The Canadian Press, "Ontario Government Officially Kills Cap-and-Trade Climate Plan," *CBC News*, October 31, 2018, https://www.cbc.ca/news/canada/toronto/ontario-officially-ends-cap-and-trade-1.4885872.
30 Financial Accountability Office, *Cap and Trade: A Financial Review of the Decision to Cancel the Cap and Trade Program* (Toronto: FAO, 2018), https://www.fao-on.org/en/blog/publications/cap-and-trade-ending.
31 Supreme Court of Canada, *References re Greenhouse Gas Pollution Pricing Act, 2021*, SCC 11, March 25, 2021, https://www.scc-csc.ca/case-dossier/cb/2021/38663-38781-39116-eng.aspx.

32 Robert Benzie, "Doug Ford's Government Abandons Unconstitutional Gas-Pump Stickers that Railed against Federal Carbon Pricing," *Toronto Star*, September 20, 2020, https://www.thestar.com/politics/provincial/doug-ford-s-government-abandons-unconstitutional-gas-pump-stickers-that-railed-against-federal-carbon-pricing/article_9810b374-0c80-5faf-b1c4-aa3c7470c3c2.html.

33 Mike Crawley, "Doug Ford Government Spent $231M to Scrap Green Energy Projects," *CBC News*, November 19, 2019, https://www.cbc.ca/news/canada/toronto/doug-ford-green-energy-wind-turbines-cancelled-230-million-1.5364815.

34 Krystalle Ramlakhan, "Ford Government Cancels Electricity Conservation Programs," *CBC News*, March 24, 2019, https://www.cbc.ca/news/canada/ottawa/ford-government-cancels-energy-electricity-efficient-programs-centralizing-1.5069318.

35 Environmental Registry of Ontario, "Removing the Timing Requirements for Releasing Ontario's Next Long-Term Energy Plan by Revoking Ontario Regulation 355/17," Government of Ontario, November 20, 2020, https://ero.ontario.ca/notice/019-2149.

36 Stefan Novakovic, "Ontario's Growth Plan Changes: The End of Smart Growth?," *Urban Toronto*, January 22, 2019, https://urbantoronto.ca/news/2019/01/ontarios-growth-plan-changes-end-smart-growth.

37 Bobby Hristova, "MZOs Have Been a Trump Card for the Ford Government – Here's Why It's a Serious Ontario Election Issue," *CBC News*, March 31, 2022, https://www.cbc.ca/news/canada/hamilton/mzo-election-2022-1.6399276.

38 Toronto Region Conservation Authority, "TRCA Calls for the Immediate Removal of Schedule 6 from Bill 229," *News Release*, December 4, 2020, https://trca.ca/news/trca-calls-for-immediate-removal-of-schedule-6-from-bill-229/.

39 Ryan Patrick Jones, "Ford Government Plan to Build New GTA Highways Imperils Emissions Targets, Critics Say," *CBC News*, November 6, 2021, https://www.cbc.ca/news/canada/toronto/highway-413-carbon-emissions-1.6238421.

40 Greg Gormick, "There is Still Time to Stop the Ontario Line," *Toronto Star*, August 26, 2021, A17; see also Matti Siemiatycki and Drew Fagan, "Transit in the Greater Toronto Area: How to Get Back on the Rails," in *IMFG Perspectives*, no. 26 (Toronto: Institute on Municipal Finance and Governance, 2019), https://tspace.library.utoronto.ca/bitstream/1807/96710/1/Perspectives-26-Siemiatycki-Fagan-Transit-GTA-October-2019.pdf.

41 Ontario Nature, David Suzuki Foundation, Bird Studies Canada, Animal Alliance, A2A – Algonquin to Adirondacks Collaborative, Alliance of Soutwestern Ontario, EcoSpark, Environmental Defence, Freshwater Future Canada, Grand River Environmental Network et al. to Public Input Coordinator, Ministry of Environment, Conservation and Parks, "Re: ERO ERO-013-5033 Review of the Endangered Species Act 2007," May 18, 2019, https://ontarionature.org/wp-content/uploads/2019/05/ERO-013-5033-ESA-May-18-2019.pdf.

42 Amanda Persico, "Ontario's Decision to Repeal 'Ineffective' Toxics Reduction Act Kills Voluntary Reduction Program," *Toronto.com*, November 27, 2019, https://www.toronto.com/news/ontarios-decision-to-repeal-ineffective-toxics-reduction-act-kills-voluntary-reduction-program/article_e920b600-1575-5f63-9f0b-6164b6244581.html.

43 Mark Winfield, "Ford Government Endangers Gains on Water Quality," *Hamilton Spectator*, June 28, 2021, https://www.thespec.com/opinion/contributors/2021/06/28/ford-government-endangers-gains-on-water-quality.html.

44 Mark Winfield, Faisal Moola, and Sheila Colla, "Scrapping Environmental Watchdog is Like Shooting the Messenger," *The Conversation*, November 22, 2018, https://theconversation.com/scrapping-environmental-watchdog-is-like-shooting-the-messenger-107345.

45 Mikaela Kyle, "Covid-19 in Ontario: An Opportunity to Degrade Environmental Law and Policy," (MES/JD Major Paper, Sustainable Energy Initiative, York University, 2021), https://sei.info.yorku.ca/files/2021/06/Mikaela-Kyle-Major-Paper-Final-Version.pdf?x60126.

46 Richard Lindgren, "Concerns Raised about Ontario's Environmental Assessment Changes," *The Lawyers' Daily*, August 20, 2020, https://www.thelawyersdaily.ca/articles/20592/concerns-raised-about-ontario-s-environmental-assessment-changes.

47 See the Government of Ontario, *Building Transit Faster Act, 2020*, S.O. 2020, c. 12, https://www.ontario.ca/laws/statute/20b12.

48 Regarding *Bill 109, More Homes for Everyone Act*, see Teviah Moro, "Ontario Legislation to Cut Housing Red Tape Is 'Bad Planning': Hamilton Mayor," *Hamilton Spectator*, April 9, 2022, https://www.thespec.com/news/hamilton-region/2022/04/09/ontario-hamilton-housing-legislation.html.

49 Government of Ontario, *A Made-in-Ontario Environment Plan* (Toronto: Queen's Printer, 2018), https://www.ontario.ca/page/made-in-ontario-environment-plan.

50 Auditor General of Ontario, *Follow-Up on Value-for-Money Audit: Climate Change: Ontario's Plan to Reduce Greenhouse Gas Emissions* (Toronto: November 2021), https://www.auditor.on.ca/en/content/annualreports/arreports/en21/ENV_FU_PAC_ClimateChange_en21.pdf.

51 Government of Canada, "How Carbon Pricing Works," accessed June 17, 2022, https://www.canada.ca/en/environment-climate-change/services/climate-change/pricing-pollution-how-it-will-work/putting-price-on-carbon-pollution.html.

52 Green Economy Law, "Fed Govt Accepts Ontario Emission Performance Standard as Satisfying Pollution Pricing Law," October 2, 2020, https://www.greeneconomylaw.com/blog/fed-govt-accepts-ontario-emission-performance-standard-as-satisfying-pollution-pricing-law.

53 Mike Crawley, "Ford Government Eyes 'Green Steel' as Way to Catch Up on Cutting Carbon Emissions," *CBC News*, February 17, 2022, https://www.cbc.ca/news/canada/toronto/ontario-climate-change-steel-co2-greenhouse-gas-emissions-1.6353814.

54 Jessica McDiarmid, "Ontario to Invest $131.6 Million in Electric Vehicle Manufacturing, but Vague on How to Increase Demand," *Canada's National Observer*, March 16, 2022, https://www.nationalobserver.com/2022/03/16/news/ontario-invest-1316-million-electric-vehicle-manufacturing-vague-how.

55 Jessica McDiarmid, "Ontario Wants to Boost Mining Exploration, Development with 5-Year Plan," *Canada's National Observer*, March 18, 2022, https://www.nationalobserver.com/2022/03/18/news/ontario-wants-boost-mining-exploration-development-5-year-plan.

56 Clifford Maynes, "Weak Ontario Hydrogen Strategy Mirrors Industry Wish List," *The Energy Mix*, April 13, 2022, https://www.theenergymix.com/2022/04/13/weak-ontario-hydrogen-strategy-mirrors-industry-wish-list/.
57 Heather Kitching, "Ontario Makes Big Promises with Critical Minerals Plans but First Nations Advocates Remain Concerned," *CBC News*, March 18, 2022, https://www.cbc.ca/news/canada/thunder-bay/critical-minerals-strategy-first-nation-concerns-1.6389154.
58 James Wilt, "The Battle for the 'Breathing Lands': Ontario's Ring of Fire and the Fate of its Carbon-rich Peatlands," *The Narwal*, July 11, 2020, https://thenarwhal.ca/ring-of-fire-ontario-peatlands-carbon-climate/.
59 Stephanie Levitz, "Doug Ford's First Term as Premier Was Upended by a Pandemic. Will His Response Earn Him an Encore?," *Toronto Star*, May 4, 2022, https://www.thestar.com/politics/provincial/doug-ford-s-first-term-as-premier-was-upended-by-a-pandemic-will-his-response/article_f94a24fb-6b0b-5178-83cd-bd40c524e857.html.
60 Mark Winfield, "The Doug Ford Doctrine: Short-Term Gain for Long-Term Pain," *The Conversation*, April 28, 2019, https://theconversation.com/the-doug-ford-doctrine-short-term-gain-for-long-term-pain-116131.
61 Mark Winfield, "How Ontario Can Recover from Doug Ford's COVID-19 Governance Disaster," *The Conversation*, April 27, 2021, https://theconversation.com/how-ontario-can-recover-from-doug-fords-covid-19-governance-disaster-159783.
62 Robyn Urback, "Ontario's COVID-19 Strategy: Waiting for Catastrophe, Then Enacting Preventative Measures," *Globe and Mail*, April 13, 2021, https://www.theglobeandmail.com/opinion/article-ontarios-covid-19-strategy-waiting-for-catastrophe-then-enacting/.
63 The Canadian Press, "Ontario Science Table to Publish New COVID-19 Projections Today," *Toronto Star*, March 17, 2022, https://www.thestar.com/news/canada/ontario-science-table-to-publish-new-covid-19-projections-today/article_c8b09e8b-161b-508e-beea-6d65c1532b86.html.
64 Intergovernmental Panel on Climate Change, *IPCC Sixth Assessment Report* (Geneva: IPCC, 2022), https://www.ipcc.ch/report/ar6/wg2/.
65 Commissioner for the Environment and Sustainable Development, *Lessons Learned from Canada's Record on Climate Change*, report no. 5 (Ottawa: Office of the Auditor General of Canada, 2021), https://www.oag-bvg.gc.ca/internet/English/parl_cesd_202111_05_e_43898.html.
66 Auditor General of Ontario, "Climate Change: Ontario's."
67 Richard Warnica, "Did Lobbyists Influence Doug Ford's COVID-19 Decisions?," *Toronto Star*, July 15, 2021, https://www.thestar.com/business/did-lobbyists-influence-doug-ford-s-covid-19-decisions-read-the-exclusive-star-series/article_d1f8e2a7-7ea4-5d35-999d-c7e0ae085f28.html.
68 Jeff Gray, "Ford Government to Rewrite Toronto's Development Plans to Allow Taller Buildings in More of Midtown, Downtown," *Globe and Mail*, June 5, 2019, updated June 6, 2019, https://www.theglobeandmail.com/canada/article-ford-government-to-majorly-revise-toronto-development-plans-and-allow/; Sheila Wang, "Ontario Issues Orders to Fast-Track Developments in Richmond Hill, Markham amid Rising Criticism," *Richmond Hill Liberal*,

April 19, 2022, https://www.yorkregion.com/news/ontario-issues-orders-to-fast-track-developments-in-richmond-hill-markham-amid-rising-criticism/article_78b24279-d920-556d-85b6-61f21b4105fc.html.

69 Kitching, "Ontario Makes Big Promises."

70 Paula Duhatshek, "Province's Plans to Change Gravel Pit Rules Could Harm Local Water, Natural Areas: Report," *CBC News*, October 19, 2019, https://www.cbc.ca/news/canada/kitchener-waterloo/province-s-plans-to-change-gravel-pit-rules-could-harm-local-water-natural-areas-report-1.5338478.

71 Mark Winfield, "Cleaning up Ontario's Hydro Mess," *Policy Options*, January 15, 2021, https://policyoptions.irpp.org/magazines/january-2021/cleaning-up-ontarios-hydro-mess/.

72 Marco Chown Oved, Kenyon Wallace, and Ed Tubb, "Doug Ford Is Spending Billions to Expand Nursing Home Chains with Some of the Worst COVID-19 Death Rates," *Toronto Star*, May 27, 2022, https://www.thestar.com/news/investigations/doug-ford-is-spending-billions-to-expand-nursing-home-chains-with-some-of-the-worst/article_7070ce98-54a6-524f-bd9f-f824f371f0ca.html.

73 Steve Buist, Noor Javed, and Emma McIntosh, "Friends with Benefits? An Inside Look at the Money, Power and Influence Behind the Ford Government's Push to Build Highway 413," *Toronto Star*, April 10, 2021, https://www.thestar.com/news/investigations/friends-with-benefits-an-inside-look-at-the-money-power-and-influence-behind-the-ford/article_9d6dcaf1-e00a-5360-a40f-8625ee6c77c5.html.

74 Toronto Star Editorial Board, "Ford's Change to Development Rules Is a Massive Overreach," *Toronto Star*, March 8, 2021, https://www.thestar.com/opinion/editorials/ford-s-change-to-development-rules-is-a-massive-overreach/article_0c596f50-6df1-5cae-aec3-238292146b30.html.

75 Jennifer Pagliaro and Robert Ferguson, "Ford Plans to Invoke Notwithstanding Clause for First Time in Province's History and Will Call Back Legislature on Bill 5," *Toronto Star*, September 12, 2018, https://www.thestar.com/news/municipal-elections/ford-plans-to-invoke-notwithstanding-clause-for-first-time-in-province-s-history-and-will/article_88bc19c6-1628-59a9-8ffe-4c9dcfb5a983.html.

76 G. Bruce Doern and Glen Toner, *The Politics of Energy: The Development and Implementation of the National Energy Program* (Toronto: Methuen, 1985); see also Leslie A. Pal, "The Accidental Theorist," in *Policy: From Ideas to Implementation*, ed. Glen Toner, Leslie A. Pal, and Michael J. Prince (Montreal: McGill-Queen's University Press, 2010), 39–58.

77 For a detailed discussion of this approach, see Winfield, *Blue-Green Province*, 3–9.

78 See, for example, Nanos Research, "Concern about Jobs/the Economy and Environment on the Rise Nanos Weekly Tracking, Ending May 6, 2022," https://nanos.co/wp-content/uploads/2022/05/Political-Package-2022-05-06-FR-HDd52.pdf. See also "Vote Compass: Economy and Environment Rate as Top Issues," *CBC News*, September 10, 2015, https://www.cbc.ca/news/politics/vote-compass-canada-election-2015-issues-canadians-1.3222945.

79 Nanos Research, "Ontarians View Investing in Healthcare as the Most Important Priority for the New Government of Ontario; Healthcare Remains the Top Issue of Concern," May 31, 2022, https://nanos.co/wp-content/uploads/2022/06/2022-2156-CTV-CP4-ELXN-ON-Tracking-Report-Wave-5-Issue-Populated-WITH-TABS.pdf.

80 Winfield, *Blue-Green Province*.
81 Winfield and Hillson, "Explaining Doug Ford's Political Durability." See also Peter Hillson, "Diagnosing Doug Ford's Durability: The Discourse and Political Economy of Right-Wing Populist Environmental Politics in Ontario" (MES/JD Major Paper, Faculty of Environmental and Urban Change, York University, 2022), https://sei.info.yorku.ca/files/2022/04/PH-FINAL-MRP.pdf?x60126.
82 "Only Doug Ford and the Ontario PC Party Will Get It Done," Ontario PC Party, accessed June 2, 2022, https://ontariopc.ca/only-doug-ford-and-the-ontario-pc-party-will-get-it-done/.
83 Emma McIntosh, "Everything You Need to Know about Doug Ford's Controversial Plans for New Highways in Ontario," *The Narwal*, November 8, 2021, https://thenarwhal.ca/highway-413-bradford-bypass-explainer/.
84 CBC News, "Ontario Government to Introduce Legislation to Cut Gas, Fuel Taxes," *CBC News*, April 4, 2022, https://www.cbc.ca/news/canada/toronto/ontario-gas-tax-1.6407385.
85 The Canadian Press, "Ontario is Ending Tolls on 2 Toronto-Area Highways This Spring," *CBC News*, February 18, 2022, https://www.cbc.ca/news/canada/toronto/highway-412-418-tolls-ending-1.6357066.
86 CBC News, "Ontario to Scrap Vehicle Licence Renewal Fees, Requirement for Stickers," *CBC News*, February 22, 2022, https://www.cbc.ca/news/canada/toronto/ontario-vehicle-licence-renewal-1.6359951.
87 Doug Anderson, Allan Gregg and Hilary Martin, "ON-Election Polling: Tracking Ontario Voters' Shifting Support," Earnscliffe Strategies, May 4, 2022, https://earnscliffe.ca/insight/on-election-polling-tracking-ontario-voters-shifting-support-2/.
88 Oved, Wallace, and Tubb, "Doug Ford Is Spending Billions."
89 Mark Winfield, "Ontario Election 2022: Summary of the PC, Liberal, NDP and Green Platforms on Climate and Energy Issues," *Mark Winfield* (blog), May 19, 2022, https://marksw.blog.yorku.ca/2022/05/19/ontario-election-2022-summary-of-the-pc-liberal-ndp-and-green-platforms-on-climate-and-energy-issues/.
90 Oliver Moore, "The Construction of Highway 413 Would Negatively Impact the Environment, Not Help It, Say Scientific Researchers," *Globe and Mail*, May 27, 2022, https://www.theglobeandmail.com/politics/article-highway-413-environmental-impact-ontario/.
91 Marco Chown Oved and Jacob Lornic, "Ontario Energy Grid Emissions Set to Skyrocket 400% as Ford Government Cranks up the Gas," *Toronto Star*, May 9, 2022, https://www.thestar.com/business/ontario-energy-grid-emissions-set-to-skyrocket-400-as-ford-government-cranks-up-the-gas/article_054c919d-ca35-51c0-a6d7-17a2321834b6.html.
92 Toronto Star Editorial Board, "Driving in the Wrong Direction," *Toronto Star*, May 14, 2022, https://www.thestar.com/opinion/editorials/voters-shouldn-t-give-ford-government-a-pass-on-the-environment/article_b3ef2d1e-22ff-5bf6-a2c6-0e165038eea3.html.
93 Mitchell Beer, "Electoral Rout: Ontario Climate Hawks Look to Next Steps and Ford Surges to Second Majority," *The Energy Mix*, June 3, 2022, https://www.theenergymix.com/2022/06/03/electoral-rout-ontario-climate-hawks-look-to-next-steps-as-ford-surges-to-second-majority-government/.

94 Mark Winfield and Colleen Kaiser, "Ontario on Track to See Major Increases in Greenhouse Gas Emissions," *Hamilton Spectator*, December 19, 2021, https://www.thespec.com/opinion/contributors/2021/12/19/ontario-on-track-to-see-major-increases-in-greenhouse-gas-emissions.html.

95 ECO, *Facing Climate Change: Greenhouse Gas Progress Report* (Toronto: ECO 2016), https://www.auditor.on.ca/en/content/reporttopics/envreports/env16/2016-Annual-GHG-Report-EN.pdf.

96 Auditor General of Ontario, "Conserving the Natural Environment with Protected Areas" (Toronto: Auditor General of Ontario, 2020), https://www.auditor.on.ca/en/content/annualreports/arreports/en20/ENV_conservingthenaturalenvironment_en20.pdf.

97 See Legislative Assembly of Ontario, Steve Clark, *Bill 3, Strong Mayors, Building Homes Act, 2022*, https://www.ola.org/en/legislative-business/bills/parliament-43/session-1/bill-3; David Crombie, Barbara Hall, Art Eggleton, David Miller, and John Sewell, "Former Toronto Mayors Warn 'Strong Mayors' Act Will Harm Local Democracy," *Toronto Star*, August 15, 2022, https://www.thestar.com/opinion/contributors/former-toronto-mayors-warn-strong-mayors-act-will-harm-local-democracy/article_10c074c8-08a4-50bd-ad71-3cdfc7462140.html.

98 See Legislative Assembly of Ontario, Steve Clark, *Bill 23, More Homes Built Faster Act, 2022*, https://www.ola.org/en/legislative-business/bills/parliament-43/session-1/bill-23; Victor Doyle, "Doug Ford's More Homes Built Faster Act Is a Trojan Horse," *The Pointer*, November 12, 2022, https://thepointer.com/article/2022-11-12/doug-ford-s-more-homes-built-faster-act-is-a-trojan-horse.

99 Ryan Patrick Jones, "Ford Government Forges Ahead with Greenbelt Development Plan Despite 'Broad Opposition' in Public Consultation," *CBC News*, December 22, 2022, https://www.cbc.ca/news/canada/toronto/greenbelt-oak-ridges-moraine-regulations-1.6692337.

100 Climate change and environment are ranked third in federal priorities, as shown in Michael Monopoli, "Abacus Election Bulletin: Climate Change and Reducing Carbon Emissions," Abacus Data, September 4, 2021, https://abacusdata.ca/climate-change-and-carbon-emissions/.

101 Climate change and environment are ranked seventh in provincial priorities, as shown in David Coletto, "Final Abacus Data Poll: Ontario PCs Lead by 13 as They Head towards Another Majority Government," Abacus Data, June 1, 2022, https://abacusdata.ca/june-1-final-ontario-poll-abacus-data/.

102 McIntosh, "Everything You Need to Know."

103 "Clean Electricity Regulations," Government of Canada, last modified August 25, 2023, accessed December 23, 2023, https://www.canada.ca/en/services/environment/weather/climatechange/climate-plan/clean-electricity-regulation.html.

104 Auditor General of Ontario, *Special Report on Changes to the Greenbelt* (Toronto: Auditor General of Ontario, 2023), https://www.auditor.on.ca/en/content/specialreports/specialreports/Greenbelt_en.pdf.

105 The Canadian Press, "A Timeline of Key Events in Ontario's Greenbelt Controversy," *CBC News*, September 21, 2023, https://www.cbc.ca/news/canada/toronto/ont-greenbelt-timeline-1.6974715.

15

The Shifting Landscape of Party-Union Relationships in Ontario

Larry Savage

INTRODUCTION

This chapter explores the shifting landscape of party-union relationships in Ontario politics. Specifically, the chapter explains how and why unions of blue-collar workers in the building and construction trades shed their long-standing opposition to the Progressive Conservatives (PCs) and endorsed Premier Doug Ford's successful bid for re-election in 2022. For context, the unions endorsing Ford represented less than 5 per cent of the province's total union membership. In contrast, the New Democratic Party (NDP) secured endorsements from much larger labour organizations. However, what made construction union support for Ford newsworthy was its novelty. Between 1999 and 2014, many construction unions were affiliated to the Working Families Coalition, a third party organization that targeted the PCs with multi-million dollar negative attack ad campaigns at election time. The Coalition worked closely with the Ontario Liberals, and its union backers funded both Liberal and NDP candidates, often whichever ones were best positioned to defeat a PC incumbent or challenger. Opposition to the PCs was fuelled by the party's persistent anti-union rhetoric and policy proposals designed to undermine unions' capacity to operate, bargain, and represent members' interests politically. Given this context, winning support from a number of construction unions was symbolically significant for the PC campaign because it fractured labour movement opposition and provided pro-worker cover for a government with a decidedly mixed record on labour rights.

But how do we explain *why* construction unions decided to embrace the PCs after so many years of fighting the party? The PC party's so-called "labour charm offensive" is the focus of the second half of the chapter. It charts the party's strategic pivot in relation to unions representing blue-collar workers specifically, and points to demographic, public policy, and interpersonal factors to explain why construction unions ultimately endorsed Ford's re-election bid.

HISTORY AND CONTEXT

Just over one in four workers in Ontario is covered by a union contract.[1] There are dozens of different unions in the province representing workers in nearly every sector of the economy. In the immediate postwar period, union membership was heavily concentrated in the private sector, and the overwhelming majority of union members were men. Today, the reverse is true. The majority of union members work in the public sector, and women in unions now outnumber men.[2] Unions are particularly dominant in health care, education, and public administration. However, they also continue to represent significant numbers of workers in the private sector, especially in transportation and warehousing, manufacturing, and construction.[3]

While unions in Ontario were historically most closely associated with the NDP, it is important to note that unions and their members have never acted as a homogeneous block. Public opinion polling has consistently shown that union members are slightly more likely than the average voter to vote NDP and slightly less likely than the average voter to vote PC.[4] Despite the fact that union status has only a modest effect on voting intentions, union activists have always been and continue to be a significant source of candidates and volunteers for the NDP, even if their unions have begun endorsing a far broader range of parties and candidates. For example, in the 2022 provincial election, the New Democrats secured the lion's share of union endorsements, but labour organizations also endorsed PC, Liberal, and Green candidates.

Historically, New Democrats had more of a lock on union endorsements. The Canadian Labour Congress (CLC) and Ontario Federation of Labour (OFL), along with many of the unions affiliated with these central labour organizations, were founding partners of the NDP when it was launched as the official political arm of organized labour in 1961.[5] Although important segments of the union movement continue to hold special status as key party stakeholders, organized labour's formal ties and influence within the party have diminished considerably in recent decades. The party's record in office, the changing composition of union membership, the impact of campaign finance reforms, and ongoing concerns about the party's electoral viability have all contributed to a weakening of the union-party link.[6]

Perhaps no single factor contributed more to the unravelling of the party-union relationship than the NDP government's decision to re-open collective agreements and impose rollbacks on public sector workers in the early 1990s. While the NDP government passed a number of significant pro-union measures early in its mandate, Premier Bob Rae's decision to address the province's growing debt and deficit by adopting the *Social Contract Act* – a fiscal austerity program that rolled back wages and suspended collective bargaining rights in the public sector through mandatory days off – was met with fierce opposition by public-sector unions and their allies.[7] Stephen McBride describes the passage of the Social Contract as a "paradigmatic event," and Leo Panitch and Donald Swartz argue that the law "shattered the confidence of the trade unions in their central political strategy: electing NDP governments."[8] In response to the Social Contract, widely viewed as betrayal by union activists, the OFL's 1993 convention voted to condemn "the Ontario NDP government for violating the principles of free collective bargaining" and called on "the OFL and its affiliated unions to disaffiliate from the Ontario NDP."[9] The OFL convention decision was highly controversial and led to a significant fragmentation in the electoral approach of unions in Ontario. While some unions, after pointing to the lack of alternatives, remained allied to the NDP, most sat out the 1995 provincial election campaign.

The NDP government's defeat in the 1995 provincial election was decisive. The party finished a distant third in both seat count and popular vote. While unions had arguably experienced both ups and downs under the NDP, things were about to get much worse for them under the unapologetically anti-union Mike Harris PCs.

CONSERVATIVES VERSUS THE UNIONS

Upon taking office, the Harris Conservatives wasted no time undoing the NDP's pro-union reforms. However, the Harris government's amendments to the *Ontario Labour Relations Act* in Bills 7 and 31 went far beyond restoring the pre-NDP status quo in the realm of labour relations. Instead, the bills, which were passed with little to no consultation with the province's unions, undid many of the postwar reforms implemented by previous PC governments. For example, Bill 7 limited unions' ability to call strike votes and eliminated card-based union certification, made it easier to decertify unions, and imposed a year-long organizing ban on unions who lost a certification vote.[10] Bill 31 repealed the Ontario Labour Relations Board's power of automatic certification at the behest of Wal-Mart.[11] The Harris government's package of reforms accompanied a number of other work-related public policy initiatives, including capping pay equity agreements, freezing minimum wage, and the ill-fated introduction of a system of work for welfare. Beyond its legislative changes, the Harris government dumped a number of key NDP appointments to the Labour Relations Board, leading some to challenge the independence of the board.[12]

The Harris years also featured significant labour unrest as unions attempted to fight back through strike action. The Ontario Public Service Employees Union (OPSEU) launched its first-ever province-wide strike in February 1996 in response to the Harris government's downsizing of the Ontario public service and the need to protect job security.[13] Province-wide teacher strikes were launched in 1997 in response to the Harris government's proposed education reforms.[14] However, the greatest mass labour mobilization against the Harris government came in the form of a series of rotating general strikes across the province known as the Days of Action.[15] After the Ontario NDP government's defeat in June 1995, the province's labour movement, momentarily disillusioned with electoral politics, sought to build alliances with progressive community organizations and social movements as part of a broad-based coalition in opposition to the right-wing and anti-union policies of the new PC government. Between 1995 and 1998, unions and their allies launched the one- to two-day protests in an effort to pressure the government to back down.[16] The Canadian Autoworkers Union (CAW) and many of the public sector unions which had opposed the NDP government's Social Contract took a leadership role in organizing the Days of Action and decried the OFL's controversial and divisive decision to jettison the rotating protests in favour of reconciliation with the NDP in the run-up to the 1999 provincial election.[17]

The OFL's decision to pull the plug on the Days of Action had the effect of pushing unions back into the electoral arena, but in an unexpected way. While most industrial unions and the Canadian Union of Public Employees (CUPE) decided to give the NDP (now led by Howard Hampton) a second chance, another group of unions, cognizant of the fact that the party was performing poorly in public opinion polls, came together under the umbrella of the Ontario Election Network (OEN) in an effort to promote strategic voting.[18] The Network, made up of teachers' unions, CAW, OPSEU, the Ontario Nurses' Association, and a number of construction unions, took the position that defeating the Harris Conservatives was labour's first electoral priority. The OEN targeted twenty-six key swing ridings, endorsing fourteen Liberals and twelve NDP candidates. In the words of OPSEU president Leah Casselman, strategic voting meant "voting NDP in strong NDP ridings, voting Liberal in strong Liberal ridings, and defeating Tories in both."[19]

However, participation in the OEN was highly divisive within the labour movement, especially among unions traditionally loyal to the NDP. While there was virtual unanimity within the labour movement on the need to defeat the Tories, union activists were sharply divided over strategy. While many longtime NDP activists in the labour movement were prepared to forgive the party for its past sins, others complained that the NDP would simply split the "non-right" vote and allow the PCs to be re-elected.[20] In the end, the Network's electoral strategy ultimately failed when the Conservatives were returned to power with an even larger share of the popular vote than in 1995, and the NDP lost official party status.

The PCs did not let up in their second term, gutting the *Employment Standards Act*, making pro-employer changes to the Workers Compensation Board and introducing new legislation requiring employers to post information in unionized workplaces on how to decertify a union.[21] The Harris government's anti-union restructuring of the province's system of labour relations appeared to be entirely driven by the corporate sector. By the end of the PC government's second term, union density had dropped from 32.1 per cent in 1995 to 28.3 per cent in 2003, and real average weekly wages dropped by 0.4 per cent, despite an economic growth rate of 3.7 per cent during the same period.[22]

THE RISE AND FALL OF THE WORKING FAMILIES COALITION

In the run-up to the 2003 provincial election, a number of construction unions came together under the banner of the newly formed Working Families Coalition and joined forces with the CAW, and nurses and teachers' unions, to launch a major third-party anti-Conservative advertising campaign blitz.[23] Riding a wave of anti-Conservative sentiment, Dalton McGuinty's Liberals

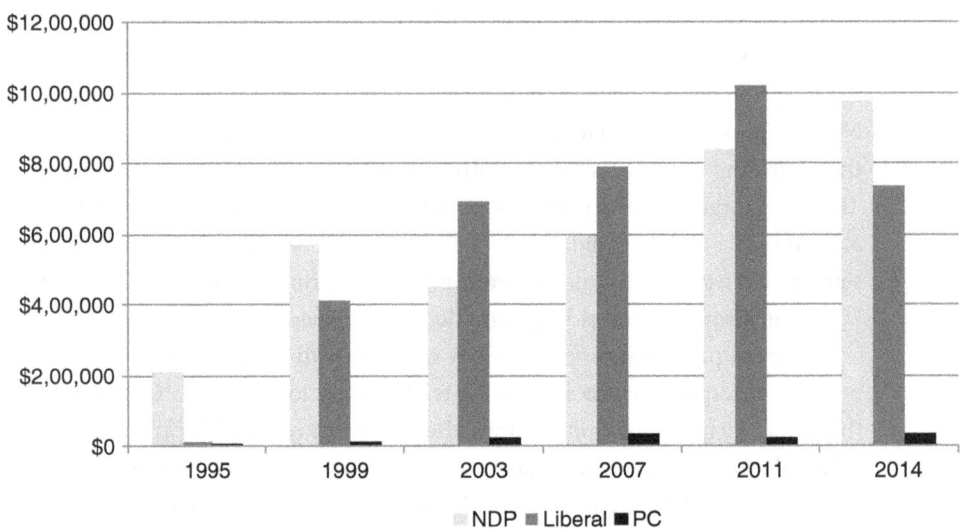

Figure 15.1. Union Campaign Donations by Party in Dollars
Source: Government of Ontario, Elections Ontario, *CR-1, CR-3 & CR-4 Financial Statements*, Ontario New Democratic Party, Progressive Conservative Party of Ontario, and Liberal Party of Ontario (1995, 1999, 2003, 2007, 2011, and 2014 Ontario General Elections).

handily defeated the PCs, now led by Ernie Eves. And for the first time in history, the Liberals collected more in union donations than the NDP during the campaign, a trend that would continue until 2014 (see figure 15.1).

Determined to avoid the labour unrest that characterized the previous government's time in office, the newly elected McGuinty Liberals promised to restore fairness and balance to the province's system of labour relations. In practice, that meant reversing some (but by no means most) of the previous government's anti-union labour law reforms.

Passed in 2005, Bill 144, the *Labour Relations Statute Law Amendment Act*, returned remedial certification authority and other powers to the Labour Relations Board and repealed the Harris government's law requiring employers to post notices explaining how to decertify their unions. However, much of the previous government's anti-union labour law reforms went untouched. For example, the Liberals maintained the Harris government's imposed year-long ban on organizing in the event a union loses a certification vote. The Liberals also refused to restore the right of farm workers to unionize and flat-out rejected calls to bring back the NDP's law banning the use of replacement workers in the event of a strike or lockout, which had been repealed by the Harris government.

Despite the McGuinty government's uneven record, the Liberals managed to satisfy the expectations of the unions that backed the ostensibly pro-Liberal Working Families Coalition. Strategically, the McGuinty government fostered transactional relationships with the unions associated with the Coalition. As a result, teacher union support for the Liberals translated into unprecedented investments in the province's education system. In return, the provincial government won education sector labour peace. Autoworker support for McGuinty through strategic voting irked the New Democrats, but helped to secure the premier's support for the province's ailing automobile industry. Construction unions, the key actors in the Working Families Coalition, were rewarded with the restoration of card-based union certification on construction sites. In many ways, the Liberals were let off the hook for their general lack of pro-union initiatives on the labour relations front because they managed to retain support from a number of influential unions whose specific priorities had been addressed by the government. While even these unions may have been critical of the McGuinty Liberals from time to time, they also recognized that the return of a PC government would surely undo many, if not all, of the gains organized labour had managed to make during this period.

Satisfied with the McGuinty government's first term in office, the Working Families Coalition redoubled its efforts in the 2007 provincial election, making explicit its desire to see the Liberals re-elected, much to the dismay of unions like the United Steelworkers (USW), CUPE, and the Communications, Energy and Paperworkers (CEP), who all continued to share strong ties to the NDP.[24] The Coalition spent $1.1 million on a third-party advertising campaign trumpeting the Liberal government's achievements and warning voters not to turn back to the PCs.[25] In the end, the Liberals were easily re-elected after the Ontario Tories fumbled badly during the campaign with an ill-fated promise to extend public funding to private religious schools.

The relative "labour peace" that characterized the McGuinty government's first term in office was shaken somewhat after the Liberals were returned to power in 2007 and the Great Recession of 2008 hit. In 2009, the Liberals legislatively ended an eighty-five-day strike by part-time instructors and teaching assistants at York University in Toronto and in 2008, McGuinty legislated striking Toronto Transit Commission (TTC) employees back to work before removing their right to strike entirely in 2011. In March 2011, the McGuinty government established the Commission on the Reform of Ontario's Public

Services, headed by former TD Bank's chief economist Donald Drummond, in order to recommend ways of eliminating the mounting provincial deficit. The establishment of the Commission sent a clear signal that the Liberals would target public sector workers to pay for an economic crisis that originated in the banking sector.

While the commission did its work, the Liberals sought re-election with the continued support of the Working Families Coalition. PC leader Tim Hudak's 2011 campaign pledge to allow union members to opt out of having their dues spent for political action purposes was aimed squarely at undermining the Coalition, which launched a $2.1 million dollar advertising blitz against Hudak, portraying the PC leader as the puppet of Bay Street capitalists.[26] The Coalition's third-party advertising budget was so impressive that the unions involved actually outspent the Ontario NDP's entire advertising campaign budget during the 2011 election campaign.[27]

Reduced to a minority after the 2011 provincial election, the McGuinty Liberals, still reeling from the economic impact of the recession, turned their attention to the findings of the Drummond Commission. The final report called for massive cuts in public spending and public services. Unsurprisingly, the recommendations were universally panned by the labour movement. According to an analysis by the Ontario Confederation of University Faculty Associations, "Drummond's model of labour relations consists primarily of hard bargaining on the part of broader public sector (BPS) employers, with government ... supporting the employer when the going gets tough."[28] The analysis continued by observing that Drummond "is counting on the devastating size of his cuts to the funding of public services to force the parties to bargain concessionary agreements, eliminate jobs, and find 'efficiencies', which obviously can only translate into dramatically higher workloads for the remaining public sector workers."[29]

With the Commission's findings in hand, the Liberals shifted gears on the education front, teaming up with the PCs to pass Bill 115, the *Putting Students First Act*, in August 2012. The new law implemented a wage freeze, clawed back sick days and extinguished meaningful collective bargaining rights for the education workers who refused to follow the lead of the Catholic and French-language teachers' unions in negotiating concessionary agreements with the provincial government.[30] Teachers' unions had been a reliable ally of the McGuinty Liberals since the late 1990s, but his government's attack on collective bargaining rights in the education sector changed the party-union dynamic overnight. After convincing long-serving PC member of provincial parliament (MPP) Elizabeth Witmer to resign her seat with the offer of a patronage appointment, the Liberals hoped to win her vacated Kitchener-Waterloo riding in order to regain its majority. However, in an unexpected twist, the NDP managed to effectively tap into the anger of teachers and other unionized public-sector workers and scored a decisive victory in the September 2012 by-election.[31] The NDP's stunning by-election victory, combined with mounting teacher protest and a number of constitutional challenges to Bill 115,[32] convinced the Liberals to re-evaluate their strategy. In the wake of all this turmoil, McGuinty announced his resignation, providing the Liberals with an opportunity to recalibrate and potentially repair its tarnished relationship with teachers and other groups of unionized workers.

In the days leading up to the January 2013 Liberal leadership convention, where delegates chose Toronto MPP and former education minister Kathleen Wynne to replace McGuinty, the government hastily announced it would repeal Bill 115 in an effort to dampen growing teacher opposition to the party. The tactic, which was more symbolic than substantive given that the bill had served its purpose, represented an olive branch of sorts. In the weeks and months that followed, the Wynne government was able to convince teachers' unions to drop their work-to-rule campaigns. A short time later, Ontario Secondary School Teachers Federation (OSSTF) president Ken Coran stunned political observers and members of his own union by announcing he would vacate his position to run for the Liberals in an August 2013 by-election in the Liberal-held riding of London West. On election day, however, the NDP candidate unexpectedly scored a decisive victory. Coran, who finished a distant third, could not overcome accusations that his candidacy was both opportunistic and unprincipled. The former union leader's disastrous campaign demonstrated that while segments of the union leadership were prepared to give the Liberals a second chance, the rank-and-file was not quite ready to forgive and forget.

While the NDP was riding high on a string of impressive by-election victories, the party's decision to precipitate a general election by toppling the minority Wynne government in May 2014 proved wildly unpopular in labour movement circles. In Kathleen Wynne, union leaders saw progressive potential and, more importantly, feared that defeating her government would open the door to a PC majority. Labour leaders argued that Hudak would unleash an unprecedented anti-union policy agenda if elected. Livid with NDP leader Andrea Horwath for pulling the plug on the minority Liberal government, important sections of the labour movement mounted a well-financed #StopHudak campaign that asked union members to vote for whichever candidate was best positioned to defeat the Tories at the riding level. The campaign was backed by resources to key ridings where unions thought they could influence the outcome. In most cases, that meant supporting Liberals. The #StopHudak campaign also dovetailed perfectly with continued efforts by the Working Families Coalition to defeat the PCs through negative ad campaigns. The NDP's electoral ambitions had, in effect, driven many unions back into the arms of the Liberal Party. On June 12, 2014, the Wynne Liberals were re-elected with a majority, winning seats from both the NDP and the PCs. Union leaders were quick to take credit for the bruising defeat of the Hudak Conservatives. The party's ill-advised commitment to cut 100,000 public-sector jobs fed directly into the labour movement's portrayal of Hudak as anti-labour and the job cut issue became a focal point of the campaign.

Wynne's re-elected government styled itself as progressive and set out to reward its labour movement backers by overhauling provincial labour standards in important ways that benefitted workers and their unions. The introduction of paid sick days and substantial increases to the minimum wage were particularly noteworthy public policy initiatives that won praise from labour organizations.[33]

Meanwhile, facing mounting criticism over the perception that her party was catering to insiders on a cash-for-access basis, Wynne's government also banned union and corporate donations to parties and introduced strict contribution limits for individuals in time for the 2018 election.[34] The Liberals also imposed limits on third-party ad spending, putting the Wynne government offside with the Working Families Coalition, which launched a constitutional challenge to the government's amendments to the *Election Finances Act*.[35] Given how much the Liberals had come to rely on corporate and union donations and the assistance of third-party advertisers, the party appeared to be shooting itself in the foot on a matter of principle. To make matters worse for the Liberals, the Wynne government's decision to privatize Hydro One proved incredibly unpopular and helped breathe new life into the NDP.[36] It was the PCs, however, who led in public opinion polls for much of Wynne's mandate and that party, now under the leadership of Doug Ford, was the odds-on favourite to win the 2018 election when the writ was dropped.

Given its unhappiness with the changes to campaign finance legislation, the Working Families Coalition sat out the campaign. Pat Dillon, the Coalition's unofficial leader, later indicated that the decision to sit out was also influenced by the fact that many construction unions had reached a détente with Ford's Conservatives ahead of the campaign. The NDP, however, was the major benefactor of the Working Families breakdown, securing support from most of the Coalition's former affiliates.

Eclipsed by a rejuvenated NDP and sinking in the polls over the course of the 2018 election campaign, the Wynne Liberals decided to concede defeat mid-campaign and turned their sights on Horwath, warning of endless strikes and a government controlled by union leaders. That strategic move destroyed any remaining goodwill between the Liberals and the labour movement. The OSSTF, which had long backed Liberal candidates, even announced it was withdrawing its endorsements of several Liberal incumbents.[37] The combined attacks of the Liberals and PCs managed to halt the NDP's growing popularity and Doug Ford's Conservatives cruised to victory on election day.

DOUG FORD AND THE PC "LABOUR CHARM OFFENSIVE"

Upon taking office, Doug Ford's PC government moved quickly to cancel the previous government's scheduled minimum wage increase and repealed paid sick days for workers. The Ford government also imposed wage restraint legislation on the broader public sector through Bill 124, limiting compensatory increases to 1 per cent per year. The province's labour movement was gearing up for a fight, just as it had under the previous PC government. But Ford and his advisors were ready, using a variety of strategies designed to neutralize, fracture, and undermine union opposition.

For example, campaign finance reforms adopted by the Ford government in advance of the 2022 provincial election placed even stricter limits on third-party ad spending. The changes were largely viewed as an attempt by the Conservatives to further undermine any potential union-backed third-party campaigns targeting the PCs.[38] While some unions cried foul over the changes, others gradually appeared to adopt an "if you can't beat them, join them" attitude towards the government. This latter approach was rendered palpable by the fact that the PCs were actively cultivating specific pockets of union support through targeted policy commitments and investments, particularly geared towards blue-collar construction workers.

This Conservative overture to segments of the union movement was dubbed a "labour charm offensive" by the media.[39] Unlike previous Conservative leaders like Mike Harris and Tim Hudak, Ford did not share the same rigid ideological opposition to unions. While he imposed wage restraint legislation on most of the public sector in 2019, he did not set out to dismantle unions and his labour minister, Monte McNaughton, routinely met with union leaders.[40] This distinguished Ford from his predecessors, who vilified unions across the board and froze their leadership out of any meaningful consultation processes. For example, Harris' anti-union reforms re-wrote labour laws to make unionization far more difficult. His government also reversed a union-supported ban on replacement workers in the event of a strike or lockout. Hudak, for his part, had proposed sweeping anti-union reforms that threatened unions' capacity to collect dues and spend money for political purposes. In short, it's not that most union leaders considered Ford pro-union. Rather, they did not consider him an existential threat to unions in the same way they viewed some previous PC leaders.

Ford's Conservatives approached the unions with a combination of carrots and sticks and effectively exploited fissures between private and public sector workers by positioning his government as a catalyst for private sector growth and opportunity, on the one hand, and public sector restraint on the other. This approach was made clear by Ontario's labour minister when he tweeted back in April 2022: "Our government is standing with hardworking people ... not those who want to 'phase out' good blue-collar jobs. We know Ontario is built by those who shower at the end of the day, not the start."[41] Of course, this dynamic is not unique to Ontario or even Canada. Conservative parties the world over have increasingly used right-wing populist frames to help construct an alternative narrative about the sources of economic insecurity experienced by working-class people and the solutions needed to bring back a Golden Age of Capitalism centred on the white male breadwinner. This was likely best exemplified by Donald Trump's nativist and populist 2016 pitch to working-class voters in the United States to "Make America Great Again." Moreover, across Europe, several conservative parties have managed to undermine the historical link between social democratic parties and working-class communities in a way that has disrupted familiar class-based voting patterns.

In Canada, Conservatives, both federally and provincially, have similarly pursued frames and strategies designed to win over blue-collar union voters traditionally hostile to the party's anti-labour policy positions by stoking divisions between these workers and what Conservative strategists refer to as the "woke urbanites" who make up much of the NDP and Liberal base.[42] Shortly after winning the leadership of the Federal Conservative Party, Erin O'Toole raised eyebrows with a 2020 Labour Day message that blamed "big business" and "bad trade deals" for Canada's ailing manufacturing, energy, and forestry sectors.[43] He followed up with a speech to the Canadian Club in October 2020 in which he made a case for unions, arguing that a high level of private-sector union density "was an essential part of the balance between what was good for business and what was good for employees. Today, that balance is dangerously disappearing. Too much power is in the hands of a few corporate and financial elites who have been only too happy to outsource jobs abroad."[44] The *Globe and Mail* columnist Robyn Urback joked that O'Toole sounded as though he was running in the 1989 NDP leadership race.[45] But the Conservative strategy was no joke. Rather, it was designed to appeal to workers experiencing real economic insecurity, often as a result of economic restructuring, who did not see their material concerns being taken up concretely by other parties. O'Toole doubled down on this strategy with his announcement during the 2021 federal election campaign that a Conservative government would require all federally regulated corporations with over 1,000 employees or $100 million in annual revenue to include worker representation on their boards of directors.[46] O'Toole's Conservatives went on to win the popular vote, but lose the election. However, Conservatives did not abandon efforts to win over blue-collar union voters. Ford and McNaughton took up the torch with aplomb.

McNaughton was the first PC labour minister in living memory to march in Toronto's annual Labour Day parade and his support for keeping the construction sector working during the pandemic won praise from skilled trades unions.[47] More broadly, Conservatives were tapping into real concerns among working-class voters over economic inequality and insecurity, but in a way that laid blame not on capitalism as an economic system, but rather "foreign" actors, "greedy elites," and a "bloated" public sector. The PCs used populist and conservative cultural appeals to union members that clearly differentiated them from other parties more closely associated with the promotion of working-class interests historically.

For example, the Conservatives framed the NDP's legitimate concerns over climate change and Indigenous sovereignty as both anti-development and anti-labour on the basis that the NDP's concern for these issues inhibited the growth and job creation that union members rely on. This is precisely the dynamic McNaughton was referring to when he argued back in 2020 "the left, truthfully, has chosen social justice and identity politics instead of things that matter to families."[48] This line of argument figured prominently in McNaughton's speeches in the lead up to election day, asserting that the opposition parties had abandoned blue-collar workers in favour of cultural flashpoints like efforts to remove statues of historical figures who were known to be racist. "They're more concerned about statues than they are about good jobs with pensions and benefits," he told the media.[49] Ford also broke with the past by making a conscious decision to not campaign on austerity. Rather, Ford's Conservatives promised to invest in building infrastructure and electric vehicles that, in turn, would create jobs for blue-collar workers.[50]

The overwhelmingly male membership, cultural conservatism, and pro-development mentality of construction unions made them a natural target for the PCs, given the party's electoral advantage with men and its own pro-development approach to public policy. It also helped that the PCs were in power and could more effectively cater to construction unions' non-ideological and transactional approach to politics. This was accomplished by reforming the Ontario College of Trades with input from the unions, investing in pre-apprenticeship programs, and guaranteeing job security through massive infrastructure projects. Reflecting on the party's strategy, one insider acknowledged to the media that "the party was wrong in the past (to vilify unions)," adding the "Big Blue Collar Machine"[51] initiative to win over union and working-class votes "aligned with the premier and who he is."[52] Whether Ford, the wealthy son of a politician and businessman, is genuinely a working-class champion is certainly up for debate, but there is no doubt he had managed to cultivate the image of someone who sticks up for the little guy. Here, Conservative frames that pit public sector unions against working-class people (both union and non-union) become very relevant.

When teachers' unions started engaging in rotating strikes in February 2020 in an effort to secure a better deal and boost student supports through the collective bargaining process, Ford slammed the union leadership, but in a way that drove a wedge between the unions, their members, and the broader working class. "I think the men and women that are serving out there work their backs off, they do a great job. I don't support the head of the unions that are causing all these problems right across the province," he said.[53] Despite the fact that front-line teachers themselves had authorized the strike action, Ford went on to assert, "this is all about lining the pockets of the unions – not protecting our children – it's about lining the pockets of our unions. Not the teachers, but the unions." The point here is to demonstrate that the PC "labour charm offensive" was both selective and contradictory. Almost none of the government's "charm" extended to public-sector unions, even though most union members work in the public sector. Thus, these unions could continue to be scapegoated by the PCs in an effort to win support from construction and other unionized blue-collar workers who, presumably, felt inconvenienced by tax increases and the potential for public sector strikes.

It is important to note, however, that the PC "labour charm offensive" was not limited to blue-collar construction unions. McNaughton also initiated legislation guaranteeing the "right to disconnect" and the extension of rights to app-based gig workers, though these measures were criticized for being more symbolic than substantive.[54] Most unions were not seduced by these strategic moves, reasoning that a leopard never changes its spots. After all, a few years earlier, McNaughton was championing US-style union-busting right-to-work legislation as a member of the Opposition.[55] Some union leaders, however, were open to the idea that the PCs were genuinely willing to turn the page on the party's demonization of organized labour, and given Ford held power, it would be foolish to not engage.

As union members from across the province gathered in Toronto at the OFL convention in November 2021 to pledge support for the NDP in the upcoming provincial election,[56] Doug Ford, flanked by two of the province's most well-known labour leaders, was holding a press conference to announce a surprise boost to the minimum wage to $15 per hour.[57] The pre-election announcement, which came three years after Ford scrapped the previous government's scheduled minimum increase, immediately shifted the media spotlight away from the OFL convention. The fact that Ford was standing alongside Unifor president Jerry Dias and OPSEU president Smokey Thomas made for headline news and left many labour activists scratching their heads. After all, both Unifor and OPSEU had campaigned hard against Ford in 2018 and were historically harsh critics of the PCs. The idea that the leader of either union would stand alongside a PC premier at a press conference seemed anathema to the political aims and objectives of the labour movement, leading some to speculate if two large unions traditionally hostile to the PCs would stand down, or even possibly back Ford come election time.

The fact that neither Thomas nor Dias were enamoured with NDP leader Andrea Horwath was an open secret, but their respective dalliances with Ford proved short-lived. Dias, who Ford later appointed to head the province's auto task force in December 2021, resigned his post and the presidency of Unifor in March 2022 amid scandal. But not before his union's Ontario Regional Council voted in favour of a policy designed to "rid Ontario of a Ford majority" through strategic voting.[58] In the case of Thomas, after fifteen years as

OPSEU president, he stepped down in April 2022, but not before delegates at the union's convention rapped his knuckles for providing pro-labour cover for Ford a few months earlier. His successor, J.P. Hornick, promptly announced that OPSEU would be endorsing the NDP.[59]

Of course, the PC war room was not banking on endorsements from OPSEU or Unifor. The fact that Ford *did* manage to secure endorsements from eight smaller construction unions would prove more than a consolation prize. The slow drip of construction union endorsements from the Laborers' International Union of North America,[60] the International Brotherhood of Electrical Workers Construction Council of Ontario, the International Union of Painters and Allied Trades, the International Brotherhood of Boilermakers, the Ontario Pipe Trades Council, Local 285 of Sheet Metal Workers' International Association, Local 787 of the United Association of HVAC&R Workers of Ontario, and Local 793 of the International Union of Operating Engineers helped build momentum for the PCs even though, combined, the endorsing unions represented less than 5 per cent of the province's union membership. To cap it off, McNaughton secured the personal backing of Pat Dillon, the infamous former Building Trades business manager who was the key architect of the Working Families Coalition.[61] In contrast, in addition to endorsements from the OFL and OPSEU, the NDP secured the backing of the United Steelworkers, the Machinists, the Amalgamated Transit Union, the United Food and Commercial Workers Unions, and CUPE. The NDP's union support was based on a combination of long-standing ties and the strength of its pro-labour commitments to raise the minimum wage, introduce permanent paid sick days, and make it easier for workers to join unions. The party also disproportionally benefitted from the endorsements of unions like Unifor, the Service Employees International Union, and teachers' unions who were pursuing anti-PC strategic voting.

While the NDP's union endorsers were much bigger and represented a much broader cross-section of workers, they did not gain nearly as much media attention as the union endorsements for Ford. The endorsements for Ford also proved much more valuable because they helped to build a media narrative that labour movement opposition to the government was not only fading, but converting into support. The endorsements also provided pro-worker cover for Ford's Conservatives that resonated far beyond the ranks of construction unions, making the PCs appear friendly to blue-collar workers more generally. How union endorsements are interpreted by the voting public is relevant here. Union support for the NDP is expected and has traditionally been met with charges of labour domination by media pundits and political opponents.[62] In contrast, union endorsements for the PCs were largely framed as an impressive game changer. This double standard was not lost on New Democrats, who have always had to walk a fine line in order to avoid the perception that unions have undue influence within the party as a result of their support.

CONCLUSION

On election night, the PC labour charm offensive appeared to pay dividends as Ford's Conservatives picked up new seats from the NDP in blue-collar ridings in Windsor, Brampton, and Hamilton on its way to re-election. Whether the new alliance between the PCs and construction unions will be sustained, however, is still an open question. Nevertheless, it is clear the NDP's weakening ties to the labour movement have invited such strategic interventions from the right. The PC labour charm offensive will no doubt also face blowback from staunchly anti-union elements within the conservative movement, as the party attempts to forge a new identity. Thus, both the left and the right face uncertain futures as the shifting landscape of party-union relations continues to transform Ontario politics.

On November 3, 2022, less than six months after the government's re-election, the PCs raised the ire of the entire labour movement by using the Charter's notwithstanding clause to pass Bill 28, the *Keeping Students in Class Act*, in order to pre-empt a strike by 55,000 CUPE education workers who made, on average, just $39,000 a year. The legislation rendered the planned strike illegal, mandated daily fines of $4,000 for individual workers who did not adhere to the law, and imposed a contract on the workers that did not come close to meeting their demands. In an act of defiance that united virtually every union in the province, CUPE members ignored the legislation and launched a two-day province-wide strike that shut down schools. Other unions in both the private and public sectors quickly lined up behind CUPE in opposition to Bill 28, threatening to trigger sympathy strikes across the province in every sector of the economy in an effort to force the government to repeal the legislation. Even Ford's allies in the construction unions condemned the premier's use of the notwithstanding clause to override the right to strike and bargain collectively. The Ford government quickly backed down as union leaders began preparing for a general strike. In exchange for a commitment by CUPE to end its strike and return to the bargaining table, the legislation was repealed and no fines were issued.[63] A negotiated settlement with improved terms was eventually reached. However, the ordeal helped to further highlight some of complexities and contradictory elements of the government's strategy vis-à-vis organized labour. Notably, while Ford's handling of Bill 28 was universally panned by union leaders, opposition parties did not immediately appear to benefit from the labour movement's successful campaign to defeat the legislation.

While, overall, union households are still consistently more likely to vote NDP than non-union households, the union leadership has more often than not failed to produce a reliable NDP voting block of rank-and-file union members capable of vaulting the party into government. This failure, however, has not convinced unions to retreat from the electoral arena. On the contrary, labour organizations are more active than ever in Ontario politics, but have largely migrated to transactional political strategies, anti-Conservative strategic voting campaigns, third-party advertising, or parallel issue campaigns as ways to educate and mobilize members and influence election outcomes. The efficacy of some of these tactics requires further examination, but what is clear is that unions' electoral strategies are more fractured than ever.

DISCUSSION QUESTIONS

1 How do we account for why some unions shifted political allegiances for the 2022 provincial election, while others maintained familiar alliances?
2 Generally speaking, which party do you think best represents union and working-class interests? Why?
3 Why do parties seek out endorsements from unions? Do you think endorsements have any effect on the voting intentions of union members and the broader public?

NOTES

1 Statistics Canada, "Union Status by Geography," table 14-10-0129-01, released January 6, 2023, https://doi.org/10.25318/1410012901-eng.
2 Stephanie Ross and Larry Savage, "Introduction: Public Sector Unions in the Age of Austerity," in *Public Sector Unions in the Age of Austerity*, ed. Stephanie Ross and Larry Savage (Halifax: Fernwood, 2013), 11.

3   Statistics Canada, "Union Status by Industry," table: 14-10-0132-01, released January 6, 2023, https://doi.org/10.25318/1410013201-eng.
4   The literature is summarized in Keith Archer, *Political Choices and Electoral Consequences* (Montreal: McGill-Queen's University Press, 1990), 56–8; Linda Erikson and David Laycock, "Building for a Breakthrough," in *Reviving Social Democracy: The Near Death and Surprising Rise of the Federal NDP*, ed. David Laycock and Linda Erickson (Vancouver: UBC Press, 2015), 49–51.
5   Gad Horowitz, *Canadian Labour in Politics* (Toronto: University of Toronto Press, 1968), 198–233.
6   Larry Savage, "Organized Labour and the NDP: Looking Back on Sixty Years of Party-Union Relations," *Labour/Le Travail* 88 (Fall 2021): 77–112, https://doi.org/10.52975/llt.2021v88.0006.
7   Panitch and Swartz, *From Consent to Coercion: The Assault on Trade Union Freedoms* (Aurora, ON: Garamond Press, 2003), 172–81; Buzz Hargrove, *Laying It on the Line: Driving a Hard Bargain in Challenging Times* (Toronto: HarperCollins, 2009), 120.
8   Stephen McBride, "'If You Don't Know Where You're Going You'll End Up Somewhere Else': Ideological and Policy Failure in the Ontario NDP," in *Challenges and Perils: Social Democracy in Neoliberal Times*, ed. William Carroll and R.S. Ratner (Halifax: Fernwood, 2005), 35; Panitch and Swartz, *From Consent to Coercion*, 178.
9   Before the convention voted on the resolution put forward by a coalition of public-sector unions and the CAW, a dozen private sector unions loyal to the NDP walked out in protest. Stephanie Ross, "The Challenges of Union Political Action in the Era of Neoliberalism," in *Divided Province: Ontario Politics in the Age of Neoliberalism*, ed. Greg Albo and Bryan M. Evans (Montreal: McGill-Queen's University Press, 2018), 526–7.
10 Government of Ontario, "Government Acts to Repeal Bill 40 to Spur Economic Growth and Create Jobs," *Canada Newswire*, October 4, 1995.
11 Daniel Girard, "Tough Labour Bill Approved Law Will Restrict Rights of Unions," *Toronto Star*, June 24, 1998, A1, A26; Judith McCormack, "Shopping for a Remedy: The Wal-Mart Case," *Canadian Labour & Employment Law Journal* 5 (1997): 341–58.
12 Kevin M. Burkett, "The Politicization of the Ontario Labour Relations Framework in the 1990s," *Canadian Labour and Employment Law Journal* 6 (1998) 178–81; Judith McCormack, "Comment on 'The Politicization of the Ontario Labour Relations Framework in the 1990s,'" *Canadian Labour & Employment Law Journal* 7 (2000): 325–53.
13 David Rapaport, *No Justice, No Peace: The 1996 OPSEU Strike against the Harris Government in Ontario* (Montreal: McGill-Queen's University Press, 1999), 107–10.
14 Alan Sears, *Retooling the Mind Factory: Education in a Lean State* (Aurora, ON: Garamond Press, 2003), 6, 233–4; Donald Kerr, "Teaching Autonomy: The Obligations of Liberal Education in Plural Societies," *Studies in Philosophy and Education* 25 (November 2006): 425–56, https://doi.org/10.1007/s11217-006-0015-y.

15 Marcella Munro, "Ontario's 'Days of Action' and Strategic Choices for the Left in Canada," *Studies in Political Economy* 53, no. 1 (1997): 125–40, https://doi.org/10.1080/19187033.1997.11675318.
16 Yonatan Reshef and Sandra Rastin, *Unions in the Time of Revolution: Government Restructuring in Alberta and Ontario* (Toronto: University of Toronto Press, 2003), 133.
17 Stephanie Ross, "The Challenges of Union Political Action," 534.
18 Reshef and Rastin, *Unions in the Time of Revolution*, 166–82; Brian Tanguay, "Parties, Organized Interests, and Electoral Democracy: The 1999 Ontario Provincial Election" in *Political Parties, Representation, and Electoral Democracy in Canada*, ed. William Cross (Don Mills, ON: Oxford University Press, 2002), 145–60.
19 President's Message, "Our Strategy in the Spotlight," Ontario Public Sector Employees Union, 1999, archived October 16, 2005, at the Wayback Machine, https://web.archive.org/web/20051016083702/http://www.opseu.org/leah/presidentmay.htm.
20 Canadian Auto Workers, *Contact* 28, no. 38 (November 15, 1998); Reshef and Rastin, *Unions in the Time of Revolution*, 168.
21 Colin Perkel, "Labour Groups to Fight Rule on Anti-Union Information," *Globe and Mail*, January 24, 2002, https://www.theglobeandmail.com/news/national/labour-groups-to-fight-rule-on-anti-union-information/article22731883/.
22 Statistics Canada, "Table 282-0078: Labour Force Survey Estimates (LFS), Employees by Union Coverage, North American Industry Classification System (NAICS), Sex and Age Group, Annually (Persons)"; Government of Ontario, Ministry of Finance, *Ontario Outlook and Fiscal Review* (Toronto: Queen's Printer, 2004), tables 2 and 27.
23 Larry Savage and Nick Ruhloff-Queiruga, "Organized Labour, Campaign Finance, and the Politics of Strategic Voting in Ontario," *Labour/Le Travail* 80 (Fall 2017): 238, https://doi.org/10.1353/llt.2017.0049; Bradley Walchuk, "Changing Union-Party Relations in Canada," *Labour Studies Journal* 35, no. 1 (March 2010): 38, https://doi.org/10.1177/0160449X09353036.
24 Larry Savage, "Contemporary Party-Union Relations in Canada," *Labour Studies Journal* 35, no. 1 (March 2010): 15–16, https://doi.org/10.1177/0160449X09353028; Walchuk, "Changing Union-Party Relations," 38–41.
25 Rob Ferguson, "Campaign Finance Rules 'Too Loose' Study Says," *Toronto Star*, October 3, 2011, https://www.thestar.com/news/canada/campaign-finance-rules-too-loose-study-says/article_4c0f67b6-9ebc-5586-a708-3eb33c73d177.html.
26 Rob Ferguson, "Campaign Finance Rules"; Rob Ferguson and Richard Brennan, "Elections Ontario Head Calls for Limits to Advertising by Interest Groups," *Toronto Star*, April 8, 2013, https://www.thestar.com/politics/provincial/elections-ontario-head-calls-for-limits-to-advertising-by-interest-groups/article_ae4ddd14-b6d3-58b1-9e55-4c25a95063e6.html.
27 Ferguson and Brennan, "Elections Ontario Head."
28 Ontario Confederation of University Faculty Associations, (OCUFA), *OCUFA Analysis of the Drummond Report: Long on Cuts, Short on Insight* (Toronto: OCUFA, 2012), http://ocufa.on.ca/wordpress/assets/OCUFA-Drummond-Report-Analysis-Feb.-22-2012Final.pdf, 3.

29 OCUFA, *OCUFA Analysis*, 3.
30 Larry Savage and Chantal Mancini, "Strategic Electoral Dilemmas and the Politics of Teachers' Unions in Ontario," *Canadian Political Science Review* 16, no. 1 (2022): 13–14.
31 Martin Regg Cohn, "Dalton McGuinty's Decision and Timing Were All Wrong," *Toronto Star*, October 23, 2012, https://www.thestar.com/news/canada/dalton-mcguinty-s-decisions-and-timing-were-all-wrong/article_7e559f5a-11d3-5c7f-a10d-ca6012031a3b.html.
32 Louise Brown, "Ontario Teachers Have Strong Case in Court Challenge, Legal Expert Says," *Toronto Star*, October 11, 2012, https://www.thestar.com/news/canada/ontario-teachers-have-strong-case-in-court-challenge-legal-expert-says/article_091e3de7-3faf-5414-b190-6ecedd1db85f.html.
33 Mike Crawley, "$15 Minimum Wage, Workplace Changes Set to Pass in Ontario," *CBC News*, November 22, 2017, https://www.cbc.ca/news/canada/toronto/15-minimum-wage-ontario-legislation-1.4412363.
34 "Ontario Passes Legislation to Transform Political Fundraising," Government of Ontario, December 1, 2016, https://news.ontario.ca/en/release/42916/ontario-passes-legislation-to-transform-political-fundraising.
35 Don Wall, "Dillon Says Working Families Weighing Options after Ford 'Tramples' Rights," *Daily Commercial News*, June 21, 2021, https://canada.constructconnect.com/dcn/news/associations/2021/06/dillon-says-working-families-weighing-options-after-ford-tramples-rights.
36 Martin Regg Cohn, "Selling off Hydro One Is Wynne's Biggest Blunder as Premier: Cohn," *Toronto Star*, June 28, 2017, https://www.thestar.com/politics/provincial/selling-off-hydro-one-is-wynne-s-biggest-blunder-as-premier-cohn/article_c498b882-1f42-5230-a206-3a68fc534cc7.html.
37 Savage and Mancini, "Strategic Electoral Dilemmas," 15.
38 "Ford Government Pushes through Controversial Election Spending Bill with Notwithstanding Clause," *CBC News*, June 14, 2021, https://www.cbc.ca/news/canada/toronto/notwithstanding-clause-vote-ontario-1.6064952.
39 "The PC Party's Labour Charm Offensive," *The Agenda with Steve Paikin*, November 25, 2021, https://www.tvo.org/transcript/2679359.
40 Jack Hauen, "Ontario PCs Spent Years Laying Groundwork for Worker-Friendly Strategy," *QP Briefing*, May 25, 2022, https://www.qpbriefing.com/archives/ontario-pcs-spent-years-laying-groundwork-for-worker-friendly-strategy.
41 Monte McNaughton (@MonteMcNaughton), "Our government is standing with hardworking people ... not those who want to 'phase out' good blue-collar jobs. We know Ontario is built by those who shower at the end of the day, not the start. #ONpoli," X (Twitter), April 12, 2022, 3:36 p.m., https://twitter.com/MonteMcNaughton/status/1514009620997541893.
42 Kory Teneycke, *The Herle Burly Podcast*, June 7, 2022, https://www.airquotesmedia.com/thb/kory-teneycke-7june2022.
43 Erin O'Toole (@erinotoole), "Do you think it's time for economic policy that puts Canadian workers first? Happy Labour Day #LabourDay," X (Twitter),

September 7, 2020, 8:26 a.m., https://twitter.com/erinotoole/status/1302991683072798721.

44 John Michael McGrath, "Why the Next Group of Voters Canada's Conservatives Will Chase is … Unions?," *TVO*, November 3, 2020, https://www.tvo.org/article/why-the-next-group-of-voters-canadas-conservatives-will-chase-is-unions.

45 Robyn Urback, "The Main Philosophy of Erin O'Toole's 'Principled Conservatism' is Winning Elections," *Globe and Mail*, November 11, 2020, https://www.theglobeandmail.com/opinion/article-the-main-philosophy-of-erin-otooles-principled-conservatism-is/.

46 "Conservative Leader Erin O'Toole to Ensure Canadian Workers have Their Voices Heard," *Conservative Party of Canada*, August 23, 2021, archived June 9, 2022, at the Wayback Machine, https://web.archive.org/web/20220609211346/https:/www.conservative.ca/conservative-leader-erin-otoole-to-ensure-canadian-workers-have-their-voices-heard/.

47 McGrath, "Why the Next Group."

48 McGrath, "Why the Next Group."

49 Brian Lilley, "LILLEY: Construction Unions Are Abandoning the Liberals for Ford," *Toronto Sun*, May 17, 2022, https://torontosun.com/opinion/columnists/lilley-construction-unions-are-abandoning-the-liberals-for-ford-and-the-pcs.

50 Graeme Frisque, "Doug Ford, Justin Trudeau Announce $1B in Subsidies for Stellantis to Build Electric Vehicles in Brampton and Windsor," *Brampton Guardian*, May 2, 2022, https://www.bramptonguardian.com/news/doug-ford-justin-trudeau-announce-1b-in-subsidies-for-stellantis-to-build-electric-vehicles-in/article_e8f6d1bf-ae95-5a4c-9ef0-22136ecb6a4f.html; Don Wall, "PCs 'Completely Aligned with LIUNA,' Says Mancinelli," *Daily Commercial News*, May 19, 2022, https://canada.constructconnect.com/dcn/news/government/2022/05/pcs-completely-aligned-with-liuna-says-mancinelli.

51 The insider's description was a nod to the earlier twentieth century PC dynasty, widely known as the "Big Blue Machine."

52 Robert Benzie, "The Inside Story of How Doug Ford Beat the NDP – and Destroyed the Liberals – in the Ontario Election," *Toronto Star*, June 9, 2022, https://www.thestar.com/politics/provincial/the-inside-story-of-how-doug-ford-beat-the-ndp-and-destroyed-the-liberals-in/article_db5b2c96-a35a-5d33-96df-4f92b04b437a.html.

53 Ryan Rocca, "'We're Losing Our Patience': Doug Ford Slams Teachers' Unions Ahead of Week Filled with Job Action," *Global News*, February 2, 2020, https://globalnews.ca/news/6496178/doug-ford-slams-teachers-unions/.

54 Solarina Ho, "Ontario's 'Right to Disconnect' Law: Who Qualifies and What Are the Loopholes?," *CTV News*, June 7, 2022, https://www.ctvnews.ca/business/ontario-s-right-to-disconnect-law-who-qualifies-and-what-are-the-loopholes-1.5936773; Mitchell Thompson, "Doug Ford's Plan to Help Gig Workers Makes It Easy to Misclassify Workers and Pay Them Less than Minimum Wage," *PressProgress*, March 1, 2022, https://pressprogress.ca/doug-fords-plan-to-help-gig-workers-makes-it-easy-to-misclassify-workers-and-pay-them-less-than-minimum-wage/.

55 Richard J. Brennan, "'Right-to-Work' U.S. States a Model for Ontario, Say Tories," *Toronto Star*, November 8, 2013, https://www.thestar.com/politics/provincial/right-to-work-u-s-states-a-model-for-ontario-say-tories/article_eeb79b43-c309-5a27-a68a-7e0d1bedbd8f.html.

56 Ontario Federation of Labour, "Ontario Federation of Labour Pledges Support for Ontario NDP," news release, November 5, 2021, https://ofl.ca/ontario-federation-of-labour-pledges-support-for-ontario-ndp/.

57 Robert Benzie, "Flanked by Union Leaders, Doug Ford Raises Ontario's Minimum Wage to $15 an Hour," *Toronto Star*, November 2, 2021, https://www.thestar.com/politics/provincial/flanked-by-union-leaders-doug-ford-raises-ontario-s-minimum-wage-to-15-an-hour/article_0ef259f2-af85-59ee-a99f-a906122cdc9a.html.

58 Unifor, "Recommendation No. 2 Ontario Election 2022," Ontario Regional Director Recommendations, March 9–10, 2022, 3.

59 Nicole Thompson "Ontario NDP and PCs Position Themselves as Labour Friendly, Each Net New Endorsements," *CBC News*, May 17, 2022, https://www.cbc.ca/news/canada/toronto/ford-unions-endorsements-labour-ndp-1.6456935.

60 LIUNA had previously endorsed the PCs and some NDP candidates in the 2018 provincial election in response to a jurisdictional change buried in the Wynne government's final budget that benefitted a rival union. Wall, "PCs 'Completely Aligned with LIUNA.'"

61 Benzie, "The Inside Story."

62 Desmond Morton with Terry Copp, *Working People: An Illustrated History of the Canadian Labour Movement* (Ottawa: Deneau Publishers, 1984), 243–4.

63 Martin Lukacs and Emma Paling, "The Inside Story of How Education Workers Beat Back Doug Ford," *The Breach*, December 14, 2022, https://breachmedia.ca/the-inside-story-of-how-education-workers-beat-back-doug-ford/.

16

Toronto and the GTA: Governing Ontario's Global City

Martin Horak

The Greater Toronto Area (GTA) is a massive, sprawling urban area that is home to nearly 7 million people. It includes the city of Toronto, with a population of 2.8 million, as well as twenty-eight surrounding suburban municipalities. This chapter looks at the changing nature of governance and policy in Toronto and the GTA, with a particular focus on the role of the provincial government. The region's large population makes it impossible for the province to ignore. In recent decades, Toronto has emerged as Canada's pre-eminent global city, a diverse and complex place that faces many policy challenges. Successive provincial governments have adopted very different approaches to engaging with these challenges, based on different ideological outlooks and shifting electoral considerations.

After introducing the city's demographics and looking back at the province's role in governing the GTA in the twentieth century, the chapter paints a portrait of the volatile and divided local politics in the city of Toronto, which lies at the heart of the GTA. It then traces the evolution of provincial engagement with Toronto and the GTA in the twenty-first century, paying special attention to two key policy challenges: constructing transit infrastructure in the city of Toronto, and managing suburban growth in the outer suburbs of the GTA. As we will see, Toronto and the GTA have been the subject of a series of provincial policy experiments and initiatives, which emerge from the interaction of local needs and the political interests of successive provincial governments. Just like the city itself, the shape of provincial engagement with Toronto and the GTA is always in flux, with little stability on the horizon.

THE GREATER TORONTO AREA: A GROWING METROPOLIS

The GTA is generally agreed to comprise the city of Toronto and the surrounding regions of Durham, York, Peel, and Halton. Any Ontario provincial government that ignores the issues and concerns of GTA residents does so at its peril. Until recently, the area's share of the provincial population has been steadily increasing. In 1951, the Toronto region had about one million residents – 20 per cent of Ontario's population.[1] By 2021, the GTA, as it is now widely known, accounted for 47 per cent of Ontario's population (see table 16.1). There are recent signs that the GTA's long population boom is slowing. For instance, the GTA accounted for 71 per cent of Ontario's population growth between 2006 and 2011, but only 37 per cent between 2016 and 2021 (calculated using table 16.1). Some of this decrease is due to a short-term drop in immigration during the COVID-19 pandemic, but longer-term factors – such as the GTA's worsening crisis of housing affordability, which is pushing residents out of the area – are probably more significant. While it remains to be seen whether the GTA has entered a new, slower-growth era for the longer term, there is no doubt that it will remain Ontario's – and Canada's – largest urban region in the decades to come.

Unsurprisingly, then, the GTA looms large in Ontario electoral politics. As table 16.2 shows, both the central city of Toronto and the outer GTA suburbs have shifted partisan allegiances more than once since 1990. With over 40 per cent of Ontario ridings located in the GTA, such swings can make or break the electoral fortunes of a provincial political party. Since 1990, no political party has formed a government without securing a majority of seats in the GTA. While the city of Toronto remains an important political battleground, the rapid growth of the outer suburbs (sometimes called the "905" region) has made them especially critical to electoral success in recent years. The resounding victories of the Conservatives in 1995 and the Liberals in 2003, as well as the Conservatives' triumphant return to power in 2018, were all built

Table 16.1. Population Growth of Toronto Area in Millions, Percentage of Ontario Population, 1986–2021

Location	1991	1996	2001	2006	2011	2016	2021
Toronto	2.28 (22.6)	2.39 (22.2)	2.48 (21.7)	2.50 (20.6)	2.62 (20.4)	2.73 (20.3)	2.79 (19.6)
GTA	4.24 (42.0)	4.63 (43.1)	5.08 (44.5)	5.56 (45.7)	6.05 (47.1)	6.42 (47.7)	6.71 (47.2)
Ontario	10.09	10.75	11.41	12.16	12.85	13.45	14.22

Note: The 1991 and 1996 data for Toronto are for the former Municipality of Metropolitan Toronto.
Sources: Calculated from Statistics Canada population and dwelling count data: Table 98-10-0002-01, https://doi.org/10.25318/3610040001-eng; Table 98-402-X2016001, https://www150.statcan.gc.ca/n1/en/catalogue/98-402-X2016001; Table 98-310-XWE2011002, https://www12.statcan.gc.ca/census-recensement/2011/dp-pd/hlt-fst/pd-pl/index-eng.cfm; Table 97-550-XWE2006002, https://www12.statcan.gc.ca/census-recensement/2006/dp-pd/hlt/97-550/Print.cfm; and Table 93F0051X, https://www150.statcan.gc.ca/n1/en/catalogue/93F0051X. Contains information licensed under the Open Government Licence – Canada.

Table 16.2. Distribution of Seats in Legislature by Major Party, 1990–2022

	City of Toronto			Outer GTA Suburbs			Total GTA			Ontario		
Election Year	PC	Lib.	NDP	PC	Lib.	NDP	PC	Lib.	NDP	PC	Lib.	NDP
1990	3	9	18	4	8	6	7	17	24	20	36	74
1995	16	9	5	18	0	0	34	9	5	82	30	17
1999	8	11	3	16	0	0	24	11	3	59	35	9
2003	0	19	3	4	12	0	4	31	3	24	72	7
2007	0	18	4	4	15	0	4	33	4	26	71	10
2011	0	17	5	4	14	1	4	31	6	37	53	17
2014	0	20	2	2	15	2	2	35	4	27	59	21
2018	11	3	11	25	0	4	36	3	15	76	7	40
2022	12	4	9	28	0	1	40	4	10	83	8	31

Notes: Prior to 1998, the area noted as "City of Toronto" was the Municipality of Metropolitan Toronto. Some provincial electoral districts cross the boundaries of the GTA; only results from ridings fully within GTA boundaries are included in this table.
Source: Calculated from Elections Ontario, "Election Results," accessed September 15, 2023, https://www.elections.on.ca/en/resource-centre/elections-results/official-past-elections-results.html.

on a near-sweep of outer suburban seats in the GTA. The GTA's role as a linchpin of Ontario electoral politics ensures that Toronto-area issues consistently receive provincial attention.

ECONOMIC AND SOCIAL TRANSFORMATION OF THE GTA

The past three decades have transformed the economic and social fabric of the GTA. After a major recession in the early 1990s, the GTA reinvented itself as the hub of Canada's new post-industrial, globally integrated economy. The outer suburbs retain significant industrial capacity in sectors such as automotive and food processing, but the central city of Toronto is largely de-industrialized – by 2021, only 6.4 per cent of its labour force worked in manufacturing.[2] Post-industrial sectors such as finance, cultural production, research and development, and higher education are major drivers of the region's economy. The Toronto region is home to 40 per cent of Canada's corporate headquarters and has the country's largest stock exchange, it has eleven colleges and universities, and it is the largest film and television production centre in the country.

Along with economic change, international immigration has transformed the social makeup of the GTA over the past generation. Immigration is the main driver of population growth. Indeed, without the 100,000 or so immigrants who settle in the GTA in an average year, the region's population would not be growing at all. Since the 1980s, the GTA has become one of the most ethnoculturally diverse urban areas in the world. In 2021, 56 per cent of the city of Toronto's residents were members of racialized minorities. Some 905-area municipalities, such as Brampton (80 per cent) and Markham (83 per cent) have even higher percentages of racialized minority residents.[3] The GTA today houses large populations of many ethnocultural groups, including Chinese, South Asian, Filipino, and Jamaican, among many others.

Together, economic transformation, social change, and rapid population growth have transformed the Toronto area into a vibrant, cosmopolitan global city. They have also shaped and defined the GTA's biggest policy challenges in recent decades. The shift to a post-industrial economy has "stretched" the income distribution – there are more high-income and low-income people, and fewer middle-income people, than there were a generation ago. This has contributed to an enduring crisis of homelessness in the central city of

Toronto, as well as to increased divides between wealthy and poor neighbourhoods.[4] Although many GTA-area local governments pride themselves on being leaders in diversity and inclusion, they have nonetheless sometimes struggled to equitably represent and serve highly diverse populations. There is a remarkable lack of diversity on many GTA-area city councils – including the city of Toronto, where half of the population is non-white, but only four out of twenty-five city councillors in the 2018–22 term identified as racialized. Racial profiling in policing, landlord discrimination against racialized tenants, and other forms of everyday racism remain disturbingly widespread.[5]

Meanwhile, sustained population growth means there is a constant need to grow and renew the "hard" infrastructure (such as roads, transit, sewers, and parks) that supports urban life, and to manage the relentless outward march of suburban development. These issues of urban infrastructure and regional development have been particularly politically salient at the provincial level. Since our focus in this chapter is on the place of Toronto in Ontario politics, we will take a detailed look at two such policy challenges that illustrate the changing nature of provincial-local relations and governance: building new rapid transit infrastructure in the core city of Toronto and managing urban growth in the 905 suburbs. Before we explore these issues, however, we will look back at the province's role in GTA governance in the twentieth century, and introduce the fascinating story of local politics in the city of Toronto.

THE PROVINCE AND GTA GOVERNANCE, 1954–98

During the second half of the twentieth century, the Ontario government repeatedly used local government restructuring as a means of dealing with Toronto-area governance issues. In 1954, the province established a two-tier local government system for Toronto that consisted of one upper-tier government called Metropolitan Toronto (or "Metro") and thirteen (later six) lower-tier governments.[6] Metro was responsible for developing major infrastructure and administering policing, transit, social housing, and social services. The lower-tier municipalities – which included the old core city of Toronto and postwar suburbs such as Scarborough and North York – had control over local planning and development, and community services such as parks, libraries, and waste collection. In the 1960s and early 1970s, Metro played a pivotal role in the development of Toronto, delivering many large provincially funded public infrastructure projects, including more than 15,000 units of public housing and major extensions to the subway system.[7]

In 1974, as new suburbs beyond the boundaries of Metro were beginning to grow quickly, the province replicated the two-tier system there. It established four upper-tier "regional municipalities" – Peel, Halton, Durham, and York. These upper-tier municipalities still exist today and encompass twenty-four lower-tier municipalities, including major centres such as Mississauga, Richmond Hill, Brampton, Markham, Oshawa, and Oakville. The suburban regional governments were established at a time when provincial investment in big infrastructure was declining, so they did not deliver public infrastructure projects on the scale that Metro had in the previous decades.[8] Nonetheless, the two-tier local government systems in the GTA were widely seen – both in Canada and abroad – as an urban governance success story. The upper-tier governments managed "big picture" development and region-wide services, while the lower-tier governments focused on property development and local services to property.

Property development in the GTA in the late twentieth century often involved tight coalitions between elected officials and private developers. Two classic examples are North York during Mel Lastman's tenure as mayor (1972–97), and Mississauga, whose rapid growth was steered for thirty-six years (1978–2014) by Mayor Hazel McCallion.[9] The former lower-tier city of Toronto took a different direction. In 1972, a "reform" movement led by young middle-class professionals swept Toronto's local elections, ushering in several decades during which the city used its rich commercial property tax base to pursue historical preservation, affordable housing development, neighbourhood planning, arts funding, and various other "progressive" local policies.[10]

Despite their early success, by the 1990s, the GTA's two-tier governance systems were in trouble. There was nearly constant political conflict between the upper- and lower-tier governments in Metro, and Metro as a whole was showing signs of social and economic decline, with many businesses and residents moving to the booming outer suburbs of the 905 region, which were quickly sprawling into the surrounding countryside. In 1993, the provincial NDP government appointed a GTA task force, which recommended creating a single upper-tier government that would span the whole Greater Toronto Area.

By the time the task force report came out in 1996, however, the NDP had been swept aside by the Conservatives under Mike Harris. The task force's proposal was a political non-starter for the Conservatives, since their support base in the 905 region strongly opposed the idea of a GTA-wide upper-tier government. So, the Harris government left the two-tier systems in the outer suburbs untouched. Instead, in 1997, it proposed to amalgamate all of the municipalities in Metro into one new City of Toronto. This move was vociferously but unsuccessfully opposed by many local politicians and residents in Metro, especially those in the old lower-tier City of Toronto; the province took advantage of its authority over all aspects of municipal affairs and pushed the merger through.[11]

LOCAL POLITICS IN TORONTO SINCE 1998

Amalgamation transformed the landscape of GTA governance. The outer suburbs retained their two-tier governing systems, but since 1998, the central city has been one huge, unified municipality. In this section, we take a closer look at local politics in the city of Toronto, the core municipality in the GTA. The city of Toronto is home to over 20 per cent of Ontario's population, and has a larger budget than most Canadian provinces. Its mayor is directly elected by more people than any other politician in Canada. The municipality's sheer size gives it some advantages in terms of governing capacity intergovernmental clout, but amalgamation has certainly not solved Toronto's governance challenges. On the contrary, as we will see, for most of its post-amalgamation history, Toronto has had a divided and volatile local politics.

Toronto has a vast and professionalized bureaucracy, which often leads the charge in developing innovative local policies in areas ranging from immigrant integration and multicultural services[12] to neighbourhood revitalization[13] and transportation planning.[14] Toronto's large population and economic weight give it the potential for significant influence on the intergovernmental stage, which its more skilful political leaders have, from time to time, effectively exercised. However, the municipality was also born with significant financial problems. The same provincial government that amalgamated Toronto also radically cut provincial funding for transit, and downloaded responsibility for social assistance and social housing – two big-ticket items in Toronto – to the municipal level. Although subsequent Liberal provincial governments restored transit funding and gave Toronto the right to levy new local taxes, public opposition and fear of losing businesses and residents to the outer suburbs has made Toronto politicians reluctant to raise local taxes to cover rising costs. As a result, for much of its existence since amalgamation, Toronto has operated in an atmosphere of fiscal shortage.

In addition, the structure of Toronto's local political institutions has made it difficult for the city to respond effectively to major policy challenges.

Toronto is run by a non-partisan council in which councillors focus heavily on ward-specific concerns.[15] Political coalitions on council are built on an issue-by-issue basis, and bigger-picture policy initiatives are typically led by the mayor and the bureaucracy. However, until very recently (see below) Toronto's mayors – like other mayors across Ontario – did not have significant executive powers, so they had to rely on their city-wide electoral mandate and their personal coalition-building skills to get things done.

Toronto's electorate is geographically divided in a way that reflects the city's Metro-era history. "Downtown" voters (those who live in what used to be the pre-amalgamation city of Toronto) tend to favour a more expansive local government that focuses on transit and arts spending and pays attention to social policy concerns. Voters in the postwar suburbs (the former municipalities of Scarborough, Etobicoke, and North York) tend to favour a more "minimalist" local government that focuses on property services and privileges automobile-based transportation. There is, as Taylor, Silver, and Doering put it, a deep "lifestyle cleavage" in Toronto between the old urban core and the postwar suburbs.[16]

Toronto's first three post-amalgamation mayors each represented one or the other of these "two solitudes" of Toronto politics. The brash and entrepreneurial Mel Lastman (1998–2003) was elected mainly with support from the inner suburbs. Support for David Miller (2003–10), a left-leaning, big-ideas mayor with a long-term policy orientation, was strongest in the city core. The election of Rob Ford in 2010 marked a dramatic swing back to a populist-conservative mayor with a suburban support base. Ford's 2010 campaign platform included a focus on cutting public spending, privatizing public services, ending "the war on the car," and building subways instead of light rail. A political outsider prone to public gaffes and controversy, Ford nonetheless secured the largest direct electoral mandate of any politician in Canadian history.[17] While Ford's actions in office largely held true to the populist-conservative vision, by late 2011, the council consensus in support of his policies crumbled, and the mayor's controversial persona and personal activities began to overshadow his policy priorities.

Ford initially ran for re-election in 2014 but dropped out due to serious health troubles, and his brother, Councillor Doug Ford, took his place as mayoral candidate. However, a critical mass of Torontonians had had enough of the Ford years and, in an election that saw a record voter turnout of more than 60 per cent, Doug Ford was defeated by John Tory. A moderate conservative whose past career included several years leading the provincial Progressive

Conservatives, Tory ran on a platform of restoring decorum to city hall and building more transit. While his electoral base was strongest in the city's core, he also secured solid support in some suburban areas, eroding the previously stark downtown-suburban electoral divide. Tory was re-elected in 2018 and 2022, handily beating challengers Jen Keesmaat (2018) and Gil Penalosa (2022) – both of them city planners who championed progressive downtown values.

Barely three months into his third term in February 2023, Tory was forced to resign after a media investigation revealed that he had an extramarital relationship with a staff member less than half his age. A mayoral by-election was quickly organized for June 26, 2023. While a number of high-profile candidates ran, the winner with 37 per cent of the vote was Olivia Chow. A former mayoral candidate, councillor, and NDP MP, Chow had strong connections to local progressive activists. At a time when housing prices were at record highs, Chow's campaign focus on affordable housing construction and renter protections resonated with voters across the core-suburbs divide, giving Toronto its first left-leaning mayor since David Miller.

THE CITY OF TORONTO ON THE MULTI-LEVEL STAGE

The relationship with the province presents a whole other set of challenges for Toronto's political leaders. Since the provincial government has full legal authority over local government, and does not hesitate to use it, this relationship can be critically important. John Tory's record of policy achievements as mayor was limited,[18] but he skilfully managed his relationship with the province – and in particular, with Conservative premier (and Tory's former rival for mayor) Doug Ford. For Olivia Chow, whose ideological position and priorities are radically different from Ford's, the relationship may prove to be more difficult.

The relationship between the City of Toronto and the provincial government has evolved significantly over the last twenty years, depending in large part on which provincial party is in power. In the early years after the Harris Conservatives imposed amalgamation, the relationship was frosty. City officials demanded new resources and powers from the province; the governing Conservatives were not interested. The election of the McGuinty Liberals in 2003, with strong support in Toronto, opened a new window of opportunity. Making good on an election promise, the Liberal government worked with the city to develop a new *Toronto Act* that came into force in 2007. While the

Act gave Toronto a number of new powers and sources of revenue, in practice its most important provision has proved to be the Municipal Land Transfer Tax, which by 2021 netted $1.2 billion in annual revenue for the city.[19]

The early 2000s also saw a brief tri-level political alignment, in which the provincial and federal governments worked together to support local policy priorities in Toronto and other big cities. In 2003, around the same time that the Liberals came to power in Ontario, Paul Martin replaced Jean Chrétien as federal prime minister. Recognizing that the federal Liberals' power base was increasingly urban in character,[20] Martin promised a federal "New Deal for Cities." Between 2004 and 2006, all three levels of government cooperated on a number of fronts. The federal government implemented a dedicated gas tax for municipal infrastructure and expanded other infrastructure funding programs; the first Canada-Ontario Immigrant Settlement agreement was developed with input from the City of Toronto;[21] and the city proposed a tri-level, $500 million initiative to support the revitalization of poor neighbourhoods.[22] However, tri-level cooperation proved difficult to sustain in the longer run. In 2006, the federal Conservatives came into office with different political priorities. While the Conservatives retained federal infrastructure funding, tri-level cooperation in many other fields fell apart, and Toronto and GTA governance once again became mainly a matter for provincial-local interaction.

During successive Ontario Liberal governments from 2003 to 2018, the province took a largely consensual approach to Toronto and GTA issues. As we will see in our discussions of transit infrastructure and regional growth management, during this time, the provincial government became increasingly involved in managing big urban issues in Toronto and the GTA, while remaining wary of appearing to step on local authority or go against local wishes. That said, the provincial Liberals were not above imposing their authority for short-term political gain: in 2017, a deeply unpopular Liberal government under Kathleen Wynne vetoed the City of Toronto's initiative to implement expressway road tolls, since the tolls would have alienated voters in the 905 region in the 2018 provincial election.[23] As it happened, the Liberals lost the 2018 election badly anyway, and the Conservatives returned to power at Queen's Park under the leadership of former Toronto councillor and mayoral candidate Doug Ford.

Only a few weeks after he was elected premier, Ford unilaterally cut the size of the Toronto City Council from forty-seven to twenty-five and cancelled planned elections of regional government Chairs in York and Peel regions – out of the blue and with no consultation with local government officials.[24]

The surprise changes came less than three months before the fall 2018 municipal elections, at a time when many candidates were already fundraising and organizing. They provoked widespread outrage in municipal circles. Progressive activists warned that Toronto and the GTA were again facing the unilateral approach to local government affairs that Ontario experienced under the Harris Conservative government at the end of the 1990s. Academics revived discussion about the need for more municipal autonomy and protection from arbitrary provincial action.[25] Notwithstanding, the fact that provincial governments have full legal control over municipalities was reaffirmed in 2021, when the Supreme Court ruled that the Ford government's cutting of the Toronto City Council was constitutional.[26]

Since 2018, the Ford government – which was re-elected with a large majority in June 2022 – has continued to pursue a top-down, directive approach to Toronto and GTA issues. For instance, in 2022, it introduced a "strong mayor" model for Toronto and Ottawa, which it expanded to twenty-six other large urban municipalities in June 2023. This model gives mayors several new executive powers, including the power to propose and veto by-laws. However, many of the powers can only be used to advance "provincial priorities," which the province has defined as building more housing. As a result, the new powers effectively make mayors the executors of the province's housing development agenda.[27] Meanwhile, in May 2023, the province addressed long-standing conflicts among the three municipalities that make up Peel Region in the GTA – Brampton, Mississauga, and Caledon – by announcing that it will dissolve the Region in 2025, only to abruptly reverse this decision six months later.[28] Despite its penchant for unilateralism, the Ford government has made a number of policy decisions that have enjoyed broad support in Toronto, not least among them an effort to cut through long-standing dysfunction in the crucial field of transit infrastructure.

TRANSIT TROUBLES: BUILDING NEW INFRASTRUCTURE IN THE CITY OF TORONTO

A large, growing city-region requires an extensive rapid transit system, but local governments in the GTA lack the resources to fund the construction of rapid transit lines on their own. Between the late 1980s and the early 2000s, the provincial government provided little to no funding for transit infrastructure, and virtually none was built. Worsening congestion across the GTA became a major provincial election issue in 2003, and a promise to address the problem helped to propel the Liberals to victory. In 2006, the province established Metrolinx, a regional transportation body whose mandate was to plan and develop a transportation network with an emphasis on rapid transit.[29] The following year, the province committed a whopping $17.5 billion for Toronto region transit projects, including four "Transit City" light rail lines proposed by Mayor David Miller of Toronto, as well as bus rapid transit in the outer GTA suburbs.[30]

By 2019, Metrolinx had spent over $20 billion building new transit infrastructure, with about 90 per cent of funding coming from the province and about 10 per cent from the federal government.[31] The results included a rail link from downtown Toronto to the airport, the reconstruction of Union Station, some improvements to existing suburban commuter rail lines, and two bus rapid transit lines in the outer GTA suburbs. However, within the city of Toronto itself, where the demand for new rapid transit lines is greatest, Metrolinx was facing huge challenges actually realizing any projects. The main problem was that rapid transit development in the city of Toronto had become a political football in the city's divided and volatile politics.

In 2010, before construction could begin on the Transit City light rail lines, newly elected mayor Rob Ford cancelled most of the initiative, saying that it would take road space away from drivers. Only one of the proposed lines – the Eglinton-Crosstown – survived; it is expected to open in 2024, after thirteen years of construction marked by delays and massive cost overruns. Mayor Ford proposed a new subway line through the inner suburban area of Scarborough, where he had strong electoral support. Successive city councils exhaustively debated the Scarborough subway over the next nine years, the planned routing changing repeatedly along with the electoral fortunes of various councillors, and progress stalled. Meanwhile, in 2014, John Tory proposed yet another different rapid transit line called "SmartTrack." It remains on the drawing board in 2024.

The Liberal government of Kathleen Wynne, anxious to respect municipal decision-making authority over transit matters, tolerated this local dysfunction and impasse. By contrast, in 2019, the Conservative government of Doug Ford adopted its trademark directive approach: without consulting local officials, it proposed a $28.5 billion rapid transit plan for Toronto that included a completely new subway line called the Ontario Line, as well as funding for the Scarborough subway and two other projects.[32] It promised to fund 40 per cent of the costs, calling on the federal government – which, under Justin Trudeau, had rolled out major new funding for transit infrastructure – to bankroll the rest. It also proposed to "upload" ownership of the whole subway system to the province. City officials successfully fended off the upload proposal, but accepted the new, imposed transit plans.[33]

In 2021, the federal government announced that it would fund most of the remaining cost of the new transit projects proposed by the Ford government.[34] Meanwhile, the provincial Ministry of Transportation assumed direct control over Metrolinx, which had previously been an arm's-length agency, and the government passed the *Building Transit Faster Act*, which allows the province to designate "transit corridors" where property can be easily expropriated and transit construction takes precedence over other activities. By March 2022, construction of the Ontario Line was underway.[35] While it remains to be seen whether the new transit projects will be successfully realized, the Ford government's top-down approach appears to have broken through the logjam in transit construction in Toronto, albeit at the cost of marginalizing the City of Toronto's role in rapid transit planning and development.

MANAGING GROWTH IN THE GTA SUBURBS

For several decades, most of the population growth in the GTA has occurred in the outer suburbs of the 905 – the regions of Peel, Halton, York, and Durham. Back in the 1970s, when those four regional governments were first developed, the province had rolled out a master plan for regional development called "The Toronto-Centred Region Plan."[36] However, soon after that, the province lost interest in managing the development of the outer suburbs, and until the early 2000s, the 905 grew steadily outward through low-density sprawl, gobbling up farmland at a breakneck pace. By 2003, suburban sprawl had become a major political issue. There was a major conflict between environmentalists and developers concerning plans to build housing on the Oak Ridges Moraine, a wooded area north of Toronto, and residents of the outer suburbs identified land development, traffic, and transit infrastructure (in that order) as the three most important local problems.[37] In this context, the provincial Liberals captured many suburban constituencies in the 2003 election by promising to deal with sprawl.

The Liberals introduced a series of regional growth management policies in the Toronto area. These policies reached well beyond the GTA, spanning the entire Greater Golden Horseshoe (GGH), an area that stretches around the western end of Lake Ontario from Niagara Falls to Oshawa, and is home to about two-thirds of Ontario's population. The province's first move was the 2004 Greenbelt Act, which froze most development in a wide arc of rural and forested land surrounding the urbanized core of the GGH. In 2005, the government passed the *Places to Grow Act*, which authorized the province to establish growth plans for designated areas in Ontario. The growth plan for the GGH was introduced in 2006. Focusing on "intensification" (increasing the density of already existing urban areas) as well as density targets for new development, the plan aimed to reduce the environmental and infrastructure costs of suburban growth by forcing municipalities throughout the GGH to plan for more compact growth.

One observer at the time called the GGH growth plan "the boldest attempt to address urban sprawl in Canada, and arguably North America."[38] It was certainly ambitious, and appeared to have strong public support. A lot of low-density sprawl had already been approved by municipal governments and was in the pipeline, however, so it would be a decade or more before the new requirements would have a major impact on the ground. In the meantime, implementation began to run up against the realities of local development politics. Ontario municipalities rely heavily on property development to boost their local tax revenues. The development industry did not like the GGH growth policies, since they threatened to steer growth away from the single-family-home subdivisions that tend to have the greatest returns on investment. Partly as a result, many municipalities were reluctant to implement the new intensification and density targets, and most – with the notable exception of the Waterloo Region – stuck with the minimum mandated densities that they could get away with under the new rules.[39]

A ten-year review of the growth plan issued in 2015 found some progress in terms of more compact growth, but called for stronger density and intensification requirements, as well as more provincial support to municipalities.[40] The Wynne government began to implement the recommended changes, but the election of the Conservatives in 2018 changed everything. Ideologically opposed to most growth restrictions and strongly aligned with the development industry, the Ford government moved quickly to undo the Liberals' "densification" policies. It began regularly using ministerial zoning orders (MZO) – which had rarely been used in the past – to exempt development proposals from local government planning regulations.[41] In 2022, it forced municipalities to set aside enough land to satisfy anticipated demand until the year 2051, ensuring that vast new development lands would be opened up,⁴² and it promised to build a major new highway, the 413, at the fringe of the GTA to support suburban growth in the area. It also opened up portions of the protected Greenbelt lands to property development, although it was forced to reverse this decision in September 2023, after a report by the provincial Auditor General found that most of the land in question belonged to developers who had lobbied Conservative appointees in the Ministry of Municipal Affairs and Housing.⁴³

The Ford government has justified its dismantling of GGH intensification policies by arguing that faster suburban development can ease the GTA's crisis of housing affordability. There is no doubt that this crisis exists. Housing prices have been growing faster than average incomes for many years, and the trend accelerated during the COVID-19 pandemic; the price of single-family homes in the GTA peaked in February 2022 at a whopping $1.86 million, beyond the reach of many middle-class families.⁴⁴ However, it is by no means clear that intensification policies – or, for that matter, a shortage of housing supply – have much to do with the housing crisis. In recent years, the housing units to population ratio in the GTA has actually improved.⁴⁵ What is clear is that the future of the provincial Liberals' big growth management experiment for suburban development in the GTA appears dim.

CONCLUSION: LOOKING TO THE FUTURE

The governance landscape of Toronto and the GTA has evolved significantly in recent decades. As we have seen, the ways in which the provincial government has engaged with the region and its needs have changed repeatedly over time, shaped by the ebb and flow of local demands, and the ideological inclinations and electoral calculus of different provincial governments. In the city of Toronto, the radical provincially imposed restructuring of the late 1990s gave way in the early 2000s to a sustained period of more collaborative provincial engagement under successive Liberal governments. While this style of engagement gave Toronto's local government substantial space to act autonomously, it did not always lead to effective solutions to key policy problems, as the torturous story of developing rapid transit infrastructure in the city of Toronto illustrates. Meanwhile, in the 905 region, ambitious Liberal plans to rein in suburban sprawl have faced implementation challenges, and are now being systematically dismantled by a Conservative government that champions market-led growth, and does not hesitate to resort to unilateral action with respect to local affairs.

As Ontario's globalized, multi-ethnic metropolis continues to grow, both local and provincial governments will be repeatedly challenged to develop policies that respond to complex and evolving urban needs: effective urban transportation, affordable housing, orderly and sustainable development, and social inclusion in the face of diversity and inequality. The Ontario provincial government cannot afford to ignore Toronto and the GTA. If the past is any guide to the future, however, provincial approaches to the evolving governance challenges of Toronto and the GTA will continue to be shaped as much by the dynamics of provincial politics as by the needs and demands of the area's local governments and their residents. For better or for worse, politics and governance in Toronto and the GTA are inextricably intertwined with the provincial politics of Ontario.

DISCUSSION QUESTIONS

1. Would Toronto and the GTA be better off if the provincial government intervened less in the region's governance?
2. What would you say is the most important policy challenge facing Toronto and the GTA at present? Justify your answer.
3. How have electoral considerations influenced the approach of provincial governments to Toronto and GTA issues since the early 1990s?
4. Should the province allow political parties in the City of Toronto? How might governance and leadership in Toronto change if this happened?

NOTES

1. Albert Rose, *Governing Metropolitan Toronto: A Social and Political Analysis, 1953–1971* (Berkeley: Institute of Governmental Studies), 164.
2. "Census Profile: 2021 Census," Statistics Canada, February 9, 2022, https://www12.statcan.gc.ca/census-recensement/2021/dp-pd/prof/index.cfm?Lang=E.
3. Statistics Canada, "Census Profile: 2021 Census."
4. David Hulchanski, *The Three Cities within Toronto: Income Polarization in Toronto's Neighborhoods, 1970–2005* (Toronto: Cities Centre, 2010), 6. Overall, the percentage of middle-income neighbourhoods in Toronto declined from 66 per cent in 1970 to 29 per cent in 2005.
5. Wendy Gillis, "'There Is Systemic Discrimination In Our Policing': New Toronto Police Data Confirms Officers Use More Force against Black People," *Toronto*

Star, June 15, 2022, https://www.thestar.com/news/gta/2022/06/15/officers-use-more-force-against-black-people-with-no-good-explanation-why-toronto-police-data.html.

6 A detailed account of the provincial government's role in governing the Toronto region in the twentieth century can be found in Frances Frisken, *The Public Metropolis: The Political Dynamics of Urban Expansion in the Toronto Region, 1924–2003* (Toronto: Canadian Scholars' Press, 2007). Zack Taylor's *Shaping the Metropolis: Institutions and Urbanization in the United States and Canada* (Montreal: McGill-Queen's University Press, 2019) places the same subject in a broader comparative and historical context.

7 Taylor, *Shaping the Metropolis*, chap. 7.

8 Taylor, 122–3.

9 For a detailed account of McCallion's remarkable career, see Tom Urbaniak, *Her Worship: Hazel McCallion and the Development of Mississauga* (Toronto: University of Toronto Press, 2009).

10 For a summary, see Martin Horak, "The Power of Local Identity: C4LD and the Anti-Amalgamation Mobilization in Toronto," *Research Paper 195* (Toronto: Centre for Urban and Community Studies, 1998).

11 Horak, "The Power of Local Identity," 35.

12 Myer Siemiatycki, "Governing Immigrant City: Immigrant Political Representation in Toronto," *American Behavioral Scientist* 55, no. 9 (September 2011): 1214–34, https://doi.org/10.1177/0002764211407840.

13 Martin Horak and Marilyn Dantico, "The Limits of Local Redistribution: Neighborhood Regeneration Initiatives in Toronto and Phoenix," *International Journal of Canadian Studies* 49 (January 2014): 135–58, https://doi.org/10.3138/ijcs.49.135.

14 "King Street Transit Priority Corridor," City of Toronto, 2020, accessed January 10, 2024, https://www.toronto.ca/city-government/planning-development/planning-studies-initiatives/king-street-pilot/.

15 Aaron A. Moore, "Trading Density for Benefits: Toronto and Vancouver Compared," in *IMFG Papers on Municipal Finance and Governance,* no. 13 (Toronto: Institute on Finance and Governance, 2013).

16 Jan Doering, Daniel Silver, and Zack Taylor, "The Spatial Articulation of Urban Political Cleavages," *Urban Affairs Review* 57, no. 4 (July 2021): 911–51, https://doi.org/10.1177/1078087420940789.

17 Christie Blatchford, "383,501 People Voted For Rob Ford – Not One Voted for the Men Behind His Ouster," *National Post*, November 26, 2012, https://nationalpost.com/opinion/rob-ford-christie-blatchford.

18 John Lorinc, "This Fall's Election Shouldn't be a Victory Lap," *Spacing Magazine*, June 27, 2022, http://spacing.ca/toronto/2022/06/27/lorinc-this-falls-election-shouldnt-be-a-victory-lap/.

19 City of Toronto, "Consolidated Financial Statements," December 30, 2021, https://www.toronto.ca/legdocs/mmis/2022/au/bgrd/backgroundfile-227976.pdf.

20 David A. Armstrong, Jack Lucas, and Zack Taylor, "The Urban-Rural Divide in Canadian Federal Elections, 1896–2019," *Canadian Journal of Political Science*

/*Revue canadienne de science politique* 55, no. 1 (March 2022): 84–106, https://doi.org/10.1017/S0008423921000792.
21. See Kristin R. Good, *Municipalities and Multiculturalism: The Politics of Immigration in Toronto and Vancouver* (Toronto: University of Toronto Press, 2009), 270–1.
22. Horak and Dantico, "The Limits of Local Redistribution."
23. Mike Crawley, "Why Kathleen Wynne Put the Brakes on Gardiner, DVP Tolls," *CBC News*, January 27, 2017, https://www.cbc.ca/news/canada/toronto/kathleen-wynne-john-tory-road-tolls-gardiner-dvp-1.3955264.
24. Robert Benzie, "Ford to Slash Toronto City Council to 25 Councillors from 47, Sources Say," *Toronto Star*, July 27, 2018, https://www.thestar.com/politics/provincial/ford-to-slash-toronto-city-council-to-25-councillors-from-47-sources-say/article_8d99a5f5-caeb-58d2-a6eb-1db261560a02.html.
25. Kristin R. Good, "The Fallacy of the 'Creatures of the Provinces' Doctrine: Recognizing and Protecting Municipalities' Constitutional Status," in *IMFG Papers on Municipal Finance and Governance*, no. 46 (Toronto: Institute on Municipal Finance and Governance, 2019).
26. Canadian Press, "Supreme Court Rules Doug Ford's Slashing of Toronto City Council in 2018 Was Constitutional," *National Post*, October 1, 2021, https://nationalpost.com/news/politics/newsalert-supreme-court-upholds-ontario-law-that-slashed-toronto-council.
27. Zack Taylor and Martin Horak, "Strong Mayor Powers in Ontario Are a Gross Violation of Democratic Principles," *Policy Options*, December 16, 2022, https://policyoptions.irpp.org/magazines/december-2022/strong-mayor-powers-in-ontario-are-a-gross-violation-of-democratic-principles/.
28. Adam Carter, "Ontario Abandoning Plans to Dissolve Peel Region," *CBC News*, December 13, 2023, https://www.cbc.ca/news/canada/toronto/peel-region-paul-calandra-1.7057628.
29. Government of Ontario, *Metrolinx Act, 2006*, S.O. 2006, c. 16.
30. Tess Kalinowski, "A $17.5B Transit Promise," *Toronto Star*, June 16, 2007, A6.
31. Metrolinx, *2021–2022 Metrolinx Business Plan* (Toronto: Metrolinx, 2021), https://assets.metrolinx.com/image/upload/v1663232126/Documents/Metrolinx/2021-22-Business-Plan-Final-English-Version.pdf.
32. John Lorinc, "Doug Ford Draws a Subway Map," *Spacing Magazine*, April 11, 2019, https://spacing.ca/toronto/2019/04/11/lorinc-doug-ford-draws-a-subway-map/.
33. Shawn Jeffords, "Ontario Drops Plan to Upload Toronto Subway as City Supports Ford Plan for 'Ontario Line,'" *National Post*, October 16, 2019, https://nationalpost.com/news/canada/ontario-drops-plan-to-upload-toronto-subway.
34. Ben Spurr, "Ottawa to Kick in More Than $10 Billion to Help Fund Doug Ford's Toronto Transit Plans," *Toronto Star*, May 11, 2021, https://www.thestar.com/news/gta/ottawa-to-kick-in-more-than-10-billion-to-help-fund-doug-ford-s-toronto/article_0af89260-ee89-5535-beea-4c88b38a0069.html.
35. Muriel Draaisma, "Ontario Premier Says Construction Underway on New Toronto Subway Line," *CBC News*, March 27, 2022, https://www.cbc.ca/news

/canada/toronto/ontario-line-official-breaking-ceremony-toronto-doug-ford-john-tory-1.6399282.
36 Taylor, *Shaping the Metropolis*, 120–4.
37 Gabriel Eidelman, "Managing Urban Sprawl in Ontario: Good Policy or Good Politics?," *Politics & Policy* 38, no. 6 (December 2010): 1211–36, https://doi.org/10.1111/j.1747-1346.2010.00275.x.
38 Eidelman, "Managing Urban Sprawl," 1212.
39 Neptis Foundation, *Understanding the Fundamentals of the Growth Plan* (Toronto: Neptis Foundation, March 2015), 19, https://neptis.org/publications/understanding-fundamentals-growth-plan.
40 Advisory Panel on the Coordinated Review of the Growth Plan, *Planning for Health, Prosperity and Growth* (Toronto: Queen's Printer for Ontario, December 2015), http://ossga.com/multimedia/0/planning_for_health_prosperity_and_growth_-_expert_panel_report.pdf.
41 Star Editorial Board, "Ford's Change to Development Rules is a Massive Overreach," *Toronto Star*, March 8, 2021, https://www.thestar.com/opinion/editorials/ford-s-change-to-development-rules-is-a-massive-overreach/article_0c596f50-6df1-5cae-aec3-238292146b30.html.
42 Noor Javed, "How 'No Sprawl' Groups are Defying Doug Ford's Toronto Area Development Plan," *Toronto Star*, March 25, 2022, https://www.thestar.com/news/gta/how-no-sprawl-groups-are-defying-doug-ford-s-toronto-area-development-plan/article_80708688-587a-5a70-bc0d-60b0b516c451.html.
43 The Canadian Press, "A Timeline of Key Events in Ontario's Greenbelt Controversy," *CBC News*, September 21, 2023, https://www.cbc.ca/news/canada/toronto/ont-greenbelt-timeline-1.6974715.
44 "GTA New Home Benchmark Price Hits a Record $1.86M," *Storeys Magazine*, March 23, 2022, https://storeys.com/gta-new-home-price-benchmark-february-2022/.
45 Brian Doucet, "Ontario's 'Affordable Housing' Task Force Does Not Address the Real Problems," *The Conversation*, February 10, 2022, https://theconversation.com/ontarios-affordable-housing-task-force-report-does-not-address-the-real-problems-176869.

17

Ontario Health Policy and Politics

Raisa B. Deber and Gregory P. Marchildon

INTRODUCTION TO HEALTH POLICY AND POLITICS IN ONTARIO

As one of the most consistently salient issues in Canadian politics, health care has been a charged and high-profile issue in electoral campaigns. In Ontario, opposition political parties have regularly criticized incumbent governments for their management of public health care and, especially, their health system reforms. During successive Liberal administrations under Premiers Dalton McGuinty (2003–13) and Kathleen Wynne (2013–18), major changes were initiated to improve primary care through new models of primary care, better coordinate health services on a regional basis through Local Health Integration Networks (LHINs), and improve access to prescription drug therapies through expanded public coverage. With the exception of primary care, these reforms were criticized by the Progressive Conservatives (PC) in the election of 2018, and then rapidly reversed by the newly elected PC government under Premier Doug Ford.

Instead, the Ford government has been modifying how care is organized. As noted below, the PC government has established Ontario Health, a single provincial health authority that took on the responsibilities of the LHINs as well as a half-dozen previously separate health agencies and is seeking to improve coordination at the level of patient care through establishing Ontario Health Teams. Before these reforms could be fully (or even partially) implemented, however, the COVID-19 pandemic produced an unexpected crisis which siphoned off scarce resources and revealed some of the weaknesses (as well as strengths) of the Ontario health system.

HEALTH CARE SYSTEMS

Analyzing health care systems involves considering many underlying factors, including how health care is financed, how it is delivered, and the distinction between public and private.[1] In addition, there are some features common to all provincial health systems, including the Ontario health system, within the Canadian federation. In this section, we review these common features.

The term "public" refers to government, but can refer to the national (federal), provincial/territorial, or local/municipal levels of government. "Private" can include corporate for-profit organizations (which seek to maximize profits), not-only-for-profit entities such as physician practices (which rely on profits to pay their bills but are also bound by ethical considerations) and not-for-profit enterprises, including the majority of hospital corporations in Ontario as well as individuals and their families, who may provide considerable unpaid care to vulnerable populations. Ontario Health is a delegated public authority, while the Ontario Health Teams are coalitions of not-for-profit enterprises and not-only-for-profit physician practices. Combining the public/private and financing/delivery dimensions leads to four potential care models, of which the following three are commonly found in health care: public financing-public delivery, public financing-private delivery, and private financing-private delivery.

In Canada, about 70 per cent of health care is publicly financed, but it is almost entirely privately delivered, although this varies considerably by the type of care. For example, almost all public health activities (which focus on disease prevention and detecting and responding to public health threats, including infectious disease outbreaks) are financed by governments and publicly delivered, since public health units are part of government. However, the public financing-private delivery model captures all medically necessary care delivered to insured persons (defined as legal residents of that province/territory) in hospitals or by physicians, because, for historical reasons, these services must be fully insured by the public payer. Other health care services may be publicly insured, but they are not required to be, and coverage can vary by location (the province or territory of residence) and personal factors (including age, income, and type of illness). Many other services, including most outpatient pharmaceuticals and much of mental health care, are privately financed and privately delivered.

FEDERALISM AND MEDICARE IN ONTARIO

Under Canada's constitution, most health care is deemed to be a provincial/territorial responsibility although the federal government has used its spending power to establish some national standards under the *Canada Health Act* for hospital, diagnostic, and medical care services that must be fully covered by provincial and territorial health insurance plans (which are called Medicare). In Ontario, this single-payer (funded solely by government) Medicare plan is called the Ontario Health Insurance Program (OHIP). To avoid deductions from its per capita share of the Canada Health Transfer (CHT), the Ontario government must ensure OHIP coverage is universal, portable, and not subject to physician extra-billing or hospital or other facility user charges on patients at the point of service.

Serving a population of almost 15 million residents (about 39 per cent of the Canadian population), the Ontario health system is the largest in the country. As the steward of much of this health system, the Ontario minister of health has the same scale and scope of responsibility as many national ministers of health in high-income countries. Supported by an extensive department and public servants with expertise in dozens of highly specialized areas as well as Ontario Health, a delegated health authority responsible for coordinating a variety of services throughout the province, the health minister is responsible for the overall effectiveness of the health system. However, any major shifts in policy or changes in the health system structure are not made by the minister alone. Often, they involve the full cabinet, with the premier playing a central role.[2]

All OHIP-funded services are financed through provincial tax revenues, and a federal contribution to the province through the Canada Health Transfer. In addition, the Ontario government provides targeted (non-universal) coverage for some recipients of long-term care, home care, outpatient prescription drugs, and other targeted health services. In fiscal year 2021–2, the Government of Ontario budgeted for a total of a total of $149 billion in operating expenses, of which $62.6 billion was allocated to the Ministry of Health (MoH), and another $6.4 billion to the Ministry of Long-Term Care.[3] This combined health and long-term care budget of $69 billion amounted to over 46 per cent of provincial operating expenses, dwarfing the next two largest spending envelopes of education ($28.7 billion) and social services (almost $18 billion). Because of the implementation of tax points as a portion of federal transfers to provinces under the Established Programs Financing in 1977,[4] which are no longer included as part of the federal transfer, most of this contribution comes from the Ontario government; the federal contribution for 2021–2 of $16.7 billion, including a one-time COVID-19 top-up of almost $1.6 billion, amounted to 24.2 per cent of the MoH's budget.[5]

Ontario's *Health Insurance Act* defines "insured services" as the "prescribed services of hospitals and health facilities" and the "prescribed medically necessary services rendered by physicians" as well as the "prescribed health care services rendered by prescribed practitioners."[6] To comply with the *Canada Health Act*, these physician services must be provided at no cost to Ontario residents. One result was that the practice of extra-billing by physicians, which had been relatively common in Ontario in the early decades of Medicare was largely eliminated within two years after the passage of the *Canada Health Act* in 1984. In 1986, the Ontario government introduced a bill requiring that doctors discontinue the practice of extra-billing in order to comply with federal requirements and get reimbursed the full amount that the Government of Canada had deducted from Ontario's share of the federal health transfer. This bill precipitated a twenty-five-day province-wide physician strike. However, without widespread public support, the Ontario Medical Association (OMA) ultimately failed in its bid to get the government to withdraw the bill.[7] There have been several confrontations between the OMA and the provincial governments since that time, but they have mainly involved the fee schedule and working conditions rather than the issue of extra-billing, avoiding a potential conflict between the Ontario government and the federal government.

The coverage model requires that hospital and medical care be provided free at the point of service for all residents with a OHIP card. OHIP coverage includes almost all diagnostic services, inpatient drugs, and most types of primary care provided by physicians; although not required by federal law, at the time of writing, it also includes primary care delivered by nurse practitioners as well as registered nurses in northern clinics. OHIP also covers some other services, such as optometry services, including one major eye exam every twelve months.[8]

Hospitals are managed almost entirely by private not-for-profit hospital corporations – a feature that differentiates Ontario from other provinces, which have shifted to models in which most hospitals have been owned and managed by government-delegated health authorities and agencies since the 1990s. Hospitals were funded largely through global budgets; these funds are provided by the provincial government (under the direction of the MoH) through Ontario Health. They can also receive some funds from charitable donations; these are used mainly for capital expansion and renewal as well as to support hospital-based research initiatives. However, this funding model has been undergoing major change in recent years.

In 2019, inspired by accountable care organizations and the pursuit of more integrated care in the United States,[9] the Ford government has begun to adopt a new approach in which hospitals have become key partners with a broad range of other providers and health organizations in newly established Ontario Health Teams (OHTs). Allocated provincial funding as a group, OHTs take responsibility for coordinating and delivering services to their patients across the continuum of care. In addition to hospital care, OHTs are responsible for a comprehensive range of services, including primary care, rehabilitative care, home and community care, residential long-term care, and mental health and addictions. Emphasis is placed on improving communication and care coordination across the team, as well as driving performance improvement through better data standardization across the network.[10] This reform, unique in Canada but slowed down due to the COVID-19 pandemic, is still in its early stages and has not yet been comprehensively evaluated. Its exact management is also unclear, particularly how tertiary and quaternary care will fit into the new model.

MIXED AND PRIVATELY FINANCED HEALTH SECTORS

The *Canada Health Act* (CHA) is a floor rather than a ceiling for universal coverage, and as noted above, the Government of Ontario has chosen to fund some services beyond those defined by the CHA as "insured services." However, for the most part, these are not provided universally, and often involve co-payments. This coverage is not part of OHIP, but largely provided through separate provincial programs, often targeting specified groups within the population. Several programs cover a portion of pharmaceutical costs for selected populations. For example, the Ontario Drug Benefit program covers a significant share of drug costs for all those with OHIP coverage who are over age sixty-five, subject to deductibles and co-payments. OHIP+ covers those under the age of twenty-four who do not have private insurance coverage for a specified list of drugs.[11] The Trillium Drug Program assists residents with very high drug costs who do not have other private or provincial health coverage.

Another mixed sector is long-term care (LTC), which can be delivered in regulated LTC homes, retirement homes, or the recipient's home. The Ontario government funds some of the costs of nursing care for high-needs patients in provincially licensed long-term care homes, although residents with the requisite means are charged for a portion of their room and board. Due to long waiting lists for publicly subsidized LTC homes, Ontario residents with the ability to pay often obtain care in non-subsidized retirement homes.[12] If they meet the necessary criteria, Ontario residents can receive subsidized home care services which provide some long-term care support in the community.[13]

Dental services are almost entirely privately funded, unless they are performed in a hospital as dental surgical services, which are a fully insured service under the CHA and OHIP. Mental health is another largely neglected area. Services are covered by OHIP if delivered by a psychiatrist or general practitioner, but not if provided by psychologists or other therapists, although some of this may be covered by private insurance. (One reason for the neglect is that when Medicare was established, it was assumed that mental health services would be provided through admission to psychiatric hospitals.) Ontario Health has highlighted improvement of mental health and addiction programs as one of their priorities.

CHANGE AGENDA: IMPROVE INTEGRATION AND COORDINATION?

The differences between universal public coverage and the areas in which coverage is mixed (part public and part private) or predominantly private can produce inappropriate incentives for both providers and patients as well as sub-optimal results for patients. As one example, non-physician services such as pharmaceuticals and rehabilitation were required to be fully publicly funded if a patient was in hospital, but not if they were discharged to another setting. The results could be cost-ineffective if patients could not afford their medications unless they were hospitalized, and so they became more sick until the point that they required admission to hospital, but it did allow governments to shift costs to the private sector. While much of the policy debate focuses on service coordination, trying to determine how to ensure that providers work together so that patients do not fall through the cracks, the problem is more profoundly one of health financing structures.

Most provinces sought to develop mechanisms to encourage coordination of services, usually on a regional basis (although recognizing that there might not be sufficient patient volume to provide certain highly specialized services in every region).[14] As noted above, one approach, taken in all provinces other than Ontario in the 1990s, was to shift hospitals from private not-for-profit organizations (which had had independent boards) into being part of regional or provincial health authorities. Ontario did allow hospitals to remain somewhat independent, and retain their own boards. However, it had previously used a variety of approaches, including seven regional offices which funded and monitored providers, and a group of sixteen advisory bodies known as District Health Councils to try and coordinate care on a voluntary basis including acute care within geographic zones. This largely voluntary approach changed when the *Local Health System Integration Act, 2006* was passed. The fourteen geographically based Local Health Integration Units (LHINs) were given a mandate to plan and fund the publicly funded services in six sectors: hospitals, long-term care homes, home care (which had formerly been managed by Community Care Access Centres – CCACs), community mental health and addiction agencies, community support service agencies, and Community Health Centres (which are described below under primary care models). However, responsibility for physician services and laboratory services was not transferred to the LHINs; neither was public health, although it was also managed at the municipal or regional level through local public health units. Accordingly, the LHINs were responsible for about half of the provincial health-care budget. They differed from the regional health models in other provinces in that they worked with, rather than replacing, the organizations providing these services; as the Auditor General Report of 2015 noted, "LHINs neither directly govern nor provide health services: all of the health-care providers, such as hospitals and long-term care homes, still maintain their own boards of directors."[15] Almost all LHIN funding went directly to the providers. However, LHINs did devote considerable attention to community engagement to identify local priorities and to accountability arrangements with the province to try to assess performance.

In the provincial election campaign of 2018, the PC Party of Ontario, under its leader Doug Ford, said it would eliminate the LHINs as an unnecessary layer of bureaucracy. After successfully defeating the incumbent Liberal government, the Ford Conservatives did so, through several pieces of legislation. One consolidated the LHINs down to six new Ontario Health regions, which took on the old LHIN functions. Another reform was to set up a new provincial agency, called Ontario Health.[16] This incorporated several previously separate organizations, some of which were responsible for service provision, and others for helping to monitor and assess aspects of the provincial health system. The organizations folded into Ontario Health included Cancer Care Ontario (which is responsible for monitoring cancer care programs and outcomes, as well as funding regional cancer programs to provide cancer prevention, screening, diagnostic, treatment, and support services, many located within specified hospitals); eHealth Ontario (which is responsible for creating a secure electronic health record information system); HealthForceOntario Marketing and Recruitment Agency (which attempts to link health care professionals, including foreign-trained providers, to available jobs); Ontario Health Quality Council (which seeks to develop quality standards and report to the public on how well the system is performing); Health Shared Services Ontario (which tries to provide shared services to local providers, including the LHINs); Ontario Telemedicine Network; Trillium Gift of Life Network (which coordinates organ donation); and CorHealth Ontario (formerly the Cardiac Care Network of Ontario and the Ontario Stroke Network). However, almost all the agencies that have been incorporated into Ontario Health note on their web pages that their functions and activities have not changed.

A subsequent associated reform has been to establish Ontario Health Teams (OHTs), which are defined as "groups of providers and organizations that, at maturity, will be clinically and fiscally accountable for delivering a full and coordinated continuum of care to a defined population."[17] The process is still being developed, but the expectations are that the coordinated services will include primary care and secondary care, as well as varying combinations of home care, community support services, mental health and addictions services, health promotion and disease prevention services, rehabilitation and complex care, palliative care, residential care, long-term care home placement, emergency health services, laboratory and diagnostic services, midwifery services, and other services as needed. Those desiring to form OHTs must apply to the Ontario Ministry of Health; the first approved cohort of twenty-four was announced in the fall of 2019, and as of February 10, 2022, the MoH had approved fifty-one.[18] The expectations are that each Ontario Health Team would receive prospective funding for their "attributed patient population" and that funding would follow the patients. The precise nature of how care will be organized and delivered is still unclear. From what has been published, this reform assumes that people will still select their care provider but does not clarify what would happen if a patient would need (or seek) care from providers outside of their Ontario Health Team. It appears that a number of select low-volume, high-cost procedures would continue to be overseen and funded provincially rather than through the Health Teams.

A major problem arising during the COVID-19 pandemic was that hospitals often could not manage their increased patient load. This was influenced by a variety of factors, including more patients with COVID-19 arriving at hospital emergency rooms, staff shortages related to outbreaks of COVID-19 and staff leaving due to burnout, and difficulties in discharging alternate level of care (ALC) patients from hospitals. ALC refers to those still occupying an acute hospital bed, but who no longer require the intensity of services that would be provided in that care setting; many (although not all) were frail elderly persons. However, once discharged, many of the costs that would be covered in the hospital for services provided by non-physicians are no longer required to be publicly covered, including nursing care, rehab, and pharmaceuticals, which gave incentives for those patients to remain in hospital. This crisis accordingly accentuated some of the problems with the public-private mix. The Ontario government has suggested a number of possible interventions. One is to encourage greater use of private clinics to provide care outside of hospitals and reduce the volume of care hospitals would need to provide, although as noted this could also involve charging patients (or their private insurers) for many of those services. The Ford government has talked about encouraging this option, and allowing for-profit clinics to perform much of this care, but this in turn has aroused opposition to those objecting to increasing the role of the private for-profit sector. If this option is pursued vigorously over the next few years, it could tip the public-private balance towards for-profit enterprise in the health system. Another option was to pass legislation allowing hospitals to send ALC patients to LTC settings (again, potentially at considerable cost to the patients and their families), regardless of whether they had consented.[19]

PRIMARY CARE MODELS

As an individual's first point of contact with the health system, primary care has long been considered critical to high-performing health systems. Governments in Canada therefore have expended considerable effort and resources to reform primary care to improve the quality of care, the continuity and coordination of care across health sectors, enhance access, address chronic care needs, and encourage more appropriate and less costly care through multi-professional teams. More than any other provincial government, Ontario has experimented with many different models of primary care over time, but all with the objective of improving patient access, the coordination of health services, and, most of all, the quality of care at what is generally the Ontario resident's first point of contact with the provincial health system.[20]

The traditional approach to primary care, as in most provinces, was for family physicians to operate as solo practitioners and be remunerated on a fee-for-service basis based on the negotiated fee schedule, although some might share overhead expenses with other physicians practicing in the same clinic location An early reform, first introduced in Ontario in the 1970s, were Community Health Centres (CHCs) with salaried physicians serving mainly lower-income and marginalized populations; there were about one hundred CHCs at that time. Between 2002 and 2007, seven other models of primary care practice were introduced in Ontario, which focused on team-based models; these could relieve the pressure on individual providers and make it easier for patients to receive care even if their own physicians were not available. The reimbursement models varied. Most of these relied on rostering, meaning that patients would register with a family practice (which could range from an individual provider to a team) and thereby commit to seeking treatment from that provider unless it was an emergency situation. These new models reimbursed providers using various combinations of fee-for-service, capitation, pay-for-performance, and salary. The most far-reaching in terms of changes to payment and practice was the Family Health Team, an interprofessional team practice which received much of its income through capitation (although if the income went to the full team, some of the team members would be paid by salaries), and who were also expected to provide after-hours service as required to rostered patients.[21] However, the capitation model provided incentives to encourage enrolling high-needs patients, who would require more care.

Although subsequent government administrations, including the Ford government, have curtailed the growth of Family Health Teams to contain costs, this model of primary care comes closest to meeting the six criteria for effective primary care reform identified in a pan-Canadian survey.[22] Most of the existing Family Health Teams, along with the providers who participate in other primary care models, are now partners in the newly formed

Ontario Health Teams. However, it remains to be seen whether the recent OHT reform will enhance or reduce the role of primary care in the provincial health system.

LONG-TERM CARE AND THE IMPACT OF COVID-19

Ontario had a variety of what it termed Home and Community Care Support Services organizations. For the most part, the provincial government was not heavily involved in funding these services (many of which do not fall into the category of care that must be publicly funded under the *Canada Health Act* requirements). Instead, they were considered to be a point of access for home and community care services, with responsibilities for assessing need, determining eligibility, and providing and arranging for home care services, school health services for children, and admissions to long-term care homes.[23] On April 1, 2021, these functions transferred from LHINs to Ontario Health.

Long-term care is complex. "LTC is defined as the services needed to meet a vulnerable person's health or personal care needs when they can no longer perform everyday activities on their own."[24] As such, it includes a variety of services that can be provided in a variety of settings by a variety of caregivers. The caregivers may include unpaid family members and friends but also paid workers. The services may include combinations of personal care "activities of daily living" (e.g., bathing, dressing, eating, mobility, taking medications), homemaker services (e.g., meals, transportation), home health care (e.g., nursing care to help a person recover from surgery or illness), and physical, occupational, or speech therapy. The settings where these services may be provided can include the hospital (if alternative locations are not available), the person's home, adult day care centres, retirement homes, and/or nursing homes. It is the latter facilities that are most often equated with LTC.

As noted above, it is important to note that most LTC services (except for medically necessary services delivered in hospitals or by physicians) do not fall under the terms of the *Canada Health Act*. As such, there is no requirement for these services to be publicly paid for in Canada, although some provinces do choose to do so for some services for some populations.[25]

In Ontario, regulated LTC facilities are designed for those with the most severe needs. Although they are subsidized by the province to cover such costs as staffing, residents must pay towards the costs of accommodations.

There is also a long waiting list. As such, many of those needing care are living in other unregulated settings.

COVID-19 made it clear that there were some major problems in the LTC facilities in Ontario. In the initial outbreak, a high proportion of COVID-19 deaths occurred in these homes. The weaknesses in the Ontario LTC system highlighted by the pandemic include the training, payment, and deployment of health human resources, chronic staffing shortages, the physical structures of the homes, and how standards were set and enforced by the provincial government.[26] This was confirmed by a report from the Canadian Armed Forces, which had been asked in April 2020 to assist several homes facing uncontrolled COVID-19 outbreaks and high death rates. In the damning report, the Canadian military medical team observed how these homes were not meeting provincial standards, and outlined the urgent need for corrective action.[27] This crisis also brought attention to the question of how long-term care needs should be managed, and the extent to which more public resources should be allocated to such services, especially in the context of facility-based LTC.

PUBLIC HEALTH

Public health involves efforts to protect and promote health, preferably by preventing disease. It includes a variety of activities, including performing research, educating people about risks, tracking disease outbreaks, setting safety standards to prevent injuries, and performing or encouraging vaccinations to prevent the spread of disease. Depending on the jurisdiction, these functions are given to different organizations. For example, public health may include efforts to ensure clean air and water, food and restaurant inspections, providing access to healthy foods, and epidemiological analyses of diseases, as well as vaccinations.

COVID-19 also highlighted issues relating to how public health is organized. Ontario has delegated responsibility for public health to thirty-four local Public Health Units, unlike other provinces where public health activities, including contagious disease monitoring and surveillance, are more centralized. These local public health units are governed by autonomous boards of health (largely composed of elected representatives from the local municipal councils for that region), and administered by a local medical officer of health. These health units are responsible for a variety of health promotion and disease prevention activities. Their costs are shared between the provincial and municipal governments.[28] Having the responsibility for public health at the local level made it relatively difficult to coordinate responses, and to ensure that accurate data was being collected. Although Canada's response to the pandemic was relatively good compared to peer countries,[29] there was clearly considerable room for improvement. An ongoing question will be the extent to which better coordination across local health units can be implemented, including whether such coordination can occur across provincial/territorial boundaries.

EMERGING INDIGENOUS HEALTH SYSTEMS

Indigenous self-government has emerged as one of the most noteworthy trends in the Canadian polity in recent decades. Associated with this shift, Indigenous-controlled health services have expanded to address health inequities often linked to interpersonal and systemic racism and to restore Indigenous healing traditions and practices. This is consistent with the Truth and Reconciliation Commission of Canada, which has called on federal, provincial and territorial governments "to acknowledge that the current state of Aboriginal health in Canada is a direct result of previous Canadian government policies, including residential schools, and to recognize and implement the health-care rights of Aboriginal people as identified in international law, constitutional law, and under the Treaties."[30]

In Ontario, this shift has been ongoing for decades. It is reflected in the 1990 establishment of the Sioux Lookout First Nations Health Authority, which administers primary and mental health services, including medical transportation, for a population of roughly 25,000 residents in thirty-three Anishinaabe communities. Seven years later, hospital services were added when the Sioux Lookout Meno Ya Min Health Centre began operating a sixty-bed hospital facility. More recently, in 2007, the Indigenous-controlled Weeneebayko Area Health Authority began operating the Weeneebayko General Hospital in Moosonee, which services Moose Factory and four other First Nations communities on the west coast of James and Hudson's Bay.[31] It is unclear at the time of writing whether this trend towards greater Indigenous control over health services, including fully insured OHIP services, will be enhanced or diminished through the Ontario Health Team reform.

2022 ELECTION AND THE FUTURE OF HEALTH SYSTEM CHANGE

Health care, in particular investing in health services, was a priority for Ontario voters in the 2022 provincial election, in large part because of the strain on resources as a result of COVID-19. Possibly due to the importance placed on health care by residents, the Progressive Conservative platform in the election, reflected in the proposed 2022 provincial budget tabled but not enacted prior to the election, promised to invest more money in hospitals ($40 billion in capital over ten years and the addition of three thousand new beds), diagnostic services, long-term care homes and home care, and Ontario's health-care workforce, including bonuses to keep nurses in the workforce. The budget also suggested that it would address wait times by providing more money for additional elective surgeries and urgent procedures. It also proposed to expand Ontario's Health Care Workforce, and to shore up domestic production of critical supplies to ensure that Ontario would be prepared for future emergencies.[32]

The Ford government was re-elected in 2022 on an election platform that, by focusing on institutional care, marginalized primary care reform as an issue. Instead, the emphasis appears to be on shoring up hospital, diagnostic, and physician services, the core elements of Medicare, and encouraging the availability of services outside of hospitals, including a debate about the potential role of private for-profit delivery. In May 2023, the government passed a health reform bill to allow more for-profit private clinics to offer selected surgeries for cataracts, hip and knee replacements, and diagnostic imaging and testing. Although the Ford government described it as part of its plan to reduce the pandemic backlog and reduce wait times, others suggested that it might be a way to shift costs and revenues to private for-profit providers, who would be able to charge for services that would have been fully covered if provided in hospitals. In response, the nurse organizations in the province have organized a campaign against what they consider a major threat to public health care, and hospitals have expressed their concerns about losing key staff to private clinics.

CONCLUSION

This chapter has explored the organization of health care, and some ongoing issues in how it will be designed and managed. Ontario has embarked on several reforms, whose impact is still unclear.

The COVID-19 crisis that began in early 2020 highlighted other long-standing challenges, particularly about service availability in more rural/remote communities, which has been aggravated by burnout among health care providers.

The pandemic also highlighted issues related to the limitations of a provincially (and regionally) based model. Accessing care has always been problematic for those living in rural/remote areas, particularly when they require specialized services. The increased use of virtual care to avoid the need for face-to-face meetings gives rise to questions about how such models should be used after the pandemic, including what fees should be paid to physicians for providing virtual compared to in-person care. There has been increased use of virtual care provided by private for-profit corporations to Ontario residents without a regular family doctor, which charged them for some of that care, and accordingly may have violated at least some provisions of the *Canada Health Act*.[33] A connected issue is that, under the Canadian model, health professionals must be licensed in the province where they treat their patients. This limits the ability to use virtual care beyond provincial borders. There has accordingly been discussion about whether mechanisms should be introduced to allow health care professionals to be licensed more easily in multiple provinces, and to provide billing numbers for non-resident physicians providing such services. Similarly, public health has found it difficult to coordinate and share information across boundaries.

The health care glass in Ontario can be seen as half full, or half empty. There is good public coverage for certain services (including hospital and physician services), although there are also workforce issues in ensuring that there will be enough providers over the next years. In addition, as the population ages, it is expected that health care costs will increase, particularly if the workforce (and their remuneration) is increased. As migrants entered the country, there was debate about the extent to which they should be eligible for coverage. There are also ongoing debates about what should be publicly covered, and what should not be. Disputes between the federal and provincial governments about how much money should be provided from the federal government, and what strings should be attached, are ongoing, and likely to continue, although Premier Doug Ford himself has taken a more conciliatory approach to Ottawa recently relative to his first years in office. Nonetheless, at least based on measures of access and outcomes, Ontario's health care system works relatively well when compared to other provincial governments and, especially, its neighbouring jurisdiction to the south.[34]

DISCUSSION QUESTIONS

1 What are the most important reforms now needed to improve the health care system in Ontario?
2 What respective roles should the Ontario and federal governments play in managing health care?
3 What are the potential strengths and weaknesses of Ontario Health Teams for delivering care?
4 To what extent should health care be organized and delivered on a regional (geographic) basis in Ontario?

NOTES

1 Raisa Deber, *Treating Health Care: How the Canadian System Works and How It Could Work Better* (Toronto: University of Toronto Press, 2018); Raisa B. Deber, "Delivering Health Care Services: Public, Not-for-Profit, or Private?," in *The Fiscal Sustainability of Health Care in Canada: Romanow Papers*, vol. 1, ed. Gregory P. Marchildon, Tom McIntosh, and Pierre-Gerlier Forest (Toronto: University of Toronto Press, 2004), 233–96.
2 Ted Glenn, "Politics, Personality and History in Ontario's Administrative Style," in *Executive Styles in Canada: Cabinet Structures and Leadership Practices in Canadian Government*, ed. Luc Bernier, Keith Brownsey, and Michael Howlett (Toronto: University of Toronto Press, 2005), 155–70; Graham White, "The Interpersonal Dynamics of Decision Making in Canadian Provincial Cabinets," in *Cabinet Ministers and Parliamentary Government*, ed. Michael Laver and Kenneth Shepsle (New York: Cambridge University Press, 1994), 251–69.
3 "Summary Table 1 – Operating (2021–22)," Government of Ontario, accessed July 4, 2022, https://www.ontario.ca/page/summary-table-1-operating-2021-22.
4 Odette Madore, *The Transfer of Tax Points to Provinces Under the Canada Health and Social Transfer* (Ottawa: Government of Canada, Library of Parliament, Research Branch, Economics Division, 1997), https://publications.gc.ca/Collection-R/LoPBdP/BP/bp450-e.htm.
5 Government of Canada, "Federal Transfers to Provinces and Territories," accessed July 4, 2022, https://www.canada.ca/en/department-finance/programs/federal-transfers/major-federal-transfers.html#Ontario.
6 Government of Ontario, *Health Insurance Act*, R.S.O. 1990, c. H.6, https://www.ontario.ca/laws/statute/90h06.
7 S. Heiber, and R. Deber, "Banning Extra-Billing in Canada: Just What the Doctor Didn't Order," *Canadian Public Policy/Analyse de politiques* 13, no. 1 (March 1987): 62–74, https://doi.org/10.2307/3550545; H. Stevenson, A. Michael, Paul Williams, and Eugene Vayda, "Medical Politics and Canadian Medicare:

Professional Response to the Canada Health Act," *The Milbank Quarterly* 66, no. 1 (1988): 65–104, https://doi.org/10.2307/3349986.
8. "What OHIP Covers," Government of Ontario, accessed July 4, 2022, https://www.ontario.ca/page/what-ohip-covers.
9. Allie Peckham, David Rudoler, Dominika Bhatia, Sara Allin, Reham Abdelhalim, and Gregory P. Marchildon, "What Can Canada Learn from Accountable Care Organizations: A Comparative Policy Analysis," *International Journal of Integrated Care* 22, no. 2 (April–June 2022): 1–15, https://doi.org/10.5334/ijic.5677.
10. Gayathri Embuldeniya, Jennifer Gutberg, Shannon S. Sibbald, and Walter P. Wodchis, "The Beginnings of Health System Transformation: How Ontario Health Teams Are Implementing Change in the Context of Uncertainty," *Health Policy* 125, no. 12 (December 2021): 1543–9, https://doi.org/10.1016/j.healthpol.2021.10.005.
11. "Learn about OHIP+," Government of Ontario, accessed July 5, 2022, https://www.ontario.ca/page/learn-about-ohip-plus.
12. Blair Roblin, Raisa Deber, Kerry Kuluski, and Michelle Pannor Silver, "Ontario's Retirement Homes and Long-Term Care Homes: A Comparison of Care Services and Funding Regimes," *Canadian Journal on Aging* 38, no. 2 (June 2019): 155–67, https://doi.org/10.1017/S0714980818000569.
13. Alla Yakerson, "Home Care in Ontario: Perspectives on Equity," *International Journal of Health Services* 49, no. 2 (April 2019): 260–72, https://doi.org/10.1177/0020731418804403.
14. Gregory P. Marchildon, "Regionalization: What Have We Learned?," *HealthcarePapers* 16, no. 1 (July 2016): 8–14, https://doi.org/10.12927/hcpap.2016.24766.
15. Auditor General of Ontario, "Chapter 3.08: LHINs – Local Health Integration Networks," in *Annual Report of the Auditor General of Ontario* (Toronto: Auditor General of Ontario), 307–62, https://www.auditor.on.ca/en/content/annualreports/arreports/en15/3.08en15.pdf.
16. "Home," Ontario Health, accessed July 6, 2022, https://www.ontariohealth.ca.
17. Ministry of Health and Ministry of Long-Term Care, "Ontario Health Teams," Government of Ontario, accessed July 6, 2022, https://health.gov.on.ca/en/pro/programs/connectedcare/oht/default.aspx.
18. Ministry of Health and Ministry of Long-Term Care, "Ontario Health Teams."
19. Government of Ontario, *More Beds, Better Care Act, 2022*, S.O. 2022, c. 16 – Bill 7, https://www.ontario.ca/laws/statute/s22016.
20. Gregory P. Marchildon and Brian Hutchison, "Primary Care in Ontario, Canada: New Proposals after 15 Years of Reform," *Health Policy* 120, no. 7 (July 2016): 732–8, https://doi.org/10.1016/j.healthpol.2016.04.010.
21. Marchildon and Hutchison, "Primary Care in Ontario."
22. Allie Peckham, Julia Ho, and Gregory P. Marchildon, *Policy Innovations in Primary Care across Canada* (Toronto: North American Observatory on

Health Systems and Policies, 2018), https://naohealthobservatory.ca/research/rapid-review-1/.
23 Ministry of Health and Ministry of Long-Term Care, "Facts about Home and Community Care Support Services," Government of Ontario, last modified April 1, 2021, https://www.health.gov.on.ca/en/common/system/services/lhin/facts.aspx.
24 "What is Long-Term Care?," NIH National Institute on Aging (NIA), accessed May 19, 2022, https://www.nia.nih.gov/health/what-long-term-care.
25 NIA, "What Is Long-Term Care?"
26 Raisa Deber, Mary-Crea Arsenio, Mélanie Lavoie-Tremblay, and Andrea Baumann, "Introduction – COVID-19 and Long-Term Care: What Have We Learned?," in "Long-Term Care in Crisis: The Reality of COVID-19," ed. Jason M. Sutherland, special issue, *Healthcare Policy* 17 (June 2022): 8–13, https://doi.org/10.12927/hcpol.2022.26858. This briefly describes the other nine articles, which deal with a number of the issues highlighted by COVID-19.
27 Karen Howlett, "Patients Died from Neglect, Not COVID-19, in Ontario LTC Homes, Military Report Finds: 'All They Needed Was Water and a Wipe Down,'" *Globe and Mail*, May 9, 2021, https://www.theglobeandmail.com/canada/article-canadian-military-report-documents-deplorable-conditions-at-two/; Noori Akhtar-Danesh, Andrea Baumann, Mary Crea-Arsenio, and Valentina Antonipillai, "Frequency of Neglect and Its Effect on Mortality in Long-Term Care before and during the COVID-19 Pandemic," in Sutherland, "Long-Term Care in Crisis," special issue, *Healthcare Policy* 17 (June 2022): 107–21, https://doi.org/10.12927/hcpol.2022.26851.
28 Ministry of Health and Ministry of Long-Term Care, "Health Services in Your Community: Public Health Units," Government of Ontario, last modified March 6, 2021, https://www.health.gov.on.ca/en/common/system/services/phu/default.aspx; Robert W. Smith, Sara Allin, Laura Rosella, Kathy Luu, Madeleine Thomas, Joyce Li, and Andrew D. Pinto, *Profiles of Public Health Systems in Canada: Ontario* (Montreal: National Collaborating Centre for Healthy Public Policy, 2021), https://ccnpps-ncchpp.ca/docs/2021-Profiles-of-Public-Health-Systems-in-Canada-Ontario.pdf.
29 Fahad Razak, Saeha Shin, C. David Naylor, and Arthur S. Slutsky, "Canada's Response to the Initial 2 years of the COVID-29 Pandemic: A Comparison with Peer Countries," *Canadian Medical Association Journal* 194, no. 25 (June 27, 2022): E870–7, https://doi.org/10.1503/cmaj.220316; Lynn Unruh, Sara Allin, Greg Marchildon, Sara Burke, Sarah Barry, Rikke Siersbaek, Steve Thomas, Selina Rajan, Andriy Koval, Mathew Alexander et al., "A Comparison of 2020 Health Policy Responses to the COVID-19 Pandemic in Canada, Ireland, the United Kingdom and the United States of America," *Health Policy* 126, no. 5 (May 2022): 427–37, https://doi.org/10.1016/j.healthpol.2021.06.012; Allin Sara, Tiffany Fitzpatrick, Gregory P. Marchildon, and Amélie Quesnel-Vallée, "The Federal Government and Canada's COVID-19 Responses: From 'We're Ready, We're Prepared' to 'Fires Are Burning,'" *Health Economics, Policy and Law* 17, no. 1 (January 2022): 76–94, https://doi.org/10.1017/S1744133121000220.

30 Truth and Reconciliation Commission of Canada, *Canada's Residential Schools: The Final Report of the Truth and Reconciliation Commission of Canada*, vol. 1 (Montreal: McGill-Queen's University Press, 2015).
31 Gregory P. Marchildon, Josée G. Lavoie, and H. James Harrold, "Typology of Indigenous Health System Governance in Canada," *Canadian Public Administration* 64, no. 4 (December 2021): 561–86, https://doi.org/10.1111/capa.12441.
32 Ontario Ministry of Finance, "Chapter 1, Section 3: A Plan to Stay Open," in *2022 Ontario Budget* (Ottawa: Queen's Printer for Ontario), accessed July 11, 2022, https://budget.ontario.ca/2022/chapter-1e.html.
33 Katherine Fierlbeck and Gregory P. Marchildon, *The Boundaries of Medicare: Public Health Care beyond the Canada Health Act* (Montreal: McGill-Queen's University Press), 124–7.
34 Gregory Marchildon, Sara Allin, and Sherry Merkur, *Health Systems in Transition: Canada*, 3rd ed. (Toronto: University of Toronto Press, 2021).

Index

Note: The letter *f* following an italicized page number denotes a figure; the letter *t*, a table.

activist/progressive governments, 273
Alberta: *Alberta Sovereignty within a United Canada Act*, 110; and backstop carbon pricing, 269; Canada Assistance Plan payments, 118–19; effect of revenue generation, 115–17; equalization payments, 115, 123; GHG emissions, 266; oil boom, 22, 29; Ottawa Valley line energy policy, 115; revenue, 121; 2019 election, 125
Albo, Greg, 24
Alcantara, Christopher, 42
AlHadidi, Janine, 145
Allen, Quaylan, 251
anti-Blackness, 253
anti-Black racism, 240–1. *See also* racism
anti-Indigenous racism, 259n7. *See also* racism, systemic
anti-racism: and Ford government, 31, 216–17, 251; policies remain underdeveloped, 229; and populism, 67. *See also* racism
auto industry: Auto Pact, 20, 118; auto plant re-fits, 126; auto task force, 301; Canadian Autoworkers Union (CAW), 29, 290–1, 293, 301, 305n9; as employer, 6, 313; and the Ford government, 31–2, 271, 300; subsidies to manufacturers, 29. *See also* capitalism; transportation; union relationships

Barrett, Toby, 167, 168
Bashevkin, Sylvia, 177
Beaulieu, Michel, 195, 199
Bevelander, Pieter, 222
bilingualism, 3, 117, 140. *See also* francophones
Black, Jerome, 225
Black Lives Matter, 216, 240
Block, Sheila, 27
Brady, Bobbi Ann, 167, 168
Brand, Dionne, 239
Brin, Colette, 139
Britain, 18, 196
British Columbia, 115, 118–19, 169
British North America Act, 56, 78
Brown, Patrick, 160, 164
Bryden, P.E., 113

Canada: effect of Confederation on Ontario's political economy, 17; free trade agreement, 20; GDP per capital, 18; and the Ontario economy, 112; strength of the dollar, 22; UNDRIP (United Nations Declaration on the Rights of Indigenous Peoples), 45–6. *See also* multiculturalism; Province of Canada
capitalism, 16–17, 298, 34n6; racial, 241
Celis, Karen, 178
Cervenan, Amy, 24–5, 26
Charania, Nadia, 202
Charlton, Sebastien, 139
Charter of Rights and Freedoms, 110–11, 117, 127, 136, 188, 218, 223, 303
child care, 101, 125, 187–90
Childs, Sarah, 178
Choudry, Sujit p 235, 223–4
Chow, Olivia, 318
Coates, Patty, 175
Cohn, Martin Regg, 127
colonialism, 3, 199, 241–2, 257
Comeau, Gina, 140–1
Conservative Party of Canada, 181, 224
Constitution Act, 1982, 38–9, 92–3, 114, 119
constitutionalism, 83
constitutional jurisdiction, 38–9, 45–6, 113
Cooper, Christopher A., 77
Coran, Ken, 295
COVID-19 pandemic: and anti-Black racism, 240; burnout among health care providers, 343; and the competitive intergovernmental dynamics, 80–1; effect on the 2022 election, 342; effect on health care delivery, 330, 332, 333; effect on housing costs, 324; effect on students, 254–6; effect on voter turnout, 168–9; Ford and federal-provincial relations, 125, 126–7; hate crimes trends, 229; impact on long-term care, 339–40; issues of organizing public health revealed, 340–41; magnification of infrastructure issues, 201; and news media, 136, 138; political communications during, 134–5; and the political economy, 15–16; political parties with roots in the, 164–6; race based discrimination during, 228–31; speed of passing emergency legislation, 67; and the spread of populism, 79–80; use of Orders of Council (OIC) during, 78, 83. *See also* COVID-19 pandemic press conferences
COVID-19 pandemic press conferences: desire for quality information, 144–5; expert appointee prominence model of leadership, 148–50; politician prominence model of leadership, 146–8, 149–50; role of, 142–3; the virtual press conference, 145–6, 151
critical actor theory, 177, 226

Davis, Bill, 8, 9, 10, 11, 115, 116, 121
Davis government, 61, 115, 121, 270
decolonization, 242
deindustrialization, 24, 25, 29, 31, 123, 126
De Lissovoy, Noah, 242
Dhamoon, Rita, 218
Dias, Jerry, 301
Dillon, Pat, 296–7, 302
Di Matteo, Livio, 203
diversity: in the Ontario press gallery, 140; and women, 177, 185–6, 192. *See also* multiculturalism
D'Mello, Colin, 150
Do, Deniz, 243, 244
Doering, Jan, 317
Doern, Bruce, 272
Drury, Ernest, 75
Du Bois, W.E.B., 222–3
Dyck, Rand, 202

Index   351

education: authority of special-purpose bodies, 94; and the Blue Party, 165; investment in, 28–9; Laurentian University closure, 201, 207; levels in Northern Ontario, 200; segregation, 230; sex education curriculum, 161; teacher strikes, 290, 300, 303. *See also* race and education; union relationships

electoral system: effect of first-past-the-post, 29, 166; *Municipal Election Modernization Act*, 97; *Municipal Elections Act*, 93, 96, 101; online voting, 96–7; turnout trends, 83–4, 96, 158. *See also* the party system

Elliott, Christine, 145–6, 147, 183

Emergencies Act, 126–7

environmental policy: average global adjustment vs. average market electricity price, 267, 267*f*; background and context, 264–8; backstop carbon pricing, 266, 269, 270–1; discursive orientation and public salience of environmental issues, 274, 275t; *Environmental Assessment Act*, 262, 264, 272; *Environmental Bill of Rights*, 262, 264, 270, 272; Ford government's approach to the environment, 268–71, 272–6; overview, 262–3; Royal Commission on the Northern Environment, 198–9, 201. *See also* Walkerton disaster; Wynne, Kathleen

Esselment, Anna Lennox, 123

Estonia, 85

Evans, 76

Eves, Ernie, 159, 188

Fafard, Patrick, 148–9

fair shares argument, 7–8, 112, 119, 123, 124, 127

farmer's movement, western Canadian, 18

federalism, balance-sheet, 119, 122

federalism, Canadian, 78–9, 87n38

federalism, emergency, 81

federalism, fiscal, 119, 120, 123, 128–9

federalism and medicare, 331–3

feminism, 177, 184, 187, 189–90, 191

Ferguson, Howard, 113

Ford, Doug: approach to federal government, 343; *Better Municipal Governance Act*, 68, 102–3; comparison of racism in Canada to the United States, 216, 231; COVID-19 pandemic press conferences, 134, 144, 145–6, 147–8, 150, 151; dissolution of the Peel Region, 104; diversity in cabinet appointments, 185; divides society into protagonists or antagonists, 67; double-standards during the COVID-19 pandemic, 230; federal-provincial relations of, 111–12, 126–7, 128; leadership during the COVID-19 pandemic, 163–4; mayoral candidate, 317; and Nicholls, 165; political background of, 102, 103; populism of, 80, 112, 123, 128–9, 263; powers of appointment and Hewitt, 167; press media tensions, 142; prioritization of Northern Ontario, 207; reduction in the size of the Toronto City Council, 102, 319–20; 2022 re-election, 83–4; re-election bid endorsed by unions, 287; relationship with Justin Trudeau, 125–6; and the PC "labour charm offensive," 297–303; 2009 election, 162; 2018 election, 160; understanding of the federal-provincial intergovernmentalism, 123–6, 129. *See also* Ford government

Ford, Michael, 227

Ford, Rob, 80, 102, 103, 317, 321

Ford government: Anti-Racism Strategic Plan, 31, 216; approach to the environmental and climate policy, 263, 268–71, 272–76, 278; approach to health care, 333, 338–9;

Ford government (*continued*)
cancellation of Indigenization of curriculum, 43–4, 47; and child care commitments, 190; commitment to combat violence against women, 191; controversial legislation of, 68; elimination of the Ministry of the Status of Women, 187; investment in transportation infrastructure, 28, 32; and Islamophobia condemnation act, 228; and the minimum wage, 30, 297, 301; *More Homes, Build Faster Act*, 104; pro-employer changes to WCB, 291; proposed rapid transit plan, 321–2; racial makeup of cabinet, 226–7; and ranked ballots in elections (2020), 97; 2022 re-election platform, 342; resistance to pay equity rulings, 188–9; reversal of Liberal health initiatives, 329; speed of implementation processes, 65–6, 102, 323; undoing GGH "densification" policies, 323–4; use of Orders in Council, 83; and women votes, 175. *See also* Ford, Doug
Ford Nation (Ford), 103
francophones, 24, 140, 200–1, 203. *See also* bilingualism
Freeland, Chrystia, 125

Galabuzi, Grace-Edward, 27
gender, 19, 165, 175–6, 191–2, 298, 300. *See also* men; women
gender equality, 187–91. *See also* pay equity
George, Dudley, 30, 40
Giasson, Thierry, 134–5
Gidengil, Elisabeth, 136
Goldman, Shelley, 260n21
government media relations: expert appointee prominence model of leadership, 148–50; political communication during the COVID-19 pandemic, 134–5; politician prominence model of leadership, 146–8, 149–50; the press gallery, 135, 136–42, 138*t*, 139*t*, 151, 152; relevance of the news media, 135–6. *See also* COVID-19 pandemic press conferences; Ford, Doug
Graefe, Peter, 123
Green Party of Ontario (GPO), 83, 158–9, 161, 162–3, 166
GTA (Greater Toronto Area): amalgamation, 93, 315–16, 318; demographics, 313–14; distribution of seats in the legislature by major party, 311, 312*t*; the electorate of, 317; growth of, 311–13, 312*t*, 313–14; managing growth in the suburbs, 322–4; new transit infrastructure in Toronto, 320–22; population of, 310, 311; post-amalgamation mayors, 317–18; reduction of the Toronto City Council, 102, 319–20; shift to post-industrial economy, 313–14; strong mayor powers, 68, 95–6, 102–3, 320; *Toronto Act*, 102. *See also* Toronto
Gueye, Abdoulaye, 221
Guzek, Damian, 145

Hall, Stuart, 219
Harper, Stephen, 120–1, 266
Harper government, 122, 141
Harris, Mike: anti-union, 297–8; changes to cabinet, 77; fair share federalism, 119; party leader, 159; *Zebra Mussels Act*, 62
Harris government: amalgamation of Toronto, 315–16, 318; amendments to the *Ontario Labour Relations Act*, 289–90; anti-union restructuring, 291, 292–3; cuts to women's policy areas, 187–8, 189; effect on the municipal sector, 102; environmental commitments, 264–265; fiscal federalism, 119–20; and the hydro system, 264, 266, 267; *Ipperwash Inquiry*, 38, 39; a neo-liberal government, 273–4; neo-liberal

restructuring reforms of, 63–4, 65, 69, 79; and pay equity, 187–8, 290; proposed highway expansion, 269; received reduced transfer to provinces, 112; returning to old same old, 10, 11; use of Early Childhood Development Agreement funds, 189; Walkerton disaster, 264–5
Hatcher, William, 144
health policy and politics: *Canada Health Act* (CHA), 114, 331, 332, 333–4, 343; Canada Health and Social Transfer, 114, 119–20, 124, 127, 331–2; creation of the Northern Ontario School of Medicine (NOSM), 206, 208; dental services, 334; federalism and medicare, 331–3; for-profit enterprise system, 337, 342; hospitals, 32, 333, 337, 343; improving integration and coordination, 334–7; insured services, 332, 333–4; Local Health Integration Networks (LHINs), 329–30, 335, 339; mental health services, 334; mixed and privately financed health sectors, 333–34; in Northern Ontario, 202, 204, 206; Ontario Drug Benefit program, 33–4, 101; Ontario Health Insurance Program (OHIP), 331–2, 333–4, 341; and the Ontario Liberal Party, 329; primary care models, 337–9; and the Progressive Conservative Party, 329–30, 342; public health, 340–1; public-private balance, 330–1, 337. *See also* COVID-19 pandemic; long-term care (LTC)
Hepburn, Mitchell, 113
Hewitt, Ken, 167–8
Hicks, Bruce, 225
Horwath, Andrea, 159, 182, 295–6, 301
Houle, René, 243, 244
housing: affordability of, 25, 31, 98, 324; Caledonia development dispute, 5; GGH Greenbelt Plan, 322–3; *More Homes, Build Faster Act*, 104; *Strong Mayors, Building Homes Act*, 102–3. *See also* long-term care (LTC)
HST, 165, 268
Hudak, Tim, 159, 294, 295–6, 297–8

Ibbitson, John, 115
immigration: Canada-Ontario Immigrant Settlement agreement, 319; and growth of the GTA, 313; health care coverage for, 343; race and education among the immigrant population, 243, 244, 245–6, 249, 258nn3–4, 260n26; racial identities and immigration status, 219–20
Indigenous Peoples: boil water advisories, 201–2, 209; child care infrastructure for, 125; and the Critical Minerals Strategy, 271; emerging Indigenous health systems, 341; employment in service sector, 26; and the Federal Economic Development Initiative for Northern Ontario (FedNor), 205; graduation coaches for students, 251; in Northern Ontario, 199, 200–2, 203; political economies of, 16–17; population, 1; and racism, 259n7, 341; recognition of, 2, 3; and reconciliation, 263; and the Ring of Fire (Northern Ontario), 206–7, 268; Royal Commission on Aboriginal Peoples, 201
Indigenous Peoples' relationship with Ontario: cancellation of Indigenization of curriculum, 43–4; and the constitutional jurisdiction, 38–9, 45–6; *Ipperwash Inquiry*, 38, 39–40, 48; *Municipal Act, 2001*, 41; municipal-Indigenous relations, 42–3; Provincial Policy Statements (PPS): 2014 and 2020, 40–2; provincial responsibilities off-loaded, 37–8, 41, 42–3, 45, 47, 49; the relationship vacuum, 38, 39, 40, 48; UNDRIP

Indigenous Peoples' relationship with Ontario (*continued*) (United Nations Declaration on the Rights of Indigenous Peoples), 45–6; unequal relationship with Ontario, 16
Innis, Harold, 196
Islamophobia, 228

Kahn, Laura, 146
Karahalios, Belinda, 165–6
Kenney, Jason, 123, 144
Key, V.O., 170
King, Adam, 205
Kumar, Martha Joynt, 143

Lastman, Mel, 315, 317
law enforcement, 39–40, 95, 101, 110–11, 126
Lecce, Stephen, 145, 147, 256
Legault, François, 79, 110–11
Lévesque, René, 117
LGBTQ issues, 75, 159, 191
Liberal Party, Ontario: and child care funding and policies, 189–90; declining popularity, 161–3; diversity in women appointed to cabinet, 185; 2022 election, 83; female leadership, 182; Hewitt as candidate, 167; initiatives on the environment, 268; minority representation, 224; in North Ontario, 203; and pay equity, 188, 191; and recent polarization of the party system, 170; regional growth management policies, 322–4; school system, 3; support for *Anti-Racism Act*, 251; time allocation in the legislature, 61; time in power, 158; and violence against women, 190–1; as "woke urbanists," 298. *See also* McGuinty, Dalton; Peterson, David; union relationships; women; Wynne, Kathleen
Liberal Party of Canada, 167, 190, 277–8, 319. *See also* Trudeau, Justin; Trudeau, Pierre

Lilleker, Darren, 151
local government: Doug Ford's interest in, 102–4; expenditures, 99–100, 100*f*; financing of, 97–101; governing municipalities in Ontario, 95–7; revenue sources, 97–8, 99*f*; special-purpose bodies, 92–3, 94–5; strong mayor powers, 95–6, 102–3; structure of, 92–5. *See also Municipal Act, 2001*; Toronto
London, Ontario, 97, 103, 216
long-term care (LTC), 334, 337, 339–40, 342
Luxton, Meg, 26

Macdonald, John A., 17, 112, 113
Maldonado-Torres, Nelson, 242
Malloy, Jonathan, 158, 168, 170
managerial/facilitative governance model, 273
Manitoba, 144, 197, 203–4
Marland, Alex, 134–5, 141
Martin, Charles, 202–3
Martin, Paul, 319
McCallion, Hazel, 315
McDermott, Patricia, 26
McDermott, Ray, 260n21
McDowell, Tom, 73, 79, 226
McGuinty, Dalton, 121; climate change responses, 264–5; environmental platform of, 264–5; improving land-use planning, 28; and Liberal Party of Ontario, 159; pledge regarding women candidates, 181; "Premier Dad," 11–12; press relations, 141–2; resignation, 10, 159, 182, 295
McGuinty government: approach to poverty, 30; child care policy, 189–90; education sector support for, 293–4; equalization payments, 112; fair share of federal dollars campaign, 7–8, 120; and Indigenous-Ontario relationships, 38; infrastructure needed for growth, 28–9; minority

representation in the, 185, 221–2, 224, 225; and municipal autonomy, 102; omnibus bills, 65; and Ontario Women's Directorate (OWD), 187; Poverty Reduction Strategy, 30; racialized inequality, 30–1
McNair, Brian, 135–6
McNaughton, Monte, 147, 298, 299–300, 301
men: numbers in cabinet, 185–6, 226; and the Progressive Conservative Party of Ontario, 175, 300; role in capitalism, 298; wage expectations, 19. *See also* gender
Mendelsohn, Matthew, 114
Mercier, Honoré, 113
Mignolo, Walter, 242
Miller, David, 317, 321
ministerial/minister's zoning orders (MZOs), 104, 269, 323
Moore, Kieran, 149, 151
Morrow, Donald, 60
Mowat, Oliver, 113
multiculturalism, 22, 43, 140, 216–20, 227, 231, 240. *See also* diversity
Municipal Act, 2001, 41, 93, 94, 96, 97, 101

National Energy Program, 116, 118, 121, 177, 272
nationalisms, 78–9
National Policy, 16–17, 24, 112–16, 118
NDP, Ontario: affirmative action nomination policy, 181–2; becomes official Opposition, 160–1; child care, 189; 2022 election, 83, 123; election performance, 167, 170, 175–6; environmental policy, 264; filibusters, 64; on minimum wage, 30; in Northern Ontario, 203, 204, 209; official party status granted, 159; and recent polarization of the party system, 170; *Standing Orders* reform, 63; time allocation in the legislature, 61; time in power, 158; as "woke urbanists," 298. *See also* Chow, Olivia; Horwath, Andrea; Rae, Bob; union relationships; women
Nelles, H.V., 197
Nelles, Jen, 42
neocolonialism, 113
neo-liberal governments, 273–4
neo-liberalism, 80, 118, 123, 128–9, 241, 273–4
New Brunswick, 113, 117
Newfoundland and Labrador, 3, 121, 169, 221
New York, 24, 103, 123
Nicholls, Rick, 165, 166
Nieguth, Tim, 204
Northern Ontario: alienation of, 197, 198, 199, 202; attraction and retention of physicians, 206; demographics, 199–202; distinctive regional subculture of, 202–3; extraction of natural resources, 196, 197, 198, 207–8; heartland-hinterland relationship, 196–7, 210; historical development, 196–9; lack of long-term planning, 205; political culture and political behaviour, 202–8; politics compared to those of Southern Ontario, 140–1; population trends, 195, 199, 200, 208–9; privatization of the Ontario Northland Transportation Commission (ONTC), 207–8, 209; Royal Commission on the Northern Environment, 198–9, 201; secessionist discussions, 197–8, 203–4, 209; wealth compared to Southern Ontario, 27–8
Notley government, 266
Nova Scotia, 107n31, 113, 169

O'Neill, Brenda, 176
Ontario: about, 1–6; and Confederation, 7–8, 48, 56; *noblesse oblige* of, 112; the political culture of, 8–13; populations of, 1–2, 3, 74, 221, 331

Ontario executive: the Cabinet Office, 76, 77, 185; centralization/decentralization of, 77–8, 79; composition of the Ontario public sector, 74, 75*t*; concept of the executive, 72–3; Emergency Orders, 82*f*, 83; the executive-legislative dynamic, 53–4, 55–6, 73–4; the Office of the Premier, 77; Orders in Council, 81, 81*t*; overview of, 74–8; power of, 78–84; role of the premier, 75; role of the secretary of the cabinet, 74–5; separation of political and administrative actors, 76–7. *See also* COVID-19 pandemic

Ontario federal-provincial relations: big brother strategy, 111–12, 125; Canada Assistance Plan payments, 118–19; Equalization program, 114, 115, 116–17, 120–2, 123, 126, 127–8; the free trade era, 117–22; industrial restructuring and populism, 122–8; National Energy Program, 116, 118, 177; and Ontario's economy, 111–12; the politics of redistribution, 112–17; the traditional strategy towards, 111. *See also* COVID-19 pandemic; Ford, Doug; Harris, Mike; McGuinty, Dalton; the National Policy

Ontario Human Rights Commission (OHRC), 240, 259n12

Ontario legislature: the classical era: 1867–1967, 56–8; the counter-reformist era: 1992–2023, 62–9; the executive-legislative dynamic, 53–54, 55–56; funding to official parties, 159; *motion of closure*, 56, 57, 61, 67–9; omnibus legislation, 63, 65, 73–4; question period, 137; the reformist era: 1967–92, 59–62; representation of minorities in, 221; sitting during COVID-19 pandemic, 144; time allocation at, 61, 63, 64, 65, 66*t*, 67, 68*t*

Ontario Liberal Party. *See* Liberal Party, Ontario

Ontario NDP. *See* NDP, Ontario
OPEC crisis, 115, 116
O'Toole, Erin, 298–9

Paikin, Steve, 148
Pal, Michael, 223–4
Panich, Leo, 289
parochialism, 196–7, 202–3
party system, the: Haldimand-Norfolk riding case study, 166–8; independent candidates, 166–7; New Blue, 165–6; Ontario Party, 164–5; overview, 157–8; party system 2003–18, 158–60; and polarization, 10, 24–6, 158, 161, 170; protest voting, 203, 209; 2022 election, 163–4; 2018 election outcome, 160–3; voter turnout, 168–9. *See also* electoral system

Passy, Pascasie Minani, 221
pay equity, 187–9, 191. *See also* gender equality
Peel Region, 104, 319–20
Pendakur, Ravi, 222
People's Party of Canada, 73, 165
Peterson, David, 76–7, 119
Peterson government, 270, 273
Pilon, Dennis, 54
Planning Act (1990), 41, 104, 272
Poland, 145
political economy: ability to increase manufacturing employment, 20–1; adoption of the US production model, 17–18, 19; approach to the welfare state, 30; average income, 27, 27*t*; COVID-19 pandemic and, 15–16; decline in manufacturing, 21, 21*t*, 22*t*, 23–4, 23*t*, 24; and dispossession of Indigenous Peoples, 17; focus on cost-competitive manufacturing, 21–2, 24, 31; industrial policies, 28, 29, 32; loss of economic competitiveness, 18–24; Ontario share of Canadian GDP by industry, 23, 23*t*; Ontario's

wealth accumulation, 16–18; politics around poverty and racialization, 27–31; role of the National Policy, 17–18, 24; share of employment by industry, 22*t*, 23, 24; share of GDP by industry, 1997-2021, 21*t*, 23; shift to the service sector, 24–7. *See also* auto industry

populism: Canadian farmers movements, 18; and constitutionalism, 83; of Ford government, 66–7, 84, 112; global spread of, 79–80, 298; and the Ontario Party, 164–5; thin ideologies, 73, 80; Toronto mayor (Rob Ford), 317. *See also* Ford, Doug; Ford government

populism, market, 263, 274–5

populism, right-wing, 66, 164, 205, 298

poverty, 26, 28, 30. *See also* wages

power relations

Progressive Conservative Party of Canada, 141

Progressive Conservative Party of Ontario: in Haldimand-Norfolk riding, 167; leadership race, 160; in North Ontario, 203; reign of, 61; school system, 3, 293; Sloan, 164; time in power, 158. *See also* Ford, Doug; Harper, Stephen; Harris, Mike; Morrow, Donald; union relationships

property development, 323, 324

Province of Canada, 3

Quebec: auction of emission permits, 266; Coalition Avenir Quebec, 110–11; COVID-19 pandemic press conferences, 144; historical relationship to Ontario, 3, 113; referendum, 119; taxation rates, 32. *See also* Legault, François; Lévesque, René

Quebec nationalism, 3, 32, 111

Queen's Park. *See* the Ontario legislature

race and education: among the immigrant population, 244, 245–6, 249, 258nn3–4, 260n26; and colonialism, 241–2; the cost of the pandemic on students, 254–6; the early schooling years, 250–4; EDI initiatives, 240–1; educational attainment of Canadian youth aged 25–9 years, 245–50; generational status, 238, 239, 245–6, 247*f*, 248*f*, 249*t*; highest level of education by race, ages 25–9, 245, 246*t*; highest level of education of black youth, ages 25–9, 247*f*; resilience, 244; segregation, 230; Statistics Canada reports on Black youths education, 236, 239, 243–5; unbelonging, 253–4. *See also* education; race and politics; women, Black

race and politics: Afzaal family murder, 216–17, 228; Black Canadian MPPs, 221–2; brokerage parties, 225; Chinese Canadian MPPs, 221; compared to ethnicity, 219; compared to the visible minority, 218–19; descriptive representation, 220–5; discrimination during the COVID-19 pandemic, 228–31; multiculturalism, 218–20, 231; party discipline, 227–8; place belonging compared to politics of belonging, 230–1; political exclusion, 223, 231; proportionality in legislatures, 220–1; substantive representation, 226–8; voter dilution, 223–4; voting patterns, 222; white supremacy, 164, 218, 228, 230. *See also* race and education

racial equality, 216

racialized equality, 27, 28, 31

racialized inequality, 30–1

racism: Ford's stance on, 216; institution, societal/structural, 252, 259n10; McNaughton on the left, 299–300; and multiculturalism, 218–19, 231, 240; and policy, 31;

raciscm (*continued*)
and power relations, 220; prevalence of in the GTA, 314; race compared to ethnicity, 219–20; and "the normal," 239. *See also* anti-Black racism; anti-racism
racism, systemic, 216, 240, 251, 341
Rae, Bob, 63, 75, 112, 119, 263, 289
Rae government, 187, 270, 273
regionalisms, 78–9, 110–11

Sartori, Giovanni, 162
Saskatchewan, 22, 110, 121, 125, 169, 202, 269
Scheer, Andrew (Conservative), 45–6
Schreiner, Mike, 161, 162–3
Segal, Hugh, 114
SEIU (Service Employees International Union) challenge, 188, 302
Silver, Daniel, 317
Sloan, Derek, 164
Small, Tamara, 134–5
Sousa, Charles, 122
Southcott, Chris, 199
staples theory, 196
Stewart, Edward E., 77
strong mayor powers, 68, 95–6, 102–3, 320
Supreme Court of Canada, 38, 92, 117, 124, 189, 269, 320
Swartz, Donald, 289
Switzerland, 85

Taylor, Zack, 317
Thomas, Smokey, 301–2
Thompson, Debra, 218–19
Toner, Glen, 272
Toronto: business services hub of Canada, 23t, 24; City Council of, 102, 103, 314, 319–20; *City of Toronto Act*, 102, 106n4; financial services hub of Canada, 24, 31, 123; population of, 92. *See also* the GTA; Tory, John
Tory, John, 125–6, 181, 317–18, 321

transportation: creation of the railway, 17, 113; delivery of services, 94, 101; Ford government's investment in infrastructure, 28, 32; funding GTA transit, 314, 316, 317, 320–1; and greenhouse gas emissions, 266; highway network expansion, 269–70, 276, 278; highways, 3, 28; Metrolinx, 95, 320–1, 322; and Northern Ontario, 197, 207–8, 209; Ontario Line, 269–70, 321–2; Toronto Transit Commission (TTC) strike, 293; transit funding formula, 127; veto on road tolls, 319. *See also* auto industry
treaty making, 39
Trudeau, Justin, 124, 125, 126, 266, 321–2
Trudeau, Justin government: relationship with press gallery, 141
Trudeau, Pierre, 117, 141
Trump, Donald, 144, 298
Truth and Reconciliation Commission (TRC) report and calls to action, 40, 43–4, 45, 341
Turcotte, Martin, 243–4, 245

union relationships: Canadian Autoworkers Union (CAW), 29, 290–1, 293, 301, 305n9; conservatives versus the unions, 289–91; free trade agreement, 20; history and context, 288–9; and the NDP, 287, 288–9, 290–1, 292–3, 294, 295, 302–3; Ontario Federation of Labour (OFL), 288, 289, 302; and the Ontario Liberal Party, 287, 291–2, 293–5; Ontario Public Service Employees Union (OPSEU), 290–1, 301–2; and the Progressive Conservative Party of Ontario, 287–8, 291, 292, 297–303; recognition of collective bargaining, 18–19; strikes, 290, 293, 300, 303–4, 332; teacher unions, 291, 293, 294, 295, 302; Unifor, 29, 301, 302; union campaign donations by party, 292,

292f; and the Working Families Coalition, 287, 291–7, 302. *See also* auto industry; Harris government
United States: free trade agreement, 20; GDP per capital, 18; health care, 333; manufacturing in and from, 21, 112; and Ontario's economy, 118
Urback, Robyn, 299

Varenne, Hérve, 260n21
violence against women, 187–9, 190–1, 259n7

Wacquant, Loïc, 241
wages: expectations and gender, 19; Ford government restraint legislation, 297–8; raising the minimum wage, 30, 297, 301; *Rebalancing the Opportunity Equation* (United Way Greater Toronto), 27, 27t; recognition of collective bargaining, 18–19. *See also* poverty
Walcott, Rinaldo, 240
Walkerton disaster, 80, 81, 264–5, 270, 276
Walsh, Catherine, 242
Watts, Ronald, 78
welfare state, 30, 114
Weller, Geoffrey, 196–7, 202, 203, 204, 205
White, Eric, 137
Williams, David, 134, 149–50, 151
Windsor, 40–1, 103, 126, 146, 147, 303
Winfield, Mark, 124
Wiseman, Nelson, 111
Witmer, Elizabeth, 295
women: in appointed office, 183–6; as cabinet ministers, 184–5, 184t, 191; and diversity, 177, 185–6, 192; elected by each party, 178, 178t; in elected office, 159, 177–83; female candidates for election, 96, 180, 180t; first woman premier, 159; and intersectionality, 177, 191–92; marginalization in the labour market, 26–7; and the NDP, 180, 180t, 181–2, 184, 189; and the Ontario Liberal Party, 180, 180t, 181, 189; the Ontario Women's Directorate (OWD), 186–7; in party caucuses, 179–80, 179f; as party leaders, 182–3; and the Progressive Conservative Party of Ontario, 180, 180t, 181, 184–5, 186, 187–8, 189; as secretaries to cabinet, 86n14; as "welfare queens," 230. *See also* child care; feminism; gender; pay equity; women, Black; Wynne, Kathleen
women, Black, 243, 244
women's movement, 19
women's policies or issues, 176
Working Families Coalition, 287
Wynne, Kathleen: claims regarding child care spaces, 190; election performances, 10, 12, 163, 182, 296; in local government, 108n52; openly gay woman premier, 13, 75, 159, 182, 183; popularity of, 160; relationship with Harper, 122
Wynne government: balance-sheet federalism during, 119, 122; Climate Change Action Plan (CCAP), 265–6; climate change responses, 263, 265–6; creation of the Ministry of the Status of Women, 175, 187; and equalization payments, 112; Fair Hydro Plan, 267–8; implementation of Greenbelt plan, 323; investment in transportation infrastructure, 28; and the minimum wage, 30, 160, 296; racialized inequality, 30–1; respect for municipal decision making, 321; and teachers' unions, 295; transportation issue under, 207–8; veto on road tolls, 319; women's representation in cabinet, 183–4, 185

Yuval-Davis, Nira, 230

Zizys, Tom, 25